I0576630

Charles Merivale

History of the Romans Under the Empire

Volume 5

Charles Merivale

History of the Romans Under the Empire
Volume 5

ISBN/EAN: 9783337121402

Printed in Europe, USA, Canada, Australia, Japan

Cover: Foto ©ninafisch / pixelio.de

More available books at **www.hansebooks.com**

HISTORY

OF THE

ROMANS UNDER THE EMPIRE.

BY THE VERY REV.

CHARLES MERIVALE, D.C.L.

DEAN OF ELY.

NEW EDITION.

IN EIGHT VOLUMES.

VOL. V.

.

LONDON:

LONGMANS, GREEN, AND CO.

1871.

CONTENTS

OF

THE FIFTH VOLUME.

———◦◦———

CHAPTER XLV.

CHAPTER XLVI.

MAP.

HISTORY

OF THE

ROMANS UNDER THE EMPIRE.

CHAPTER XL.

The great cities of the Roman empire.—The cities of Greece: Corinth, Sparta, Athens, Delos.—The cities of Asia: Ephesus and others. —Antioch in Syria.—The Grecian cities in Italy: the cities on the Campanian coast.—Approach to Rome.—The hills of Rome.—The valleys of Rome.—The Forum, Velabrum, &c.—The Transtiberina. —The Campus Martius.—The streets and domestic architecture of Rome.—The Domus and Insulæ.—Population estimated: 1. From the area of the city. 2. From the number of houses. 3. From the number of recipients of grain.—Concluding remarks.

THE progress of the Greeks and Romans in the arts of peace and civilization may be ascribed in a great measure to the skill they early attained in self-defence. When assailed by a superior foe whom they were unable to

The idea of the city first absorbed in that of the empire under the Cæsars.

meet in the field, they withdrew behind the shelter of their walls, constructed for the permanent security of their temples and dwellings, and derided from the heights of their airy citadels the fruitless challenge of the adversary who pined inactive beneath them. Hence the political importance which the city, the place of common refuge, the hearth of the national gods, the stronghold of national independence, acquired among them, and the comparative insignificance to which they resigned their domains and villages, which they held themselves ever ready, at the first sign of invasion, to abandon to the enemy.

Even when their conquests extended far and wide
over islands and continents, Rome and Athens, Syracuse and Sparta, still continued, unlike England and
France, Russia and Turkey, in modern times, to be
the names of cities, rather than of countries; all
political privileges centred in them, and flowed
thence with slow and measured pace to the more
favoured of their subject communities.   It is to this
principle of their polity that we owe much of the
intense national life, the deep-marked lines of
national character, of faith, manners, and opinions,
which severally distinguished them, and which seem
to have received their form and pressure from the
mould of the city walls in which they were first
fused together.   We have seen, however, in the last
chapter, how the exclusive pretensions of the greatest of these conquering cities were eventually modified by the exigencies of a wide-extended sovereignty.
The Roman empire claims at last, the first in civilized antiquity, to be considered as in itself a political
body, independent of its connexion with Rome, the
residence of its chief governor.   Our history becomes
a review of the affairs of a vast unit, the aggregate
of a multitude of smaller members, the sum of many
combined elements.   The title affixed to it, the
History of the Romans rather than of Rome, may
serve to mark this important feature in its character;
and accordingly it seemed most fitting to commence
our survey of the condition of the Roman people
under Augustus with a general view of the empire
itself, and the social and political bands by which it
was held together and compacted into one system.
I have reserved for a second chapter the more special
examination of the features of the illustrious city
from which it must still derive its chief interest, as
well as its celebrated name.

    Before entering, however, on this survey of the
Eternal City, we will pass in rapid review the most

conspicuous of her rivals in fame and splendour, such as they appeared at this period of eclipse, *Proposed survey of the city itself, as compared with the other great cities of the empire.* if not of degradation. The grandeur of Rome, great and striking as it must seem in itself, may not disdain to borrow additional lustre from comparison with her noblest contemporaries.

No Roman traveller of gentle birth and training could enter the precincts of an Hellenic *The cities of Greece under Augustus.* community, and fail to imbibe a portion of the sacred glow with which it regarded the beautiful in the world either of sense or imagination. The young patrician, sent forth to acquire lessons of taste or wisdom at Rhodes and Athens, returned to his own rude Penates an altered man. A citizen who had visited Greece might be recognised, no doubt, in the Via Sacra almost at sight. He had worshipped in the temple of a real divinity; he had been initiated into the genuine mysteries of nature; he had received illumination from above. Yet the Greece which he had traversed and admired, though still full of restless stir and motion, still occupied upon thoughts that never die, and forms that never tire, was *living Greece* no more: she was the shadow of her former self, the ghost of her ancient being, still lingering among the haunts of her pride and beauty, more attractive perhaps to the imagination than in the bloom of her living existence. He had threaded, perhaps, with Cicero's graceful friend, the narrow channels of the Ægean, crowned by the Athenian acropolis. Behind him had lain Ægina, before him Megara, on his right the Piræus, Corinth on his left.[1] It was indeed a scene of mournful recollections. Ægina, the handmaid of haughty *Ægina and Megara.* Athens, had shared her latest disasters, but had never revived with her recent renovation. Me-

---

[1] See the famous consolations of Sulpicius to Cicero (*Div.* iv. 5.), written in the year 709.

gara, the fatal cause of the great war of the Pelopon-
nesus, had sunk into a state of decay and insignificance in which she could no longer tempt an
Corinth and
the Piræus. unhallowed ambition. The sight of Corinth,
still desolate and in ruins, might awake a
painful remembrance of the sack of Mummius, the
most shameful page in the annals of Roman devas-
tation; while the Piræus reflected still more recent
traditions of outrage, when Sulla wreaked on her the
vengeance which he affected to spare to the venerable glories of Athens. No spot on earth could read
the Roman moralist a more instructive lesson on the
vanity of human greatness, or display to him more
melancholy trophies of the lust of rapine and conquest.

Such mementos might have their use and appro-
priateness as addressed to a child of the
Restoration of
Corinth by
Julius Cæsar. capitol and the forum on crossing the
threshold of illustrious Greece; but we are
not to infer from them that decay and misery had
fallen as a blight upon the whole realm of Hellas.
Corinth herself was at that moment about to rise
from her ashes under the auspices of a generous
Roman, and to take her place once more among the
most distinguished of cities. Her position, in respect to commerce and navigation, was not less
admirable than that of Alexandria or Constantinople;
and nothing but the deliberate pressure of a conqueror's arm could keep her permanently prostrate.
Placed at the head of two almost commingling gulfs,
and commanding by them the commerce of Italy and
Asia, which shrank in conscious imbecility from the
stormy navigation of the Malean Cape, Corinth, restored to life and freedom by the decree of Julius
Cæsar, entered at once on a new career of prosperity,
in which she was destined speedily to outstrip the
fame of her earlier successes. It is probable indeed
that some of her chief buildings and temples had

survived, though defaced and desecrated by the ruthless Mummius.[1]   A squalid and degraded population
still crouched under their shelter; but these poor
wretches gained their livelihood, not by returning to
the pursuits of commerce, which were checked by
wars and piracy, and the now triumphant rivalry of
Rhodes and Delos, but by groping among their ruins
for the buried remnants of Corinthian bronze which
had escaped the cupidity of the first captors, and had
since become of priceless value.[2]   The restoration of
Corinth was one of Cæsar's noblest projects, and
he was fortunately permitted to accomplish it.   In
gratitude for his services the new inhabitants gave
it the name of the *Praise of Julius*.[3]   But the lazy
plebeians of Rome had shown no inclination to earn
wealth by industry; no mercantile community could
have sprung from the seed of the licentious veterans.
The good sense of the dictator was strongly marked
in his disregarding the prejudices of his countrymen,
and transplanting to his new establishment a colony
of enfranchised slaves.[4]   Corinth rapidly rose under
these auspices, became a centre of commerce and
art, and took the lead among the cities of European
Hellas.   Here was established the seat of the Roman
government of Achaia, and its population, though
the representations we have received of it are extravagant, undoubtedly exceeded that of any Grecian

---

[1] This. it seems, may be inferred from the way in which Pausanias,
in his account of Corinth, speaks of these edifices as monuments of
antiquity.

[2] Comp. Strabo, viii. 6. p. 381.; Plin. *Hist. Nat.* xxxiv. 2., xxxvii.
3.; Stat. *Sylv.* ii. 2. 68. : "Æraque ab Isthmiacis auro potiora favillis."
Cicero (*Tusc. Disp.* iii 22.) laments the indifference these people
evinced to their degraded condition.   He was more moved by the
sight of their ruins than they were themselves: "Magis me moverunt
Corinthi subito aspectæ parietinæ quam ipsos Corinthios, quorum
animis diuturna cogitatio callum vetustatis obduxerat."

[3] "Laus Julia" upon the medals.   Eckhel, ii. 238.

[4] Strabo, viii. 6. p. 381.; Pausan. ii. 1, 2.; Plut. *Cæs.* 57.; Dion,
xliii. 50.; Plin. *Hist. Nat.* iv. 4 ; Crinagoras in *Anthol. Gr.* ii. 145.

rival.[1] The beauty of its situation, the splendour of
its edifices, the florid graces of its architecture, and
the voluptuous charms of its parks and pleasure
grounds, delighted the stranger whom its commerce
had attracted. The security it now enjoyed allowed
it to expand its ample streets far beyond the precincts of its defences, and the light and airy arcades
which connected it with its harbour at Lechæum
might be advantageously contrasted with the weary
length of dead wall which extended from Athens to
the Piræus.[2]

The restoration of Corinth exalted her to higher
eminence in every respect, except historic

Sparta favoured by Augustus.

fame, than either of the rivals who had
formerly outshone her. Of these, indeed,
Sparta, in the days of Augustus, had fallen almost
to the lowest depths of humiliation. Enjoying no
advantages of position, she had suffered more than
her share in the general decline of the Grecian cities
after their loss of independence. In the late troubles,
however, she had prudently sided with Octavius,
while Athens was dazzled by the more brilliant pretensions of Antonius. She had been rewarded with
the boon of immunity from Roman taxation, as well
as self-government, and these privileges she continued
to retain.[3] But at the same time she was allowed to

---

[1] Comp. Apuleius, *Metam.* x. p. 247.; Hierocles, p. 646.: Κόρινθος
μητρόπολις πάσης ‘Ελλάδος. Athenæus (vi. 20.) declares that its slaves
amounted to 460,000. This number may bear perhaps to be shorn of
its last figure ; but we may as well suspect exaggeration in the writer
as corruption in the MSS.

[2] Stat. *Sylv.* ii. 2. 25.:

    " Qualis ubi subeas Ephyres Baccheidos altum
    Culmen, ab Inoo fert semita tecta Lechæo."

There was more than one such " via tecta " for the convenience
of shade at Rome. At a much later period such an arcade ran from
the Lateran gate to the basilica of St. Paul, and one structure of
the kind now leads from Bologna to a favourite shrine some miles
distant.

[3] Strabo, viii. 5. p. 365.: ἐτιμήθησαν διαφερόντως, καὶ ἔμειναν ἐλεύθεροι,

exercise no supremacy over the descendants of her Helots and Perioeci, who retained, under the name of free Laconians, complete independence of her authority in four-and-twenty townships along her coasts; and of the hundred burghs she boasted in the days of her prosperity, she could now count no more than thirty, all of which were sunk in squalid insignificance.

Nevertheless in this reverse of fortune, the Spartans could still vaunt themselves genuine children of the Dorian heroes, who had conquered the sons of Hercules, and made themselves more than once the tyrants of the Hellenic world. Did their ancient rivals the Athenians venture to put forth similar pretensions of race and pedigree, they were met with a contemptuous smile from the rest of Greece and the enlightened all over the world, who well knew how little of pure Attic blood really flowed in their veins. The genuine race of Cecrops, the earth-born Eupatrids, had long mingled with strangers, before the fatal massacre of Sulla, which almost exterminated them. The edifices of their city, which the Roman general deigned to leave standing, were now repeopled by a motley crowd of immigrants from all parts.[1] With the name, however, of Athenians, these new citizens inherited the pride of their presumed ancestry. They paraded a spirit of independence even before the fasces of the praetor, refusing, when urged by one Roman consular, to allow sepulture within their walls to another, and declining to repeat the cele-

The Athenians debased in blood.

πλὴν τῶν φιλικῶν λειτουργιῶν ἄλλο συντελοῦντες οὐδέν. Comp. Plin. *Hist. Nat.* iv. 5: "ager Laconicæ gentis" Pausan. iii. iv.

[1] Cic. *Orat.* 44.: "Athenis mos est quotannis laudare in concione eos qui sunt in proeliis interfecti, recitato Platonis Menexeno" Tacitus (*Ann.* ii. 55.) tells how the pride of Rome rebuked these pretensions: "quod contra decus Rom. nominis non Atheniensis *tot cladibus exstinctos,* sed colluviem omnium nationum comitate nimia coluisset."

bration of their mysteries at the solicitation of Crassus.[1]

The splendour of the old Athenian glory still cast a mild declining ray over the land of Phœbus and the Muses; but the most accomplished of its foreign votaries could not but observe, that in his time the home of science and letters was more justly appreciated by strangers than by its own degenerate citizens.[2] Strangers indeed still continued to flock to it, and none were so numerous, none such enthusiasts in admiring it, as the sons of its Italian conquerors. The contemporaries of Cicero fully recognised the fact that the fame of ancient Hellas was mainly a reflex from the preeminent glory of Athens.[3] The jealousies of ancient rivals were extinguished in their common humiliation, and the men of Rhodes and Sparta regarded Athens as the last prop of their national renown, and sought the honour of enrolment among her citizens.[4] The noblest of the Romans were fain to follow this example. In vain did Cicero remind them of a principle of their own law, better known, perhaps, to constitutional antiquarians than to practical jurists, that every Roman who inscribed his name on the rolls of another republic, thereby forfeited the privileges of his own.[5]

With the destruction of the Piræus by Sulla the commercial ascendancy of Athens had suffered an eclipse whence it never again emerged. In the time of Augustus her naval arsenal had dwindled into a small straggling

Architectural splendour of Athens.

---

[1] See the letter of Sulpicius on the death of M. Marcellus. Cic. *ad Div.* iv. 12. 5.; and comp. Cic. *de Orat.* iii. 20.

[2] Cic. *de Orat.* iii. 11.: "Athenis jam diu doctrina ipsorum Atheniensium interiit, domicilium tantum in illa urbe remanet studiorum, quibus vacant cives, peregrini utuntur."

[3] Cic. *Brut.* 13. . . . "dicendi studium non erat commune Græciæ sed proprium Athenarum."

[4] Cic. *pro Flacc.* 26.: "Auctoritate tanta est, ut jam fractum et debilitatum Græciæ nomen hujus urbis laude nitatur."

[5] Cic. *pro Balb.* 12.

village, and the three state galleys which she still
maintained, like the Bucentaur of falling Venice,
merely preserved the tradition of her former greatness.[1] Nevertheless, though shorn of the resources
of industry and independence, the splendour of the
illustrious city was maintained by the pious vene-
ration of her foreign visitors, who regarded her not
unjustly with a feeling akin to religious. The Athens
of the Augustan era might still, perhaps, claim to be
the finest city in the world. Since the fall of her
liberty 300 years before, kings and potentates had
vied with one another in embellishing her streets and
public places; and if she presented, like more modern
cities, no capacious squares or long vistas lined on
either side with superb edifices, it was owing to the
unevenness of her original site, and the scruples
which had spared her narrow and tortuous lanes in
so many capitulations. The great temple of Zeus
Olympius, first designed by the dynasty of Pisistratus,
had risen, column after column, under Antiochus
Epiphanes, and having been partially spoiled by
Sulla, was carried on almost to completion by the
joint efforts, already commemorated, of many royal
associates.[2] Attalus, king of Pergamus, had crowned
the walls of the Acropolis with statues. Ptolemy
Philadelphus had erected a magnificent gymnasium.
The groves of Academus which Sulla had cut down

[1] Strabo, ix. 1. p. 395. Athens contributed all her remaining forces
to the cause of Pompeius, retaining only the three official galleys,
Theoris, Paralus, and Salaminia, the last tokens of her ancient glory.
Lucan, iii. 381.:

> "Exhausit veteres quamvis delectus Athenas,
> Exiguæ Phœbea tenent navalia puppes ;
> Tresque petunt veram credi Salamina carinæ."

The passage is crabbed, and there is no satisfactory explanation to be
given of the word *Phœbea*. None of the Athenian havens was consecrated to Apollo, but the Munychia had a temple of Diana.

[2] Livy (xli. 20.): speaks of it perhaps before the undertaking of
the confederate potentates: "templum Jovis Olympii unum in terris
inchoatum pro magnitudine Dei."

to construct machinery for his siege were planted
anew in the regin of Augustus, and continued for
many ages to furnish a shade to sophists and rhetoricians.   The walls of Athens, however, once overthrown, lay henceforth in ruins.   The weakness of
the city of Minerva became now her best defence.
Both Julius and Augustus contributed to the erection of a portico dedicated to the goddess, and Agrippa
placed his own statue, together with that of his imperator, upon a single pedestal by the side of the
Propylæa of the Acropolis.   A temple of Rome and
Augustus was erected before the eastern front of
the Parthenon.   The munificence of a private bene-
factor, the censor Appius Claudius, had decorated
the hamlet of the Attic Eleusis; and we may indulge,
perhaps, in the idea that Cicero himself displayed
his gratitude to his Alma Mater by dedicating to
her a votive memorial within the precincts of the
Academy.[1]

Exempt from the direct control of a Roman officer,
the university of Athens was governed by a
senate and assembly of its own.   It was
permitted to retain its ancient laws, and
the august tribunals, such as the Areopagus, which
had continued for so many ages to administer them.
Under the shadow of the free republic of thought and
letters, art, science, and philosophy were still taught
and cultivated.   The professors of ethics and physics,
of oratory and grammar, still held forth to admiring
audiences, each in his own lecture-room; every theory
had its special teacher, every paradox its sworn defender; but strangers flocked to Athens, not to ascertain the truth from the collision of minds, but to hear
how the doctrines of Epicurus were modified by Patro,
how Phædrus handled the dialectics of Zeno, or what

Cultivation of art and letters at Athens.

---

[1] Cic. *ad Att.* vi. 1. 26.: "Audio Appium προπύλαιον Eleusine facere:
num inepti fuerimus si nos quoque Academiæ fecerimus?   Equidem
valde ipsas Athenas amo: volo esse quoddam monumentum."

was the latest qualification of the doubts of the Academy.[1] The place of the poets had been taken by lecturers on poetry: but versification still had its votaries, and the epigram's *humble plot of ground* was cultivated at least with exquisite taste. The arts of sculpture and architecture had long lost their originality and simplicity; yet there was no department of excellence in which the genius of Greece seemed so nearly inexhaustible as in these.[2]

The destruction of Corinth by the Romans had driven the commerce of Greece to the Isle of Delos, which, besides the convenience of its situation at the entrance of the Ægean, enjoyed the advantage of a reputation for special sanctity. It was the natural emporium of four seas, and offered an interchange between the products of Greece and Asia, Libya and Sarmatia. It became the centre of the slave trade of the ancient world, the most constant, and perhaps the most extensive, of all traffics. The piracy of the Mediterranean, which threatened to sweep away all other maritime employments, was the feeder and sustainer of this. Hither it converged in its regular and legitimate course from Thrace and Pontus on the Euxine, from Phrygia and Caria, from Egypt and Cyrene; even

Commercial emporium of Delos.

---

[1] Propert. iii. 21.:

> " Inde ubi Piræi capient me litora portus,
>   Scandam ego Theseæ brachia longa viæ.
> Illic aut spatiis animum emendare Platonis
>   Incipiam, aut hortis, docte Epicure, tuis.
> Persequar aut studium linguæ, Demosthenis arma,
>   Librorumque tuos, munde Menandre, sales ;
> Aut certe tabulæ captent mea lumina pictæ,
>   Sive ebore exactæ, seu magis ære, manus."

[2] Enthusiasts for Grecian art, such as Visconti, have maintained that its excellence in sculpture lasted without decline for six centuries. On the other hand, Velleius Paterculus asserts the famous paradox, " Eminentissima ingenia in idem arctati temporis spatium congregari," and illustrates it by the assumed confinement of the excellence of all arts in Greece within the limits of a single generation. Vell. i. 16, 17.

the cities of European Hellas furnished a class of victims, selected for the beauty of their persons or the refinement of their manners. But wherever piracy was in the ascendant, captives from every coast, and even noble Romans among them, were wafted to the great depôt of Delos, and transferred without remorse to the dealers who awaited their arrival.[1] Not less than 5,000 slaves had thus been bought and sold in a single day. But the prosperity of the guilty island was more shortlived than even the crimes on which it throve. The pirates were still roaming the seas with impunity when the wealth of Delos tempted the cupidity of Menophanes, one of the captains of Mithridates, by whom it was stormed and ransacked.[2] Its commercial eminence migrated to the securer stronghold of Rhodes, which had the singular good fortune to escape the sword both of the Romans and their adversaries. The ruin of Delos was consummated by the restoration of Corinth; and in the age of Augustus it still lay prostrate, nor did it ever again recover a portion of its earlier importance.[3]

Notwithstanding many vexatious restrictions on the natural course of trade imposed by fiscal ignorance, the unity of the Roman empire conspired on the whole to restore commerce to its legitimate channels. The spot on the Asiatic coast which corresponded most nearly with Corinth on the European was Ephesus, a city which, in the time of Herodotus, had been the start-

Cities of Asia:

Ephesus,

---

[1] After the suppression of the Cilician piracy, the practice survived of kidnapping free men and selling them into slavery. Cicero (*de Off.* ii. 16.) praises the benevolence of those who redeemed the victims of the crimps or corsairs. Even in Italy, during the civil wars, free men were seized by armed bands and carried into the ergastula of the great proprietors. Both Augustus and his successor attempted to remedy this violence (Suet. *Oct.* 32., *Tiber.* 8.): nevertheless the crime continued. Senec. *Controv.* x. 4. The *Digest,* xxxix. 4., recognises the existence of freemen made slaves.

[2] Cicero, at a little later period still, contrasts the security of Delos with the dangers of Italy, and even the Appian Way, under the reign of maritime piracy. *Pro Leg. Manil.* 18.

[3] Strabo, x. 5. p. 486.

ing-point of caravans for Upper Asia, but which, under the change of dynasties and ruin of empires, had dwindled into a mere provincial town. The mild sway of Augustus restored it to wealth and eminence, and as the official capital of the province of Asia, it was reputed to be the metropolis of no less than 500 cities.[1]   It shared with Smyrna, Pergamus, and Nicæa the honour of erecting a temple to the emperor. Apamea, in Phrygia, the centre of trade with the interior, was reputed the second commercial city in the peninsula.   Synnada was celebrated for its variegated marbles, Laodicea for its woollens and tapestries, Hierapolis and Cibyra, the first for its dyes, the second for its iron manufactures. To these may be added the commercial activity of Miletus, and the royal magnificence of decoration which distinguished Cyzicus, Sinope, and Cnidus, in each of which kings had once resided.[2]   These numerous hives of population were supported, not only by the exchange of their industry for foreign articles, but by the abundant fertility of the soil around them : the plains of Sardis and the valleys of the Caicus, the Hermus and the Cayster, were remarkable for their harvests, and the wines of Asia were among the choicest in the world.[3]

Apamea, Synnada, Laodicea, Cibyra.

Miletus.

Such was the condition of the most famous cities of the old world, reviving under the exercise of their native usages, or protected by the vigilance and equity of a strong metropolitan administration.   There was, however, another class of cities in the East, of more modern origin

Cities of Macedonian origin in Asia.

---

[1] Eckhel, *Doctr. Numm.* ii. 559, &c.; Ulpian. *de Off. Procons.* in *Digest.* iv. 5.; Strabo xiv. 1. p. 640. foll.

[2] Strabo, xii., xiii.; Joseph. *Bell. Jud.* ii. 16, § 4.

[3] Strabo, *ll. cc.* For the natural resources of Asia, the rapidity with which it recovered its losses by war and tyranny, and the importance of its revenues to the empire, see particularly Cicero, *ad Qu. Fr.* i. 1. and *pro Leg. Manil.* 6. ad *Att.* vi. 2.

and character, of which it will be sufficient to notice
one specimen. The Macedonian rulers of the East
were a race of builders. After the manner of the
kings and satraps to whom they succeeded, they fed
their pride by sweeping the inhabitants of towns and
villages into cities laid out with pomp and splendour, on sites the most convenient and commanding,
to which they gave their own names, or those of their
kinsmen or consorts. Antioch flourished
on the fall of Tyre. It was erected by
Seleucus Nicator, the greatest of all builders of the
class, on the banks of the Orontes, about fifteen miles
from the sea, in a plain celebrated for the beauty of
its climate, the abundance of its water, and conse-
quent fertility. It was laid out, after the usual type
of the Macedonian cities, on a symmetrical plan, the
chief street being a straight line four miles in length,
bordered throughout with double colonnades. Four
cities, contiguous to one another, coalesced into a
single metropolis; but, from some inequality of
ground or other cause, the common arrangement of
two transverse streets was not adopted at Antioch.[1]
The character of Grecian architecture, with its in-
definite prolongation of horizontal lines, its regularity
of outline, and constant repetition of similar forms,
must have given a peculiar air of magnificence to this
style of construction, and conveyed an impression of
the enormous power of the hand which could thus
strike out as it were at one blow a fabric capable of
infinite extension in every direction. Antioch contained, we are told, in the third century, 300,000
free citizens, and was then surpassed in numbers only

Antioch.

---

[1] Strabo, xvi. 2. p. 750. See the description and map of Antioch
from Malelas and Libanius, in Lewin's or Conybeare and Howson's
Life of St. Paul. Nicæa, mentioned above, should be included among
the cities of Macedonian origin. Strabo describes it as a square of
sixteen stadia in circumference, divided into equal rectangles by two
straight avenues, so that the four gates could be seen from a pillar in
the public place in the centre. Strabo, xii. 4. p. 506.

by Rome and Seleucia on the Tigris. Alexandria perhaps nearly equalled it, but every other city throughout the world yielded to it the palm of grandeur and population.[1]

The Grecian cities of Syria, and Antioch at the head of them, were notorious for their Greek cities luxury and voluptuousness: and the idle in Italy. and dissolute native, relaxed by long servitude to his kings and priests, received the polish of Hellenic culture only to make his degradation more conspicuous. The refinements of Grecian life had found a home also on the fairest shores of Italy, and had exercised no less debasing influence on the sterner character of the Romans themselves. From ages long lost in the darkness of legendary history, settlers from Greece had established themselves on the coast of the Tyrrhene or Sicilian Sea: hill and headland, pool and river, village and city, had received from them a Grecian appellation, and had been admitted within the hallowed circle of their national traditions. Misenum and Leucosia, Posidonia and Cumæ, Acheron and Avernus, Neapolis and Herculaneum, attested the ancient settlement of the Greeks on the coast of Campania; while cities of native growth, such as Baiæ and Stabiæ, Surrentum, Pompeii and Salernum, grew up by the side of the foreign colonies, and partook of their splendour and prosperity.[2] From the period of the conquest of this region by the Romans, its beauty and salubrity had attracted their notice; the medicinal qualities of its

---

[1] Herodian. iv. 5.: ἢ τὴν Ἀντιόχειαν ἢ τὴν Ἀλεξάνδρειαν, οὐ πολύ τι τῆς Ῥώμης, ὡς ᾤετο, μεγέθει ὑπολειπούσας. Seleucia on the Tigris was built also by Seleucus Nicator. In the time of Pliny it was supposed to contain 400,000 free inhabitants (Plin. *Hist. Nat.* vi. 36.), although the Parthians had built Ctesiphon by its side to rival and control it. I suspect that Pliny's estimate applies properly to the two cities conjointly

[2] Pæstum was the Italian name of Posidonia, Puteoli of Dicæarchia, which eventually prevailed over the Grecian.

warm vapours and sulphureous springs were appreciated by them : while the mountains which encircled
it had not yet revealed their latent fires, or the activity they may have displayed in remote ages was
remembered only in obscure traditions.[1]

Roman imperators, from the time of the Scipios
The life of the Romans on the Campanian coast. and the Gracchi, had sought repose in this
favoured tract : on the heights of Misenum
Hortensius and Lucullus, Cæsar and Pom-
peius, had erected their villas, their camps, as Seneca
would rather call them, from the dignity of their
position, and the wide prospect they commanded.[2]
The cities which lined the gulf or crater embraced
by the sweeping arms of Misenum and Surrentum,
were governed by Grecian laws, and surrendered to
the sway of Grecian usages and customs. To them
the Roman, wearied with the ceaseless occupations
and rigid formality of life at Rome, gladly retired
for bodily relaxation, to be ennobled, as he might
pretend, by intellectual exercises. Neapolis had its
schools and colleges, as well as Athens ; its society
abounded in artists and men of letters, and it enjoyed
among the Romans the title of the learned, which
comprehended in their view the praise of elegance
as well as knowledge.[3] Every fifth year the festival
of the Quinquennia was celebrated with athletic contests in the arena ; in its theatre the genteel comedy

[1] It has been conjectured that the Homeric or Phœnician tradition,
that here were the ends of the earth covered with Cimmerian darkness, was derived from the reports of navigators, who had found the
sun obscured by volcanic smoke and ashes, such as have been known
to extinguish the light in Iceland for months together.

[2] Seneca, *Ep.* 51.: "Videbatur hoc magis militare ex edito specu-
lari late longeque subjecta. Adspice quam positionem elegerunt,
quibus ædificia excitaverunt locis et qualia: scias non villas esse sed
castra." It is curious that the vast remains of the Lucullan substructions, grottoes, and arcades, received in the middle ages the name of
Castrum Lucullanum.

[3] Columell. x. 134.: "Docta Parthenope." The epithet implies,
besides mere knowledge, the polish and refinement of manners imparted by a liberal education.

of the school of Menander combined in due proportions the decorousness of Rome and the licence of its
native country.[1] Here the patrician might throw off
the toga, the sandal and the cap, and lounge in a
trailing robe barefooted, his head lightly bound with
the Oriental fillet, attended at every step by obe-
dient slaves and cringing parasites, but relieved from
the gaze of clients and lictors, from the duty of
answering questions and the necessity of issuing
commands.[2] Such was the indolent life of the Romans at Neapolis and its neighbour Palæpolis; such
it was at Herculaneum and Pompeii. But Baiæ, the
most fashionable of the Roman spas, presented another and more lively spectacle. Here idleness had
assumed the form of dissipation, and the senator
displayed as much energy in amusing himself as he
had elsewhere shown in serving his country or pro-
moting his own fortunes. As soon as the reviving
heats of April gave token of advancing summer, the
noble and the rich hurried from Rome to this choice
retreat; and here, till the raging dogstar forbade
the toils even of amusement, they disported themselves on shore or on sea, in the thick groves or on
the placid lakes, in litters and chariots, in gilded
boats with painted sails, lulled by day and night with
the sweetest symphonies of song and music, or gazing

---

[1] Stat. *Sylv.* ii. 5. 89.:

> " Quid nunc magnificas species cultusque locorum,
> Templaque, et innumeris spatia interstincta columnis;
> Quid geminam molem nudi tectique theatri,
> Et Capitolinis Quinquennia proxima lustris;
> Quid laudem risus libertatemque Menandri,
> Quam Romanus honos et Graia licentia miscent?"

It must be observed, however, that the Quinquennial games of Neapolis were an institution of Domitian, seventy years after Augustus.

[2] Cicero, *pro Rabir. Post.* 10.: "Deliciarum causa et voluptatis
non modo cives Romanos sed et nobiles adolescentes, et quosdam
etiam senatores, summo loco natos, non in hortis et suburbanis suis,
sed Neapoli in celeberrimo oppido, cum mitella sæpe vidimus." See
in the same place what scandal might be caused by the use of the
pallium.

indolently on the wanton movements of male and female dancers. The bath, elsewhere their relaxation, was here the business of the day: besides using the native warm springs and the vapours which issued from the treacherous soil, they turned the pools of Avernus and Lucrinus into tanks for swimming; and in these pleasant waters both sexes met familiarly together, and conversed amidst the roses sprinkled lavishly on their surface.[1]

But I have brought the reader from the provinces to Italy: I now assume the graver task of introducing him to Rome.

From whichever side of Italy the stranger approached the imperial city, he emerged from the defiles of an amphitheatre of hills upon a wide open plain, near the centre of which an isolated cluster of eminences, moderate in height and volume, crowned with a vast assemblage of stately edifices, announced the goal towards which for many a hundred miles his road had been conducting him.

Approach to Rome.

There were two main routes which might have thus led him from the provinces to the capital, the Appian from Greece and Africa, and the Flaminian from Gaul; but the lines of the Servian wall, which still bounded Rome in the age of Augustus, were pierced with eighteen apertures, each of which admitted a well-appointed road from the nearer districts of the peninsula. The approach to the greatest of cities was indicated also by works of an-

The roads.

---

[1] For the amusements of Baiæ see Tibullus, iii. 5.; Martial, iv. 57., x. 30., xi. 80.; Ovid, *Art. Amand.* i. 255.; and especially Seneca, *Ep.* 51.: "Videre ebrios per litora errantes, et comissationes navigantium, et symphoniarum cantibus perstrepentes lacus . . . præternavigantes adulteras dinumerare, et aspicere tot genera cymbarum variis coloribus picta, et fluitantem toto lacu rosam, et audire canentium nocturna convicia." He also calls it, more compendiously, "diversorium vitiorum." Ovid, *l. c.*:

"Hinc aliquis vulnus referens in pectore dixit:
Non hæc, ut fama est, unda salubris erat."

other kind, the most magnificent and imposing in their character of any Roman constructions. In the time of Augustus seven aqueducts brought water from distant sources to Rome. Some of these streams indeed were conveyed underground in leaden pipes throughout their whole course, till they were received into reservoirs within the walls, where they rose to the level required for the supply of the highest sites. Others, however, entered the city on a succession of stone arches, and of these the Aqua Marcia, which was derived from the Volscian mountains, was thus sumptuously conducted for a distance of 7000 paces before it reached the brow of the Esquiline Hill.[1] These monuments of the pomp and power of the people to whose wants they ostentatiously ministered, were rendered the more impressive from the solitudes in which for many miles they planted their giant footsteps. The Campagna, or plain of Rome, at the present day the most awful image of death in the bosom of life anywhere to be witnessed, was already deserted by the swarms of population which three centuries before had made it the hive of Italy. The fertile fields of the Hernici and Æqui had been converted into pasture land, and the cultivators of the soil, once the denizens of a hundred towns and villages, had gone to swell the numbers of the cities on the coast. Even the fastnesses in the hills had been abandoned in the general security from external attack; while the patrician villas, with which central Italy was studded, were buried in the shade of woods or the cool recesses of the mountains. For many months, it may be added, the heat was too oppressive for journeying by day, whenever it could be avoided; the commerce of Rome was chiefly carried on by means of the river[2]; and the

The aqueducts.

Solitude of the country round Rome.

---

[1] Strabo, v. 3.; Plin. *Hist. Nat.* xxxi. 3. 24. Corrected by Frontinus in his special treatise on the aqueducts, c. 7.

[2] There are picturesque allusions to the movement on the river in

necessities of warfare no longer required the constant passing and repassing at all hours of soldiers, couriers, and munitions. The practice of riding by night seems to have been generally adopted, so that the movement on the roads gave little sign by daylight of the vicinity of so vast a haunt of human beings with their manifold interests and occupations.[1] Nor was the proximity of so great a city indicated long before arriving at its gates by suburbs stretching far into the surrounding plain. The rhetorical flights of certain writers who would assure us of the contrary, and persuade us that Rome sent forth her feelers as far as Aricia and Tibur, and that many cities were attached to it by continuous lines of building, are plainly refuted by the fact that groves, villages, and separate houses are repeatedly mentioned as existing within three or four miles of the capital.[2]

The solemn feeling with which, under such circumstances, a great city would naturally be approached, was redoubled by the wayside spectacle, peculiarly Roman, of the memorials of the dead. The sepulchres of twenty generations lined the high roads for several miles beyond the gates; and many of these were edifices of considerable size and architectural pretension: for it was the nobles only whose houses were thus distinguished, and each

Tombs by the roadside.

Propertius, i. 14.:

"Et modo tam celeres mireris currere lintres,
    Et modo tam tardas funibus ire rates:"

and Martial, iv. 64.:

"Quem nec rumpere nauticum celeusma,
    Nec clamor valet helciariorum."

[1] Many indications might be alleged of the frequency of night travelling. The Allobroges were circumvented on their leaving Rome in the evening. Catilina made his exit from the city at night; so did Curio and Antonius. Comp. Juvenal, x. 19.:

"Pauca licet portes argenti vascula puri
    Nocte iter ingressus."

[2] See the passages of the ancients, and ill-considered inferences of the moderns, in De la Malle, *Econ. Pol.* i. 375.

patrician family pointed with pride to its own mausoleum, in which it gathered the ashes of its members, and often of its slaves and freedmen, beneath a
common roof. Flanked by such rows of historic
marble, and crossed by the gaunt shadows of funereal
cypresses, the Appian, the queen, as it was proudly
termed, of all Ways, as the oldest, the longest, and the
most frequented, approached the city from the south.[1]
At five miles' distance from the walls it traversed the
famous plain where the Horatii decided the fate of
the young republic, and where the monuments of the
Roman and Sabine champions indicated the spots on
which each had fallen.[2] Nearly at the first milestone,
as measured from the Servian gates, it passed under
the arch of Drusus, and thence descended a gentle
slope into the hollow of the Aqua Crabra.[3] The monuments of the dead now lay closer together. Here
were the sepulchres of the Scipios, the Furii, the
Manilii, the Servilii, Calatini and Marcelli; of which
the first four have been already discovered, the rest
still await the exploration of the curious.[4] Here were
laid under a common dome in cells arranged along the
walls, the ashes of the slaves of Augustus and Livia.

---

[1] Stat. *Sylv.* ii. 2. 12.: " Appia longarum teritur Regina viarum."

[2] Liv. i. 25.; Dionys. Hal. *Antiq. Rom.* iii. 18.: The modern topographer Canina accounts for a bend in the road at this point, as
meant to avoid the desecration of these sacred memorials. *Annali
del Instituto,* &c., 1852, p. 268. He thinks that the actual monuments
have been discovered in the most recent excavations.

[3] Fragments of the first milestone have been discovered at 512
palms (about 120 yards) beyond the Porta S. Sebastiano. Canina,
Annali, 1851, p. 317. The arch of Drusus stands a little within that
modern gate.

[4] Cic. *Tusc. Disp.* i. 5. The excavations of the last few years
extend from the fourth to the ninth milestone. Besides the foundations of villas, temples, and sepulchres, many inscriptions have been
brought to light, which appear, however, in almost every case to
belong to the later periods of the empire. It is *possible,* from the single
word " Cotta," which can now be read upon the Casal rotondo, a
monument of similar character to that known by the name of Cæcilia
Metella, that this was the tomb of Messala Corvinus. See Canina,
in *Annali,* 1851.

Hard by the gate reposed the remains of the base
Horatia, slain by a patriot brother for her devotion
to a foreign lover. Beside the rivulet, on the
southern slope, perhaps of the Cælian Hill, was the
reputed grotto of Egeria, once rudely scooped out of
the rock; but its native simplicity had long been
violated by the gaudy pomp of architecture and
sculpture.[1] On the descent to the Aqua Crabra, the
temple of Mars crowned the eminence which fronted
the gate of the city, the spot from which the procession
of the knights to the Capitol on the Ides of Julius took
its commencement.[2] Still nearer to the gate, on
the right side of the road, were the twin temples of
Honour and Virtue, vowed by the great Marcellus
for his conquest of Syracuse, which he had adorned
with the earliest spoils of foreign painting. From
the steps of these temples the populace had greeted
Cicero on his return from exile. The gate, surnamed
Capena, dripped constantly with the overflowings
of the Aqua Appia, and of a branch of the Marcia
brought there to join it: the united stream was
carried over the arch on its way to the Aventine.

Entrance to Rome. Here we enter Rome: the road has become
a street; houses, hitherto interspersed between monuments and temples, have now become
dense and continuous. The avenue is still, however,
broad and straight for the convenience of military
processions. Soon it forks into two ways, still following the direction of the hollows between the hills:
the one, turning to the right between the Palatine

---

[1] Juvenal. iii. 18.

[2] The temple of Mars stood on an acclivity (Clivus Martis), and
faced the Porta Capena: " quem prospicit ipsa Appositum tectæ porta
Capena viæ." It was probably, therefore, on the descent to the Aqua
Crabra, in going towards the city. That there was some interval
between it and the gate appears from Livy, x. 33.: " semitam saxo
quadrato a Capena Porta ad Martis struxerunt." The lowering of
this hill is recorded on an inscription in Gruter: " Clivum Martis
pec. publica in planitiem redegerant."

and Cælian, was conducted to the Velia, the Esquiline and the Forum, till it arrived at the golden milestone at the foot of the Capitol; the other, to the left, entered one extremity of the Circus Maximus, beneath the Palatine and Aventine, to pass out of it at the other, and reach the same termination through the Forum Boarium and the Velabrum.[1]

The seven hills of Rome have been diversely enumerated, and admit, indeed, of being multiplied to a much greater number, or, regarding them from a different point of view, of being not less considerably reduced.   The Aventine is the only eminence among them wholly distinct and separated from the others.   The Palatine is connected with the Esquiline by the low ridge or saddle of the Velia, and the Capitoline was in like manner attached at its northern extremity to the Quirinal, till severed from it by an artificial cutting a century after Augustus.   The Quirinal, the Viminal, the Esquiline, and the Cælian, to which may be added the extramural eminence of the Pincian, are in fact merely tongues or spurs of hill projecting inwards from a common base, the broad table-land which slopes on the other side almost imperceptibly into the Campagna. On approaching Rome from the north the eye was at once arrested by the abrupt escarpment of the Capitoline, which sufficed to exclude from it all view of the city; but from the south or east it was carried gently upwards along the rising slopes, and allowed

The seven hills of Rome.

---

[1] There was unquestionably a communication through the circus longitudinally for the triumphal processions; but it is not likely that this was kept open for ordinary traffic. The usual thoroughfare must have run alongside the outer wall of the circus, and was perhaps conducted under the arcades which supported the upper seats of that edifice. The upper part of the circus was connected with the buildings on the Palatine on one side, and probably with those on the Aventine on the other, the whole width of the valley between being thus occupied by its extensive structures. The Aqua Crabra, we must suppose, was carried in a tunnel beneath it.

to overleap the depressions which lay beyond them, of the Suburra, the Circus, the Velabrum and the Forum, in which the densest buildings of the city nestled, till it lighted on the heights of the Capitoline and the summits of the Etruscan mountains in the distance.

The Palatine Hill, which was closely embraced by the double arms of the Appian Way,—the site of the city of Romulus, the cradle of imperial Rome,—was an elevation of about 130 feet above the level of the sea.[1] With some assistance from art it was made to slope abruptly on every side, though at its junction with the Velia its height was not more than half that which has been ascribed to the mass in general. It formed a trapezium of solid rock, two sides of which were about 300 yards in length, and the others about 400: the area of its summit, to compare it with a familiar object, was nearly equal to the space between Pall Mall and Piccadilly, in London. Along the brow of the escarpment ran, we must suppose, the original walls; but no fragments of them remain, nor have our authorities preserved any notice of their exact position. The site of two of the gates may be pointed out perhaps at the base of the cliffs; but it is possible that these mark the apertures, not in the defences themselves, but in the sacred enclosure of the pomœrium beyond them.[2] This fanciful limitation had been

The Palatine.

---

[1] This and subsequent measurements, taken from M. Bunsen's work on Rome, refer of course to the present elevation. Some allowance must be made for the degradation of the summits. At the same time the hollows have been filled up to the depth, in some places, of fifteen or twenty feet. It must be remembered that the bed and water-line of the Tiber have also risen, though probably in a less degree. The crown of the arch of the Cloaca at its embouchure stands now very little above the mean level of the river. We are told that in ancient times the tunnel could be navigated by boats, and admitted a waggon loaded with hay: but this perhaps supposes the water at its lowest.

[2] The Porta Mugionis, the present access to the Palatine from the north near the arch of Titus, and the Porta Romana on the west, near

traced round the foot of the hill, after the Etruscan fashion, with a plough drawn by a bull and a heifer, the furrow being carefully made to fall inwards, and the heifer yoked on the near side, to signify that strength and courage are required without, obedience and fertility within the city.[1]   The broad ways which encircled the Palatine skirted the borders of the pomœrium, and formed the route of the triumphal march, and of the religious and political processions.[2]

The locality thus doubly inclosed was reserved for the temples of the gods and the residence of the ruling race, the class of patricians, or burghers, as Niebuhr has taught us to entitle them, which predominated over the dependent commons, and only suffered them to crouch for security under the shadow of the walls of Romulus.   The Palatine was never occupied by the plebs.   In the last age of the republic, long after the removal of this partition, or of the civil distinctions between the great classes of the state, here was still the chosen site of the mansions of the highest nobility.   Here stood the famous dwelling of the

The Palatine occupied by temples and patrician residences.

the church of S. Teodoro. There was probably a third gate at the south-eastern corner of the hill, where Severus afterwards built his Septizonium, to make the approach to the city from Africa, *i.e.* by the Appian Way, more imposing.

[1] Varro, *L. L.* v. 32.; Plut. *Rom.* 11.   From Tac. *Ann.* xii. 26., it appears that this Etruscan fashion referred to the pomœrium, not to the walls.

[2] The line of the Triumphal Way has been referred to in another place (cl. xix.).   Becker has described it more closely.   It seems to have run from the Porta Carmentalis (I omit the difficult question about the Porta Triumphalis), along the Vicus Jugarius, up one side of the Velabrum, and down the other again by the Via Nova, thence through the circus, &c.   In this way it made a complete circuit of the original city on the Palatine, and had doubtless a religious significance.   Compare also the lustral procession round the pomœria, in Lucan, i. 592.:

> " Tum jubet et totam pavidis a civibus Urbem
> Ambiri, et festo purgantes mœnia lustro
> Longa per extremos pomœria cingere fines
> Pontifices, sacri quibus est permissa potestas. . . ."

tribune Drusus, whose architect proposed so to fence
it with walls and curtains that its owner should be
secluded from the observation of the citizens below.
The tribune's answer, *Rather build it so that all my
countrymen may see me*, implied not only that he
would be visible by all, but accessible to all also.
The site of this house cannot be fixed with certainty;
but it seems probable from this anecdote, that it
overlooked the Forum, and stood therefore on the
north side of the hill, not far from the Porta Mugionis.   It became the property of Crassus, and was
bought of him by Cicero; it was razed, as we have
seen, by Clodius, but the vacant space was restored
to its recent possessor, after whose death we hear of
its passing into the hands of a noble named Censo-
rinus.   The house of Æmilius Scaurus was another
patrician mansion in this locality.   There seems
reason to believe that it stood at the north-eastern
angle of the hill, overlooking the valley since occupied by the Colosseum and the arch of Constantine.[1]
This mansion also passed through various hands in
the course of two or three generations: it was famous
for the size and splendour of its columns, of the
costly marble afterwards distinguished by the name
of Lucullus.[2]   Contiguous to the dwelling of Cicero
was that of his enemy Clodius: the price the tribune
had given for it, says Pliny, agreed with the madness
of a king rather than the dignity of a Roman senator.[3]   The Regia, the official residence of Cæsar as
chief pontiff, which lay at the foot of the hill, abut-

---

[1] See Dezobry, *Rome sous Auguste*, i. 156.   The topographical
part of this generally valuable book is founded on some inveterate
errors, and can only occas onally be made serviceable.

[2] Pliny, *Hist. Nat.* xxxvi. 2.   These columns, four in number,
were thirty-eight feet in height, and adorned the atrium of the house.
They were the largest of the whole number of three hundred and
sixty which Scaurus had conveyed, in his ædileship, to Rome (A.U.
696) for the decoration of a temporary theatre.   They were afterwards used in the theatre of Marcellus.   Ascon. *in Orat. pro Scaur.*

[3] Plin. *H. N.* xxxvi. 24. 2.

ting on the forum, may have thus been placed immediately below it.   We may amuse ourselves with
imagining the flight of steps and the wicket in the
garden wall, which admitted Pompeia's gallant to
the mysteries of the Bona Dea.   Agrippa, and after
him Messala, occupied the house which had belonged
to Antonius on the Palatine; and Domitius Calvinus,
who triumphed over Spain in 715, devoted a large
portion of his spoils to the construction of a mansion
in this quarter also.[1]   But a spot of more interest
than these in the imperial annals was that which
bore the residence of Augustus himself.   From the
modest house in which he first saw the The palace of
light, the dwelling of his father Octavius, Augustus.
which was also on the Palatine, he removed at a later
period to the mansion of Hortensius, on the same
hill, and there he continued to abide, though lodged
far beneath the dignity of his position, in the height
of his power, till it was destroyed by fire in 748.[2]
The citizens insisted on contributing to its restoration on a grander scale; and their subscriptions
must have been universal if, as we read, the emperor
refused to accept more than a single denarius from
each.   The residence of the chief of the state began
already to be known from its situation as the Palatium
or palace.   Augustus, in his care not to press on the
limits of popular favour, pretended to regard the
dwelling thus erected for him as the property of the
public, and relinquished a large portion of it for the
recreation of the citizens.[3]   It was probably connected with the Regia, and its remains are accordingly
to be looked for in the north-westen angle of the hill,

---

[1] Dion, xlviii. 42., liii. 27.

[2] For the emperor's changes of residence see Suetonius, *Oct.* 5, 51,
72.; and Dion, liii. 16., lv. 12.   The house of Octavius was probably
on the Germalus, a portion of the Palatine Hill, and the Scalæ
Annulariæ descended from it to the Velabrum.

[3] Dion, lv. 12.: τὴν οἰκίαν οἰκοδομήσας ἐδημοσίωσε πᾶσαν .   . ἵν'
ἐν τοῖς ἰδίοις ἅμα καὶ ἐν τοῖς κοινοῖς οἰκοίη.

where indeed some foundations have been discovered which may have really appertained to it. Tiberius also built a mansion by the side of the Augustan, with which he eventually connected it, and thus embraced within the precincts of the imperial residence a large part of the western side of the Palatine. We shall see hereafter how later emperors extended these limits, and connected dome with dome, and at last hill with hill, by arcades, bridges, and substructions of enormous dimensions.

The Palatine was ascended in more than one direction by flights of steps, and if there was *Temples on the Palatine:* any road for wheel-carriages to its summit, it was used perhaps only for the convenience of religious solemnities. The houses of the nobility here, as in other parts of Rome, were isolated structures, placed at the caprice of their owners, surrounded by gardens, and never regularly disposed in streets, an arrangement which was confined to the lower level and inferior habitations of the city. They were interspersed with temples, colonnades and sacred groves. On the summit of the Palatine stood, among many others, the temples of Cybele and Juno Sospita, of Luna, of Febris, of Faith and Fortune, of Mars and Vesta: but none of these was so illustrious as that of Apollo, the emperor's patron, which was dignified by a spacious area inclosed by porticos, where the trophies of all nations were suspended. To this temple was also attached the celebrated library, in two compartments, devoted respectively to the writings of the Greeks and the Romans.[1] On the slopes of the hill, or immediately at its foot, were temples of Victory and of Jupiter Stator, bordering upon the Forum: the shrine of Pan, called also the Lupercal, stood at the entrance to the Velabrum.[2] On the

---

[1] Suet. *Oct.* 29.; Vell. iii. 81.; Dion, liii. 1.
[2] Virgil, *Æn.* viii. extr.:

> " Ipse sedens niveo candentis limine Phœbi,
> Dona recognoscit populorum, aptatque superbis
> Postibus."

crest which overlooked the circus was a venerable
monument, which pretended to be the regia of Romulus and Numa, and also a square mass of masonry, to
which was given the name of Roma Quadrata, supposed to have some mysterious connexion with the
fortunes of the city, beneath which certain precious
amulets were deposited.[1]

While the Romans were fortifying themselves on
the Palatine, the neighbouring summits did
not remain unoccupied.   The Quirinal, the   The Quirinal,
Viminal, and the Esquiline, the three prin-   Viminal, and Esquiline.
cipal spurs of the great northern ridge, were separated
from the Palatine by a swampy jungle, and their
crests were crowned with the strongholds of a rival
tribe.   The Quirinal at least was in the hands of a
Sabine colony; and we may conjecture that the
settlers on the other eminences were closely connected with these, from the tradition of the earthen
mound which seems to have closed, in remote antiquity, the mouth of the valley between them.[2]   The
Romans and the Sabines contended for the possession
of the Capitoline.   This hill, the smallest   The Capito-
of the seven, was flung across the hollow   line.
which descended westward from the Velia, and while it

We may remember how throughout this book the poet revels in allusions to the objects on the Palatine, and surrounds the residence of
his patron with a halo of historic associations.

[1] Festus, in v. Quadrata, p. 258.: "Quadrata Roma in Palatio ante
templum Apollinis (it lay towards the circus) dicitur, ubi reposita
sunt quæ solent boni ominis gratia in urbe condenda adhiberi (they
were bones of animals and implements) quia saxo munitus est initio
in speciem quadratam."

[2] The early Sabine occupation of the Quirinal is attested by the
presence here of many shrines of Sabine divinities, such as those of
Sancus, of Quirinus, and perhaps of Flora.   The college of the Salii
was at the Colline Gate.   Here was a house of Numa, the Sabine
king, and, at a later period, the temples of the Sabine emperors of the
Flavian house.   The antiquity of its occupation is shown by the Capitolium Vetus, the rival Capitol, in which, as in the other, was a temple
common to Jupiter, Juno, and Minerva.   Varro, de Ling. Lat. v. 32.
It stood probably on the crest of the hill, facing the Forum.

touched the Quirinal of the Sabines at one end, was
separated from the Palatine of the Romans by the
valley of the Velabrum at the other. It rose in two
summits: the Sabines seized the northern; the Romans established themselves on the southern.[1] A
small rectangular space lay depressed between them,
which for convenience we may call the Intermontium,
and this the Romans seem to have been the first to
make their own. The sacred grove, or asylum, in
which they offered a retreat for fugitives, was meant,
we may suppose, to encourage desertion from the
enemy. The disputes between the two powers ended
in their union and coalition; the morasses of the
valley were drained for their comitium or place of
meeting, and their common forum or thoroughfare;
while the fortress of the united confederacy was
founded on the northern summit of the hill they
shared between them, and the great temple of their
common patron Jupiter on the opposite extremity:
The Arx and the one was called specifically the Arx or
Capitolium. Citadel; the other bore the august name of
Capitolium.[2] The former contained only one important civil edifice, the temple of Juno Moneta, or
the Roman mint; the latter was the centre of the
religious system of the city, the spot where the holiest
mysteries of her faith were solemnised by the chief
of her priesthood, the consul or the dictator; to which
the imperator led his conquering legions preceded by
the spoils and captives of his triumph, and where he
returned his thanks for victory with appointed sacrifices. This was that rock eternal and immovable, to
which the empire of the world was promised, and
which the race of Julius and Æneas should inherit

---

[1] The northern summit, now known as the Araceli, is the higher
of the two, and rises 151 feet above the sea.

[2] The respective sites of the Arx and Capitolium are still a matter
of controversy on which it would hardly be proper to enter in this
work. I shall have further occasion to notice the question.

for ever and ever. The temple of Jupiter Capitolinus was divided into three cells, occupied The Temple of
by statues of the king of gods and Juno and Jupiter, Tarpeius or Capi-
Minerva, his assessors; the ancient divini- tolinus.
ties Terminus and Juventas, who refused to quit their
wonted stations on the foundation of the Capitol, were
accommodated with places within the sacred walls.
Here the images of the gods, on occasions of peculiar
solemnity, after being paraded through the city on
litters, were reclined on costly cushions, and invited
to a gorgeous banquet. The Jupiter of the Capitol
was called also the Tarpeian, from the name of the
cliff which fronted the Palatine, a precipice eighty
feet in height; and this was the direction in which
his temple looked.[1] On the same summit was a
second shrine of Jupiter, under the title of Of Jupiter
Feretrius, or the spoil-bearer, and another Feretrius, and
Tonans.
was erected here also to the same divinity
by Augustus, under the name of the Thunderer.[2] The
Capitoline was climbed perhaps by three paths; of
which two, the Clivus Asyli and the Clivus Clivus Asyli
Capitolinus, sprang from the Forum and and Clivus
Capitolinus.
ascended to the Intermontium, on the right
and left hand respectively. The first of these, the
existence of which is matter of question, was probably
a mere flight of steps; the other was practicable for
carriages, and for this purpose was made to climb
the acclivity with a zigzag. The triumphal chariot
rolled up this path, and was admitted within the
fortress through the gate Pandana, midway on the
ascent. There was a third access by the flight of
the Hundred Stairs from the southern extremity,
where the hill approached within three hundred yards

[1] Becker has fully shown that Mons Tarpeius and Mons Capitolinus
are convertible terms; the first, at least, being only the earlier, the
second the later designation: hence the Jupiter of the Capitol is
called sometimes by the one name, sometimes by the other.
[2] Dion, liv. 4.

of the river. The chief approach in modern times, that from the west, or the Campus Martius, was then a sheer declivity, and the spot most jealously guarded along the whole crest of the hill.

The Capitoline was the great bulwark of Rome against the Etruscans descending the Tiber from the north. But a colony of that people settled at a very early period on an eminence in the opposite quarter, which derived its name of Cælius from their leader Cæles Vibenna. These strangers, it is said, were transplanted, under a convention with the holders of the Palatine, to the valley between that hill and the Capitoline, the memory of which event was preserved in the appellation of the Tuscan Street, which led through the Velabrum from the Forum to the river side. The Cælius then fell into the possession of the Romans, who repeopled it with a colony of Latins transplanted from Alba Longa, their recent conquest.[1] In consequence perhaps of this early destination, this hill was never a strictly patrician quarter, although many noble mansions and particularly that of Cæsar's officer, Mamurra, were to be found there; it was covered with the houses of all classes indiscriminately, and became, at least under the empire, one of the most populous regions of the city.[2]

The Aventine, which from its position might well have become the most formidable rival of the Palatine, was condemned by the same caprice of fortune which had robbed it of the August Augury, on which the life of the city depended, to play an obscure and insignificant part in the early

The Cælian Hill.

The Aventine.

---

[1] Liv. i. 30.; Strabo, v. 3. p. 234.

[2] For the palace of Mamurra, who first encrusted his walls with marble, see Pliny, *Hist. Nat.* xxxvi. 6.:—for the number of noble residences, Martial, xii. 18.: "Dum per limina te potentiorum Sudatrix toga ventilat, vagumque Major Cælius et minor fatigant:"—for the mixture of all classes, Vell. ii. 130., describing a fire which ravaged the Cælian Hill: "omnis ordinis hominum jactura."

history of the Romans. This hill was a holy spot reserved by the neighbouring tribes for the meetings
of their confederacy, of which Rome herself was the
head, and was consecrated to Diana, whose temple
continued for ages to be the most conspicuous object
upon it.[1] When appropriated by the Romans under
Ancus, it was assigned as public domain to the use
of the patricians. The ruling caste placed on it some
bands of Latins as their tenants and clients, and it
was thus converted into a plebeian suburb of the
haughty Palatine.[2] The space which lay between the
two hills, the valley of the Aqua Crabra, had been
devoted by Romulus to the public games; and here,
after the stream was arched over and the area levelled
and strown with sand, the Great Circus, a stadium
600 yards in length, furnished seats for 150,000
spectators of the national races. Such was the extent of the city and its dependencies when Servius
Tullius, according to the tradition, resolved
to embrace the whole together within a
common line of defences. The summits indeed of
the precipitous cliffs might require no artificial forti-
fications, and it would seem that the Capitoline itself
had no other protection at some points than the
steepness of its natural escarpment; but dykes were
thrown across the hollows, and the most accessible
spots on the hills were strengthened with mounds of
earth or masonry. The long level ridge from which,
as has been described, the Esquiline, Viminal, and
Quirinal spring, was fortified by a continuous ditch
and rampart, which obtained the special appellation
of the Servian Agger. That there was no stone wall
here may be inferred not only from this title, but also

The walls of Servius.

---

[1] Servius compares the Latin worship of the Aventine Diana with
that of the Ephesian by the Ionian confederacy. Livy considers it
an acknowledgment of the supremacy of Rome by her Latin allies.
i. 45.

[2] Liv. i. 33.

from the fact, already noticed, that Mæcenas extended
the gardens of his palace on either side of the mound.
It is hardly to be supposed that he would have ventured to level a wall of masonry, but it was easy to
convert an earthen terrace, by sloping and planting,
into a pleasant promenade for the public.[1]　The Servian lines continued, however, still to form the nominal boundary of the city, though the idea of maintaining them for defence had long been abandoned as
superfluous.　While the temples of the gods and the
palaces of the wealthy were planted, as we have seen,
for the most part, on the airy summits of the hills,
the dwellings of the lower classes were clustered together in the narrow valleys between them.　The
roads were measured from the gates of the Servian
inclosure; and here began the straight lines of their
interminable avenues.　Within the walls the streets
The valleys of Rome.　were laid out with no such regularity, or
rather they may be said to have grown up
as caprice or accident dictated, so that the names
of few of these confined and tortuous alleys have
been preserved, and of these few we can seldom ascertain the direction.　The Forum alone of all the
The Forum Romanum.　public places of the city was designed
with any approach to regularity.　Its open
space, nearly rectangular in form, was inclosed by

---

[1] Hor. *Sat.* i. 8. 14., referred to in a former chapter.　This account
of the real character of the Servian walls is confirmed by the almost
total absence of any actual traces of them, though the topographers
have pitched here and there upon substructions in the face of the
cliffs as remains of this primitive fortification.　Already in the time
of Augustus the Greek antiquarian could find few portions of them,
on account of the private dwellings which had encroached upon
them: δυσεύρετον διὰ τὰς περιλαμβανούσας αὐτὸ πυλλαχόθεν οἰκήσεις,
ἴχνη δέ τινα φύλαττον κατὰ πόλλους τόπους τῆς ἀρχαίας κατασκευῆς.
Dion. Hal. *Ant. Rom.* iv. 13.　Strabo certainly was no believer in a
continuous Servian wall.　After noticing the agger as a defence or a
special point, he accounts for its exceptional character, διότι Ῥωμαίοις
προσῆκεν οὐκ ἀπὸ τῶν ἐρυμάτων, ἀλλὰ ἀπὸ τῶν ὅπλων καὶ τῆς οἰκείας
ἀρετῆς ἔχειν τὴν ἀσφάλειαν καὶ τὴν ἄλλην εὐπορίαν, προβλήματα νομίζοντες
οὐ τὰ τείχη τοῖς ἀνδράσιν, ἀλλὰ τοὺς ἄνδρας τοῖς τείχεσι (v. 3. p. 234.).

paved roads which skirted its border, and were specially intended for processions. These roads were
lined, on the edge where they approached the bases
of the hills, by rows of temples and public edifices;
and the limits of the most famous area in the world
may be distinctly traced to this day by the remains
of these historic monuments. Strange it is to observe
within how small a space the affairs of the greatest
of empires were transacted. From the slope of the
Velia to the foot of the Capitoline its length does not
exceed three hundred yards, and its breadth, which
increases as it advances westward, varies from about
fifty to one hundred. The temple of Julius on the
one height fronted that of Jupiter on the other. On
the right stood the ancient temple of the Penates and
that of the twin heroes, Romulus and Remus, with
the spacious hall of Paulus Æmilius; on the left the
shrine of Vesta, in which the sacred flame was ever
burning, with the mansion of the chief pontiff annexed, the temple of the twin gods Castor and Pollux,
and the basilica of Julius Cæsar. In the time of the
republic the sides of the Forum had been lined with
shops, having dwellings over them; but these had
been latterly displaced by sacred and civil buildings,
such as have been noticed. The line of the Sacra
Via, which descended from the Velia, under the arch
of Fabius, and skirted the Forum on the right, was
bordered on one side by these public edifices, on the
other by a range of statues on pedestals, or columns,
forming an august approach to the Capitol, which it
mounted by an oblique and gradual ascent before the
temples of Concord and of Saturn. To this avenue,
similarly adorned and directed towards the same
point, corresponded the Nova Via on the left. But
the whole space thus described generally as the Forum
Romanum was more properly divided into two portions, of which one slightly elevated above the other
was strictly denominated the Comitium, and was ori-

ginally the place of honour assigned to the Populus
as distinguished from the Plebs. The Rostrum, or
tribunal for public speaking, which stood in the
centre of the open space, was turned at first towards
the Comitium, and away from the Forum: the harangues of the orators were addressed to the curies,
and not to the centuries. The bold change by which
the Rostrum was directed towards the opposite quarter was the manœuvre of Livius Drusus, the popular
tribune: but at that time the distinction of plebs and
populus had almost ceased to exist; the Comitium
soon lost its political significance; and while the
senators transacted their affairs under the cover of
halls and temples, the mighty multitude of the Roman
people occupied without dispute the whole vacant
space between the Sacred and the New street, and
crowded without order or distinction of places around
the occupant of the political pulpit. The meetings of
the senate were held most frequently in the Curia
Hostilia, which stood beneath the north-west angle
of the Palatine, and was flanked, a little in advance,
by a small building called the Græcostasis, in which
foreign envoys awaited the summons of the imperial
assembly. But this curia had been consumed in the
Clodian conflagration, and other halls or temples were
at different times adopted at the caprice of the consuls or the emperor. Year after year the
Roman Forum received fresh accessions of
splendour and convenience. The fire just
referred to cleared a space for nobler constructions,
and first suggested the idea of more important changes
and additions. With the surrender of political privileges grew the taste for ostentatious display in the
enlargement and decoration of the site which had
once been consecrated to their exercise. The colonnades by which the place became surrounded, connecting hall with hall, and temple with temple, were
in the morning the thoroughfare of men of business,

Enlargement and decoration of the Forum Romanum.

but at a later hour were almost abandoned to the
seekers of pleasure and dissipation.　The area of the
ancient Forum was found, however, too narrow either
for the one use or the other.　Various attempts had
been made to gain additional space; and it was with
this view perhaps that the rows of shops or stalls
which formerly inclosed it, had been recently demo-
lished.　It was not so easy to remove the temples and
other consecrated objects, which continued to present
impassable barriers to extension at almost every
point.　Behind them, however, on the right, there
was still a space nearly level, reaching to the foot of
the Esquiline and Quirinal; and here on the site of
the ancient grove of Argiletum, and in the jaws of the
Suburra, the population of Rome was most densely
crowded together.　Overlooked by the temples and
patrician mansions of the Carinæ and other surrounding heights, the Argiletum and the Suburra were the
abodes of artificers of all kinds, the workers
in metals and in leather, the clothiers and The Argi-
letum and
Suburra.
perfume-sellers.　This, moreover, was the
quarter of the booksellers, and the publicans, of the
retailers, in short, of every article of luxury and necessity.　Here was concentrated much of the vicious
dissipation of a large capital; and here the young
gentlemen of Rome, just emerged from dependence
on their parents and tutors, might lounge with friends
or flatterers, and glance without control on every
object of interest or amusement.[1]　In earlier times
the Suburra had been the residence of many noble
families, and here Julius Cæsar had himself been
born; but as they advanced to the highest pinnacles
of greatness, they had migrated to the more conspicuous quarters of the Palatine or the Esquiline.

---

[1] "Quales in media sedent Suburra." Martial, vi. 66. Compare
Persius, Sat. v. 32.:
　　　　"Cum blandi comites, totaque impune Suburra
　　　　Permissit sparsisse oculos jam candidus umbo."

and fashion had now generally deserted the lower parts of the city.   From the entrance of the Suburra branched out the long streets which penetrated the hollows between the Quirinal, Viminal, and Esquiline, to the gates pierced in the mound of Servius.   It was in this direction that Cæsar effected the first exten-

The Forums of the Cæsars. sion of the Forum, by converting the site of certain streets into an open space which he surrounded with arcades, and in the centre of which he erected his temple of Venus.   By the side of the Julian Forum, or perhaps in its rear, Augustus constructed a still ampler inclosure, which he adorned with the temple of Mars the Avenger.   Succeeding emperors, hereafter to be specified, continued to work out the same idea, till the Argiletum, on the one hand, and the saddle of the Capitoline and Quirinal, excavated for the purpose, on the other, were both occupied by these constructions, the dwellings of the populace being swept away before them ; and a space running nearly parallel to the length of the Roman Forum, and exceeding it in size, was thus devoted to public use, extending from the pillar of Trajan to the basilica of Constantine.[1]

Next to the quarter of the Suburra, that of the

The Velabrum. Velabrum, on the opposite side of the Forum, was the most crowded portion of the city.   The hollow which descended from the

---

[1] The reader will understand that these are the conclusions at which I have arrived, chiefly under the guidance of Becker's Handbook, upon a subject on which the views of various schools of Roman topographers have been widely divergent.   It would be superfluous to specify the ancient authorities.   The general arrangement of the Roman Forum by Bunsen and Becker, and the German school as opposed to the Italian, ought to be considered as settled by the recent excavations, which have revealed beyond dispute the sites of the Æmilian and Julian basilicas.   At the same time, it cannot be denied that the Italians, headed by Canina, have not yet surrendered their theory, that the Forum extended longitudinally towards the Tiber, and not towards the Velia, and maintain that the Julian basilica was an encroachment upon the ancient area.

Velia, after meeting that of the Suburra, turned obliquely towards the Tiber; and the Nova Via, which skirted the base of the Palatine, followed its flexure from the temple of Castor and Pollux, and formed the boundary of the Velabrum on one side, as it had before limited the Forum. But the Velabrum, the space between the Palatine and the Capitoline, was wide enough to admit of two other streets running parallel to the Nova, the Vicus Tuscus and the Vicus Jugarius. These avenues, descending from the Forum Romanum, opened upon the Forum Boarium, the spot perhaps where the cattle destined for the consumption of Rome were landed from the barks on the Tiber: but they were also the great outlets of the multitudes which hurried from the heart of the city to the shows of the circus, and the recreations of the Campus Martius. The Vicus Tuscus, the middle street of the three, was perhaps *the most crowded thoroughfare of all, the Cheapside of Rome. The public buildings in this quarter were comparatively few and insignificant, and we may believe that the whole space of the Velabrum was densely packed with the cabins of the industrious classes.

The Forum Boarium.

The streets which traversed the Velabrum led direct to the bank of the Tiber, and to the oldest of the bridges of Rome, the Sublicius, or bridge of piles, which connected the city with the Transtiberine quarter, called also Janiculan, from the slope on which it stood. This district, rising in terraces from the river, enjoyed a noble view of the seven hills on the opposite bank, and was also celebrated for its salubrity, which circumstances combined to attract to it the wealthier citizens under the later republic and the empire, who spread themselves along the crest of the adjoining eminences, and gradually occupied the whole ridge of the Vatican. The lower part continued to be the resort of the poorer

The Transtiberine quarter.

classes. But the importance of this region may be inferred from the aqueducts which were constructed to supply it, the numerous bridges which connected it with other quarters, the venerableness of its shrines, especially that of the goddess Fortuna, and the station there of one cohort of the city police, or Vigiles. The island in the Tiber, fashioned at either end into some rude resemblance to a ship, was also included in the Transtiberine, and was densely crowded with habitations. The gardens of Cæsar on the right bank of the river have been already described. Augustus excavated a naumachia, or basin for the exhibition of naval engagements, by their side. He surrounded it with groves and walks, to which he gave the names of his grandsons Caius and Lucius, and supplied it with water, not, as might have been expected, from the adjacent river, but by means of an aqueduct from the lake Alsietinus, or Bracciano, in Etruria.

We have still to notice the two regions beyond the Servian walls, in the broad plain to the north of the city, which may be designated by the comprehensive name of the Campus Martius, though that appellation, as we shall presently see, was more strictly confined to a certain portion only. From the earliest period the grassy meadows which here skirted the Tiber had been a resort for military exercises, and the recreations of leaping, running, and bathing. From the Porta Ratumena and the Carmentalis, on either side of the Capitoline, the citizens poured after the business of the day, to indulge in these sports, a custom which survived, through the whole period of the republic, late into the times of the emperors. Gradually, however, the space between the walls and the reach of the river was encroached upon by buildings of various kinds; and Cæsar contemplated, as we have seen, its extension, by giving a wider sweep to the Tiber. Here stood some of the principal temples of the gods, and here, from an

early period, were the septa, or booths, at which the
centuries polled. The elections were originally a
military institution, and on this account the citizens
were summoned outside the walls to solemnize them.[1]
The regulation that no imperator might enter the
city, led to the practice of convening the senate also
in the Campus Martius. Here too was the gate from
which the victor, returned from distant frontiers, commenced his triumphal procession to the Capitol. Here
was the gorgeous theatre of Pompeius, with its groves
and porticos, and halls for business or amusement.
Here stood the Flaminian circus, second only in size
to the great circus beneath the Palatine; and here
were the theatre of Marcellus and the portico of Octavia, the contributions of Augustus himself to the
attractions of this splendid region. Here also, further
from the city and precisely in the centre of the plain,
still stands the magnificent Pantheon of Agrippa,
which constituted a portion only of his extensive constructions in this quarter. Beyond it rose the amphitheatre of Taurus, and adjacent to the banks of the
river the conspicuous mausoleum of the Cæsarean
family. Up to this point the area was perhaps almost
covered with edifices, but beyond it there was still a
tract of open meadow, preserved for the martial sports
of the Roman people, extending to the modern Ripetta
and the Porta del Popolo. The whole of this district
north of the Capitoline is now thronged with houses,
and comprehends the chief part of modern Rome : the
remains of some of the most interesting buildings of
the ancient city lie buried beneath the masses of mediæval construction ; and no portion of it has been of
necessity so imperfectly explored, or presents so many

---

[1] The division of the Roman people into classes and centuries had
a military object, and the word classis had originally the meaning of
exercitus. Gell xv. 27., quoting an ancient writer : "Centuriata
comitia intra pomœrium fieri nefas esse, quia exercitum extra urbem
imperari oporteat, intra urbem jus non sit."

insoluble problems to the topographer. It was divided into two unequal portions by the straight line
of the Flaminian Way, which issued from the city at
the northern angle of the Capitoline. The first portion of this road was known perhaps by the title of
the Via Lata, which gave its name to the region on
the right, extending beyond the level of the plain
over the slope of the Pincian hill. In the course of
time this road was bordered with houses, and the
Corso of the modern city runs at least for some distance on its track.[1] The Pincian itself was
occupied by villas shrouded in extensive
parks or gardens, such as those of Lucullus and
Sallust, from whence it derived the name of Collis
Hortulorum. From its flank descended the arches
of the aqueduct called Aqua Virgo, one of the most
stupendous works of Agrippa, by which water was
conveyed to the septa in the Campus Martius.[2] The
Campus Agrippæ, the site of which is not determined,
was a portion of the plain which the same great bene-
factor laid out in gardens and porticos for the recreation of the citizens, and the convenience of the
bathers. It contained the thermæ which he constructed for the public; and two of its colonnades,
styled the Europa and the Neptune, were celebrated
for the elegance of their fresco paintings.[3] Augustus
peopled the Campus with a host of statues taken
chiefly from the Capitol, where they had accumulated, as the spoils of war or the votive offerings of

The Pincian hill.

---

[1] Martial (x. 6.) describes the Via Flaminia as running through
the plain, with trees and detached houses by its sides:

> " Quando erit illa dies, qua campus et arbor et omnis
>   Lucebit Latia culta fenestra nuru?
> Quando moræ dulces, longusque a Cæsare pulvis,
>   Totaque Flaminia Roma videnda via?"

[2] Frontin. *de Aquæduct.* 22.

[3] See the allusions in Martial, ii. 14., vii. 32., iii. 20. It has been
imagined that the Pantheon was originally constructed for a central
hall, some think for a swimming bath, to the thermæ of Agrippa.
See Bunsen's *Rom.* iii. 3. 123. 341.

conquerors, to an inconvenient extent. At a later period the Forum and other public places were deliberately thinned of their overgrowths of sculpture, which amounted, it may be supposed, to many thousands of specimens, to enrich the halls, the baths, and the colonnades of the Palaces of the People.[1]

It would appear from this review that the densely populated parts of Rome covered but a small part of its whole area, for the summits of the hills were generally occupied by temples and aristocratic mansions, and large spaces even in the intervening hollows were devoted to places of public resort. The vici, or streets of Rome, as far as their names and directions are known to us, were confined to the valleys. The houses on the hills were generally detached mansions, surrounded in many cases by gardens. It must be allowed, however, that the clients of the nobles often clustered their obscure tenements against the outer walls of their patrons' palaces. But in the districts where the masses of the population were collected, such as the Suburra and Velabrum, every available inch of ground was seized for building, and the want of space was compensated by elevation. Perched upon the precipitous ledges of the hills, the houses rose to an enormous height in front, while in the rear their elevation might often be far more moderate. Rome, says Cicero, rhetorically, is suspended in the air: Rome, avers the more guarded Vitruvius, is built vertically; Tacitus speaks of houses rising from the plain to the level of the Capitoline summit.[2]

The population of Rome chiefly clustered in the lower parts of the city.

---

[1] Suet. *Calig.* 34.; Dion. lx. 6. The Campus Martius is described by Strabo with more vivacity than is usual with him (v. 3. p. 236.). I have avoided the debateable parts of his description, over which a furious battle still rages. Preller, however, the last combatant who has entered the field, especially against Becker, seems to me captious and unreasonable.

[2] Cic. *Leg. Agr.* ii. 35.: "Romam in montibus positam et convallibus, cœnaculis sublatam atque suspensam." He compares it dis-

Augustus was the first to impose a limit by law to
their daring ascent, and he was satisfied with fixing
the greatest height at the liberal allowance of seventy
feet.   At the same time for no other purpose, as far
as we can divine, than to economize space, their ex-
terior walls were forbidden, we are told, to exceed a
foot and a half in thickness, the minimum, perhaps,
which was calculated to bear the weight of the super-
incumbent mass.[1]   The streets, following the tracks
of the cattle and herdsmen of primitive antiquity to
their pastures and watering-places, were narrow and
winding; and this may account for the fact that so
few of them were important enough to transmit their
names to history.[2]   It was not till the gates had been
passed that the direction of the roads began to be
marked out deliberately; and except the avenues
which were designed for sacred processions, or the
course of which was shaped by the narrow gorges
through which they ran, few perhaps preserved for
many yards together the irksome uniformity of a
right line.[3]   Narrow as these alleys were, and little

advantageously with the broad open spaces of the Greek city of
Capua.   Vitruvius says: " Roma in altum propter civium frequentiam
ædificata."   Tacitus, *Hist.* iii. 71.: " Ædificia quæ in altum edita
Capitolii solum æquabant."   Aristides, in his *Encomium Romæ,* compares the stories of Rome with the strata of the earth's crust, and
pretends that, if they were all laid out on one level, they would
occupy the whole area of Italy from sea to sea.
    [1] Vitruvius, ii. 8.   Comp. Juvenal, iii. 193.: " Nos urbem colimus
tenui tibicine fultam."
    [2] See the description of the hurried and irregular manner in which
the city was rebuilt after its burning by the Gauls, in Livy, v. 55.
(Comp. Diodor. xiv. 116.)   The lines of the old streets were probably
preserved, for the most part, as with us after the fire of London.
Livy, indeed, would have us believe that every citizen built for himself, as suited his convenience, without reference to his neighbours,
or to any common plan; but this cannot, I conceive, have been
generally the case.   The preservation, indeed, of the names of the
ancient streets sufficiently attests the contrary.
    [3] Strabo contrasts the style in which Rome was laid out with the
elegant designs of the Greek city builders: τῶν γὰρ Ἑλλήνων περὶ
τὰς κτίσεις μάλιστα εὐτυχῆσαι δοξάντων ὅτι κάλλους ἐστοχάζοντο. v. 3.

adapted for the passage of wheel carriages, which indeed till a late period were hardly used in Rome, they were still more confined above, by the device of projecting balconies from the upper stories. These were known by the name of Mæniana, from the tribune Mænius, who first invented them to accommodate the spectators of the processions in the streets below. It is probable, though we have no express testimony to the fact, that these balconies were afterwards improved into hanging stories, the occupants of which could sometimes shake hands with their neighbours opposite.[1]

It may be believed that the roofs of the houses in Rome were adapted to a climate abounding in violent storms of rain, and rose in steep ridges, presenting sometimes a gable (a spread eagle the Greeks would have called it) to the street.[2] The want of glass, which was hardly known up to the imperial era, and but little used for dwelling windows to a late period, compelled the Romans to make the apertures of their houses few and narrow compared with those of modern architecture[3]; but the habit of living through the day almost entirely out of doors would render this deprivation of light less intolerable. In the better class of houses, however, there were windows protected by shutters of lattice work with double

Style of domestic architecture.

---

[1] See Festus in voc. Mæniana : "Mænius . . . . primus ultra columnas extendit tigna, quo ampliarentur superiora." The *Digest,* l. 16. 242. speaks of mæniana and suggrundia, projecting eaves. These projections, together with the narrowness of the streets, gave a grateful shade (comp. Cic. *Acad.* ii. 22.), and on that account were considered to contribute to salubrity. Tac. *Ann.* xv. 43. Martial, i. 87.: "Vicinus meus est manuque tangi De nostris Novius potest fenestris." But this may apply to a next-door neighbour.

[2] "Fastigia, pectinata tecta:" Gr. ἀέτωμα, τρίχωρος. Upon this subject, on which our information is indistinct, see the note of Salmasius, on Spartian. *Pescenn.* 12.

[3] Plin. xxxvi. 66.: "Neronis principatu reperta vitri arte." This can only refer to its employment for windows. Comp. Senec. *Ep.* 90.: "Quædam nostra demum prodisse memoria scimus, ut speculariorum usum, perlucente testa, clarum transmittentium lumen."

valves.[1] The most common material for private dwellings was brick, which not only superseded the primitive wood, but was preferred for the purpose to the stone of the country, whether extracted from beneath the soil of Rome itself, or dug from the quarries of Alba, Gabii, and Tibur.   Although this stone was as easily obtained, and was perhaps the cheaper material, the Romans gave a preference to brick, from its applicability to the construction of the arch, and also for the extreme hardness and durability it assumed in their hands.   The old consuls of the republic truly built for eternity, when they ranged tile upon tile, and embedded them in their concrete sand and gypsum. It was a famous boast of Augustus, when he pointed to the sumptuous halls and temples with which he had eclipsed the modest merit of preceding builders, that he had found Rome of clay and had left her of marble : but after eighteen centuries the marble has mostly vanished and crumbled into dust, while huge strata of brick-work still crop out from under the soil, a Titanic formation as imperishable as the rock itself.[2]

The temples of ancient Rome were all, as far as we can trace them, constructed on the Grecian

Style of temple architecture. pattern; that is, generally in oblong masses of masonry, with long low roofs, corresponding with the apex of the pediment.   Though crowned perhaps with statues on the summit, they scarcely overtopped, except from their position, the meaner buildings around them : the invention of bells, the greatest of all boons to architecture, had not yet afforded a motive or excuse for raising the many storied

---

[1] Hor. *Od.* i. 25. 1.: "*Junctas* quatiunt fenestras." Pers. iii. 1.: " Jam clarum mane fenestras Intrat, et angusto distendit lumine *rimas.*"

[2] This saying has been referred to in an earlier chapter.   Strabo remarks that the ancients, occupied with more urgent cares, paid little attention to the decoration of the city, a merit which was reserved for Pompeius, Cæsar and Augustus, with his friends and relatives.

turret, or suggested the arrowy flight of the spire or steeple.   Here and there perhaps the watch-tower of some palace or fortress might break the horizon of stone ; but these were too few and unimportant in character to lead the eye of the spectator upwards, or divert him from the sights of splendour or squalor nearer to his own level.   Nevertheless there was a grand significance in the crests of the hills encompassing the Forum, crowned with a range almost unbroken of columned temples, the dwellings of the gods, who thus seemed to keep eternal watch over the secure recesses of the city.   If neither the architecture nor religion of the Roman pointed heavenwards, or led to spiritual aspirations, not the less did they combine to impress upon him, in their harmonious development, the great idea of Paganism, the temporal protection with which the Powers of Nature, duly honoured and propitiated, encircle their favourites among men.

The dwellings of the citizens were of two general classes, the domus and the insulæ.   The former of these, which we may call mansions, were the abodes of the nobility, and were constructed originally as separate buildings, inclosed within courts or gardens, and adapted, at least since the latter years of the republic, to the Greek fashion, covering a considerable surface with a single, or at most two stories.   The application to the private mansion of the ornamental architecture of Greece, which had been long reserved at Rome for temples and public edifices, soon demanded the use of the rich and polished material with which Greece abounded, of their own wealth in which the Italians were perhaps hardly yet aware.   When the nobles began to build their long columnar corridors, they required marble to give variety by its colour to the interminable repetition of pillar after pillar, and the vast expanse of their level pavements.   Crassus, the

The domus and insulæ.

The mansions of the nobles.

orator, was said to have first introduced into his house six columns of Hymettian marble. This was about the middle of the seventh century. Soon afterwards Lepidus paved his arcades with polished slabs from the quarries of Numidia. This nobleman's palace was reputed at that time the finest domestic edifice in Rome, but thirty-five years later it was excelled by not less than a hundred rivals.[1] Nevertheless, at a still later period, the Romans continued to wonder at the inordinate luxury of the Orientals, who piled the richest marbles block upon block, while the lords of the world could only afford to use them in thin flags.[2]

The domus, it has been said, were generally insu-
The cabins of the poorer citizens. lated dwellings; the insulæ, or islands, on the other hand, were precisely the contrary of what their name should import, the smaller abodes of the lower classes, closely connected together in large blocks of building, and covered with a continuous roof.[3] These little dwellings were generally built over the rows of shops which lined the area of

---

[1] Plin. *Hist. Nat.* xxxvi. 2, 8, 24.

[2] Lucan contrasts the magnificence of Cleopatra's palace with those of Rome in language which expresses the feeling probably of his own time:

> "Nec summis crustata domus sectisque nitebat
> Marmoribus: stabatque sibi non segnis Achates,
> Purpureusque lapis; totaque effusus in aula
> Calcabatur onyx."   *Pharsal.* x. 114.

[3] A law of the twelve tables required, for security against fire, that every house should stand separate; but it is impossible that this can have applied, even at that early time, to every single chamber in which a separate family was lodged. I consider the insula to have originally been a block of chambers, such as are represented in the fragment of the ancient plan of Rome still preserved on marble, which corresponds with the style of arrangement observed at Pompeii. These rows of building were often constructed round public edifices, and the clients, operative slaves, and freedmen of the noble were often thus lodged against the walls of his domus. If insula was the term originally given to the aggregate of such dwellings, it came afterwards to be applied to the component members. Thus Tacitus uses insulæ as synonymous with tabernæ. *Ann.* vi. 45., xv. 38. See De la Malle, *Econ. Pol.* i. 364.

the streets, and were entered by stairs from the outside, having no connexion with the resorts of trade and
industry below them.   In a height of seventy feet
there were probably from seven to ten stories, and each
of these stories, and often each chamber in them, might
be occupied by a separate family.[1]   Being used as
little else than sleeping apartments, they accommodated, in the fashion of the age and country, a multitude of inmates, the amount of which, however, we
are totally at a loss to estimate.   The subject, indeed,
of the population of Rome has exercised the ingenuity of many inquirers, but with widely differing results.   As regards the accommodation the tract covered
by the city may have afforded, when we have carefully
measured the circuit of the walls, and estimated the
area they inclosed, we are still ignorant both of the
capacity of the houses, and of the amount of empty
space within the inclosure.   In drawing a comparison,
however, from experience in our own day, we may observe that, if modern cities on the one hand are not so
closely built, nor their houses so densely inhabited as
was the case with ancient Rome, on the other they
have no such proportion of vacant space appropriated
to gardens, and courts, and public places.   Setting one
of these conditions, therefore, against the other, it may
seem not unreasonable to form an approximate estimate of the population of Rome from the numbers
domiciled on an equal area in some modern capital.

I. According to an ancient definition, the space within the walls was specifically denominated the Urbs, or City, while the term Rome was applied to the whole un-broken extent of buildings which reached to the ex-

Data for calculating the population of Rome. 1. From the area of the city.

---

[1] Thus a house of four stories is indicated in the account of one of Livy's portents, xxi. 65.: "foro boario bovem in tertiam contigna-tionem sua sponte escendisse atque inde tumultu habitatorum ter-ritum sese dejecisse."

tremity of the suburbs.[1]   The Roman urbs, then,
was included at this period within the walls or lines
of Servius; and this area had been divided by Augustus, for administrative purposes, into eleven regions, to which he had added three others outside
the walls, to embrace, we may suppose, the most
frequented quarters of the suburbs.[2]   The area of the
eleven urban regions has been found by measurement
on an accurate map to equal about one-fifth of that
of the modern city of Paris within the barrier.[3]   The
population therefore of the urbs, if calculated on the
basis of that of Paris (equal 1,050,000), would not
amount to more than two hundred and ten thousand;
nor is it easy to adduce any direct proof that it
actually exceeded this very moderate number.   Bearing in mind what has been said of the character of
the buildings which prevailed in different parts of
this space, the number of temples and public edifices,
the extent of many private residences, the space
devoted to theatres, circuses, and baths (of which last

[1] Paulus in *Digest*. l. 16, 2.: "Urbis appellatio muris, Romæ
autem continentibus ædificiis finitur, quod latius patet."
[2] These three were (Reg. i.) Porta Capena; (vii.) Via Lata; (ix.)
Circus Flaminius.   It may be conjectured that these were included
within the pomœrium as extended by Augustus in the year 746
(Dion, lv. 6.).   See Becker, *Ræm. Alter*. ii. 105.
[3] For this important statement I cite the words of Dureau de
la Malle (i. 347.): "La superficie de Paris (*i. e.* within the barrière
de l'octroi) est. d'après les mesures exactes, de 3439 hect. 68 ar.
16c.; celle de Rome, 638 hect. 72 ar. 34c.   J'ai calculé la superficie
d'après le grand plan de Nolli, dont l'exactitude est reconnue.   Mon
savant confrère M. Jomard a eu l'extrème obligéance de revoir mes
calculs; je les ai fait vérifier de nouveau par un habile mathématicien.
On s'est servi du périmètre déterminé par d'Anville pour la *première
enceinte* de Rome, et vérifié de nouveau sur les lieux par M. Nibby
et par Brocchi."   He adds in a note that his calculations of the area
of the city were again verified by Tournon, the learned prefect of
Napoleon's department of Rome.   De la Malle's calculations were
made about 1824, and his statement of the population of Paris
(714,000) refers to the year 1817.   *Econ. Pol.* i. 369.   The estimate
in McCulloch's *Dict. of Geography* for 1846 is, 1,050,000.   There has
been a great extent of building within the barrier during that
interval.

Agrippa alone established, within and without the urbs, no less than a hundred and seventy), the numerous groves and gardens which existed even within the walls, it will be allowed that the surface actually covered with the abodes of the masses can hardly have exceeded that similarly occupied in Paris, or any of our cities at the present day.[1] It has been shown, however, how closely the houses of the densest quarters were packed together; and we may also believe that the space required, man by man, at Rome was much smaller than accords with our modern habits. This arises from the outdoor mode of life practised in ancient Italy, from the number of slaves, who were huddled together without respect to health or comfort, and from the sordid notions of domestic comfort common even to the higher classes. Thus, while they allotted ample space to their halls for banquets and recreation, their sleeping rooms were of the smallest possible dimensions. The habitations indeed of mediæval Europe were far more densely crowded than our own, and such we may easily believe was the case with the ancient urbs also. Assuming, however, that from these considerations we may double the amount of its population as compared with modern Paris, we shall still be surprised, and perhaps even startled, to find that we cannot raise it above four hundred and twenty thousand.

If we now look to suburban Rome, and seek for compensation in that quarter for the slender amount of population within the walls, we shall still be disappointed. From the time indeed of the retreat of Hannibal the citizens had ceased to require the protection of military defences for their dwellings, and there was no impediment, except in the reserved space of the pomœrium, to their constructing their houses outside the ancient lines, and

Extent of the suburbs.

---

[1] There were, according to Pliny (*Hist. Nat.* iii. 9.), not less than 265 open places in Rome.

at as great a distance from them as they pleased. Modern Vienna, with its central urbs, surrounded by a broad vacant glacis, and again by a second belt of houses beyond it, may offer a considerable resemblance to the Rome of Augustus.[1] These outer buildings continued no doubt to increase both in extent and density, through the two following centuries, before they were finally inclosed in the second and wider circumvallation, which still marks the greatest spread of the imperial metropolis, embracing an area rather more than twice the size of the Servian city, or than two-fifths of that of Paris.[2] But in the Augustan period this outer area was only partially occupied with buildings. Augustus, when he added three Suburban regions, the Via Lata, the Circus Flaminius, and the Porta Capena, to the eleven Urban, included in them a portion only of this intermural space, and of these the Circus at least can have had very few private dwellings of any kind. It may be wrong, however, to assume that the rest of the space uncomprised in these three regions was not also encroached on by numerous habitations; for so London runs into extensive and populous suburbs, though they are excluded from the limits of its component boroughs, and known perhaps by no distinctive appellations. On the other hand, however, the great number and extent of private villas and gardens,

---

[1] There is no statement, I believe, of the ordinary width of the pomœrium, which probably varied very much in different quarters. I do not suppose that it was anywhere nearly equal to that of the glacis at Vienna; and indeed, in the time of Augustus, it had been greatly encroached upon. If, as Dionysius tells us, the lines of Servius could no longer be traced throughout in his days, neither certainly could the pomœrium.

[2] De la Malle (i. 347.) calculates the area of the Aurelian inclosure at 1396 hect. 9 centiar.: it seems on the map much more than double the Servian. D'Anville (cited by De la Malle) states the length of the Servian walls at 6187½ toises, or 8186 Roman passus; that of the Aurelian, at 12,345 toises. Hence his happy correction of Pliny, VIII. M.CC. for XIII. M.CC., *Hist. Nat.* iii. 9.

such as those of Mæcenas, of Pallas, of Sallust, of the Lamiæ and Laterani, of Cæsar, and many others of historical celebrity, which occupied large sites between the Servian and Aurelian walls, though some of them eventually gave way to the extension of streets and lanes, clearly indicate that at an earlier period that area was far from filled with ordinary dwellings. Nor, again, is it possible to give a high estimate to the more distant suburbs of Rome. Up to the gates of the city the Campagna yields few vestiges of ancient habitation, except here and there the foundations of isolated villas; and the roads, as we have seen, were lined, not with rows of tradesmen's lodgings, but with a succession of sepulchral monuments, which the feelings of the Romans would have shrunk from desecrating by proximity to the abodes of life.[1] It seems unreasonable, then, to estimate the extramural population at more than one-half of that within the walls, which will raise the sum total to six hundred and thirty, or, making a liberal allowance for soldiers and public slaves, who occupied the baths and temples, about seven hundred thousand.[2]

II. But any estimate formed on such grounds as these only must at best be very uncertain, and it will be well to inquire whether the arguments which may be drawn from other sources

2. The recorded number of houses.

---

[1] It is difficult to resist the strong expressions of Pliny, Dionysius, and others: but we must shut our ears to their reckless exaggerations; such as, Plin. iii. 5.: "Exspatiantia tecta multas addidere urbes." Dion. Hal. iv. 13.: οὕτω συνύφανται τῷ ἄστει ἡ χώρα, καὶ εἰς ἄπειρον ἐκμηκυνομένης πόλεως ὑπόληψιν τοῖς θεωμένοις παρέχεται; and the passage of Aristides, before referred to, *Encom. Rom.* vol. i. p. 324.: εἴ τις αὐτὴν ἐθελήσειε καθαρῶς ἀναπτύξαι, καὶ τὰς νῦν μετεώρους πόλεις ἐπὶ γῆς ἐρείσας θεῖναι ἄλλην παρ' ἄλλην, ὅσον νῦν Ἰταλίας διάλειπον ἐστιν ἀναπληρωθῆναι, τοῦτο πᾶν ἄν μοι δοκεῖ, καὶ γενέσθαι πόλις συνεχὴς μία ἐπὶ τὸν Ἰόνιον τείνουσα.

[2] De la Malle fixes the population of the Servian urbs at 266,684, that of the Aurelian at 382,695, and of Rome, including the suburbs at their furthest extent, at 502,000. To these he adds 30,000 for strangers, and an equal number for soldiers, making a total of 562,000. i. 403.

serve to confirm or to invalidate it. There exists
an ancient statistical account of Rome, in which,
among other specific numerical notices, the number of the domus and insulæ respectively is given
for each of the fourteen regions.[1] The date of
this little work cannot perhaps be fixed very nearly,
but the substance of the information it conveys may
be referred to the third century of our era, after the
building of the Aurelian walls, and at the period
probably of the greatest extension of the city. We
must bear in mind, therefore, on the one hand, that
the density of habitation in the urbs was unquestionably reduced after the time of Augustus; and on the
other, that the whole enlarged area was more uniformly occupied with dwellings. If these circumstances may be supposed nearly to balance one another, we may be allowed perhaps to assume that the
numbers given in the *Notitia* do not far exceed the
actual amount at the earlier period,—namely, 46,602
insulæ and 1,790 domus. The numbers, however, of
individuals accommodated in each domus and insula
respectively must still be a matter of mere conjecture,
nor can we find any close analogy to guide us. The
average ratio of dwellers to houses in London or
Liverpool is said to be about five to one; in Paris
and Vienna it is much greater; and we may, perhaps,
fairly double it for the insulæ of Rome, although
these were in many cases, as I have said, merely
single chambers. The capacity of the domus must
have been still more varied, and I confess that I am
merely speaking at random in assigning to them an
average of eighty occupants.[2] The result, however,

---

[1] See Preller's comparative edition of the *Curiosum* and *Notitia*.

[2] Brotier guesses the average at eighty-four, nor does De la Malle
see reason to dissent from him. I should prefer a smaller number,
because, in my view, multitudes of slaves belonging to great houses
were lodged in the insulæ appended to them. Such would generally
be the case with the artificers whose skill was turned to the profit of
their masters. The chief argument for the great numbers of do-

of such a calculation will be found somewhat to exceed six hundred thousand for the domus and insulæ together, which does not fall greatly short of the estimate at which we have arrived from the basis previously assumed.

III. There is, however, still a third datum to be considered, which may seem at first sight to lead us to very different results, though possibly, on further examination, it may be found rather to confirm our original estimate. Augustus, as we learn from his own statement, reduced the recipients of the ordinary dole of grain to the number of two hundred thousand. When, however, he bestowed upon the plebs urbana, the populace of the city, an extraordinary donative, the numbers who partook of his bounty swelled again to three hundred and twenty thousand. The smaller of these amounts may represent, perhaps, the poorer sort of the citizens; the larger the whole population, male and free, below the senatorial and equestrian ranks.[1] This last has been assumed accordingly by many inquirers as the actual number of the commons of Rome; and this they have doubled, at one stroke of the pen, to comprehend the females, and quadrupled at another, to embrace the slaves also. When to this aggregate has been added a reasonable proportion for the noble classes, together with their wives and families, it has been thought that the enormous sum of two millions of souls is not too large for the whole amount of the inhabitants of Rome. Now, whatever we may think of the capacity of the domus and insulæ, it seems almost demonstrable, from what has been said above,

3. The number of recipients of grain.

---

mestic slaves is taken from the well-known case of the *family* of Pedanius, amounting to 400, who were all put to death for their master's murder. Tac. *Ann.* xiv. 45. Allowance, however, must be made for the houseless, and the slaves of the temples and public buildings.

[1] Before the time of Augustus children below the age of ten years were excluded, but he extended the gratuity to all. Suet. *Oct.* 41.

that the limits of the city can never have contained such a mass of human beings; nor, on fair examination of the data, are we driven in fact to so extravagant a conclusion. I have little doubt that the plebs urbana, as they are called, who were allowed to receive the extraordinary largess, comprehended not merely the actual residents, but as many citizens as could present themselves in person, or possibly even by proxy, from the country round. If this be so, it is evident that the specified number of three hundred and twenty thousand may far exceed that of the actual free male residents.[1] Again, with regard to the proportion of females to males, to suppose it, according to the ordinary law of nature, to be nearly equal is, I fear, in this case an unwarrantable assumption. The licence of infanticide was, we know, a principle recognised generally in the ancient polities: there can be no doubt that the crime was regularly and systematically practised by the civilized as well as the barbarous.[2] Solon enjoined, and even the gentle Plutarch approved of it; and if it is rarely noticed in books, it is perhaps only because it was too common to remark upon. Nor can there be any doubt that, under these circumstances, exposure would befall the female far more commonly than the male infants. There is, indeed, one passage of antiquity which expressly asserts the disproportion of the female to the male adults, where Dion tells us that Augustus allowed the Roman citizens below

---

[1] In the same manner, it may be presumed that the numbers of the census, before the time of Augustus, included not merely the residents in Rome, nor, on the other hand, the whole number of citizens within and without it, but precisely as many as could present themselves to the censors from the city and the country round.

[2] The frequency of this practice among the Romans, insinuated by Tertullian, *Apol.* 9., is painfully confirmed by the cursory remark of Tacitus on the abstinence of the Germans: "Numerum liberorum finire . . . flagitium habetur." *Germ.* 19.

the rank of senators to intermarry with freedwomen, for this very reason, because the females of ingenuous birth were not numerous enough to mate them.[1] With respect to the numbers of the slave population, the estimate I have referred to is not less gratuitous. The most careful and conscientious inquirer into this intricate subject declares himself unable to form any conjecture as to its amount, and though he remarks the vast size of the *families* of the Roman magnates, and the multitude also of public slaves, it is most probable that the mass of the commonalty possessed no slaves at all.[2] The nearest analogy to which we can refer, perhaps, would be that of the great Oriental cities of our time, such as Cairo or Constantinople, in which there are nearly the same striking contrasts as in ancient Rome of luxury and squalid misery; the same extravagance among the few rich in building, amusements and decorations, and the same stolid apathy among the many poor in enduring life on a crust of bread and a sup of water.   Although a few pashas and emirs may dazzle the eyes of the Frank with the ostentatious display of hundreds of male and female slaves, an immense proportion of their countrymen are entirely destitute of them; and the total number of this class, as far as I can learn, forms an inconsiderable element in the whole population.[3]

While, therefore, there are some apparent data for the opinion not uncommonly advanced by moderate and judicious critics, that the inhabitants of Rome amounted to a million or twelve hundred thousand souls, it would seem that

Exaggerations of ancient and modern authorities.

[1] Dion, liv. 16., referred to in vol. iv. chapter xxxiii.

[2] Wallon, *Hist. de l'Esclavage*, &c., pt. ii. chap. 3.

[3] Mr. McCulloch, in his *Dictionary of Geography*, tells us that the estimates of the population of European Turkey by M. Boué and Mr. Urquhart (strangely discrepant as they are) are those on which most reliance may be placed. Neither of these makes any mention of the class of slaves.

the grounds for this conclusion are at best questionable, while it is hardly possible to assign more than
seven hundred thousand to the extent of area on
which they were domiciled.[1]   Accustomed as we are
to contemplate much larger collections of human
beings within the limits of a single city, and to
connect the idea of the capital of a vast and rich
empire with a much higher amount of population,
we may feel surprised and disappointed at such a
result of our calculations, and the more so from the
enormous numbers which the extravagance of certain
earlier authorities has ascribed to imperial Rome.[2]
Little stress, however, can be placed upon the vague
generalities of the native writers, who indulged in
the grossest hyperboles in representing the vastness,
as they supposed it, of the Roman population : they
were not accustomed to weigh and compare statistical

[1] There is another important statement upon this subject in the
Hist. August. in Sever. 23.: "Moriens septem annorum canonem, ita
ut quotidiana septuaginta quinque millia modiorum expendi possent,
reliquit." De la Malle argues that this amount of 75,000 modii per
diem was the estimated consumption of the whole population of Rome.
He goes on to show that this quantity equals 1,012,000 pounds, and
represents, at two pounds per head, a number of 506,000 persons.
Econ. Pol. i. 274, 404. But Wallon, in his admirable work (ii. 84.),
has shown that this standard of consumption is too high in the
ratio of 5 to 3; while Dezobry, comparing it with the returns of
consumption in Paris, reckons it too high in the ratio of 2 to 1.
Rome, iii. 534. But this datum, it will be observed, refers to a period
two centuries later than the Augustan ; nor can we affirm that the
towns and villages round Rome were not partly supplied from the
granaries of the capital.

[2] Lipsius computed the population of Rome at 4,000,000 ; Mengotti,
as late as 1781, at the same. Brotier and Gibbon have reduced it
to 1,200,000, and this is the number assigned to it by Jacob: *On the
Precious Metals.* That Chateaubriand should raise it to 3,000,000
might, perhaps, be expected; but I am surprised at the sum of
2,000,000 assigned to it, on very futile grounds, in the elaborate
description of Rome by M. Bunsen and his learned associates. See
Rom. i. 185. Hoeck, on more critical, but still, as I maintain, on
quite erroneous principles, would raise it to 2,265,000. *Röm. Reich.*
i. 2. 390.

data; and though we have reason to believe that the amount of the inhabitants of every city was registered and made known to the government, it may be admitted that there was no general curiosity on the subject, and no conception of the moral and social purposes to which such knowledge might be applied. Even on the lowest computation which has been made, it is plain that the density of habitation in Rome must have far exceeded all modern experience; and when we remember how much the Romans lived out of doors, how gregarious were their habits, how universal their custom of frequenting the baths, visiting the theatre, and attending the games of the circus, we may well believe that the movement and aggregation of the people at certain spots was far greater than what we ordinarily witness in our own cities. We should be led to expect that the great places of public resort, such as those just mentioned, would be expressly calculated to accommodate the whole mass of the free male population; but the theatres which existed in the time of Augustus could not, at the highest statement, contain above ninety thousand, and the Circus Maximus, the general place of assemblage for all citizens within reach of Rome, on the greatest national solemnities, afforded seats at this period to not more than a hundred and fifty thousand.[1]

---

[1] The theatre of Pompeius held, as Pliny assures us (*H. N.* xxxvi. 15.), 40,000; but according to the *Curiosum* only 17,580; that of Balbus 11,500, according to this last authority, but the *Notitia* gives the number of 30,000. The theatre of Marcellus held, according to the *Curiosum* again, 20,000. To the Circus Maximus, Dionysius assigns (*Ant. Rom.* iii. 68.) 150,000 places: Pliny gives 260,000, and the last spurious edition of the *Curiosum*, which goes by the name of Victor, 385,000. The accommodation of the circus was probably increased from time to time by the addition of wooden galleries, as we know was the case with the Colosseum. We need not trouble ourselves with the statement of the so-called Publius Victor. In the circus the citizens were originally seated according

Nor indeed was Rome calculated, from the position
The circum- it held among the cities of the empire, to
stances of
Rome do not attain any extraordinary population. It
admit of a very was neither a commercial nor a manufac-
large popula-
tion. turing city. It was not the emporium of a
great transit trade, like Alexandria, nor the centre of
exchange among a host of opulent neighbours, like
Antioch. It was not surrounded by the teeming hives
of life which encircled Babylon or Seleucia. Nor was
it increased by the ever-accumulating wealth of all
classes of society, like modern London, or by the
constant tightening of the bands of centralization, by
which the lifeblood of the provinces is flooded back
upon Paris. It was not the natural focus of attraction
for the indolent and luxurious; but every one who
had the means escaped from it as often and as much
as he could, and exchanged its ungenial climate for
the cool breezes of the mountains or the coast, and
the voluptuous recreations of a Campanian watering-
place. The country around it was almost abandoned,
in the imperial period, to the maintenance of cattle,
and the drain of human life caused by its crowded
state and baneful atmosphere was only replenished by
immigration from distant shores. I will not compare
it with Madrid, a mere royal residence, nor with the
marble exhalation of St. Petersburg; but of modern
capitals Vienna may perhaps be considered most
nearly to resemble it. Its great social characteristic

to their classes; the chief magistrate presided, the senators and knights
attended in their places, and every order was arrived in its proper
garb. It was, in fact, the civil camp of the Roman people. When
Juvenal says, " Totam hodie Romam circus capit," his hyperbole is
only the tradition of an ancient reality. Tacitus (*Ann.* xiii. 24.)
expresses nearly the same idea: " Intraverunt Pompeii theatrum
quo magnitudinem populi viserent." Comp. Senec. *de Ira.* ii. 7.:
" Illum circum in quo maximam sui partem populus ostendit." Yet
from the time of the later republic women were not excluded from
the theatres or circus. Plut. *Sull.* 35.; Ovid. *Art. Amand.* i. 139.;
Calpurn. *Ecl.* vii. 26.

was the entire absence of a middle class, the bone
and sinew of cities as well as of empires; and its
population mainly consisted of the two orders of
wealthy nobles on the one hand, whose means were
in process of trituration under the pressure of the
imperial imposts, and the poor citizens on the other,
who clung to the forum and the circus for the sake
of their amusements and largesses.

CHAPTER XLI.

Life in Rome.—Thronging of the streets.—Places of recreation.—
Theatres, circus, and amphitheatres.—Exhibitions of wild beasts
and gladiators.—Baths.—The day of a Roman noble: the forum,
the campus, the bath, and the supper.—Custom of recitation.—
The schools of the rhetoricians.—Authors: Livy, Virgil, Horace,
Propertius, Tibullus, Ovid, each reflecting in his own way the
sentiments of the Augustan age.

WE will now proceed to people with human figures
the expanse of brick and marble which has
been presented to our view, and realize, as
we may, the actual movement of life in the
great metropolis, hearkening to the surging murmurs .
which still seem to resound across the abyss of eighteen
centuries.[1] Rome, at the time of which we are speaking,
was in the crisis of that transitional state which most
great capitals have experienced, when a rapid increase
in their population and the transactions of daily life
has begun to outstrip the extension of their means of
accommodation. The increase of numbers must necessarily multiply the operations of industry, which cross
and recross each other in the streets; and though
neither the commerce nor manufactures of Rome
were conducted on the scale to which our ideas are
accustomed, the retail traffic which passed from
hand to hand, and the ordinary affairs of business
and pleasure, must have caused an ever-increasing
stir and circulation among the multitude of human
beings collected within its walls. The uninterrupted
progress of building operations, and the extension of
the suburbs simultaneously with the restoration of

Thronging of the streets of Rome.

[1] Stat. *Sylv.* i. 1. 65.: "Magnæ vaga murmura Romæ."

the city, must have kept every avenue constantly thronged with waggons and vehicles of all sorts, engaged in the transport of cumbrous materials: the crush of these heavy-laden machines, and the portentous swinging of the long beams they carried round the corners of the narrow streets, are mentioned among the worst nuisances and even terrors of the citizen's daily walk.[1] Neither of the rival institutions of the shop and the bazaar had been developed to any great extent in ancient Rome. Numerous trades were exercised there by itinerant vendors. The street cries, which *Trades exercised in the streets.* have almost ceased within our own memory in London, were rife in the city of the Cæsars. The incessant din of these discordant sounds is complained of as making life intolerable to the poor gentleman who is compelled to reside in the midst of them.[2] The streets were not contrived, nor was it possible generally to adapt them, for the passage of the well-attended litters and cumbrous carriages of the wealthy, which began to traverse them with the pomp and circumstance of our own aristocratic vehicles of a century since[3]; while the police of the city seems never to have contemplated the removal of the most obvious causes of crowd and obstruction, in the display of gymnastic and gladiatorial feats, of conjurors' tricks and the buffoonery of the lowest stage-players, amidst the most frequented thoroughfares.[4] The noble seldom crossed his threshold without a numerous train of clients and retainers; *Crowds of loungers and gazers.* the lower people collected at the corners of the streets to hear the gossip of the day, and

---

[1] Juvenal, iii. 236, 255. In the second century it became necessary to forbid loaded waggons to traverse the city. "Orbicula cum ingentibus sarcinis urbem ingredi prohibuit." Spartian. *Hadrian.* 22.

[2] Martial, i. 42., x. 3., xii. 57.

[3] The Appian Way was the fashionable drive of the Roman nobility. Hor. *Epod.* 4. 14.; *Epist.* i. 6. 26.

[4] Suet. *Oct.* 74.: "Triviales ex Circo ludii."

discuss the merits of racers and dancers; the slaves
hovered over the steam of the open cook-shops,
or loitered on their errands, to gaze on the rude
drawings or pore over the placards on the walls.
The last century had filled the imperial capital with
multitudes of foreigners, attracted by curiosity as
much as by business to the renowned emporium of
the wonders of the world, who added to the host of
idlers and gazers in the streets of Rome; men of
strange costumes and figures, and, when they spoke,
of speech still stranger, who, while they gazed around
them with awe and admiration, became themselves
objects of interest to a crowd of lounging citizens.
The marked though casual manner in which the
throng of the streets is noticed by the Roman writers,
shows in the strongest way how ordinary a feature it
was of life in the city.[1]

The streets, or rather the narrow and winding alleys,
Interruptions to traffic. of Rome were miserably inadequate to the
circulation of the people who thus encum-
bered them; for the vici were no better than lanes
Paucity of thoroughfares. or alleys, and there were only two viæ, or
paved ways, fit for the transport of heavy
carriages, the Sacra and the Nova, in the central
parts of the city. The three interior hills, the Palatine, the Aventine, and the Capitoline, were sore
impediments to traffic; for no carriages could pass
over them, and it may be doubted whether there were

Comp., for instance, Hor. *Sat.* ii. 6. 28.:

"Luctandum in turba, facienda injuria tardis;"

and Cicero, in the passage so important for the topography of Rome
(*pro Planc.* 7.): "Equidem si quando, ut fit, jactor in turba, non
illum accuso qui est in summa Sacra Via, cum ego ad Fabium
fornicem impellor, sed cum qui in me ipsum incurrit et incidit."
Such an illustration would not occur to an English speaker. Comp.
Plaut. *Mercat.* i. 1. 8.: "Tres simitu res agendæ sunt . . . . et cur-
rendum, et pugnandum, et autem jurgandum est in via." Dezobry,
Rome, i. 218.

even thoroughfares for foot-passengers. The occurrence of a fire or an inundation, or the casual *Demolition of*
fall of a house, must have choked the cir- *houses. Fires.*
culation of the lifeblood of the city.[1] The first, indeed,
and the last of these, were accidents to which every
place of human resort is liable; but the *Inundations.*
inundations of Rome were a marked and
peculiar feature of her ancient existence. The central
quarters of the city were founded in a morass little
raised above the ordinary level of the Tiber, a river
peculiarly subject to rapid and violent risings. The
Romans might complain that, from the configuration
of the spot, the masses of water brought down from
above were flung from the right bank, where the high
grounds descended directly into the stream, and
driven with increased violence against the left, just
at the point where nature had left an opening into
the heart of the city.[2] It might have been easy to
maintain a mound or levée on this bank, and curb
the overflows at least of ordinary years; but the seven
hills were themselves great attractors of rain, which
they cast off from their sides into the pool of the
Forum and the trough of the Velabrum, and this
discharge it required a stupendous under-drainage
to convey safely into the river.[3] When the Tiber

---

[1] Strabo speaks very strongly of the constant fall and demolition
of houses (v. 3. p. 235.): αἱ συμπτώσεις καὶ ἐμπρήσεις καὶ μεταπράσεις,
ἀδιάλειπτοι καὶ αὗται οὖσαι· καὶ γὰρ αἱ μεταπράσεις ἑκούσιοί τινες συμπτώσεις εἰσι, καταβαλόντων καὶ ἀνοικοδομούντων πρὸς τὰς ἐπιθυμίας ἕτερα
ἐξ ἑτέρων.

[2] Such is the interpretation sometimes given to the well-known
lines of Horace:
> "Vidimus flavum Tiberim retortis
> Litore Etrusco violenter undis."

It may be more correct to understand by the litus Etruscum, the
coast of the Mediterranean; but I remember the happy boldness of
the Ovidian, "pro ripis litora poscunt," and am willing to adopt it
here.

[3] Strabo describes the drainage of the city, v. 3. p. 235.: τοσοῦτον

was high, the torrents of the sewers, or cloacæ, were
of course ponded back, and no ingenuity could prevent
the flooding of the lower levels of the city to a depth
of several feet. Nor was it in the Forum and Velabrum only that these disastrous effects were produced :
the little Aqua Crabra, which descended into the city
from the Porta Capena, and was carried beneath the
arena of the circus into the Cloaca Maxima, often
overspread the low grounds at the foot of the Cælian
Hill, and the grotto of Egeria was sometimes, we
may believe, thus converted into an abode more
worthy of the water-nymph to whom it was dedicated.[1]

The efforts made to expand the sides of the Forum,
and give more play to the lungs of the great animated
machine, were very feeble and imperfect, till Julius
Cæsar, and after him Augustus, removed large masses
of 'habitations in this quarter, and threw open to
traffic and movement the space thus seasonably acquired. But if the Roman people was ill accommodated in its streets, it might derive compensation in
the vast constructions erected for its amusement, the
Places of re-
creation for
the citizens.
Parks and
gardens.
ample walks and gardens devoted to its
recreation, and the area which was sedulously preserved for its exercise in the
Campus Martius, and the circuses of Romulus and
Flaminius. The theatre of Pompeius, the first built
Theatres.
of stone for permanent use, was rivalled
by that of Balbus, and Augustus dedicated
a third to the pleasures of the citizens under the

δ' ἐστὶ τὸ εἰσαγώγιμον ὕδωρ διὰ τῶν ὑδραγωγείων, ὥστε ποταμοὺς διὰ τῆς
πόλεως καὶ τῶν ὑπονόμων ῥεῖν. Here occurs his remarkable statement
that a waggon loaded with hay could enter the great cloaca.

[1] Cicero describes the effect of a flood in this quarter in a passage
of some topographical importance. "Romæ et maxime Appia ad
Martis mira proluvies ; Crassipedis ambulatio ablata ; horti, tabernæ
plurimæ ; magna vis aquæ usque ad Piscinam publicam." *Ad Qu.*
Fr. iii. 7.

title of the theatre of Marcellus.[1] From the enormous size of these celebrated edifices, it is clear that the idea of reserving them for dramatic performances hardly entered into the views of their builders. The Roman theatres were an institution very different from ours, where a select audience pay the price of admission to a private spectacle on however large a scale: they were the houses of the Roman people, to which every citizen claimed the right of entrance; for they were given him for his own by their munificent founders, and the performances which took place in them were provided gratuitously by the magistrates. The first object, therefore, was to seat the greatest number of the people possible; and when that was accomplished, the question followed of how they should be safely and conveniently entertained. An assemblage of 30,000 spectators, gathering excitement from the consciousness of their own multitude, could not sit tamely under the blaze of an Italian sun, tempered only by an awning, in the steam and dust of their own creating, which streams of perfumed waters were required to allay[2], to hear the formal dialogue of the ancient tragedy declaimed by human puppets from brass-lipped

---

[1] Ovid, *Trist.* iii. 12.: " Cumque tribus resonant terna theatra foris." The three forums are those of Julius and Augustus, with the Boarium. It is not quite clear what was the construction or what the fate of the theatre of Scaurus. It was adorned with costly pillars of marble, but the walls and seats may have been chiefly of wood ; and if it was not pulled down, it must have been destroyed by fire before the erection of the Pompeian a few years later.

[2] These were recent inventions: in simpler times, according to Propertius (iv. 1. 15.):

" Non sinuosa vago pendebant vela theatro ;
Pulpita solennes non oluere crocos."

In the amphitheatres which were too spacious for complete awnings the spectators were refreshed by the play of jets d'eau, which rose to the full height of the building. Senec. *Nat. Quæst.* ii. 9.

masks, staggering on the stilted cothurnus.[1]   Whatever might be the case with the Greeks, it was impossible, at least for the plainer Romans, so to abstract their imaginations from the ungraceful realities thus placed before them, as to behold in them a symbolic adumbration of the heroic and the divine.   For the

Theatrical exhibitions. charms, however, both of music and dancing, which are also considered pleasures of the imagination, they appear to have had a genuine, though perhaps a rude, taste.   Their dramatic representations, accordingly, were mostly conducted in pantomime; this form at least of the drama was that which most flourished among them, and produced

Pantomime. men of genius, inventors and creators in their own line.   Some of the most famous of the mimic actors were themselves Romans; but the ancient prejudice against the exercise of histrionic art by citizens was never perhaps wholly overcome. Accordingly Greek names figure more conspicuously than Roman in the roll of actors on the Roman stage; and two of these, Bathyllus and Pylades, divided between them, under the mild autocracy of Augustus, the dearest sympathies and favours of the masters of the world.   The rivalry of these two competitors for public applause, or rather of their admirers and adherents, broke out into tumultuous disorders, which engaged at last the interference of the emperor himself.   *It is better for your government*, said one of them to him, when required to desist from a professional emulation which emperilled the tranquillity of the city—*it is better that the citizens should quarrel*

---

[1] "Like mice roaring," to apply an expression of Mrs. F. Kemble's. I cannot reconcile the use of the mask and buskin with the keen appreciation of the graceful in form ascribed so liberally to the Greeks; nor can I understand how the audiences of Aristophanes could be the same people who gravely witnessed Agamemnon's shuffle across the stage:—χαμαὶ τιθεὶς Τὸν σὸν πόδ', ὦναξ, 'Ιλίου πορθήτορα.

*about Pylades and Bathyllus than about a Pom-
peius and a Cæsar.*[1]

But whatever claims pantomime might have as a
legitimate child of the drama, the Roman
stage was invaded by another class of ex-   Spectacles.
hibitions, for which no such pretensions could be
advanced. The grand proportions of the theatre
invited more display of scenic effects than could be
supplied by the chaste simplicity of the Greek chorus,
in which the priests or virgins, whatever their number, presented only so many repetitions of a single
type. The finer sentiment of the upper classes was
overpowered by the vulgar multitude, who demanded
with noisy violence the gratification of their coarse and
rude tastes.[2] Processions swept before their eyes of
horses and chariots, of wild and unfamiliar animals;
the long show of a triumph wound its way across the
stage; the spoils of captured cities, and the figures of
the cities themselves were represented in painting
or sculpture; the boards were occupied in every interval of more serious entertainment by crowds of
rope-dancers, conjurors, boxers, clowns, and posture-
makers, men who walked on their hands, or stood on
their heads, or let themselves be whirled aloft by
machinery, or suspended upon wires, or who danced
on stilts, or exhibited feats of skill with cups and
balls.[3] But these degenerate spectacles were not the

---

[1] Dion, liv. 17.; Macrob. *Saturn.* ii. 7.

[2] Hor. *Epist.* ii. 1. 184.:

> "Indocti stolidique, et depugnare parati
> Si discordet eques, media inter carmina poscunt
> Aut ursum aut pugiles," &c.

[3] The learned Bulenger (*de Theatro*, i. 34. foll. in Grœv. *Thes.*) has
given a list of the kinds of performers who thus encroached upon the
domain of Melpomene and Thalia: "Ingens utique hujusmodi
hominum sylva fuit, quorum alii miracula patrarent, Grœci vocant
θαυματοποιούς, Latini prœstigiatores, acetabulos, alii per catadro-
mum decurrerent, cernuarent, petauristæ essent, petaminarii, gralla-
tores, phonasci, pantomimi, crotochoraulæ, citharœdi, satyri, lentuli,
tibicines, parasiti, atellani, dictiosi, ridiculi, rhapsodi, urbicarii, psal-

lowest degradation to which the theatres were subjected. They were polluted with the grossest in-
decencies; and the luxury of the stage, as the Romans
delicately phrased it, drew down the loudest indignation of the reformers of a later age.[1] Hitherto at
least legislators and moralists had been content with
branding with civil infamy the instruments of the
people's licentious pleasures; but the pretext even
for this was rather the supposed baseness of exhibiting
oneself for money, than the iniquity of the performances themselves. The legitimate drama, which was
still an exercise of skill among the Romans, was relegated, perhaps, to the smaller theatres of wood,
which were erected year by year for temporary use.
There were also certain private theatres, in which
knights and senators could exercise their genius for
singing and acting without incurring the stigma of
public representation.

The appetite for grandeur and magnificence, developed so rapidly among the Romans by
the pride of opulence and power, was stimulated by the rivalry of the great nobles. The
bold and ingenious tribune Curio, whose talents
found a more fatal arena in the contests of the civil
wars, was the first to imagine the form of the double
hemicycle, which he executed with an immense wooden
structure and a mechanical apparatus, by which two
theatres, after doing their legitimate duty to the
drama, could be wheeled front to front, and combined

*The amphi-
theatres.*

---

triæ, sabulones, planipedes, mimi, mastigophori, apinarii, moriones,
miriones, sanniones, iambi, salii, musici, poetæ, curiones, præcones,
agonarchæ: " all which he proceeds severally to describe.

[1] This coarseness dated, indeed, from a period of high and honourable feeling. The impurities of the Floralia offended the elder Cato,
according to Martial's well-known epigram, i. 1. The same licentiousness continued to please, through a period of six centuries, down
to the time of Ausonius, who says,

" Nec non lascivi Floralia læta theatri,
    Quæ spectasse volunt qui voluisse negant."

into a single amphitheatre for gladiatorial spectacles.[1]
There can be no doubt that this extraordinary edifice
was adapted to contain many thousands of spectators;
and there are few, perhaps, even of our own engineers,
who build tubular bridges, and suspend acres of iron
network over our heads, who would not shrink from
the problem of moving the population of a great city
on a single pair of pivots.[2] The amphitheatre of
Julius Cæsar in the Campus was of wood also, and
this, as well as its predecessors, seems to have been
taken down after serving the purpose of the day. It
remained for Statilius Taurus, the legate of Augustus,
to construct the first edifice of this character in stone,
and to bequeath to future ages the original model of
the magnificent structures which bear that name,
some of which still attest the grandeur of the empire
in her provinces; but the most amazing specimen of
which, and indeed the noblest existing monument of
all ancient architecture, is the glorious Colosseum at
Rome. Like most of the splendid buildings of this
period, the amphitheatre of Taurus was erected in
the Campus Martius, the interior of the city not
admitting of the dedication of so large a space to the
purpose; though it was rumoured indeed that Augustus had purposed to crown the series of his public
works by an edifice of this nature, in the centre of
his capital.[3] While the amphitheatre, however, was

---

[1] Plin. *Hist. Nat.* xxxvi. 24. § 8.: "Theatra juxta fecit amplissima
e ligno, cardinum singulorum versatili suspensa libramento, in quibus
utrisque ante-meridiano ludorum spectaculo edito inter sese aversis,
ne invicem obstreperent scenæ, repente circumactis ut contra starent,
postremo jam die discedentibus tabulis et cornibus in se coeuntibus,
faciebat amphitheatrum, et gladiatorum spectacula edebat, ipsum
magis auctoratum populum Romanum circumferens."

[2] Plin. *l. c.*: "Super omnia erit populi furor, sedere ausa tam infida
instabilique sede . . . . ecce populus Romanus universus, velut
duobus navigiis impositus, binis cardinibus sustinctur."

[3] Suetonius, remarking particularly that the Colosseum, or amphitheatre of Vespasian, was in the centre of the city, tells us that it was
erected there in order to carry out a design of Augustus. *Vespas.* 9.

a novel invention, the circus, to which it was in a manner supplementary, was one of the most ancient institutions of the city. The founder himself had convened his subjects in the Murcian valley, beneath his cabin on the Palatine, to celebrate games of riding, hunting, and charioteering. The inclosure in which these shows were annually exhibited was an oblong, curved at the further end, above six hundred yards in length, but comparatively narrow. The seats which ranged round the two larger sides and extremity of this area were originally cut out of the rising ground, and covered with turf: less rude accommodation was afterwards supplied by wooden scaffoldings; but the whole space was eventually surrounded by masonry, and decorated with all the forms and members of Roman architecture.

The arena was adapted for chariot racing by a partition, a dwarf wall, surmounted with various emblematic devices, which ran along the middle and terminated at either end in goals or ornamented pillars, round which the contending cars were driven a stated number of times. The eye of the spectator, from his position aloft, was carried over this spinal ridge, and he obtained a complete view of the contest, which thus passed and repassed amidst clouds of dust and roars of sympathizing excitement, before his feet. The Romans had from the first an intense delight in these races; and many of the most graphic passages of their poets describe the ardour of the horses, the emulation of their drivers, and the tumultuous enthusiasm of the spectators.[1] These contests main-

The Circus.

Chariot races.

---

[1] Most of us have been struck with the spectacle of an audience of three or four thousand in one of our theatres rising simultaneously at the first sound of the national anthem. The Romans were deeply impressed with the grandeur of such a movement, on the very different scale with which they were familiar. Comp. Stat. *Theb.* vi. 448.:
"Subit astra fragor, cœlumque tremiscit,
Omniaque excusso patuere sedilia vulgo."

tained their interest from the cradle to the very grave of the Roman people. The circus of Constantinople, under the Greek designation of Hippodrome, was copied from the pattern of the Roman; and the *factions* which divided the favour of the tribes almost from the beginning of the empire, continued to agitate the city of Theodosius and Justinian. The citizens were never satiated with this spectacle, and could sit without flagging through a hundred heats, which the liberality of the exhibitor sometimes provided for them. But the races were more commonly varied with contests of other kinds. All the varieties of the Greek Pancratium, such as boxing, wrestling, and running, were exhibited in the circus; gladiators fought one another with naked swords, sometimes in single combat, sometimes with opposing bands. The immense size of the arena, un- Exhibition of favourable for the exhibition of the duel, wild beasts. was turned to advantage for the display of multitudes of wild animals, which were let loose in it to be transfixed with spears and arrows. This practice seems to date from the sixth century, when victorious generals first returned to Rome from the far regions of the East, and ingratiated themselves with the populace by exhibiting strange monsters of unknown continents, lions and elephants, giraffes and hippopotami. As in other things, the rivalry of the nobles soon displayed itself in the number of these creatures they produced for massacre; and the favour of the citizens appears to have followed with constancy the champion who treated them with the largest effusion of blood. The circus was too spacious for the eye to gloat on the expression of conflicting passions, and watch the last ebbings of life; but the amphitheatre brought the greatest possible number of spectators within easy distance of the dead and dying, and fostered the passion for the sight of blood, which continued for centuries to vie in interest with the harmless excitement of the race.[1]

The idea of the theatre is representation and illu-
Gladiatorial combats. sion, and the stage is, as it were, magic ground, over which the imagination may glance without restraint and wander at will, *from Thebes to Athens*, from the present to the past or future. But in the amphitheatre all is reality. The citizen, seated face to face with his fellow citizens, could not for a moment forget either his country or his times. The spectacles here presented to him made no appeal to the discursive faculties; they brought before his senses, in all the hardness of actuality, the consummation of those efforts of strength, skill, and dexterity in the use of arms, to which much of his own time and thoughts was necessarily directed. The exhibition of gladiatorial combats, which preceded the departure of a general for a foreign campaign, was part of the soldier's training (and every citizen was regarded as a soldier), from which he received the last finish of his education, and was taught to regard wounds and death as the natural incidents of his calling. These were probably the most ancient of the military spectacles. The combats of wild beasts, and of men with beasts, were a corruption of the noble science of war which the gladiatorial contests were supposed to teach; they were a concession to the prurient appetite for excitement, engendered by an indulgence which, however natural in a rude and barbarous age, was actually hardening and degrading. The interest these exercises at first naturally excited degenerated into a mere passion for the sight of death; and as the imagination

---

[1] Favourable as the long extent of the circus might have been for the exhibition of pageants and processions, the people, in their eagerness for spectacles of bloodshed, witnessed them here with great impatience. M. Seneca thus closes one of his prefaces: " Sed jam non sustineo vos morari. Scio quam odiosa res sit circensibus pompa." *Controv.* i. præf.

can never be wholly inactive in the face of the barest realities, the Romans learnt to feast their thoughts on the deepest mystery of humanity, and to pry with insatiate curiosity into the secrets of the last moments of existence : in proportion as they lost their faith in a future life, they became more restlessly inquisitive into the conditions of the present.

The eagerness with which the great mass of the citizens crowded to witness these bloody shows, on every occasion of their exhibition, became one of the most striking features of Roman society, and none of their customs has attracted more of the notice of the ancient writers who profess to describe the manners of their times. By them they are often represented as an idle and frivolous recreation, unworthy of the great nation of kings ; nor do we find the excuse officially offered for the combats of gladiators, as a means of cherishing courage and fostering the ruder virtues of antiquity, generally put forward as their apology by private moralists.[1] Men of reflection, who were far themselves from sharing the vulgar delight in these horrid spectacles (and it should be noticed that no Roman author speaks of them with favour, or gloats with interest on their abominations), acquiesced in the belief that it was necessary to amuse the multitude, and was better to gratify them with any indulgence they craved for, than risk the more fearful

Sentiments of antiquity on these bloody spectacles.

---

[1] Capitolin. *Max. et Balb.* 8. Cicero (*Tusc.* ii. 17.), even while offering this vindication, cannot help remarking: "Crudele gladiatorium spectaculum nonnullis videri solet; et haud scio an ita sit, ut nunc fit." Compare also his remarks to Marius (*ad Div.* vii. 1.): "quæ potest homini polito esse delectatio quum homo imbecillus a valentissima bestia laniatur," &c. See also a passage to the same effect in Seneca, *de Brev. Vit.* 13., and the preaching of Apollonius at Athens (Philostr. *Vit. Apoll.* iv. 22.). Tertullian and Prudentius have some declamations against the exhibition; but far the most interesting passage on the subject is the description in St. Augustine's *Confessions* (vi. 13.) of the youth Alypius yielding against his will to its horrid fascination: "Quid plura? spectavit, clamavit, exarsit," &c.

consequences of thwarting and controlling them.
The blood thus shed on the arena was the price they
were content to pay for the safety and tranquillity of
the realm. In theory, at least, the men who were
thus thrust forth to engage the wild beasts were condemned criminals : but it was often necessary to hire
volunteers to complete the numbers required; and
this seems to prove that the advantage was generally
on the side of the human combatant. The gladiators,
although their profession might be traced by antiquarians to the combats of armed slaves around the
pyre of their master, ending in their mutual destruction in his honour, were devoted to no certain death.[1]
They were generally slaves purchased for the purpose,
but not unfrequently free men tempted by liberal
wages; and they were in either case too costly articles
to be thrown away with indifference. They were
entitled to their discharge after a few years' service,
and their profession was regarded in many respects
as a public service, conducted under fixed regulations.[2]
Under the emperors, indeed, express laws were required to moderate the ardour even of knights and
senators to *descend into the arena*, where they delighted to exhibit their courage and address in the
face of danger. Such was the ferocity engendered
by the habitual use of arms, so soothing to the
swordsman's vanity the consciousness of skill and
valour, so stimulating to his pride the thunders of
applause from a hundred thousand admirers, that
the practice of mortal combat, however unsophisti-
cated nature may blench at its horrors, was actually
the source perhaps of more pleasure than pain to
these Roman prize-fighters. If the companions of
Spartacus revolted and slew their trainers and mas-

---

[1] Servius in *Æneid*. iii. 67.; Tertull. *de Spectac.* 12.
[2] Hor. *Epist.* i. 1. 4.:   " Veianius armis
          Herculis ad postem fixis, latet abditus agro,
          Ne populum extrema toties exoret arena."

ters, we may set against this instance of despair and
fury the devotion of the gladiators of Antonius, who
cut their way through so many obstacles in an effort
to succour him.   But the effect of such shows on the
spectators themselves was wholly evil; for while they
utterly failed in supplying the bastard courage for
which they were said to be designed, they destroyed
the nerve of sympathy for suffering, which distin-
guishes the human from the brute creation.

The Romans, however, had another popular passion,
innocent at least of blood and pain, but
perhaps little less pernicious to the moral
character, in the excess to which they indulged it, than that which we have just reviewed.
This was their universal appetite for the bath, a
refreshment which degenerated, in their immoderate
use of it, into an enervating luxury.   The houses of
the opulent were always furnished with chambers
for this purpose; they had their warm and cold
baths, as well as their steam apparatus; and the
application of oil and perfumes was equally universal
among them.   From the earliest times there were
perhaps places of more general resort, where the
plebeian paid a trifling sum for the enjoyment of
this luxury; and among other ways of courting
popular favour was that of subsidizing the owners of
these common baths, and giving the people the free
use of them for one or more days.   The extent to
which Agrippa carried this mode of bribery has been
before mentioned.   Besides the erection of lesser
baths to the number of a hundred and seventy, he
was the first to construct public establishments of
the kind, or Thermæ, in which the citizens might
assemble in large numbers, and combine the pleasure
of purification with the exercise of gymnastic sports,
while at the same time they might be amused by the
contemplation of paintings and sculptures, and by
listening to song and music.   The Roman, however,

Fondness of the Romans for the bath.

had his peculiar notion of personal dignity, and it
was not without a feeling of uneasiness that he
stripped himself in public below the waist, however
accustomed he might be to exhibit his chest and
shoulders in the performance of his manly exercises.[1]
The baths of Mæcenas and Agrippa remained without rivals for more than one generation, though they
were ultimately supplanted by imperial constructions
on a far grander scale.   In the time of Augustus the
resort of women to the public baths was forbidden,
if indeed such an indecorum had yet been imagined.

The manners of the baths. At a later period, whatever might be the
absence of costume among the men, the
women at least were partially covered.[2]   An ingenious writer has remarked on the effect produced on
the spirits by the action of air and water upon the
naked body.   The unusual lightness and coolness,
the disembarrassment of the limbs, the elasticity of
the circulation, combine to stimulate the sensibility
of the nervous system.   Hence the Thermæ of the
great city resounded with the shouts and laughter of
the bathers, who when risen from the water and
resigned to the manipulations of the barbers and
perfumers, gazed with voluptuous languor on the
brilliant decorations of the halls around them, or
listened with charmed ears to the singers and mu-
sicians, and even to the poets who presumed on
their helplessness to recite to them their choicest
compositions.[3]

Such were the amusements of the great mass of
the citizens; and their amusements were now their
most serious occupations.   But the magnanimous

---

[1] Valerius Maximus (ii. 1. 7.) states as an instance of this modest
reserve that, " aliquando nec pater cum filio, nec socer cum genero
lavabatur."   The dislike of the Romans, at their best period, to be
represented by naked statues, has been already noticed.

[2] Martial, iii. 87.   See Walckenaer, Vie d'Horace, i. 126.

[3] Two of the most interesting passages on the manners of the
baths are Senec. Ep. 56. and Petron. Satyr. 73.   See Walckenaer, l.c.

Roman of the caste which once ruled the ~~ght before~~
was still permitted to administer it, con- ~~he would~~
tinued to be trained on other principles, and ~~Rom~~ while
was still taught to combine in no unfair proportiion,
attention to business, cultivation of mind, the exer~~ts~~
cise of the body, and indulgence in social relaxations.
Bred up in the traditions of an antique education,
these men could not soon be reduced, under any
change of government, to become mere loungers and
triflers. Augustus at least had no such aim or desire;
on the contrary, he was anxious to employ all men
of rank and breeding in practical business, while at
the same time he proposed to them his own example
as a follower both of the Muses and the Graces. The
Roman noble rose ordinarily at daybreak, and received
at his levée the crowd of clients and retainers who
had thronged his doorstep from the hours of darkness.[1]
A few words of greeting were expected on either side,
and then, as the sun mounted the eastern sky, he
descended from his elevated mansion into the Forum.[2]
He might walk surrounded by the still lingering
crowd, or he might be carried in a litter; but to ride
in a wheeled vehicle on such occasions was no Roman
fashion.[3] Once arrived in the Forum he
was quickly immersed in the business of the
day. He presided as a judge in one of the
basilicas, or he appeared himself before the judges

The business of the morning.

[1] For the disposal of the Roman's day see particularly Martial,
iv. 8.: " Prima salutantes atque altera continet hora," &c.   Comp.
the younger Pliny's account of his uncle's day. *Epist.* iii. 5.;
cf. iii. 1.

[2] The phrases, *descendere in forum* or *in campum* (so Hor. iii. 1.,
" Descendit in campum petitor ") . refer to the comparative level of
the noble mansion on the hill, and the public places in the valley or
plain. Champagny, *Césars,* ii. 256.

[3] The Romans rode in carriages on a journey, but rarely for
amusement, and never within the city. Even beyond the walls it
was considered disreputable to hold the reins oneself, such being the
occupation of the slave or hired driver. Juvenal ranks the consul,
who creeps out at night to drive his own chariot, with the most de

as an advocate, a witness, or a suitor. He transacted his private affairs with his banker or notary; he perused the Public Journal of yesterday, and inquired how his friend's cause had sped before the tribunal of the prætor. At every step he crossed the path of some of the notables of his own class, and the news of the day and interests of the hour were discussed between them with dignified politeness.

Such were the morning occupations of a *dies fastus*, or working day: the holy-day had its appropriate occupation in attendance on the temple services, in offering prayers for the safety of the emperor and people, in sprinkling frankincense on the altar, and, on occasions of special devotion, appeasing the gods with a sacrifice. But all transactions of business, secular or *divine*, ceased at once when the voice of the herald on the steps of the Hostilian Curia proclaimed that the shadow of the sun had passed the line on the pavement before him, which marked the hour of midday.[1] Every door was now

The midday siesta. closed; every citizen, at least in summer, plunged into the dark recess of his sleeping chamber for the enjoyment of his meridian slumber. The midday siesta generally terminated the affairs of the day, and every man was now released from duty and free to devote himself, on rising again, to relaxation or amusement till the return of night. If the senate had been used sometimes to prolong or renew its sittings, there was a rule that after the tenth hour, or

graded of characters: that he should venture to drive by daylight, while still in office, is an excess of turpitude transcending the imagination of the most sarcastic painter of manners as they were. And this was a hundred years later than the age of Augustus. See Juvenal, viii. 145. foll.

[1] I allude to the passage, well known to the topographers, in Pliny, *Hist. Nat.* vii. 60.: "Meridies . . . . accenso consulum id pronuntiante, quum a curia inter rostra et Græcostasim prospexisset solem." The reader will observe that this refers in strictness to an earlier period, and that the Curia Hostilia was destroyed in the year 52 B.C.

four o'clock, no new business could be brought before
it, and we are told of Asinius Pollio, that he would
not even open a letter after that hour.[1] Meanwhile
Rome had awakened to amusements and recreation,
and the grave man of business had his amusements
as well as the idler of the Forum. The exercises of
the Field of Mars were the relaxation of
the soldiers of the republic; and when the
urban populace had withdrawn from mili-
tary service, the traditions of the Campus were still
cherished by the upper ranks, and the practice of its
mimic war confined, perhaps, exclusively to them.
The swimming, running, riding, and javelin-throwing
of this public ground became under the emperors a
fashion of the nobility[2]: the populace had no taste
for such labours, and witnessed with some surprise
the toils to which men voluntarily devoted themselves,
who possessed slaves to relieve them from the most
ordinary exertions. But the young competitors in
these athletic contests were not without a throng of
spectators: the porticos which bordered the field
were crowded with the elder people and the women,
who shunned the heat of the declining sun: many a
private dwelling looked upon it from the opposite
side of the river, which was esteemed on that account
a desirable place of residence. Augustus had promised his favour to every revival of the gallant customs of antiquity, and all the Roman world that lived
in his smiles hastened to the scene of these antique
amusements to gratify the emperor, if not to amuse
themselves.[3]

The after-noon: the Field of Mars.

---

[1] Senec. *de Tranq. Anim.* 15.: "Quidam nullum non diem inter
et otium et curas dividebant ; qualem Pollionem Asinium, oratorem
magnum, meminimus, quem nulla res ultra decimam retinuit ; ne
epistolas quidem post eam h ram legebat, ne quid novæ curæ nas-
ceretur."

[2] See for the exercises of the Campus, Hor. *Od.* i. 13., *Art. Poet.*
379.

[3] Horace knew how to please his patron by frequent allusions to

The ancients, it was said, had made choice of the
Field of Mars for the scene of their mimic warfare
for the convenience of the stream of the Tiber, in
which the wearied combatants might wash off the
sweat and dust, and return to their companions in
the glow of recruited health and vigour.[1]   But the
youth of Rome in more refined days were not satisfied with these genial ablutions.   They resorted to
warm and vapour baths, to the use of perfumes and
cosmetics, to enhance the luxury of refreshment; and
sought by various exquisite devices to stimulate the
appetite for the banquet which crowned the evening.

The evening:
the supper.
The cœna or supper of the Romans deserves
to be described as a national institution : it
had from the first its prescriptions and traditions, its
laws and usages; it was sanctified by religious observances, and its whole system of etiquette was held
as binding as if it had had a religious significance.[2]
Under the protection of the gods to whom they poured
their libations, friends met together for the recreation equally of mind and body.   If the conversation
flagged, it was relieved by the aid of minstrels, who

the exercises of the Campus. It is probable that they declined in
interest at a subsequent period. and the mention of them becomes
comparatively rare.   But they still constituted a part of the ordinary
occupation of the day in the second century of the empire (Martial,
ii. 14. iv. 8.), and were not disused in the third.   Trebell. Poll.
Claud. 13.: "Fecerat hoc adolescens in militia quum ludicro Mar-
tiali in campo luctamen inter fortissimos quosque celebraret."

[1] Veget. *de Re Milit.* i. 10.   What life and spirit this gives to
Virgil's lines at the end of the ninth book of the Æneid:

> "Tum toto corpore sudor
> Liquitur, et piceum, nec respirare potestas,
> Flumen agit; fessos quatit æger anhelitos artus:
> Tum demum præceps saltu sese omnibus armis
> In fluvium dedit: ille suo cum gurgite flavo
> Accepit venientem, ac mollibus extulit undis,
> Et lætum sociis abluta cæde remisit."

[2] Hor. *Sat.* ii. 6. 66.:

> "Ante Larem proprium vescor, vernasque loquaces
> Pasco libatis dapibus."

Comp. Ovid. *Fast.* ii. 631.

recited the famous deeds of the national heroes[1] : but in the best days of the republic the guests of the noble Roman were men of speech not less than of deeds, men consummately trained in all the knowledge of their times ; and we may imagine there was more room to fear lest their converse should degenerate into the argumentative and didactic than languish from the want of matter or interest. It is probable, however, that the table-talk of the higher classes at Rome was peculiarly terse and epigrammatic. Many specimens have been preserved to us of the dry sententious style which they seemed to have cultivated : their remarks on life and manners were commonly conveyed in solemn or caustic aphorisms, and they condemned as undignified and Greekish any superfluous abundance of words. The graceful and flowing conversations of Cicero's dialogues were imitated from Athenian writings, rather than drawn after the types of actual life around him. *People at supper*, said Varro, himself not the least sententious of his nation, *should neither be loquacious nor mute ; eloquence is for the forum, silence for the bedchamber.*[2] Another rule of the same master of etiquette, that the number of the guests should not exceed nine, the number of the Muses, nor fall short of three, the number of the Graces, was dictated by a sense of the proprieties of the Roman banquet, which the love of ostentation and pride of wealth were now constantly violating. Luxury and the appetite for excitement were engaged in multiplying occasions of more than ordinary festivity, on which the most rigid of the sumptuary laws allowed a wider licence to the expenses of the table. On such high days the number of the guests was limited neither by law nor custom : the entertainer, the master or

---

[1] Cic. *Tusc.* i. 2., iv. 2.; Nonius, in Assa voce; Val. Max. ii. 1. 10.
[2] Varro, quoted by A. Gellius, xiii. 11.

father, as he was called, of the supper, was required
to abdicate the ordinary functions of·host, and, according to the Greek custom, *a king of the wine,* or
arbiter of drinking, was chosen from among themselves by lot, or for his convivial qualities, by the
Bacchanalian crew around him.[1]

Our own more polished but not unmanly taste
Coarseness of must look with amazement and even dis-
the luxury of gust at the convivial excesses of the Ro-
the Roman table. mans at this period, such as they have
themselves represented them. Their luxury was a
coarse and low imitation of Greek voluptuousness;
and for nothing perhaps did the Greeks more despise
their rude conquerors than for the manifest failure
of their attempts at imitating the vices of their
betters. The Romans vied with one another in the
cost rather than the elegance of their banquets, and
accumulated with absurd pride the rarest and most
expensive viands on their boards, to excite the admiration of their parasites, not to gratify their palates.
Cleopatra's famous conceit, in dissolving the pearl in
vinegar, may have been the fine satire of an elegant
Grecian on the tasteless extravagance of her barbarian
lover. Antonius, indeed, though he degraded himself to the manners of a gladiator, was a man of noble
birth, and might have imbibed purer tastes at the
tables of the men of his own class; but the establishment of the imperial regime thrust into the high
places of society a number of low-born upstarts, the
sons of the speculators and contractors of the preceding generation, who knew not how to dispense
with grace the unbounded wealth amassed by their

---

[1] Cicero, *de Senect.* 14.: "Me vero magisteria delectant a majoribus instituta." This refers, I conceive, to the legitimate ordering
of the feast by the host himself: the "pater coenæ" (Hor. *Sat.* ii. 8. 7.).
The Thaliarchus, or, as the Romans styled him, "Rex vini," represented a Greek innovation.

sires.[1] Augustus would fain have restrained these
excesses, which shamed the dignified reserve he
wished to characterize his court: he strove by counsel
and example, as well as by formal enactments, to train
his people in the simpler tastes of the olden time,
refined but not yet enervated by the infusion of
Hellenic culture.[2]   His laws indeed shared the fate
of the sumptuary regulations of his predecessors,
and soon passed from neglect into oblivion. His
example was too austere, perhaps, to be generally
followed even by the most sedulous of his own courtiers. He ate but little, and was content with the
simplest fare: his bread was of the second quality, at
a time when the best was far less fine than ours;[3]
and he was satisfied with dining on a few small
fishes, curds or cheese, figs and dates, taken at any
hour when he had an appetite rather than at regular
and formal meals. He was careful, however, to keep
a moderately furnished table for his associates, at
which he commonly appeared himself, though, as has
been before remarked, he was often the last to arrive,
and the first to retire from it.[4]

The ordinary arrangement of a Roman supper
consisted of three low couches, on three
sides of a low table, at which the attendant   *Ordering of a Roman sup-*
slaves could minister without incommoding   *per.*
the recumbent guests.   Upon each couch three
persons reclined, a mode which had been introduced
from Greece, where it had been in use for centuries,
though not from the heroic times. The Egyptians

[1] Tacitus (*Ann.* xii. 55.) refers to the "luxus mensæ a fine Actiaci belli . . . . per C annos profusis sumptibus exerciti."

[2] The leges Juliæ allowed 200 sesterces for a repast on ordinary days, 300 on holidays, 1000 for special occasions, such as a wedding, &c. Gell. ii. 24.

[3] De la Malle, in his work often cited, has some elaborate calcu- lations of the comparative loss of nourishment in a given weight of flour from the imperfect grinding of the Romans.

[4] Suet. *Oct.* 74, 76.

and Persians sat at meat; so till the Greeks corrupted them did also the Jews: the poetical traditions
of Hellas represented the gods as sitting at their
celestial banquets. The Macedonians, also, down to
the time of Alexander, are said to have adopted the
more ordinary practice; and such was the custom at
Rome till a late period.[1] When the men first allowed
themselves the indulgence of reclining, they required
boys and women to maintain an erect posture, from
notions of delicacy; but in the time of Augustus no
such distinction was observed, and the inferiority of
the weaker sex was only marked by setting them
together on one of the side couches, the place of
honour being always in the centre. Reclined on
stuffed and cushioned sofas, leaning on the left elbow,
the neck and right arm bare, and his sandals removed,
the Roman abandoned himself, after the exhaustion
of the palæstra and the bath, to all the luxury of
languor. His slaves relieved him from every effort,
however trifling[2]: they carved for him, filled his cup
for him, supplied every dish for him with such fragmentary viands as he could raise to his mouth with
his fingers only, and poured water on his hands at
every remove.[3] Men of genius and learning might

[1] The primitive Romans sat at meals. Serv. *in Æn.* vii. 176.
Afterwards men reclined, boys and women sat; finally women reclined also. Val. Max. ii. 1, 2. Homer represents his heroes as
sitting; and such was the posture of the gods of Olympus. Catull.
lxiv. 304.: " Qui postquam niveos flexerunt sedibus artus."

[2] The structor or carver was an important officer at the side-
board. Carving was even taught as an art, which, as the ancients
had no forks (χειρονομᾶν, to manipulate, was the Greek term for
it), must have required grace as well as dexterity. Moreau de
Jonnès observes, with some reason, that the invention of the fork, apparently so simple, deserves to be considered difficult and recon-
dite. The Chinese, with their ancient and elaborate civilization,
have failed to attain to it. " Cinquante siècles ne leur ont pas per-
mis d'imaginer l'usage des fourchettes." *Statist. des Anciens Peuples,*
p. 506.

[3] For some of the most extravagant refinements of the luxury of
the table see Martial, iii. 82.:

amuse themselves with conversation only; those to whom this resource was insufficient had other means of entertainment to resort to. Music and dancing were performed before them; actors and clowns exhibited in their presence;' dwarfs and hunchbacks were introduced to make sport for them; Augustus himself sometimes escaped from these levities by playing at dice between the courses; but the stale wit and practical humour, with which in many houses the banquet seems to have been seasoned, give us a lower idea of the manners of Roman gentlemen than any perhaps of these trifling pastimes.[1] The vulgarity, however, of the revellers of Rome was less shocking than their indecency, and nothing perhaps contributed more to break down the sense of dignity and self-respect, the last safeguard of Pagan virtue, than the easy familiarity engendered by their attitude at meals.

Some persons, indeed, men no doubt of peculiar assurance and conceit, ventured to startle the voluptuous languor of the supper-table by repeating their own compositions to the captive guests.[2] But for the most part the last sentiments of expiring liberty revolted against this odious oppression. The Romans compounded for the inviolate sanctity of their convivial hours by surrendering to the inevitable enemy a solid portion of the day. They resigned themselves to the task of listening as a part of the business of the morning. The custom of re-

Custom of recitation.

> " Stat exoletus suggeritque ructanti
>   Pinnas rubentes cuspidesque lentisci. . . .
>   Percurrit agili corpus arte tractatrix,
>   Manumque doctam spargit omnibus membris. . . . ."

[1] Suet. *Oct.* 77.; Macrob. *Saturn.* ii. 4. Horace's wit is exquisite, but it must be allowed that his convivial humour is intolerable. The silliness of his butt Nasidienus is far less odious than the vulgarity of his genteel associates. Comp. the supper, *Sat.* ii. 8., and the festive scenes in the journey to Brundisium, *Sat.* i. 5.

[2] Cic. *ad Att.* xvi. 2. in fin.

citation is said to have been introduced by Asinius
Pollio, the prince, at this period, of Roman literature.[1]
It was in fact a practice of somewhat older date; the
influence, however, of so distinguished a patron may
have brought it more into fashion, and established it
as a permanent institution. The rich and noble
author could easily secure himself an audience by
merely throwing wide his doors, and he was hardly
less secure of their acclamations; but when the usage
descended to the inferior herd of literature, who
were obliged to hire rooms to receive the guests they
summoned, it was far more difficult to attract flattering or even courteous listeners.[2] Such, however,
was the influence of the mode, that even under these
discouragements, the practice seems to have maintained its ground: attendance on these solemn occasions, whatever natural jeers or murmurs they
excited, was esteemed a social duty, and among other
habits of higher importance, though always evil
spoken of, it was still faithfully observed. Much,
indeed, of the best poetry of the day was thus recited
as an experiment on the taste of the town; and the
practice served in some degree the purpose of our
literary reviews, in pointing out the works which
deserved to be purchased and perused. But it owed
its popularity still more, perhaps, to the national
love of acting and declamation; and while few of
the company might care to listen to the reciter's
language, all intently observed his gestures and the
studied modulations of his voice. It was the glory
of the author to throw his audience into a fever of
excitement, till they screamed and gesticulated themselves in turn, and almost overwhelmed the blushing

---

[1] M. Seneca, *Controv.* iv. proem.
[2] Plin. *Epist.* viii. 12.; Juvenal, vii. 40.; Tac. *de Orator.* 9.:
Quorum exitus hic est, ut . . . . rogare ultro et ambire cogatur, ut
sint qui dignentur audire: et ne id quidem gratis; nam et domum
mutuatur et auditorium exstruit et subsellia conducit et libellos dis-
pergit," &c.

declaimer with the vehement demonstrations of their applause.[1]   The tendency of such a system to stimulate false taste and discountenance modest merit may easily be imagined.   In the age of Augustus the evil had not reached its highest point.   Horace, who describes himself as weakly in voice and limb, and devoid of personal graces, might shrink from the ordeal of recitation from a consciousness of these deficiencies rather than from greater delicacy of taste; but his calm and judicious style of composition was not the less honourably appreciated for the want of these spurious recommendations.[2]   At a later period the ear of the public was accessible perhaps by no other means.

The Romans, it will be observed, were not a people of readers: the invention of printing would have been thrown away upon them; or rather, had they had a strong appetency for reading, they would undoubtedly have discovered the means (on the verge of which they arrived from more sides than one) of abridging the labour of copying, and diminishing the cost of books.[3]   But to hear recitation with its kindred accompaniment of action, of which they were earnest and critical admirers, was to them a genuine delight, nor were they content with being merely hearers.   With the buoyant spirits and healthy enjoyment of children, the Romans seem to have derived pleasure, akin to that of children, in the free exercise of their voice and lungs.   If the

Habits of declamation.

---

[1] Hor. *Art. Poet.* 428.: "Pulchre, bene, recte!" Pers. i. 49.; Juvenal, vi. 582.; Martial, i. 77.: " At circum pulpita nostra Et steriles cathedras basia sola crepant."

[2] Hor. *Sat.* i. 4. 22.: " Cum mea nemo Scripta legat vulgo recitare timentis." Comp. *Epist.* i. 19. 39.

[3] The figures on the tesserae or tablets of admission to the theatres were undoubtedly stamped, and there is considerable reason to believe that a method had been discovered of taking off copies of a drawing or painting. See Plin. *Hist. Nat.* xxxv. 2.: " M. Varro benignissimo invento . . . . non passus intercidere figuras . . . . in omnes terras misit ut praesentes essent ubique . . . ."

Greeks were great talkers, the Romans were eminently a nation of speakers. Their earliest education
was directed to conning and repeating old saws and
legends; such as the laws of the twelve tables, the
national ballads, and rhythmical histories; and from
their tender years they were trained to the practice
of debate and declamation. Rhetoric was taught
them by technical rules, and reduced, indeed, to so
formal a system, that children of twelve years, or
even under, could come forward and deliver set
harangues on the most solemn of public occasions.
Julius Cæsar pronounced the funeral oration of his
aunt in his twelfth year; nor was Augustus older
when he performed a similar feat. But, in fact, such
tours de force were merely school exercises ; the form,
the turns of thoughts, the cadences, everything but
the actual words was modelled to a pattern, allowing neither opportunity for genius nor risk of failure.
Under the free state these scholastic prolusions were
soon exchanged for the genuine warfare of the forum
or the tribunals. The ever-varying demands of those
mighty arenas on the talents and resources of the
noble Roman required incessant study, and compelled
the orator to devote every leisure hour to the toils of
practice and preparation. Augustus never allowed
a day to pass without reserving an hour for declamation, to keep his lungs in regular exercise, and
maintain the armoury of dialectics furbished for ready
use. Yet the speeches of Augustus were not discussions or contests, but merely proclamations of
his policy. With the firmer application of a central
authority to control the vices of the magistrates, and
check the ebullitions of party violence, the occupation of his contemporary orators was lost.[1] The age

---

[1] The 37th chapter of the treatise *De Oratoribus* is an eloquent
exposition of this thesis: "Quæ mala sicut non accidere melius est,
isque optimus civitatis status habendus est quo nihil tale patimur;
ita, quum acciderent, ingentem eloquentiæ materiam subministra-

of the first princeps was perhaps the period of the lowest decline of Roman eloquence; it rose again, as we shall see, to a state of feverish activity under the reign of his successors, when the favour of the emperor might be secured by ardour in denouncing crimes against his honour and safety. The law of Treason evoked a more copious stream of rhetoric than those of Violence and Rapine. Nevertheless, the want of worthy subjects for their powers seems to have availed little in checking the passion for oratorical distinction among the young declaimers of the schools. After Augustus had *pacified eloquence along with all things else*, the mature orators of the falling republic, such as Pollio and Messala, had retired with suppressed indignation from the rostra, and disdained to degrade their talent by exercising it in false and frivolous declamation.[1] But the rising generation, to whom the fresh air of liberty was unknown, had no such honourable scruples. The practice of the art in private, by which Cicero and his rivals had kept the edge of their weapons keen for the encounters of the forum, became, under the new regime, an end, and not a means. The counterfeit or shadow was adopted for the substance of oratory. The schools of the rhetoricians, who professed instruction in eloquence, were more frequented than the forum, the senate-house, and the tribunals. They became the resort, not of learners merely, but of amateur practitioners; and the verdict of the select audience they

The schools of the rhetoricians.

bant." In the next chapter the author adduces as a further cause of the decline of eloquence, the limitation of time, first imposed on the orators by Pompeius. That such a limitation, once imposed, should never have been removed again, seems to show that it must have had great practical advantages.

[1] Tacitus, *de Orator.* 38.: " Postquam longa temporum quies et continuum populi otium et assidua senatus tranquillitas et maximi principis disciplina ipsam quoque eloquentiam, sicut omnia alia, pacaverat."

entertained was more highly prized than the suffrage of the judges, or the applause of the populace. Around this new centre of exertion, traditions of its own began speedily to gather. It had its examples and authorities, its dictators and legislators, men whose maxims became axioms, and whose sayings were remembered, quoted, imitated, and pointed afresh by each succeeding generation. It had a manner and almost a language of its own. One declaimer was reproved for addressing the mixed assemblage of a public place in the style reserved for the initiated of the School[1]; another, when called upon to plead in the open air, lost his presence of mind, committed a solecism in his first sentence, and called in his dismay for the close walls, the familiar benches, and the select auditory before which alone he was fluent and self-possessed.[2]

What then was this declamation, which for the space of a hundred years from the battle of Actium was the most really active and flourishing of all intellectual exercises at Rome? We happen to possess a great collection of its remains, preserved to us by one who was perhaps the most renowned professor of the art; a man who rose in some respects superior to its trivialities, and lived to perceive its fatal tendency, and lament its degeneracy. M. Annæus Seneca, the father of the celebrated philosopher, and generally distinguished from him by the title of the Rhetorician, after giving instruction in Rome, whither he had repaired, at the close of the civil wars, from Spain, for more than half a century, was induced, in extreme old age, to put on record for his sons the wittiest and finest

M. Annæus Seneca, the rhetorician.

---

[1] M. Senec. præf. *Controv.* v.: "Nihil indecentius quam ubi scholasticus forum, quod non novit, imitatur."

[2] M. Senec. præf. *Controv.* iv.: "Nec ante potuisse confirmari tectum ac parietes desiderantem quam impetravit ut judicium ex foro in basilicam transferretur."

sayings of the declaimers of his own best days, which had fallen under the principate of Augustus.[1] He divides into the two classes of Suasives and Controversies the subjects of their scholastic exercises. The first are quasi-historical; as, whether Alexander should have launched on the ocean; whether Cicero should have burnt his Philippics: the second refer to debateable points in ethics or casuistry, ingeniously intricate, and perversely indeterminable; points on which the cleverest things that can be said prove only how much better it were to be silent.[2] On all these subjects the compiler has cited entirely, as he says, from memory a multitude of subtle and sparkling sentiments from the most illustrious wits of the period; while in his prefaces he marks with strong and rapid touches the literary characters of a large company of declaimers. In these pages Porcius Latro, Albucius Silo, Arellius Fuscus, Cestius, Gallio, Montanus, and many others have each their distinct individuality; and the anecdotes related of them are often piquant in themselves, as well as historically curious.[3] The fashion of epigram and antithesis,

[1] M. Seneca, or Seneca Rhetor, was a native of Corduba in Spain, and born about the close of the seventh century of the city. He came to Rome at the termination of the civil wars, and became a fashionable teacher of rhetoric. He wrote also a history of his own times, of which only two short fragments have been recovered. Towards the end of his life, which was protracted into the reign of Caius Caligula, he addressed to his three sons, Lucius Seneca, Lucius Mela, and M. Novatus, the compilation on rhetoric which is now extant. If his declaration that it is made from memory is accurate, the work is a very extraordinary one. He gives other portentous instances of his powers in this respect. See præf. *Controv.* i. The remains of Seneca Rhetor are well analysed by Egger. *Historiens d'Auguste,* ch. iv.

[2] Champagny (*Césars,* i. 212. foll.) has painted the schools of the declaimers with great force and brilliancy.

[3] Thus, for instance, it is interesting at least to learn that Ovid's fine saying, "Arma viri fortis medios mittantur in hostes," &c., was taken from a declamation of Latro. There is also an amusing story of the poet's friends asking leave to select three of his lines to be expunged, and his consenting, on condition that he might also select

which these rhetoricians introduced, was more fatal
to truth and justness of sentiment than even the
florid exuberance of Cicero and his imitators. The
habit of estimating logical arguments by the accessories of style alone soon leapt from the schools to
the tribunals. The noblest of the Romans, accused
of plunder or extortion in the provinces, and assailed
with virulent licence of tongue as a thief or brigand,
could reply, not by refuting the charges with evidence
or reason, but by curiously poising them in a balance
of antitheses, and receive, if not his acquittal, that
which perhaps for the moment he valued higher, the
admiration and applause of his judges.[1]

A glimpse of this curious fragment of Roman
literary life may leave a feeling of wonder,
not unmixed with pity, at the exuberance
of animal spirits fostered by the training
of the Campus and Palæstra, which found a vent, in
the silence imposed on serious and sober thought, in
vociferating conceits and puerilities with all the force
of the lungs, and the by-play of attitudes and gestures. If the subject of the debate was merely
moonshine, if its *schemes* and *colours* and *sentences*
were in a great degree conventional, yet the manner,
the movements, the arrangement of the dress, the
management of the voice, all these came more and
more to take the place of real meaning and purpose,
and were subjected themselves to rule and rigid

Conventional rules for the declaimers.

three to retain. The lines, on being produced, were found to be *the
same.* Two of them are mentioned : " Semibovemque virum, semi-
virumque bovem," was one; "Egelidum Borean, egelidumque Noton,"
another. I think Ovid was right. It is added ; "Aiebat interim
decentiorem faciem esse in qua aliquis nævus esset." I am inclined
to agree with him again. The saying is very characteristic. For
historical anecdotes I may refer to those about Cicero, Cremutius
Cordus, and other celebrated personages.

[1] Persius, i. 85.:

> " Fur es ait Pedio; Pedius quid ? crimina rasis
> Librat in antithetis; doctas posuisse figuras
> Laudatur."

censure. The hair was to be sedulously coifed; directions were given for the conduct of the hand-kerchief; the steps in advance or retreat, to the right hand or to the left, which the orator might safely take were numbered. He was to rest so many instants only on each foot alternately, to advance one so many inches only before the other; the elbow must not be raised above a certain angle; the fingers should be set off with rings, but not too many, nor too large; and in elevating the hand to exhibit them, he must be careful not to disarrange his head-dress. Every emotion had its prescribed index in the gesture appropriated to it. The audience of scholars and amateurs who crowded to these private theatricals, applauded with intense enthusiasm not the passion nor even the conceit so much as the correctness of the pantomime. From the schools all these conventions were transferred to the tribunals; and a century after Augustus, a judicious professor of the art of speaking, could devote several pages of his elaborate treatise on the Institution of an Orator to the discussion of these and many other points of etiquette in dress, manners, and attitude.[1]

The pernicious effects of this solemn trifling seem to have perverted the moral sense of the Romans more speedily than even their literary style. Itself the creation in part of an era of hollow pretensions, it reacted *General purity and terseness of style in the Augustan writers.* still more powerfully upon it, and produced the tone of insincerity which pervades the monuments of its mind and intellect. Yet it was long before it affected that justness of thought, that purity of taste, and that accuracy of diction which distinguished the

---

[1] Quintilian, *Inst. Orat.* xi. 3. His examples are in a great measure derived from the usage of Cicero, and even Demosthenes; and it must be admitted that the physical accessories of oratory were studied with a care which was not altogether superfluous in the best ages of Greek and Roman eloquence.

compositions of the Augustan age; and it must be remembered that the declaimers themselves, of whom mention has been made, were of the same generation as the men who could cheer with correct discrimination a Livy, a Virgil, and a Horace.   Seneca himself was not unconscious of the meanness of his art, and contrived to keep his language but little corrupted by the conceits with which he burdened his memory. The purest master of Latin prose we possess, the illustrious Titus Livius, was himself a fre-

Titus Livius.

quenter of the schools, and, perhaps, even a professor of rhetoric.[1]   If his style escaped the contagion of such evil influences, if his judgment and fancy retained their well-adjusted balance, he may still have lost in that baneful atmosphere the clear perceptions of truth and candour, and the abiding sense of moral obligation, which should hold sleepless vigil round the desk of the historian.   Devoid of these, the passion for liberty is as rank a perverter of justice as the meanest servility; the truth of history was sacrificed as much by the few indomitable spirits who still thundered against tyranny, as by the supple flatterers who painted the tyrant in the colours of a patriot and a demigod.   If we possessed the Annals of the surly republican Labienus, we should doubtless find them no more to be relied on than the panegyrical biographies of the courtier Nicolaus.   It is mentioned as a proof of the freedom with which Labienus had lashed the crimes of the great and powerful, that in reciting to his friends, he would sometimes roll up whole paragraphs of the volume, saying, *What I now pass over will be read after my death.*[2]   But the man who writes, under

---

[1] This may be inferred, perhaps, from comparing Senec. *Epist.* 100. —" Scripsit enim et dialogos, quos non magis philosophiæ annumerare possis quam historiæ, et ex professo philosophiam continentes libros "—with Quintil. *Inst. Orat.* viii. 2. 18., x. 1. 39., and Suet. *Claud.* 41.

[2] M. Senec. præf. *Controv.* v.: "Memini aliquando cum recitaret historiam magnam partem convolvisse et dixisse, hæc quæ transeo

such circumstances, for posterity what he dares not divulge to his contemporaries, subjects himself to a temptation to gratify malice by calumny, which few can withstand, and which none should venture to disregard.

It was in the schools, we may believe, that Livy learnt that indifference to historical accu- Character of racy, that sacrifice of the substance to the Livy's history. form of truth, which has ·cast a shade over the lustre of his immortal work. As a friend of the ancient oligarchy, and an aristocrat in prejudices and temper, he would scarcely have carried his Roman history down to his own times, had he not submitted to veil his real sentiments, and made his book such as Augustus himself might sanction for the perusal of his subjects. The emperor, indeed, is said to have called him a Pompeian, and to have complained of the colours in which he portrayed the men of the opposite side; but this could only have been in jest; the favour in which he was held by the courtiers of the empire, and his being suffered to assist the studies of Claudius Germanicus, show that he was not seriously regarded as a disaffected politician.[1] The scorn which Livy heaps on the tribunes and demagogues, and his ignorant contempt for the Plebs, evince the leaning of his mind to the side of the nobility. But these are obviously the views of the rhetorician rather than of the historian; and Augustus, tribune and demagogue as he was, could distinguish between the hollow commonplaces of a perverted education and the stern judgment of genuine conviction. The loss

post mortem meam legentur." His books were burnt by a decree of the senate. Cassius Severus said: " Nunc me vivum uri oportet, qui illos edidici."

[1] Tac. *Ann.* iv. 34.; Suet. *Claud.* 41. Nevertheless, in the preface to his work, Livy alludes with deep feeling to the misery of the times he had witnessed: and his presentiment of national decline—" Hæc tempora quibus nec vitia nostra nec remedia pati possumus "—must have been highly unpalatable to the reigning powers.

of the latter portions of this extensive work must be
deplored for the number of facts it has swept into
oblivion; but the facts would have been valuable
rather from the inferences modern science might
deduce from them, than from the light in which the
author would himself have placed them. Livy,
taking the pen in middle life, and continuing to
pour forth his volumes in interminable succession,
perhaps to the end of his long career,—for born in
the year 695, he died in 771—left it still apparently
unfinished, at the close of his hundred and forty-
second book, and with the decease of Drusus Germanicus.[1] It may be conjectured that the latter
portions of the work were overtaken by the garrulity
of old age, and were suffered to fall into oblivion
from their want of political or literary value.[2]

It is in the earlier books, however, that the spirit
of Livy found its most congenial sphere;
the first and third decades, containing the
early history of the kings and consuls, and
again the grand epic of the war with Hannibal, have

The service Livy performed for his countrymen.

---

[1] Niebuhr's remarks on the dates of Livy's history (*Rom. Hist.* iv.)
may be compared with the more common view given in Smith's Dictionary and elsewhere. I think the beginning of the work must be
placed in 725—730; but adopting the idea that it was originally
divided into decades, the fact, now demonstrated, that it reached to a
142nd book, seems to show that it was not left complete according to
the author's intentions. It is also well remarked that the death of
Drusus does not furnish a point of sufficient importance for the termination of the great epic of Roman history. This view is supported
by the interesting statement of Pliny, that in one of his latter books
Livy had declared: " Satis jam sibi gloriæ quæsitum; et potuisse se
desinere, nisi animus inquies pasceretur opere." Plin. *Hist. Nat.*
præf. A period of more than forty years thus devoted to the elabo-
ration of a single work is not unparalleled. Froissart was engaged
forty years upon his Chronicles.

[2] We have sustained undoubtedly a great loss in the characters of
the chief men of later Roman history, such as Livy so frequently
inserted into his narrative, and of which we have one fine example
in the fragment on the death of Cicero. The ancients declared
him, " Candidissimus magnorum ingeniorum æstimator." M. Senec.
Suasor. 7.

always retained their preeminence in general esteem as the noblest specimens of narration. The greatest minds of Rome at this period seem to have kindled with inspiration from the genius of the founder of the empire; and of these Livy at least appears to have conceived unconsciously the idea of attaching his countrymen to the early records of their city, by encircling it with a halo of poetical associations. The imagination of the Romans of that age was inflamed by the conservative reaction which sought to bridge the chaos of the last century, and revive the sense of national continuity. The thanks the race of Romulus owed to Livy, for making them acquainted with their ancestors and proud of their descent, were akin to those which Englishmen acknowledge to the historical dramas of Shakspeare. He took the dry chronicles, in which alone their first affairs were written, drew forth from them the poetic life of half-forgotten traditions, and clothed it again in forms of ideal beauty. His narrative, glowing in all the colours of imagination and fancy, is just as faithful to its authorities as the dramatized histories of the English bard to theirs; indeed, the myths of Romulus and Tarquin cannot lie farther from the truth of facts than the tragedies of Lear and Cymbeline; and when he begins to tread the domain of sober history, his painted Hannibals and Scipios approach as nearly to the men themselves as the Richards and Henrys of our own mighty master. The charms of Livy's style befitted the happy conjunction of circumstances under which he wrote, and combined with it to give him that preeminence among Roman historians which he never afterwards lost. The events and characters of deepest interest became immutably fixed in the lines in which he had represented them. Henceforth every Roman received from Livy his first impressions of his country's career, which thus became graven for ever in the mind of the nation. It was in vain that the inaccuracy of these relations, and in many cases their direct falsehood, were pointed out by the votaries of truth, or by jealous and unsuccessful rivals; henceforth it was treason to the majesty of Rome to doubt that Porsena was driven in confusion from her walls, or that the spoils of the Capitol were wrested again from the triumphant legions of Brennus.[1]

The poets lie under no such obligation to speak the truth, and Virgil requires no excuse for his endeavour to inflame the patriotism of his countrymen by a fanciful account of their origin. But, writing as he did a few years earlier than Livy, and in all the glow of patriotic fervour, the spirit which animated him was doubtless far more genuine. The simplicity of his genius shrank from the subtle inventions of the schools, to which, indeed, his youth had been a stranger; he uttered the convictions of an imagination which he felt as an inspiration, and he spoke from a sense of duty which had almost the force of compulsion. We have seen how this child of the Muses, born and bred in rustic retirement, was expelled from his patrimony by an intruding soldier, and restored beyond expectation by the kindly interference of Pollio. We have traced him under the shadow of the gracious patronage of Mæcenas, and the generous countenance of Octavius himself. We have marked the enthusiasm of gratitude for himself, and hope for his country, with which he seized the popular sentiment in favour of the Western triumvir, in his contest with the pirate Sextus and the renegade Antonius. His ardour in the cause of law, order, and tradition assumed the character of a religious sentiment, and he conceived himself devoted to a great moral mission. His purpose widened, and his enthusiasm grew deeper, as

Virgil an enthusiast.

---

[1] Comp. Plin. *Hist. Nat.* xxxiv. 39.; Tac. *Ann.* iii. 72.

he contemplated the sins of his countrymen, and the means by which alone they might be expiated : their abandonment, on the one hand, of the first duties of their being; on the other, the restoration of belief, and a return to the principles of the past. The character of Virgil deserves the interest and awe which, however grotesquely delineated, it excited in the middle ages. His spirit belonged to the Ages of Faith. In the twelfth century he might have founded an order of monkery or of knighthood.

It is not in his first known compositions, the Eclogues, the dates of which extend from 713 to 717, or from his twenty-ninth to his *The Eclogues.* thirty-third year, that this sense of a religious mission can be generally traced. There is, however, a certain earnestness of feeling in the fourth and sixth, which seems to show that the depths of the poet's soul were already stirring within him; and the ardent love of peace and justice they commonly exhibit, may have sufficed to attract the observation of Mæcenas, as the adviser of the new sovereignty, and lead him to enlist the young enthusiast in the service of the government, to expound in an attractive form the principles it pretended to assert. The tradition that Mæcenas himself suggested the composition of the Georgics may be accepted, not in the lite- *The Georgics.* ral sense which has generally been attached to it, as a means of reviving the art of husbandry, and the cultivation of the devastated soil of Italy ; but rather to recommend the principles of the ancient Romans, their love of home, of labour, of piety, and order; to magnify their domestic happiness and greatness; to make men proud of their country, on better grounds than the mere glory of its arms and the extent of its conquests. It would be absurd to suppose that Virgil's verses induced any Roman to put his hand to the plough, or take from his bailiff the management of his own estates ; but they served undoubtedly to

revive some of the simple tastes and sentiments of
the olden time, and perpetuated, amidst the vices and
corruptions of the empire, a pure stream of sober and
innocent enjoyments, of which, as we journey onward,
we shall rejoice to catch at least occasional glimpses.

To comprehend the moral grandeur of the Georgics,
in point of mere style the most perfect piece
of Roman literature, we must regard it as
the glorification of Labour. In the better
times of Rome, when manual labour was still in
honour, it was to husbandry and arms that its exercise
was confined. It was not for the reviver of antiquity
to cast his eye over newer fields of industry, such as
the occupations of trade and science, and direct to
them the minds of his countrymen; and of arms
there had been already more than enough : it is on
husbandry, accordingly, that Virgil fixes his admiration, and throws on the labours of the husbandman,
hard and coarse as they seem to the unpurged vision,
all the colours of the radiant heaven of the imagination. *Labor improbus*, incessant, importunate labour,
conquers all things; subdues the soil, baffles the in-
clemency of the seasons, defeats the machinations of
Nature, that cruel stepmother, and wins the favour
and patronage of the gods.[1] *For gods there are* who
have ever looked with kindness on the industry and
piety of man, who have shown to him the excellent
uses of every product of the soil, who have blest his
labour with increase, and averted evil from his roof.[2]
The first Georgic may be viewed as the poet's protest against the unbelief of philosophy; the shield of

The moral grandeur of the Georgics.

---

[1] Virgil, *Georg.* i. 121.:

        " Pater ipse colendi
Haud facilem esse viam voluit . . . . Labor omnia vincit
Improbus . . . ."

[2] *Georg.* i. 125. 147.:

    " Ante Jovem nulli subigebant arva coloni . . . .
      Prima Ceres ferro mortales vertere glebam . . . ."

Lucretius is pierced through and through by the fiery blade of Virgil; the frigid pleas of naturalism dissolve in the blaze of lightning which *Jove himself, with his red right hand, hurls from the night of the thunder clouds. . . . . Then before all things*, says the preacher, *venerate the Gods*.[1] Nor is religion harsh and exacting in its rites. Though it prescribes many days of repose, and gives no success to ordinary labour on some others, yet certain works there are which are not even then prohibited; the husbandman is never bidden by the Gods to fold his hands in idleness.[2] *May they now*, he continues, *save the saviour of the state, the support of this sinking age.* Octavius was the object against whom all the daggers which had met in his father's bosom were once more levelled; he was exposed to perils in war, to perils by sea and land; his frame was weak, his health was precarious; and the most pious of the Romans were offering vows for his safety, and engaging their heirs to sacrifice to the Gods in their name, in gratitude for the blessing of leaving him their survivor.[3]

The praise of Italy might wean the restless Romans from the visions of an Atlantis, a paradise beyond the sea, which had flitted before their eyes since the days of Sertorius, and which they too often sought to realize by quitting the stern duties of their fatherland for the pleasant indulgences of the East. Its fields and river

The Æneid: the glorification of the Romans and of Augustus.

---

[1] *Georg.* i. 328. 338.:

    "Ipse Pater media nimborum in nocte corusca
    Fulmina molitur dextra . . . .
    In primis venerare Deos . . . ."

[2] *Georg.* i. 268.:

    "Quippe etiam festis quædam exercere diebus
    Fas et jura sinunt."

[3] Suet. *Oct.* 59.; *Georg.* i. 498.:

    "Di patrii Indigetes . . .
    Hunc saltem everso juvenem succurrere sæclo
    Ne prohibete . . . ."

sides might supply those charms of indolent repose, for which the wearied warrior too often repaired to the blandishments of Athens or Ephesus. The institutions of an imperial republic might be aptly recommended by the example of the prudent bees, the insects which nature has herself endued with the instinct of divine order.[1] But the pious sentiment of Virgil receives its strongest expression in the monument he has erected to the glories of his countrymen, and of their tutelary saint Augustus. The grand

The religious idea which pervades it. religious idea which breathes throughout his Æneid, is the persuasion that the Romans are the sons and successors of the Trojans, the chosen race of heaven, of divine lineage and royal pretensions, whose destinies have engaged all the care of Olympus from the beginning, till they reach at last their consummation in the blissful regeneration of the empire. It maintains the existence of Providence as the bond of the Roman commonwealth. *Yes! there are Gods*, it proclaims, and the glories of Rome demonstrate it. Yes: there are Gods above, and the Romans are their children and their ministers upon earth, exercising in their name a delegated sovereignty, sparing those who yield, but beating down the proud. This is the mission of the race of Assaracus, to vindicate the ways of God to man, to impose upon him the yoke of an eternal peace, and bring all wars to an end for ever![2]

But the government of Olympus is monarchical:

Its vindication of monarchy. the Jove-born demigods and heroes have all been kings themselves, ruling their children and descendants with the dignity and authority of patriarchs. Hence the Romans may submit without dishonour to the sceptre of a patriarch of their

---

[1] *Georg.* ii. iv.
[2] Virg. *Æn.* ix. 643.:

<blockquote>
" Jure omnia bella
Gente sub Assaraci fato ventura resident."
</blockquote>

own.   He has recovered, indeed, with the sword the kingdom of his ancestors, but the divine effulgence of his countenance suffices to attest his claims.   His legitimate right may be traced through his illustrious ancestors, and is impressed upon us by many a sounding reference to the faith of ancient days.   Virgil read in the legend of Rome that it was founded by the descendants of Æneas; but this Æneas, though he traced his descent from Trojan kings, and, like other heroes, from Jove himself, neither in this nor in other respects stood preeminent above his peers.   In the glories of the Trojan war he had borne no superior part: what claim could be advanced for him to rule over the Trojans, or centre in himself and his posterity the interest of all the offspring of Dardanus and Tros?   To raise Æneas to the place of Hector, to make him the virtual successor of Priam, the last and greatest of the heroes, this was the enterprise Virgil undertook.   Accordingly, we may observe how everything is made to conspire to thrust this preeminence upon him.   Hector himself, when all hope has vanished, counsels his flight from the crumbling city; Hector commends to him the Penates of his land; Hector foretells to him the new city he shall found beyond the seas.   Troy has been utterly overthrown, Priam and all his sons have vanished from the stage, Astyanax, the hope of Troy, has perished.   Helenus, the last survivor of the race, pious and resigned, speeds the fated hero on his voyage, and assures him of the favour of the Gods. The house of Ilus, the elder branch of the Dardanian stem, is prostrate on the ground; all its rights and honours, its hopes and aspirations, have reverted to the offspring of the cadet Assaracus.[1]   Around him

---

[1] The stemma of the royal race of Troy was this:—1. Dardanus. 2. Erichthonius.   3. Tros.   4. Ilus and Assaracus.

Ilus had 5. Laomedon, 6. Priam, 7. Hector, &c.
Assaracus had 5. Capys, 6. Anchises, 7. Æneas, &c.

the gods of Troy now watch with peculiar care. All
his steps are guided or controlled by omens. He
submits himself in all things to the will of heaven
thus visibly revealed to him.   At its bidding he
surrenders every natural desire, the desire to perish
sword in hand among the flames of Troy, to recover
his wandering wife Creusa, to yield to love and repose in the sweet embrace of Dido.   The oracles of
the Gods still marshal him on his way: they go before him to Italy, and king Latinus is already apprised
that he must yield his daughter to a stranger, ere
Æneas steps on the Lavinian shore, and presents himself as her suitor.[1]   In vain the Furies and Demons
interpose, with even the envious Juno at their head;
the foe must be overthrown, the bride be won; the
chosen race of Dardanus and Assaracus, bearing with
it the destinies of Ilus and Priam, must unite with
the native dynasty of Alba, and the line of kings
which springs from this triple legitimacy combine
every right to reign, and fulfil every augury of fortune.   To complete the poetic justice of this development of fate, we are reminded that Dardanus himself,
the first of the Trojans, was of Italian origin, and his
descendants are not really strangers in the land of
their adoption.[2]   Henceforth the mingled blood of
Troy and Latium flows in many channels: in one
it descends, through Silvius, Numitor, and Ilia, to
Romulus; in another it animates the race of the
Julii; and thus Augustus becomes by legitimate
adoption the offspring of Iulus and Æneas, of Venus
and Jove.   Once more, the family of his mother Atia

Homer, *Ill.* xx. 219. fol.   This genealogy, though not distinctly asserted, is supposed throughout the Æneid.
    [1] Virg. *Æn.* vii. 255.:
        " Hunc illum fatis externâ ab sede profectum
          Portendi generum."
    [2] Virg. *Æn.* vii. 206.:
            " His ortus ut agris
        Dardanus Idæas Phrygiæ penetrârit ad urbes."

derives from Atys, the companion of Iulus, and thus
Augustus is Trojan on either side.[1]

Such is the career of piety and such is its reward.
The children of Assaracus the Just inherit   Augustus
in the room of the family of Ilus, attainted   shadowed
for the treason of Laomedon.   The pious   gil's Æneas.
Æneas recovers the patrimony of his first ancestor
Dardanus, deprived by violence of his legitimate
rights.   And thus, too, in the mind of the poet, the
pious Augustus recovered the empire of his father
Julius, slain by the daggers of faction.   Urged by
his patron Apollo, and the voice of many oracles,
Augustus had crossed the sea to the promised shore
of Italy, to claim his rightful inheritance.   He, too,
had been tost for many years both on land and sea.
He had suffered much in wars, while laying the foundations of his everlasting polity.   He had traversed
a wider realm than Hercules or Bacchus.[2]   He had
subdued many nations, and overthrown many cities.
With noble constancy and firmness he had accomplished the divine designs; no temptations had al-
lured him from the path of duty, and persuaded him
to found his state on any foreign soil.   The anxiety
of the Romans about the often rumoured translation
of the seat of empire, whether to Ilium or to Alexandria, had a particular significance.   They expected
that the victorious triumvir would aspire to found a
monarchy, and yet they clung to the belief that no

---

[1] *Æn.* v. 568. :
> " Alter Atys, genus unde Atium duxere Latini:
> Parvus Atys, pueroque puer dilectus Iulo."

These remarks on the poems of Virgil have been derived in a good
measure from my recollection of some interesting essays on the Roman
poets by a French writer named Legris, in his work entitled *Rome,
ou Etudes sur Lucrece, Catulle, Virgile, et Horace,* whose ingenuity,
though indulged with too little restraint, has brought out in very
striking relief the ideas and sentiments of the period.

[2] *Æn.* vi. 802.:
> " Nec vero Alcides tantum telluris obivit, ...
> Nec qui pampineis victor juga flectit habenis . . . . "

king could reign at Rome. That the name of the republic would be suffered to remain, while the yoke of royal rule was really fixed upon them, was beyond their power to conceive; accordingly, they were convinced that he meditated establishing himself with his army in some Oriental city, and governing Rome and the world from its regal acropolis. His long sojourns in the East kept this notion constantly alive; the example of Antonius, who had reigned there for ten years, of Julius, whose half-revealed design was nipped, as they imagined, in the bud, and the common passion for escaping from the duties of the citizen to live in licentious independence abroad, all conspired to impress on the minds of the Romans the persuasion that Augustus would sacrifice Rome to a foreign capital. The Æneid may be read as a continued protest against such a crime. Nevertheless, the opinion that Augustus himself is specially represented by its hero cannot be admitted without great reservation. Æneas, ever alarmed by some apparition, always led by soothsayers, flitting from oracle to oracle, believing in dreams, predictions, days and omens, if he resembles Augustus, reflects no less the general type of the slavish superstition of the time. Æneas weeping at every crisis instead of acting, may suit the popular notion of the triumvir, whose effeminacy was the theme of many a lampoon; but surely the poet would have refrained from so far pushing his parallel. The baseness of the hero in deserting Dido, and his slender excuse for abandoning the search for Creusa, at which the moral sense revolts, whatever religious pretext may be devised for them, show how wanting Virgil himself was in delicacy; and the plain injustice of the attack on Turnus has been cited in proof of the blunted sensibility of his age.

The composition of the Æneid occupied the interval between 727 and 735, the year of the poet's death. During this period Virgil made his principal residence at Naples, and though an honoured guest at the tables of the great at Rome, he Melancholy seems to have easily yielded the post of court of Virgil. favourite to rivals of a gayer and perhaps a more supple temper. The honour his writings pay to the principle of religious belief was certainly not assumed for a political purpose. But with a temper naturally inclined to melancholy, neither the objects of his faith nor the prospects it presented to him, were such as to cheer and enliven it. After describing with mournful enthusiasm the virtues of the ancient Romans, it was impossible even for a more sanguine Cæsarean than Virgil to augur a revival of those simple manners which were to him the pledges of happiness and goodness. His view of the progress of the world was the reverse of the Lucretian : but it is hard to say which of the two was the least reasonable; that of the believer who anticipates under the sway of Providence a constant decline of happiness and virtue; or of the sceptic, who, casting man on his own unaided energies, expects him to subdue the evil around him and within him, and to grow from strength to strength, by the force of philosophy and culture. Virgil, we may imagine, in his retirement began already to see the shades closing around the public life of his countrymen, and feared that he had bestowed on the idol of the day a premature and excessive adoration. Possibly he repented the course he had taken, the flattery to which he had pledged his talents and consecrated his existence; and when on his death-bed he desired that his unfinished poem should be destroyed, he may have been moved, not by regret at its imperfections, but by the remorse of an accusing conscience. His last breath, like that of his own gallant Turnus, may have passed away with a groan of indignation. But Augustus knew too well the political value of the Æneid to sacrifice it to a morbid sensibility. He placed it in the hands

of Varius and Plotius for the necessary correction,
but strictly charged them to make no additions, nor
even to complete the few unfinished lines at which
the hand of the master had paused or faltered.[1]
Great, undoubtedly, is the debt we owe him for this
delicate consideration. The Roman epic abounds in
moral and poetical defects : nevertheless it remains
the most complete picture of the national mind at its
highest elevation, the most precious document of
national history, if the history of an age is revealed
in its ideas, no less than in its events and incidents.
This is the consideration which, with many of us,
must raise the interest of the Æneid above that of
any other poem of antiquity, and justify the saying
of I know not what Virgilian enthusiast, that if
Homer really *made Virgil*, undoubtedly it was his
greatest work.

The remark of an ancient biographer that there
was a shade of rusticity in the expression
of Virgil's countenance, has been amplified
by later critics ; and the lines of Horace,
describing a friend, of many sterling qualities indeed
and of fine genius, but coarse in figure, moody in
temper, and causing a smile in the ranks of fashion
by the carriage of his gown, the cut of his hair, and
the fit of his slipper, have been applied to him on the
testimony of an early scholiast.[2] The bashfulness and
reserve which have been attributed to the poet may
at least be accepted as facts : and even these trifling
defects of manner might, under the circumstances of
society at Rome, be deemed worthy of remark and
gentle correction. Under the imperial system, which

Personal appearance of Virgil.

----

[1] Donat. *in Vit. Virgil*, 15.

[2] Donatus, *vit. Virgil*, 5.; Acron. *in Horat. Sat.* i. 3, 30, foll.:

> " Iracundior est paulo, minus aptus acutis
>   Naribus horum hominum . . . . . at ingenium ingens
>   Inculto latet hoc sub corpore."

Comp. also *Sat.* i. 4, 35.

sought to mould all men to a common type of complacent mediocrity, the apparition of a single visitant
of independent thought and manners, whose honesty
and genius condemned the creeping servility of his
associates, could not fail to alarm and irritate.   In a
company whose festivity depended on their success in
forgetting themselves, and who disguised their own
littleness by mutual applause, the society of the *sacred
poet* might be felt as a restraint, and even Augustus
and Mæcenas may have breathed more freely when
relieved from it.

We must not fail, indeed, to observe how the emperor himself, much as he set his heart on
the high moral principles of conservation   The political
mission of
and renewal, much as he had on his lips   Horace.
the words, religion and devotion, the sanctity of marriage, the purity of the life philosophical, was not
unwilling to encourage by his countenance, and even
by his example, such libertinage and dissipation as
could be kept within certain conventional limits, and
do no violence to public feeling.   Looking back for
a moment to the age of Cæsar, and to Catullus, who
holds up the mirror to its sins, we shall remark how
vice, as reflected in his pages, is imbued with the
spirit of freedom and independence, which has not yet
fled from the atmosphere of Rome.   It raises its forehead with the insolence of the tyrant aristocrats born
to triumph and rule mankind; it walks abroad, shameless and lusty, gazing and to be gazed at.   But when
we turn to view it in the days of Augustus, we see it
cowering beneath the control of a master, who has
subjected it to forms and regulations, removed it from
the centre to the side of the street, from the forum
to the lanes and alleys, and constrained it to assume,
at proper times and places, a show of decency or even
a pretence of virtue.   Rome is full of hypocrites,
who affect gravity and austerity, men who commit
every excess in private, but profess in public the so-

briety of the Curii and the Catos.[1]   Horace himself,
who is charged with the office of chasing the truant
vices back to their covert, knows well the limits of
his commission: if sin appears in his pictures less
coarse and naked than in those of his predecessor, it
is because he is only permitted to lift a corner of the
veil, to allure his compatriots to indulgence, but not
to disgust them by effrontery.[2]

Examples are not wanting to aid us in conceiving
the effect of the great revolution which had

Attempts of Augustus to correct the deterioration of manners among his courtiers.

recently been accomplished in the social
deportment of the Romans.   The régime
of the first Napoleon which followed the
extirpation of the old nobility, and the proscription of their fashions, was marked by vulgarity
and rudeness, by a careless affectation of indifference
to the manners of polite society, or by absurd attempts to imitate them.   The emperor himself had
no tact for such conventionalities, and the influence
of his consort was at best ill-directed.   One of the
weak points of his government was the handle given
by his court to the mockery of the frivolous and idle.
It is interesting to observe the good sense of Augustus
and his advisers in perceiving the disadvantage to
which his system was subjected by the folly of the
classes he called on to support it.   To form or correct
the habits of the day was no mean part of the policy
of the founder of the empire.   But all that he did in
public as prefect of manners, all his regulations for
the conservation of religious and moral principles,
were of far less importance towards establishing his
power than the means he employed for moulding the
demeanour of the citizens, so that it should obtain

---

[1] Hor. *Epist.* i. 16, 57.:

   " Vir bonus, omne forum quem spectat et omne tribunal. . . ."

[2] There can be no doubt that the scandalous anecdote told of
Horace's private habits, in the life of him ascribed to Suetonius, really
refers to another person.

general respect, and trample on no prejudices. The aristocracy of birth and honours had been almost swept away: it was necessary to replace it; and for this no other materials were at hand but the clever officials, the trusty soldiers, the astute freedmen of noble houses, the bankers, usurers, and traders, who, in waiting upon the necessities of their betters, had taken the varnish of their manners. The senate of Augustus was in short an assembly of plebeians, but of plebeians more vain of their position than an Æmilius or Valerius, a Marcius or an Hortensius: while Gorgonius was boorish and rude even to affectation, Rufillus was not less offensive from his pretensions to excessive refinement.[1] These men were to be fashioned to the mode, first by tailors and wig-makers, and next by the parasite or poet of the court, the master of ceremonies to the emperor, or rather, that his own influence might be less apparent, to his minister and confidant. They were to be taught not only to wear their toga decorously, but to bear themselves politely at the table, or at the theatre and circus. If Domitius Marsus, a favourite writer of the day, devoted a treatise to instruction in *urbanity*, or the graces of town conversation, the whole philosophy of good breeding was reviewed by Horace in the poetical discourses, to which he gave the old Roman name of Satires or Medleys.[2]

The part Horace had taken in the civil wars, to which a boyish enthusiasm had impelled him, was soon over. After Philippi, his first and only field, he abjured the service of liberty, Career of Horace.

---

[1] Hor. *Sat.* i. 4, 92.:

> "Pastillum Rufillus olet, Gorgonius hircum."

[2] Quintilian (*Inst. Orat.* vi. 3, 102.) speaks of such a treatise by Domitius Marsus, a poet of the Augustan age: "Qui de urbanitate diligentissime scripsit." But the *urbanitas* of Marsus is rather pleasantry than politeness. "Urbanitas est virtus quædam in breve dictum coacta et apta ad delectandos movendesque homines," &c.

and finding his way almost friendless to Rome, began writing verses and making himself a name, while solicitous only for his daily bread. Careless and incorrect as his first pieces are, sometimes vapid in sense and ill-conditioned in their object, there were not wanting among them some of a better character, fitted to impress a sagacious reader with a high idea of his genius. Virgil is said in the popular tradition to have been the first to make the discovery, and to have introduced Horace in all simplicity to Mæcenas as a man of poetical promise. But this, however he might affect to patronize literature for its own sake, was not all the minister required; and for some time, a few courteous words were all the notice he thought fit to take of his new acquaintance. But Horace improved his own fortunes. He continued to write with more earnestness and in a tone of greater self-respect; he mingled with his compositions compliments to the minister so delicate that neither could be ashamed of them. He acquired the great man's friendship, and was received gradually into closer intimacy and even confidence. But we know not how far this confidence really went. The citizens doubtless surmised that it extended to public affairs, and that Horace was consulted by Mæcenas on the disposal of his patronage, or the assignment of colonial territories. It was the business of the poet to laugh away these conjectures, possibly to put the guessers on a wrong scent, and represent himself as totally unconnected with politics, absolutely devoid of ambition, satisfied with the smallest favours, a sincere, independent friend of the minister, and even of the emperor himself. Certain it is that Horace, however strict may have been the attachment between himself and the men in power, obtained neither riches nor office. He was gratified with the present of a moderate estate, the Sabine farm, of which he sings with such pleasing anima-

The nature of his connexion with Augustus and Mæcenas.

tion; and professing himself simple in his tastes, with few wants, being unmarried, and apparently without kinsmen, he was satisfied with the golden mean of fortune which entailed on him neither trouble nor anxiety.[1] To the Roman, whose pleasures and amusements were mostly public, and who might satiate every lawful taste with the libraries, the baths, the shows, and the galleries of the great city, the want of large personal means brought no sensible deprivations. It was the policy of Augustus to curtail the excessive affluence of the few, and make the masses dependent for their enjoyments on the government itself. It was doing him good service therefore to expose to scorn or ridicule the men who made a parade of their wealth, or betrayed anxiety to amass it; to sing the praise of simplicity and indifference, and contrast with the smoke, the noise and splendour of Rome, the languid indolence of midday slumbers in the meadow.[2] At the same time the jealousy of the new nobility might demand some consolation from their patrons for the mortification they experienced at the sneers of the survivors of the true aristocracy. For them Horace had a salve in his specious disparagement of illustrious parentage, and descent from generations of official notabilities.[3] But whether he rebukes the vain, or ministers comfort to wounded susceptibility, he knows the art of sweetening his potions by his tone of good-humoured levity and banter. Angry passions, he suggests, have been ex-

---

[1] *Epist.* ii. 2, 159.: " Qui te pascit ager tuus est."

[2] Compare Horace's sneers at the " Fumum et opes strepitumque Romæ," &c., with the conclusion of Virgil's second Georgic—the " Quid bellicosus Cantaber et Scythes," of the one, &c., with the " Non res Romanæ perituraque regna," or the " Conjurato descendens Dacus ab Istro," of the other. Surely both drew their inspiration from the same official source.

[3] Hor. *Sat.* i. 6, fin.:
> " Ilis me consolor victurum suavius, ac si
> Quæstor avus, pater atque meus, patruusque fuisset."

cited more than enough; it is time to allay irritation, to relieve men of their fears, to surround the throne with cheerful countenances; to let all men know each other's weaknesses, and rely upon mutual indulgence. The genial magician who shall thus transform society must have special qualifications for a task so delicate. He must be of no family illustration himself, to make the new men jealous; he must be a man of courtly manners, to satisfy the taste of the refined; he must dress with faultless neatness rather than elegance, trim his hair and beard carefully but not fantastically, have a tender indulgence for the vices of good company, and if his own stomach is too weak for an occasional excess, he must sit through the festive meetings of his companions, and enjoy at least their enjoyment.[1] He must be fond of music and poetry; and if he is able to entertain others with his wit, if, above all, he can strike the lyre to notes of genial harmony himself, he will become the soul of fellowship, the emperor's viceroy in the realms of fashion. He must be able to invest ordinary ideas with elegant language, and appeal to educated mediocrity by sentiments level with its understanding; and then, if he can sometimes take a higher flight, and utter bursts of inspiration, solemn, passionate, and tender, if he can assume an enthusiasm worthy of a Roman freeman or a Grecian bard, and emulate the fire of Pindar with the steady glow of a sustained dignity, he will combine the voices of the generous and the vulgar,

---

[1] Accordingly Augustus, we are told, used to call him *homuncionem lepidissimum*. Suet. *vit. Hor.* Some pleasing fragments of the emperor's letters to the poet are given in this biography, and may not improbably be genuine. Horace says of himself:

> "Quem tenues decuere comæ, nitidique capilli;
> Quem scis immunem Cinaræ placuisse rapaci;
> Quem bibulum liquidi media de nocte Falerni
> Cœna juvat."
>
> *Epist.* i. 14, 32. Comp. i. 7, 26.

of the future and of the present, and become a fixed
star in the heaven of poetry.

A further task remains, however, for the favoured
instrument of ministerial conservatism. Ho- *Horace's pre-*
race must teach the Roman gentlemen to be *tensions to re-*
ligious senti-
religious, or at least to appear so.   Horace *ment.*
was himself, so he seems to confess, something of a
scapegrace in his youth: one who could be so wrong
and foolish as to embrace the cause of the murderers
of divine Julius, must have imbibed some very false
notions from the sources of his philosophy. He had
dallied with the Greek ideologists, the corrupters
of youth, in the schools of Athens; he had fancied
himself a disciple of Epicurus: child as he was, he
had affected to renounce allegiance to all sound principles of religion as well as of politics.   Under the
change of his fortunes he has had the grace to re-
pent; he has become devout; he wishes his countrymen to know how highly he now thinks of Jupiter
and Apollo, no less than of Augustus and Mæcenas.
A man of ardent imagination and of delicate sensibility, a man who questioned the world and his own
conscience both solemnly and sternly,—such a man
as Virgil, for instance,—might well persuade himself
that the miseries he had witnessed attested the mortal
sin of renouncing the worship of the Gods, and compassing the destruction of their hero; but Horace
has no such claim on our indulgent interpretation,
and the palinodes of his lyric muse ring false to an
attentive ear.[1]

---

[1] Horace is indiscreet in assigning the motives of his conversion,
which have caused much perplexity to the critics who wished to believe him in earnest. *Od.* i. 34.:

      "Parcus Deorum cultor et infrequens . . . .
      . . . . Namque Diespiter
   Igni corusco nubila dividens
   Plerumque, per sudum tonantes
      Egit equos."

Compare i. 22.: "Namque me sylva lupus in Sabina . . . ."
    ii. 17.: "Me truncus illapsus cerebro . . . ."
    iii. 4.: "Non sine Dis animosus infans."

It can hardly be mere accident that the pieces in
which this subtle moralist inculcates tem-
perance and sobriety of thought and action,
which denounce the vanity of ambition and
the cares of greatness, are addressed in almost every case to scions of the noblest and
proudest houses. Such is the character of the odes
to Lollius and Licinius, to Torquatus and Quinctius,
to Postumus and Dellius, Antonius, Pompeius, and
Plancus.[1] When we remember that these men were
precisely of the class to which the regards of Augustus
and his minister were most jealously directed, such
a concurrence of similar warnings, repeated to more
than satiety, seems to admit of only one explanation.
The minion of the usurping dynasty would not have
been countenanced in such frequent and familiar addresses to men whose restless ambition, whose exalted birth and ample means made them formidable
to the court, more than one of whom had been found
in open or secret array against it, unless on condition
of exerting his influence to curb their impatience,
and chastise their illicit aspirations.[2] Horace re-
sounds the praises of Italy in strains not dissimilar
to those of Virgil; and we are again reminded, by
his fervid encomiums on the beauties of that sacred
soil, of the anxiety of his master to recall the truant
spirits of his subjects from the charms of Greece and
Asia to the post of piety and duty.[3]

*Horace em-
ployed to re-
commend mo-
deration and
contentment
to the restless
nobles.*

---

[1] Comp. *Epist.* i. 6.: To Numicius: " Nil admirari . . . ." We
have met with several of these names ranged on the side of the
senate against Cæsar, or of the Eastern against the Western triumvir.

[2] Legris ventures to explain the perplexing ode to Plancus (*Od.* i.
7.), with its preference of Tiber and the Anio over Argos and Larissa,
as a covert .invitation to renounce the service of the tyrant of the
East, and join the defender of his native land. It is difficult to see
why a poet should make any mystery of such an object. Yet the
well-known political poem (*Epod.* 16.: " Altera jam teritur ") bears
considerable analogy to this, and other odes of Horace have unquestionably a covert allusion to the state of public affairs.

[3] Compare, also, Propert. iii. 22.:

" Omnia Romanæ cedent miracula terræ," &c.

We cannot, perhaps, easily exaggerate the influence which the cheerful subservience of the Dissatisfaction of Horace in his later years. Horatian muse exerted upon patriots willing to be persuaded, and pleased to have their weakness gilded with the names of good sense and philosophy. Horace was rewarded, if not splendidly, at least to the extent of his desires : he enjoyed ease, reputation, the fellowship of the good and witty; he who had commenced life in search of a patron, finished it as the observed of all observers. Yet it may be true that the attainment of every wish left him despondent and dissatisfied with himself. If I rightly understand the chronology of his compositions, those which seem to be among the latest betray a spirit of mortification, rather than the cheerfulness to which he at least pretended in his earlier years.[1] He now longs for retirement; he seeks to be released from servitude; he seems even ashamed of his success in seconding the policy of his masters. He quits the thorny path of politics, and the transparent shades of his assumed philosophy, and sickens at last over the long-abused refrain of all his poetry, that wisdom is better than wealth and honours, liberty and beauty, acknowledging with a bitter smile that contentment depends more on the digestion than the finest precepts of the schools.[2] Finally, he amuses himself with meditation on literature, and the innocent recreations of abstract criticism. The *Art of Poetry* is a curious, perhaps we may say an instructive, eutha-

---

[1] Compare, for instance, Hor. *Epist.* i. 1, 2, 7, 8, 10.: "Non eadem est ætas non mens—Solve senescentem—Sic mihi tarda fluunt ingrataque tempora—Sapere aude, Incipe—Quod si me noles unquam discedere—Mihi jam non regia Roma—Vivere nec pulchre nec suaviter—Mente minus validus quam corpore—Vivo et regno simul ista reliqui."

[2] Hor. *Epist.* i. 1, fin.:

"Ad summum sapiens uno minor est Jove, dives,
Liber, honoratus, pulcher, rex denique regum,
Præcipue sanus, nisi *cum pituita molesta* est."

nasia to the fervid exaltation of his youth, and the decorous accommodation of his maturer years.[1]

A dissertation has been written to show that the disagreeable acquaintance whom Horace sought in vain to shake off in the Via Sacra was no other than the poet Propertius. The hypothesis, fanciful as it seems, is not altogether devoid of probability; but whether it be correct or not, there is undoubtedly something in the character of Propertius, as we trace it in his writings, which harmonizes with such an estimate of him.   While the

Propertius.

---

[1] The commentators have found a golden key to the chronology of Horace's writings in the lines which terminate his address to the first book of the Epistles:

"Forte meum si te quis percontabitur ævum,
Me quater undenos sciat implevisse Decembres,
Collegam Lepidum quo duxit Lollius anno."

This consulship was A.U. 733. But this allusion proves nothing except of course that the book was not published earlier than that date. There is no reason why it should not have been sent forth some years later; and such I believe, from the evidence both of style and matter, was really the case. The Epodes, most of which were among the writer's earliest compositions, which were circulated, like his other pieces, from hand to hand long before they were collected into a volume, breathe the freshness and independence, together with the inaccuracy, of youth. The two books of Satires and the first three of Odes were composed probably together during a series of years, and belong to the period in which Horace was actively employed in the service of his patrons. The last book of Odes, we are told, was published at the express desire of Augustus, and the few pieces it contains were probably strung together as a vehicle for the exhibition of the fine poems in praise of the imperial family. But in the first book of the Epistles we find the poet complaining that he has no longer the spirit for composition ("Non eadem est ætas non mens"), and parrying the solicitations of Mæcenas to resume the task. He shows an inclination to withdraw from political service: he complains of himself and of the world. Finally, the three long pieces which conclude the collection are evidently the work of a single period, when he had at last succeeded in throwing off the yoke of servitude, and could indulge himself, and perhaps seek forgetfulness, in polished and sensible, but not very profound nor very careful, remarks on the literary taste of his day. Horace was born in 689, and died in 746, within a few days perhaps of Mæcenas, but later, if we may believe the story that the dying minister recommended him to Augustus with the words, "Horatii Flacci ut mei memor esto." Suet. in *vit. Hor.*

favour of the rulers of the commonwealth was showered upon Virgil and Horace, Varius and Plotius, recommended by the eminence of their commanding genius, or the exquisiteness of their tact, there were doubtless other men, of considerable pretensions to literary talent, who sought a share in their distinctions, and were eager to barter the incense they could offer for the smiles and sunshine of the court. Among these, none perhaps was more distinguished than Propertius; yet in the race of favour he seems to have fallen far behind his more fortunate rivals. He started, indeed, in early life from the same common goal with them, being introduced to the notice of Mæcenas as a victim of the revolution. His abilities gave ample promise; and he qualified himself for the minister's consideration by the zeal with which he sought to gild with all the ornaments of verse the false idols of the day, in making vice and voluptuousness graceful, in singing in sounding verse the legends of Roman mythology, and in praising to the skies the glories of Augustus, and the virtues of his trusty counsellor. But on all these topics, similar as they are to those which Horace has so delicately recommended to us, we feel sensibly the inferior powers of his less successful competitor. Propertius is deficient in that light touch and exquisitely polished taste which volatilize the sensuality and flattery of Horace. The playfulness of the Sabine bard is that of the lapdog, while the Umbrian reminds us of the pranks of a clumsier and less tolerated quadruped.[1] Amidst all his affected indifference, the art of Mæcenas must have been constantly exercised in keeping importunate suitors at a distance. The assiduity of Propertius was perhaps too officious, and it was necessary to repel without offending him. Like all his unfortunate class, he could not understand how,

---

[1] Propert. iv. 1, 64.: "Umbria Romani patria Callimachi."

with undoubted talents and acknowledged industry, his pursuit of the great was through life a failure, while that of his rivals, who seemed so much less eager in it, was crowned with such distinguished rewards. Nevertheless, this disappointment was not wholly merited. Although Propertius is often frigid and pedantic in his sentiments, though he takes his learning from dictionaries and his gallantry from romances, and retails at second hand the flattery of his contemporaries, there is notwithstanding a strength, and sometimes a grandeur in his language, which would have been more highly relished in the sterner age of Lucretius. His rustic muse, though brought as a willing captive to the tables of the great at Rome, seems sometimes to break her silken fetters, and bound along in the wilder measures of her native mountains. Propertius stands alone among the Roman poets in the force and fervour he imparts to elegiac verse: he alone raises the soft and languid pentameter to the dignity of its heroic consort.[r] But it is in the weight of single lines, and the manly savour of occasional expressions, that the charm of this writer is to be found: he has none of the form of poetical invention, and is alike deficient in sustained majesty, in natural grace, and in flowing rhythm.

A contemporary of Propertius, and also a writer of elegiac poetry, is Albius Tibullus, the sweet-

Tibullus.

ness of whose versification, deficient though it is both in variety and strength, is remarkable at least from the early period to which it belongs. But Tibullus deserves our consideration on a more im-

---

[1] As for instance in the lines:

iii. 7, 56.: "Cum moribunda niger clauderet ora liquor.'

iii. 11, 56.: " Jura dare et statuas inter et arma Mari."

iv. 6, 42.: " Imposuit prorœ publica vota tuœ."

iv. 11, 46.: " Viximus insignes inter utramque facem."

Rutilius, in the fourth century of our era, is the only writer who deserves to be compared in this respect with Propertius.

portant ground, for the singular independence of character he exhibits in relation to the court of Augustus. Like so many of his most distinguished contemporaries, he had been dispossessed of his estates at Pedum, near Præneste, by the soldiers of Octavius ; but he too, like them, had the fortune to recover his patrimony, at least in part, and this probably through the good offices of Messala. To Messala accordingly, as his patron, he attached himself through life, following him throughout his campaigns in Aquitania, and sharing the glory and merits of his success. Tibullus sings of this distant warfare with more than usual animation, though generally he expresses a poet's aversion to the toils of military life : nevertheless the heroic poem, specially dedicated to the praise of Messala, which passes under his name, can perhaps hardly be ascribed to him. The most virtuous of the Roman nobles seems to have exacted no unworthy compliances of his grateful client. Messala, it would appear, was himself surrounded, like Mæcenas or Agrippa, with a retinue of versifiers as well as of warriors, and kept a mimic court of his own, as a chief of the ancient aristocracy. Certain it is that Tibullus refrained from all flattery of the rival following of Octavius. Throughout his works there is no mention made either of Augustus or of his ministers and associates. Yet the imperial court, on its part, was not indisposed to flatter and solicit him. Horace addressed him more than once in kindly and complimentary strains, which seem to invite him to enrol himself also in the cohort of the bards of the empire.[1] If such was Horace's view, it would appear that he was wholly unsuccessful. The muse of Tibullus, constant to its chosen theme, was devoted to singing his generally unprosperous loves; yet the tone of tender melancholy which pervades its elegies

---

[1] Hor. *Od.* i. 23.; *Epist.* i. 4.

may have had a deeper and purer source than the caprices of three inconstant paramours. The spirit of Tibullus is eminently religious; but his religion bids him fold his hands in resignation rather than open them in hope[1] : there is something soothing at least in the idea that he alone of the great poets of his day remained undazzled by the glitter of the Cæsarean usurpation, and pined away in unavailing despondency in beholding the subjugation of his country.[2]

Virgil and Horace may have had, besides the common throng of admirers, the audience fit, though few, of some solitary students ; but Ovid is eminently the poet of society, and the various styles of composition in which he excelled, disclose to us the tastes and interests of the day, and reflect the tone of ordinary sentiment in the higher ranks of the capital. Fatigued as they were with the unbending exaltation of the epic and the lyric, the *Elegies* and *Art of Love* attracted and delighted them as the representation, but slightly disguised or idealized, of actual manners and habits. Ovid was the successor in elegy of Propertius and Tibullus, of Gallus and Marsus ; but it is probable that all these writers drew from the common fountain of Grecian inspiration, and even from the effusions of a single author, Parthenius. Born at Nicæa, and carried captive as a child to Rome in the wars of Mithridates, the talents of Parthenius, and his powers of pleasing, had obtained him freedom and reception among the highest circles. He was the author of erotic elegies in verse, some of them lively and joyous, others of a

Ovid,

an imitator of Parthenius.

---

[1] "Cœlo *supinas* si tuleris manus." For the indications of this religious spirit, see particularly i. 1, 37., ii. 80., iii. 57., and Ovid, *Amor.* iii. 9, 37.

[2] See some remarks on Tibullus in Legris's second volume. Tibullus died young, according to the epigram ascribed to Marsus:

> " Te quoque Virgilio comitem non æqua, Tibulle,
> Mors juvenem campos misit ad Elysios."

funereal strain. Among the first of his disciples were
Gallus and Virgil, and some lines of the Georgics, it
is said, were fashioned directly upon his models.
Tiberius Cæsar, who affected himself to compose
Greek verses, had such admiration for this poet,
that he caused his bust and writings to be placed
in the public libraries among the most famous notabilities of his nation. His influence may
be traced in the *Heroids* of Ovid, in which   The Heroic.
the most tragic love stories of ancient legend are
versified under the form of epistles, and which seem
to have been founded on the summaries Parthenius
had specially drawn up for the use of Cornelius Gallus.[1] But however elegant the Grecian may have
been in his style, or copious in the flow of his language, it was doubtless to his training in the schools
of the rhetoricians that Ovid owed the wonderful
variety he has been able to introduce into a set of
subjects so similar in character, in which the universal passion, deserted or unsuccessful, is made to
breathe from the mouths of Sappho or Œnone, Ari-
adne or Medea. If the poet has failed to catch the
simplicity of the best heroic models, he has at least
imbibed a portion of their purity and depth of feeling.
The *Loves of the Heroines* is the most elevated and
refined in sentiment of all elegiac compositions of the
Romans. If we may argue back from Ovid to Parthenius, the marked predilection of Tiberius for the
Grecian poetaster will appear not discreditable to
that prince's taste and feeling.

It is possible that the same author suggested to
Ovid the idea of his extraordinary poem on   The Meta-
the *Metamorphoses*, or *Transformations*,   morphoses.
of Greek and Roman mythology, in which the wealth
of his fancy is displayed still more abundantly, and is

---

[1] See Walckenaer's *Histoire d'Horace*, ii. 197., from Suidas in voc.
Gellius, ix. 9., xiii. 26.; Suet. *Tiber.* 70.

at times combined with an epic majesty of diction. Its structure betrays at once the occasions for which it was written; for the slender thread of connexion which runs through it is unable to sustain any continued interest, while the repetition of similar incidents, however ingeniously varied in relation, would become inexpressibly wearisome in a continuous perusal. But viewed as a series of sketches intended for successive recitation to the same, and often to different audiences, the Metamorphoses is perfectly adapted to the author's object. The work rolls on in an uniform line, without a catastrophe or a climax, to its chronological termination : yet the Romans may have drawn a political moral from the philosophy of Pythagoras in the concluding book, which taught that all things change, but nothing perishes; and may have felt that the transformation of the republic into an empire was no more than a crowning illustration of the ruling principle of the work.[1]

The *Fasti* assumes a character of considerable importance when we regard Ovid, not as a poet

The Fasti.

giving utterance to his own enthusiasm, but as the fashionable author addressing himself always to the current taste or interest of society. The work which goes under that name may be described as the pontifical ritual in verse : it gives the rationale of the calendar, and of the stated observances of the national religion : it digests *the Seasons and the Reasons* of every special cult and ceremony.[2] Such a work, it would appear, must have been calculated to meet a popular demand. The Roman people required an explanation, in the courtly and graceful style to which

---

[1] Ovid, *Metam.* xv. 165.: "Omnia mutantur, nihil interit."

[2] Ovid, *Fast.* i. 1.: "Tempora cum causis Latium digesta per annum." The Fasti is remarkable, even among the works of Ovid, for its combination of ease with dignity. No where else are his stories told with such vivacity and perspicuousness. There is no better example, perhaps, of narrative in verse than in the legend of Anna Perenna. iii. 557, foll.

alone they would listen, of the usages to which they had solemnly devoted themselves. With these fair and sounding verses the poet satisfied the ecclesiastical spirit of the times, which leant with fond reliance on forms and traditions, and was less a thing to be felt than to be talked about. From the appearance of such a work, we may feel assured that the decree of Augustus, that the Romans should become again a religious people, was duly accepted on their part and ratified by their outward practice; that they actually set themselves to worship the gods after the manner of their fathers on the emperor's admonition. It would be idle to say that this was mere hypocrisy or flattery: doubtless there was felt a spiritual want, and multitudes blindly followed the blind leaders who offered themselves, and took their faith in all sincerity from Augustus, and their ritual complacently from Ovid.

The gloom and despondency which pervade this poet's later writings, the *Tristia*, or *Sorrows*, and the *Epistles from the Euxine*, are explained and excused by the painful circumstances under which they were composed: the exile of the Roman Siberia speaks the natural language of a spoilt child in suffering.[1] Yet there is something instructive here also, in witnessing the breaking down of the old Roman fortitude, which seems to have been among the first of the virtues of the republic to wither under the shadow of the empire. Neither the melancholy of Virgil, nor the self-dissatisfaction we have remarked in Horace, would have been betrayed in word or deed in the period of true pride and self-reliance.[2] We should

The Tristia and Epistles ex Ponto.

---

[1] The *Ibis*, however, an attack upon some nameless slanderer, who had trampled on him in his misfortunes, is as energetic as could be desired; while the address to his wife (*Trist.* iii. 7.) reaches a lofty pitch of manly endurance.

[2] We may be allowed, however, to question whether even a Coriolanus could have used such an expression as, *Romans, I banish you!* which Shakspeare has transferred to him from the mouth of the cynic Diogenes. Shaksp. *Coriol.* act iii.

be curious to learn how the lamentations of the banished poet were received by his associates at home. They moved the compassion neither of Augustus nor of his successor; and there is too much reason to fear that neither the friends he so piteously intercedes with, nor the wife he praises so feelingly, ventured to move in his behalf. Long before his death, Ovid, we may believe, was forgotten in the land he so miserably yearned for; and it was not perhaps till after his own tongue had grown cold, that the verses it poured forth in so copious a stream were brought from the desks of his correspondents, and published for the interest of the world. In the course of time the empire teemed with a society of fellow-sufferers, who learnt perhaps, from their own woes, to sympathize with the lamentations of the first generation of exiles. The *Tristia* of Ovid became the common expression of the sentiments of a whole class of unfortunates.

I have thus sought to give a view of the ideas of the Augustan era, from a few representative examples; but it would detain us too long from our narrative were we to examine the subject of its literature through all its elements and features. For the same reason, and because indeed the remains we possess of them are still more fragmentary, not from undervaluing their significance in expressing the mind of their age, I omit all reference, here at least, to the arts and sciences of the period, to its painting, architecture and sculpture, as well as to its investigations in ethics and physics. The moral character of these times is indeed a subject of still deeper interest, and one which it will become us to study with all the resources of knowledge and application we can command; but it will be well to postpone this survey till we can compare the Roman principles and practice with the Christian, and scrutinize both by the light which they will throw recipro-

Conclusion.

cally upon each other.   Meanwhile I return to the
political history of the empire, as far as we can succeed in penetrating its obscurity; for the guides who
deign to aid us will prove too often blind or treacherous; and we shall march like the hero of Virgil in
the infernal twilight, by the malign rays of Tacitus
and Suetonius, through the gloom of a tyranny which
has overshadowed men and things, and confused the
various colours of events and characters.[1]

[1] Virgil, _Æn._ vi. 270.:

> "Quale per incertam lunam sub luce maligna
> Est iter in sylvis, ubi cœlum condidit umbra
> Jupiter, et rebus nox abstulit atra colorem."

CHAPTER XLII.

Tiberius succeeds to the empire.—His condescension to the senate, and pretended reluctance to accept power.—Mutiny of the legions in Pannonia and on the Rhine, quelled by Drusus and Germanicus. —Character of Germanicus.—His popularity awakens the jealousy of Tiberius.—Campaigns of Germanicus beyond the Rhine in 767, 768, and 769.—He revisits the scene of the slaughter of Varus.— Disaster on his return by sea.—Germanicus reaches the Weser.— Quarrel between Arminius and his brother Flavius.— Battle of Idistavisus.—Successive defeats of the Germans, and barren trophies of the Romans.—Second disaster by sea.—The eagles of Varus recovered.—The frontier of the empire recedes finally to the Rhine.—Return of Germanicus to Rome, and triumph there. —Gloomy forebodings of the people. (A.D. 14—17, A.U. 767— 770.)

IT may be recorded in praise of Augustus, among few other sovereigns who have long survived the date of their early popularity, that no burst of general satisfaction hailed the announcement of his decease. The old man had no doubt become stale and wearisome to his countrymen; a damp had been cast on their spirits by the dull shade of a monotonous rule, which had long ceased to be relieved by gleams of adventitious splendour. The prosperity of his latter years had been clouded by alarming disasters; yet these had not so depressed the feelings of the nation as the leaden weight of an administration which seemed concerned only to avert motives of popular excitement. The generation which had admired Augustus as the genius of beneficent government had descended into the tomb: it had been succeeded by one which regarded him only as a despot, or, more unfavourably still, as a pedant. Whatever discontent, however, might lie smothered beneath the external forms of

The Romans ready to acquiesce in the succession of Tiberius.

loyal submission, the approaching end of his long domination was anticipated in no quarter as the advent of a new era.[1] Augustus himself justly presumed that no party contemplated the restoration of the republic on his decease; he was content to warn his successor against the personal ambition of the most eminent nobles, those who might be expected to covet the sovereignty, and those who without coveting might be deemed fit to wield it.[2] But the great mass of the citizens acquiesced at this crisis in the conviction that the man who had shared his later counsels would be appointed heir to his relinquished powers. They contemplated without a murmur the succession of Tiberius to the complete cycle of the imperial functions, from no personal regard or admiration, nor from any deliberate belief that he was the fittest of the citizens to assume preeminence, but from a half-conscious acknowledgment of his divine or legitimate right as the adopted son of the hero Augustus, himself the adopted son of the divine Julius. Such is the proneness of the human mind to discover a right for a once established and uncontested might; so smooth is the path of usurpation, when it has once succeeded in scaling the barriers of the law. It was not in vain that Augustus had cherished among his subjects the remnant of religious feeling; he was rewarded by becoming himself the centre of their idolatry, and imparting a ray of his own adorable godhead to the heir of his name and titles.

But with the fortunes of Augustus, Tiberius did not inherit that reliance on his personal merits which nerved the arm of his predecessor, and imbued him with so lofty a sense of his

Self-distrust of Tiberius.

---

[1] Tac. *Ann.* i. 4.: "Postquam provecta jam senectus ægro et corpore fatigabatur, aderatque finis et spes novæ: pauci bona libertatis incassum disserere: plures bellum pavescere, alii cupere: pars multo maxima imminentes dominos variis rumoribus disserere.'

[2] Tac. *Ann.* i. 13.

mission. Though certainly with no mean ability,
both military and administrative, he seems to have
been wanting in the higher quality of genius which
seizes or makes its opportunities, and floats on the
crest of the swelling waves of a national inspiration.
Of this he was himself painfully sensible; and it was
the consciousness that he could neither kindle the
imagination of the soldiers like Julius, nor of the
citizens like Augustus, that made him feel less secure
of their obedience than he really was. He had suffered, indeed, though mainly through his own perverseness, a fall from power, which rendered him
keenly alive to the precariousness of his elevation,
and to the dangers which attend on infirmities of
temper in the great. The secret of his predecessor's
success had lain, as he was perhaps aware, in the
perfect equilibrium of his abilities and his temper,
in the combination of genius with self-command; his
own conscious deficiency in this particular chilled
him as an omen of ultimate failure, as it had already
been the cause of his temporary disgrace. Tiberius
reigned in the constant apprehension of the crash
which he expected to overwhelm him; the sword of
Damocles seemed ever suspended over him; and he
scanned with angry perturbation the countenances
of all who approached him, to discover whether they
too saw the fatal spectre which was never absent from
his own imagination.[1]

At the critical moment he might himself have
hesitated and looked timidly around him;
but he was fortunate, if one may say so, in
having in his mother Livia an ally endued
with the unity of object and promptness in action
which so strongly characterize her sex. Augustus, it
seems probable, had not yet breathed his last, and

*Death of Au-
gustus an-
nounced.*

---

[1] One passing stroke from Pliny on this subject rivals in effect the
elaborate paintings of Tacitus: "Tiberius tristissimus, ut constat,
hominum." *Hist. Nat.* xxviii. 5.

his step-son, hastily recalled from the Dalmatian coast, was not yet in attendance on his death-bed, when the empress boldly ventured to take the necessary measures to prevent the tidings of his decease being too soon made public. When, however, Tiberius was himself on the spot, there was no further occasion for disguise, and the decease of the late imperator was proclaimed at the same moment with the substitution of a successor.[1] The fidelity of the few troops about the capital, already bound by the military sacrament to their actual chief's coadjutor, was sufficiently assured; obedience to the orders of Tiberius had become habitual to them. Nor was there any real cause for apprehension lest a rival should start up among the nobility of the capital. Of the possible competitors already designated by Augustus, Lepidus, he had said, was equal to empire, but would disdain it; Asinius Gallus might be ambitious of it, but was unequal to the post; and one only, the rich and high-born Arruntius, had the spirit both to desire, and, if occasion served, to contend for it.[2] But Arruntius bore no official distinction or military reputation; no circumstances had combined to smooth his way to such an elevation, and the only immediate risk of competition lay in the members of the Cæsarean family itself. Of these, Germanicus was at the moment absent: Drusus, the youthful child of Tibe-

---

[1] Tac. *Ann.* i. 5.: "Provisis quæ tempus monebat, simul excessisse Augustum et rerum potiri Neronem, fama eadem tulit."

[2] Tac. *Ann.* i. 13.: "M. Lepidum dixerat capacem, sed aspernantem; Gallum Asinium avidum, et minorem; L. Arruntium non indignum, et si casus daretur ausurum." M. Æmilius Lepidus was brother of the Paulus Æmilius, husband of the younger Julia, who conspired against Augustus. See vol. iv. chap. xxxviii. He continued in the enjoyment of favour and dignity till his death, A. U. 786. Tac. *Ann.* vi. 27.; see below. C. Asinius Gallus was son of Asinius Pollio, and married to Vipsania, the divorced wife of Tiberius. For his death, 783, see below. L. Arruntius was son of a lieutenant of Augustus in the battle of Actium (consul A. U. 732). His suicide, A. U. 790, will be mentioned in its place.

rius, had yet acquired no independent position; but the wretched Agrippa still lingered in his island-prison, and the. rumour that Augustus had recently visited him in secret, and held out, not without tokens of affection, some hopes of release and favour,

Rumoured assassination of Agrippa Postumus.

had excited the jealous fears both of Livia and her son. As soon as Augustus ceased to breathe, and even before his decease was proclaimed, an order was conveyed to the centurion in guard over the captive to put him to death. Such was the belief of the times; but whether the order was issued by Livia, without her son's privity, or whether it was the first act of the new Cæsar's authority, the propagators of the rumour were not agreed. A hint seems indeed to have been thrown out that Augustus had instructed the keepers to kill their prisoner as soon as his own death should be known, to anticipate the risk of disturbance in the succession; and Tiberius publicly declared that the deed was not commanded by him; nevertheless he took no steps to explain the mystery, and the perpetrators of a crime thus officially acknowledged were allowed to remain unquestioned.[1]

With the announcement of the emperor's decease Tiberius summoned the senate by virtue of his tribunitian power.[2] The consuls Appuleius and Pompeius

---

[1] Tacitus ascribes the act without hesitation to Tiberius: " Primum facinus novi principatus fuit Postumi Agrippæ cædes " . . . . and Dion follows him. Suetonius speaks more dubiously: " Quos codicillos dubium fuit Augustusne moriens reliquisset quo materiam tumultus post se subduceret, an nomine Augusti Livia, et ea conscio Tiberio an ignaro dictâsset." Velleius seems to insinuate that Agrippa died before Augustus. In the will of the emperor, made sixteen months before his own decease, he made no mention of this grandson ; but nothing can be built on this omission. Tacitus and Suetonius both agree that the centurion reported to Tiberius, " Factum esse quod imperasset," and that Tiberius replied with anger, " Neque imperasse se, et rationem facti reddendam apud senatum; " but took no further notice of the affair. See Tac. Ann. i. 6.; Suet. Tib. 22.; Dion, lvii. 3.

[2] Suet. Tib. 23.: " Jure tribunitiæ potestatis coacto senatu."

came forward, as the first magistrates of the republic, to swear obedience to him as their impe-
rator, and the formula was repeated by all the officers of the state, and echoed by the soldiers and the citizens.[1] Tiberius con-
venes the
senate.   The ceremony passed smoothly without demur or scruple. Tiberius alone, perhaps, was astonished at the readiness with which his fellow-citizens accepted from the lips of their magistrates the obligation to maintain the imperial system in his person. The terms in which he had convoked the fathers had been studiously moderate and cautious. He had carefully avoided committing himself to any personal views : he had only requested that they should consult about the honours due to the deceased; while for himself he proposed to continue meanwhile in attendance on the venerated remains, the sole public function which he claimed the right to discharge. Yet he had not scrupled to assume the ordinary ensigns of power at the emperor's death-bed, he had disposed the sentinels and given the watch-word without reserve; even in presenting himself in the forum and the senate he had adopted a military escort: still more, he had despatched his own orders to the legions in the provinces; in short, he had shown no signs of hesitation in anything but his address to the senators themselves.[2] As associated indeed in the imperium he was perfectly competent

---

[1] Tac. *Ann.* i. 7.: "Primi Coss. in verba Tiberii Cæsaris juravere." In the camp from which the usage was derived the legatus Imperatoris first uttered the oath of obedience—" præstitit sacramentum "—to his general ; then the centurions, and finally, the soldiers—" jurabant in verba legati "—took his oath upon themselves. But the military sacrament had now become a general oath of allegiance, which the consuls proposed, and the rest of the citizens repeated after them. Comp. Suet. *Jul.* 84.; Appian, *Bell. Civ.* ii. 145.

[2] Tac. *Ann. l. c.*: "Defuncto Augusto signum prætoriis cohortibus ut imperator dederat ; excubiæ, arma, cætera aulæ ; miles in Forum miles in Curiam comitabatur ; literas ad exercitus, tanquam adepto principatu, misit; nusquam cunctabundus nisi quum in Senatu loqueretur." Comp. Suet. *Tib.* 24.; Dion, lvii. 2.

to take these military measures; but the motive which impelled him to act so promptly was his fear of Germanicus, the commander of several legions and the favourite of the people, who, it might be apprehended, would rather choose to seize the supreme power at once than wait for its descent to him hereafter.[1] Tiberius had a further reason for courting the suffrages of the senate, rather than commanding them: he was anxious to appear to owe his election to the national voice, rather than slip into the succession as the adopted heir of a woman-ruled dotard. It suited his temper, moreover—and in estimating the acts of the moody Tiberius we must regard his temper even more than his policy—thus to ascertain the real sentiments of the courtiers, whose voices he could have easily constrained.

Already, sixteen months before his death, Augustus had sealed his will, and placed it beyond his own reach in the custody of the Vestals.[2] By this instrument he had made a careful disposition of his property, after the manner of a private citizen. The bulk of it he had bequeathed, after expressing his regret at the loss of Caius and Lucius, to Tiberius and Livia in unequal proportions, the former receiving two-thirds, the latter one-third only; but even this share was beyond what the law allowed to a widow, and required a special exemption from the senate.[3] It was provided at the same time that Livia should be adopted into the Julian family, and distinguished with the title of Augusta. In

Private testament of Augustus.

---

[1] Tac. *l. c* : "Causa praecipua ex formidine ne Germanicus, in cujus manu tot legiones, immensa sociorum auxilia, mirus apud populum favor, habere imperium quam exspectare mallet."

[2] Suet *Oct.* 101.; Tac. *Ann.* i. 8.; Dion, lvi. 32, 33.

[3] The lex Voconia had allowed a widow to inherit only a fourth, and this had been reduced to a fifth by the lex Papia Poppæa. It may be said, however, that Livia had been released from the severity of this law by receiving the Jus trium liberorum. Dion, lv. 2. See Reimar's note on Dion, lvi. 32.

default of the survival of these his first-named heirs,
he called his grandsons and their children to the inheritance, one-third of which was to descend to Drusus,
the son of Tiberius, the remainder to be apportioned
among Germanicus and his three male children.
The unfortunate Julias were specially excepted from
all benefit in this arrangement, and a clause was
added by which their remains were forbidden to rest
in the Cæsarean mausoleum. Of Agrippa Postumus
no mention seems to have been made. Failing all
natural or adoptive successors, the emperor had taken
the precaution of inserting some names of the chief
nobility, even such as he was known to have regarded
during his lifetime with distrust and dislike, either
to conciliate their favour towards his descendants, or
as an empty display of generosity. But the property
which, after fifty years of power, the emperor had to
bestow, did not exceed what might be expected from
a citizen of the first rank ; and it was burdened by
liberal donations to the public treasury, to the citizens
individually, to the legionaries and the guards of the
palace, and also to a few private friends.[1] As regarded public affairs, the last counsels he Last public counsels.
gave his children and the commonwealth
were exhortations to prudence and moderation. He
requested that no ostentation of magnificence should
induce them to emancipate many slaves at his funeral;
that they should abstain from admitting the subjects
of the empire indiscriminately to the honours and
privileges of the ruling race ; that they should summon all men capable of affairs to a share in their
administration, and not accumulate all public functions in a single hand ; lastly, that they should rest
satisfied with the actual extent of the frontiers, nor
risk, by the lust of further conquests, the loss of the

---

[1] Tac. *l. c.*: " Populo et plebi ccccxxxv., prætoriarum cohortium
militibus singula nummum millia, legionariis ccc., cohortibus civium
Rom. ccccc. nummos viritim dedit."

provinces they possessed : for so he had paused himself in the career of his own successes, and preferred
to present gain or personal glory the permanent interests of the republic.[1]

Tiberius was anxious that the citizens should notice
the deference paid by the deceased ruler to
their presumed supremacy, and fancy that
the empire, with its various powers and prerogatives, was still their own to give or to withhold.
The senate and people vied in the honours they
heaped on the memory of so loyal a sovereign.   The
body, it was decreed, should be borne into the field
of Mars through the gate of triumph, but Tiberius
himself interfered to moderate the officious zeal of
individual courtiers.   The populace signified their
resolve to consume the remains in the forum, and an
armed guard was required to prevent this irregularity, to avert the riots which might have ensued,
and spare the superstitious feelings which would be
hurt by it.   But the vapid admiration of the sated
sight-seers of Rome was finally contented with the
decorous solemnities of a national apotheosis.   The
senate, the same body, at least in name, which had
struck down another Cæsar sixty years before, which
had conceded honours to his corpse under bitter compulsion, and driven his adorers from his shrine with
blows and menaces, now combined with all classes of
the citizens in a common act of extravagant adulation.
The procession of the knights who attended on the
bier held its march from the suburban station of
Bovillæ to the centre of the city ; orations in praise of
the deceased were pronounced by Tiberius and his

Funeral honours de-creed him.

---

[1] Dion, lvi. 33.   These counsels seem to have been appended to
the register of the empire (its forces, revenues, &c.), which Augustus
bequeathed to the state.   Tac. *Ann.* i. 11.: " Proferri libellum reci-
tarique jussit : opes publicæ continebantur, &c. . . . . . addideratque
consilium coercendi intra terminos imperii." See vol. iv. chap. xxxix.
It was still a question, however, whether this last advice was the
result of care for the public weal, or of envy towards his successor.

son Drusus from the steps of the Julian temple and from the rostra; from the forum the honoured remains were borne upon the shoulders of the senators to the place of cremation in the Campus Martius. Temples, priests, and holy observances were decreed to the divine Augustus, as before to the divine Julius, for a prætor was found to affirm that he had seen his soul ascend from his ashes into the celestial abodes. This testimony, such as it was, followed an ancient and auspicious precedent, and was rewarded with a splendid present from Livia.[1] On the death of Cæsar, no such vision had been required : Rome and the world believed without a witness, that a spirit more than human had exchanged life for immortality.

Meanwhile a scene was being enacted in the Senate House of much more importance to the interests of the citizens than that which concerned the remains of fallen greatness just consigned to the tomb. Tiberius had learnt from the policy of his sire that, however bold and decided his movements might be, in the camp and the provinces, he must govern the nobles in the city by craft and management. Following implicitly the example which had been set him on more than one solemn occasion, he now met the professions of submission to his authority, which the senators eagerly tendered, with pretending to shrink from its acceptance. He began with uttering ambiguous generalities about the vast extent of the empire, and the arduousness of the task of governing it.[2] From thence he proceeded to insinuate that the charge was in fact too great for a single hand, and might tax the powers of more than one associate. He hinted, perhaps, at the policy of appointing a third triumvirate, to divide the cares to

Tiberius in the senate.

---

[1] Suet. *Oct.* 100.; Dion, lvi. 46.

[2] Vell. ii. 124. : "Veluti luctatio civitatis fuit pugnantis cum Cæsare senatus populique, ut stationi paternæ succederet ; illius ut potius æqualem civem quam eminentem liceret agere principem."

which Augustus had alone been equal; as it had required the vigour of three combined imperators to
wield the sword of Cæsar. He was not unaware that
among the traditions of the republic the triumvirate
was more obnoxious than even the monarchy, and he
might anticipate that the fear of returning to a rule
stamped with the fatal impress of massacre and civil
war, would throw his hearers on the only other feas-
ible alternative, the perpetuation of imperial supremacy. The senators received his harangue in silence,
rather from uncertainty as to his real wishes than
from any hesitation of their own; for with the exception of the few among them who might cherish
schemes of personal aggrandisement, there can be no
doubt that the general disposition was to acquiesce,
however reluctantly, in the substitution of Tiberius
for Augustus. But the smooth progress of the trick
was presently interrupted by the captious question of
Asinius, who ventured to ask the speaker what part
of the imperial functions he was prepared himself to
accept. Tiberius was for a moment embarrassed;
but recovering himself, he replied adroitly, that it
was not for him to choose or to reject any particular
charge, when for his own part he would willingly be
excused from all. The rash or petulant inquirer
sought to cover his retreat by declaring he had no
other motive in asking, but to show by the answer
he should elicit that the state was one and indivisible,
and could only be governed by a single head. The
session ended with the understanding of all
parties that the government should continue
in the hands of Tiberius, with all the functions amassed by his predecessor.[1] No formal decree, however, was pronounced to this effect;

*All the func-
tions of empire
left by tacit
understanding
in the hands of
Tiberius.*

---

[1] Tac. *Ann.* i. 11—13.; Suet. *Tib.* 24.; comp. Dion, lvii. 2. That
there was no regular decree on this occasion, as was usual in later
times, for conferring the imperial prerogatives, appears from the fact
that Tacitus and Suetonius are not agreed as to the turn the discus-

he already possessed the imperium, which required no further intsrument to give him the control of the legions and provinces; the tribunitian and proconsular power had been granted on a previous occasion, and the prerogatives of the consular were sufficiently understood without a distinct and formal recognition. The principate was, perhaps, virtually conferred without a special act, by tacitly yielding the first voice in the senate, while the popular suffrage, in which lay the disposal of the chief pontificate, might be easily taken for granted. The time had come when, whatever artifices might still be required for the management of the senate, the chief of the state need keep terms no longer with the popular assemblies. The appointment of the consuls, with the forms of voting, was now finally withdrawn from the centuries, and therewith the last frail remnant of the political privileges of the Roman people was substantially abolished. The emperor henceforth nominated four candidates, and allowed the senate simply to make choice of two among them; but the aspirants for honour were no longer subjected to the humiliation of suing, or the pain of being refused, and the express recommendation of the emperor himself was considered as in fact authoritative. The senators accepted with gratitude the relief from a delicate and invidious responsibility, and the people submitted to the change with scarce an audible murmur.[1]

The last political privileges of the people abolished.

sion ultimately took: the former gives us to understand that Tiberius broke up the meeting without any specific declaration of assuming the empire; but Suetonius says, expressly, that he agreed to undertake the charge, at least for a season.

[1] Tac. *Ann.* i. 15.: "Tum primum a campo comitia ad Patres translata sunt," etc.; but at the close of this book (c. 81.) the same author remarks, in apparent contradiction to this statement, " De comitiis consularibus, quæ tum primum illo principe ac deinceps fuere, vix quidquam firmare ausim," etc. The subject will be treated more fully in a subsequent chapter.

While the supreme power was thus quietly changing
hands at the centre of the empire, events
of no little moment were happening on the
frontiers, where the seeds of future revolutions were sown by a mutinous soldiery.   The insubordination which Cæsar had experienced more
than once among his own legionaries, was the effect
of his indiscriminate enlistments, and the licentious
principles he had instilled into his followers.   The
three legions which now occupied Pannonia under
Julius Blæsus were composed in a great measure of
recruits promiscuously levied to repress the recent
revolt.   Though among these many veterans were
mingled, it seems impossible that the complaints
they put forth of having served thirty or even forty
years without obtaining their discharge, could have
been true of any large number.   Harassed as the
actual veterans may have been by a service protracted,
under the necessities of the times, far beyond the
legitimate period, we may conjecture that the turbulence of the recent levies had given an impulse to
their dissatisfaction.   They complained of their
wounds and privations; of the intolerable harshness
of camp discipline; of the meagreness of their daily
dole; of the miserable and distant recompense of
allotments on a barbarous frontier.   The few days
of rest or rejoicing which the legate allowed them,
on the confirmation of the empire to Tiberius, were
occupied by the most ardent spirits in fanning the
sparks of sedition; yet it must be observed, that
among all their murmurs, they never pretended that
the death of Augustus released them from their legitimate subjection to his associate.[1]

Discontent of the legions in Pannonia.

The authority of Blæsus was soon overthrown.   The troops insisted that the term
of their service should be definitely fixed at sixteen

Drusus is sent to quell the mutiny.

[1] Tac. *Ann.* i. 16.

years.[1]   They demanded also a further advance
in the rate of the legionary's pay, which Julius
Cæsar had already raised to double the earlier
standard of the republic.[2]   The legatus was compelled to send his son to Rome as the bearer of these
requisitions, which wore the character of a defiance,
for the Roman in the camp lost every right of the
freeman; his only patron was the tribune in the
Forum, his sole means of redress his vote in the
Comitia.   Nor while awaiting a reply from the emperor and senate, did the soldiers return frankly to
obedience.   Conscious of the crime of indiscipline,
they broke into frenzies of anger and jealousy, struck
or slew their centurions, and insulted their commanders.   Drusus, being despatched promptly with
some prætorian cohorts to recover their fidelity,
found them in open mutiny, occupying their camp
and drawing their rations, but refusing every work
and exercise.   The prince was furnished with no
definite instructions; his father had withheld from
him the requisite authority for conceding demands
which he still hoped to evade.   The soldiers were
infuriated at this disappointment.   Drusus was actually attacked by tumultuary bands and with diffi-

---

[1] Hitherto the term of service for the legionary was twenty years,
and sixteen for the prætorian, the name by which the guards of the
emperor's person, and tent or palace, came now to be distinguished.
But even at the end of that period Augustus had introduced the
custom ‹ f exauctoratio, by which the legionaries were relieved from
some of the more severe duties of the service, but still retained under
their colours, instead of missio or complete discharge.

[2] The soldiers demanded the denarius per day instead of the ten
ases.   The denarius had been raised to the value of sixteen, or, as
some say, twelve ases, and such was apparently the increased demand.   But if I understand Pliny rightly, this point they never
actually gained : the denarius continuing always to be counted as
ten ases in military payments.   *Hist. Nat.* xxxiii. 3.: "Denarium
in militari stipendio semper pro x assibus datum." But the whole
question is involved in great difficulty.   See Lipsius, Excurs. vi. and
vii. in Tac. and the notes of Walther, Ritter, and other commentators.

culty rescued; night intervened, but the morning seemed about to dawn on the entire defection of three legions. Suddenly the moon became eclipsed, and before it emerged from the ominous shadow, clouds had gathered in the sky, and seemed, to the affrighted and ignorant multitude, to threaten its total extinction. The men were struck with dismay; and while the fit of fear or remorse was upon them, Drusus seized the moment for promises and caresses. In return for some vague assurances of redress from the emperor, he engaged them to surrender their ringleaders, on whom he inflicted the full vengeance of outraged discipline, with the consent and approbation of the fickle multitude.[1]

Almost at the same moment, and from similar *Insubordination among the legions on the Rhine.* motives of discontent, a mutiny had broken out also among the legions on the Rhine. The danger was far greater in this case than in the other; the army of the Rhenish frontier numbered not less than eight legions, posted in two divisions in the Upper and Lower Germania; and the direction of the entire force was intrusted to Germanicus, as commanding in chief throughout the whole province of Gaul. Not only did the mutineers clamour for higher pay and more indulgent treatment, but the legions of the lower province proclaimed that they would carry the youthful Cæsar in triumph to Rome, and gird him with the sword of their deceased leader. They obtained complete mastery over their officers, and the legate Aulus Cæcina; and their outbreak was scarcely kept in check by the yet undecided attitude of the upper division, which C. Silius still restrained from open mutiny. Germanicus was absent at Lugdunum, where he was presiding over the census of the Gaulish states. Here he received

---

[1] Tac. *Ann.* i. 16—30.: "Promptum ad asperiora ingenium Druso erat: vocatos Vibulenum et Percennium interfici jubet." But could any commander have done otherwise?

the news of the late emperor's death, with orders
from Tiberius to tender to the provincials the oath
of allegiance to the elect of the senate. This duty
he was intent on discharging, without apprehension
of any military outbreak, when the report of the state
of affairs in his camp interrupted his proceedings.
The soldiers had assailed their officers with violence;
they had murdered tribunes and centurions; obedience was at an end, and the legate himself was
constrained to deliver into their hands the objects
of their bitterest hatred.[1]

The Roman quarters among the Ubii had been
for some days in a state of confusion and *Germanicus*
anarchy, when Germanicus arrived and *hastens from*
Lugdunum to
threw himself boldly into the midst. The *suppress it.*
young Cæsar was personally adored by the soldiers;
nor, had it been otherwise, were any of them prepared
to discard the authority of a scion of the imperial
house. On his appearance among them they cast
themselves at his feet, imploring his sympathy with
their just complaints, the most aged of the veterans
seizing his hands, it was said, and thrusting them,
as if to kiss them, within their lips, that he might
feel their toothless gums, and learn to appreciate
the length of their ill-requited services. Some
showed him the scars of their wounds, others the
marks of the centurion's vine-rod. The men soon
lashed themselves into fresh fury, and with loud cries
adjured Germanicus to lead them straight to Rome,
and assume the empire under their protection. The
young Cæsar shrank with horror from such a treason,
and possibly they might in their frenzy have done
violence to his person had not his attendants snatched
him hastily from their grasp. But meanwhile their
emissaries were soliciting the adhesion of the legions
of the Upper Germania, stationed at Moguntiacum;

---

[1] Tac. *Ann.* i. 31, 32.; Suet. *Tib.* 25.; Dion, lvii. 5.

and while undecided as to their ultimate objects,
they already talked of commencing their rebellion by
the plunder of the Ubii and the cities of Gaul.   The
military chiefs were well aware that this dissolution
of discipline on the frontier would bring the Germans
immediately across it, and the civil war which must
ensue between the faithful allies of Rome and her
own insurgent children would be aggravated by
foreign invasion, and possibly by provincial revolt.
Assembled in the imperator's tent, they hastily concerted an offer of terms to the soldiers, to which they
pledged the name of Tiberius himself.   Besides the
required revision of the term of service, ample dona-
tives in money were promised, as soon as the legions
should return to winter quarters.   This was not
enough.   The insurgents demanded that the stipu-
lated sum should be paid down on the instant, and
the private coffers of Germanicus and his officers, as
well as of the emperor himself, were ransacked to
satisfy them.[1]

This sacrifice was after all unavailing.   The appearance of envoys from the senate, charged
to examine the soldiers' demands, was the
signal for a fresh disturbance; for the alarm
quickly spread that the concessions made
on the spur of momentary danger would fail to be
ratified on maturer deliberation.   The more violent
of the mutineers persuaded their comrades to refuse
all accommodation, and so formidable was the attitude
now assumed, that Germanicus was forced to surrender the eagles to the keeping of the rebellious
legionaries, and in fact to relinquish the command.
At most he could only secure a retreat for the envoys, on whom the fury of the insurgents was about
to fall, and at the same time for his wife and children,
whom he was anxious to remove to a place of safety.

The popularity of Germanicus, and his success in quelling the mutiny.

---

[1] Tac. *Ann.* i. 34—36.

Agrippina, a woman of masculine spirit and devoted to her husband, could hardly be persuaded to quit his side. When she at last took leave, with a few female attendants, carrying in her arms her infant child Caius, the pet and playfellow of the soldiers, the feelings of the spectators were moved to remorse. Germanicus seized the moment to remind them of the claims of his own family upon them, and of the love they had borne to his father Drusus; nor did he fail to recall to remembrance the glories of Augustus, the victories of Tiberius, and the spirit with which the immortal Julius had quelled the mutiny of his soldiers by addressing them as *citizens*. This last passionate appeal proved successful. The insurgents fell on their knees, and implored him to punish the guilty, to spare the penitent, and lead the pardoned host directly against the enemy. They conjured him to recall his wife and child, and not leave them as hostages in the land of the Gauls, but retain them under the safeguard of the Roman legions. Nor did they fail to deliver of their own accord to the punishment of the axe and rod those whom they regarded as their ringleaders, whom their officers gladly left it to themselves to point out. The ferocious zeal with which each offender denounced such as he chose to think more guilty than himself presents a fearful picture of human passion.[1]

When we meet among the scions of the imperial house with one described as eminently vir- Character of Germanicus. tuous and noble, we must prepare to hear that his career was melancholy, that his promise ended in disappointment, and his death was premature. Such a death at least doubly gilds his virtues, while it may anticipate the development of crimes or vices. Of all the chiefs of Roman history, none has been represented in fairer colours than the ill-fated

---

[1] Tac. *Ann.* i. 37—44.

Germanicus. We have seen already that he was the nephew of Tiberius, being the son of the gallant Drusus, whose title he was permitted to inherit, by a daughter of the triumvir Antonius.[1] Augustus had connected him still more closely with himself, by uniting him to the child of Agrippa by his own daughter Julia. Adopted by Tiberius, he was placed on the same line of succession as his cousin Drusus, to whom he was two or three years senior; and after the deaths of Caius and Lucius Cæsar, who had shone so briefly as twin stars in the firmament, the fortunes of the two adopted brothers seemed to rise together in auspicious conjunction.[2] Whatever brilliant future might be in store for Germanicus, the Romans, if we may believe their posthumous testimony to his merits, were fully persuaded that he deserved it. His natural abilities had been carefully cultivated. He had been trained equally in the art of war and the exercise of civil employment. His first laurels had been gained in his twenty-second year, in the wars of Pannonia and Dalmatia, the successful issue of which was in a great measure ascribed to his energy and conduct.[3] In the year 765 he had been summoned to the consulship, and in the highest rank of magistracy, young as he was, his countrymen had marked in him all the skill in affairs which is commonly attained only by experience. The government of the Gaulish provinces, too extensive a command to be entitled a mere proconsulate, followed on the expiration of his functions in the city; and there, at the head of eight legions, before the most formidable opponents of the Roman power, he stood in the eyes

---

[1] Suet, *Claud.* 1.; *Calig.*1.; Plut. *Anton.* 87.

[2] Germanicus, born in September 739 (see vol. iv., ch. xxxviii.), was now, at the close of 767, in his twenty-ninth year. The date of the birth of Drusus is not accurately known; it was probably a short time before the separation of Tiberius from his mother Vipsania, in 742.

[3] Dion, lvi. 15. See above.

of the soldiers and provincials as little less than an
emperor himself. The large training of the highest
Roman education had fitted him, amidst these public
avocations, to take a graceful interest in literature.
His compositions in Greek and Latin verse were
varied, and perhaps more than respectable for school
exercises, with which only they should be compared.[1]
Nor did he neglect the practice of oratory, which he
employed, as was always especially recorded of those
whose memory the Romans delighted to honour, in
the defence rather than the prosecution of the accused.[2] His manners were eminently *civil* both at
home and abroad, such as became the son of the man
who, according to the fond belief of the citizens,
would have restored the commonwealth ; and while
he comported himself towards his countrymen as an
equal, his demeanour to foreigners and allies was
affable and condescending. In the camp his behaviour was in striking contrast both with the reserve
of Augustus and the mal-address of Tiberius. He
lived freely among his soldiers, whose humours he
sought to flatter, like the first and greatest of the
Cæsars, by sympathy and kindness. When he explored his men's sentiments on the eve of a perilous
undertaking, by traversing their quarters disguised
at night, he might hear his own merits made the
theme of their conversation, and assure himself of the
confidence they reposed in his valour and fortune.[3]

---

[1] The Greek comedy of Germanicus (Suet. *Calig.* 3.) was probably
a mere scholastic imitation, such as was generally the character of
the Greek verses of the young Roman nobles. The translation of
Aratus which is, I think properly, ascribed to him, was a *tour de
force*, to which we can hardly attach any practical use, though even
Cicero occupied himself in a similar version of the poet of astronomy.
But Ovid solicits his patronage for the most learned of his own works,
at a time when such applications were not merely compliments. *Fast.*
i. init. Comp. *Ex Pont.* iv. 8. 67.

[2] Suet. *l. c.*; Dion, lvi. 26.; Ovid, *Fast.* i. 21. :
"Quæ sit enim culti facundia sensimus oris,
Civica pro trepidis cum tulit arma reis."

[3] Tac. *Ann.* ii. 13. The occasion will be specified below.

His popularity with all classes, especially with the soldiers, was fully shared by his consort. The greatest praise they could bestow on a woman was to liken her to the Roman matrons of a hallowed antiquity, and to bless her for her love to her husband, and the fertility which they hailed as its surest token.[1]

The strong contrast which the character of Germanicus thus presented to that of his uncle *Jealousy of Tiberius.* might have given cause for jealousy and distrust even in a private family: between members of a ruling dynasty, the course and succession of which were established on known and long-respected principles, it would have led no doubt to estrangement and mutual dislike; but the misfortune of Tiberius and his nephew lay in the vagueness of the title by which the one enjoyed power, and the other might be expected to aspire to it. The claim of Julius Cæsar to reign over the Romans was emphatically that of the worthiest. He founded his usurpation on the virtual presumption that the republic required a chief, and he was himself the fittest to become such. It was the aim of Augustus, of which he never lost sight for a moment, to strengthen his human right as the heir of Julius by the divine right, to which he also pretended, of moral fitness. This human right, if I may so call it, of inheritance might be strengthened in the third descent; but Tiberius, painfully alive to his own deficiencies, and conscious of no personal claim to the reverence of his countrymen, felt that the divine right no longer pertained to him, and was constantly harassed by the apprehension that the Romans, still looking for the

---

[1] Agrippina bore her husband nine children, of whom three died in infancy, the others, three sons and as many daughters, survived their father, and will all find a place in these pages. Suet. *Calig.* 7. With regard to one who died in childhood, a pleasing trait is recorded of Augustus: "Insigni festivitate, cujus effigiem habitu Cupidinis in æde Capitolinæ Veneris Livia dedicavit, Augustus in cubiculo suo positam, quotiescunque introiret, exosculabatur."

worthiest to reign over them, would turn from him
to the younger scion of the worthiest of Roman
houses. Every despot is discontented at being outshone by the rising glories of his presumptive successor; but few have the excuse of the unfortunate
Tiberius, who felt that every laurel placed on the
brow of Germanicus constituted a claim, not to succeed
him on the throne, but to eject him from it. Other
usurpers have stepped at once within the circle of
admitted principles of descent. The subjects of a
Napoleon or a Cromwell were familiar with the idea
of dynastic sovereignty; but it was otherwise with
the children of the old Roman republic. The Cæsars
had every rule and principle of monarchy to create;
and it was not till they had established the rights of.
legitimacy, that the emperors could feel the personal
security, which was the best guarantee for their
temperate exercise of power. The mutiny of the
German legions revealed to Tiberius a secret of fatal
significance. The cries of the legionaries, *Cæsar
Germanicus will not endure to be a subject*, confirmed
the presentiment of his own self-disparaging conscience.[1]

After all, this distrust of his own abilities, which
were certainly considerable, was the great
and fatal defect in the character of the self-
tormentor. The state of pupilage in which
he had been held by Augustus may account perhaps
for this self-disparagement, and for the meanness
with which he ultimately threw himself on the support of a favourite far less able than himself. The
trifling results of his own last campaign in Germany
made him the more jealous of the plans now urged
by Germanicus for the entire subjugation of the insolent victors of Teutoburg. Yet it was more than
ever necessary to employ the discontented legions,

He determines to employ the discontented soldiers.

---

[1] Tac. *Ann.* i. 31.: " Magna spe fore ut Germanicus Cæsar imperium alterius pati nequiret."

who had placed themselves without reserve under their young Cæsar's orders, and to precipitate them headlong on the Elbe was the surest way of averting a march upon the Tiber. The soldiers themselves were burning for occupation : they were anxious to wash out in blood the stain of mutiny which ever left a dark and burning spot on the conscience of the Roman legionary.

During the crisis of these military outbreaks, the emperor's conduct was marked by consummate artifice and caution. He successfully evaded binding himself to any precise stipulation by which his supreme authority could be compromised, while he allowed his son and nephew to treat with the mutineers, and amuse them with specious hopes beyond their power to confirm.[1] His advisers at Rome urged him to go in person and quell the sedition by the majesty of his presence, as, until the latest periods of his reign, Augustus, on every great emergency, had quitted the city for the provinces. Always professing to be about to take some decided step, Tiberius continued to allege excuses for indecision and inactivity. He was aware that at Rome he was supported by the name and influence of the senate, which as a body was entirely devoted to the imperial government. In the camp, on the contrary, he knew not on whom he might depend, or how far the traditions of military allegiance still retained their potency. By remaining within the precincts of the city he could escape direct comparison with Drusus and Germanicus, from which he shrank with the instinct of self-distrust; and there he was under the protection of the armed force of

His artifice in dealing with them.

---

[1] The cry for a sixteen years' service seems to have been listened to, but Tiberius soon afterwards took occasion to disregard his concession, and fixed twenty years for the regular legionary term. Tac. *Ann.* i. 78.: " Ita proximæ seditionis male consulta . . . . abolita in posterum."

the capital, which at the moment of assuming power he had bound to his service by the most solemn formulas. Moreover, his own jealous nature suggested that to whichever of the two camps, the Pannonian or the German, he should repair, he might awaken the jealousy of the other. Finally he argued, it rather befitted the majesty of the imperial power to judge of the complaints of its subjects at a distance, than to wrangle with them on the spot. Nevertheless, to break the force of the petulant murmurs which assailed him, Tiberius pretended to have resolved to quit Rome for the frontiers, and caused preparations to be made for his anticipated departure. But first the winter season, and when that was past, the pressure of business at home, still furnished him with pleas for delay. His own ministers and intimates were long deceived as to his real intentions, the citizens still longer, and longest of all the provinces themselves.[1] Meanwhile he was anxious to court the good opinion of the senators by the general conduct of his administration at home. In matters of personal concern he rivalled and even exceeded the moderation of Augustus himself. He interposed with specious words to restrain the extravagant compliments showered on him by the nobles, and checked the servile impatience with which they pressed forward to swear obedience to his enactments, not only past but future. In the senate he suffered all men to discuss his measures with freedom, and propose motions of their own, on which he was often among the last to declare his sentiments. He was proud of the appellation of Prince, but would not endure to be addressed as Imperator or Dominus.[2] While he en-

Policy of Tiberius in the senate.

---

[1] Tac. *Ann.* i. 47.: "Ceterum, ut jam jamque iturus, legit comites, conquisivit impedimenta, adornavit naves : mox hiemem aut negotia varie causatus, primo prudentes, dein vulgum, diutissime provincias fefellit."   [2] Dion, lvii. 7, 8.

couraged the appointment of priests, rituals, and
games in honour of his deified predecessor, he vehemently repelled the preposterous adoration proffered
to himself by citizens or provincials. Yet the moderation of Tiberius was simply politic, and was
tinged by no ray of generosity or clemency. The
hapless Ovid he suffered still to languish in the
exile from which neither entreaties nor flatteries
availed to release him.[1] The lapse of fifteen years
had not softened his spite against his miserable
consort, who was now treated with even increased
rigour in her confinement at Rhegium, till she sank
under her sorrows and possibly under the most cruel
privations, in the first months of her husband's elevation.[2] Her paramour, Sempronius Gracchus, retained in an island off the coast of Africa during the
lifetime of Augustus, was slain by one of the earliest
mandates of his successor. The only trait of gentle-
ness the new ruler exhibited was in his behaviour to
his mother, whom he never ceased to regard with
respect and even with awe, allowing himself to be
guided or thwarted by her to the last, with the
docility of his childish years.[3] Nevertheless, though
he suffered Livia to assume great authority over
himself, he strictly forbade, as a Roman matron, her
taking any ostensible share in public affairs, and
curtailed the excessive honours the senate would
have lavished upon her.

But we must return from Rome to the frontiers
once more, with the historian Tacitus, and
follow the culminating star of the hero
Germanicus. No sooner had he quelled

*Germanicus
leads the le-
gions across the
Rhine.*

---

[1] The date of Ovid's death, "æt. 60," may range between April
770 and April 771.

[2] Tac. *Ann.* i. 53. The death of the elder Julia is placed by this
writer within the year 767, which embraced little more than three
months of the new principate. Yet he speaks of her death as the
result of the long and deliberate severities of the new emperor :
"Inopia ac tabe longa peremit, obscuram fore necem longinquitate
exilii ratus."   [3] Dion, lvii. 12.

the sedition in his camp, than the young Cæsar, postponing to a fitter moment the business of the census at Lugdunum, transported his impatient soldiers across the Rhine, and promised them an opportunity of effacing the stain of disaffection in the blood of the national enemies. The slaughter of Varus was yet unavenged, and the last incursion of Tiberius had failed to restore the authority of the empire on the right bank of the river. An attempt, indeed, had been made to define the frontier of a Transrhenane province between the Lippe and the Ruhr by the line of the Cæsian forest, and a supplemental rampart of wood and earth; but this work had been left incomplete, and Germanicus now cut his way through it without hesitation.[1] He was resolved to place the bulwarks of the Roman empire much farther to the east. Dividing his forces into four corps (wedges the Romans called them, and the name was well applied to the service in which they were employed, of breaking their way through every obstacle, and splitting to the heart the vast region before them), he swept a large extent of territory with fire and sword, and startled from their lairs the warriors of many formidable nations. The Marsi, whom he first reached, were taken unprepared, and made to suffer severely; the Bructeri, Tubantes, and Usipetes retreated before him, or evaded his onset, and wide as he spread his battalions he could not force them to join battle. Harassed on the flanks and rear, it was only by a great effort that he succeeded in shaking off the enemy whom he could not assail, and eventually bringing back his troops with no great loss to their winter quarters. This incur-

---

[1] Tac. *Ann.* i. 50.: "Propero agmine sylvam Cæsiam, limitemque a Tiberio cœptum, scindit." Of the Cæsian forest nothing is known except from this passage. It extended probably along the right bank of the Rhine between the streams mentioned in the text, and the lines commenced by Tiberius were a rampart of earth and palisades beyond it."

sion, it must be remembered, was made towards the
close of the year, when he could not expect to obtain
any considerable results. Tiberius, it is said, received the account of these proceedings with mixed
feelings. The suppression of the mutiny relieved
him from anxiety; but he was far from satisfied with
the sacrifice, as he deemed it, of dignity, and the
compromise of state principles by which it had been
achieved.[1] Nevertheless he consented to sanction
the pledges his son and nephew had given; and in
addressing the senate he enlarged on the merits of
Germanicus, while he affected to speak with modest
reserve on those of his own son Drusus. Nor did
he fail to crown the trifling exploits of this desultory
incursion with the honour of a triumph, the cele-
bration of which, however, was to be deferred till
the conclusion of the war, and the anticipated conquest of Germany.

In the following year, A. D. 768, Germanicus re-
commenced his operations at an earlier
season, and with more definite plans. He
had equipped a force of eight legions for
the field, with perhaps an equal number
of auxiliaries and irregular skirmishers; four of
these legions were directed to cross the Rhine from
the great camp at Vetera, under the command of
the able and experienced Cæcina, and penetrate into
the territory of the Cherusci; the other four were
led by the Cæsar himself into the district of the
Taunus, and were destined to keep in check the
Chatti, whose powerful confederation was ever ready
to harass the flank of a Roman armament in the
north, or even to seize the opportunity of invading

*Renewed ope-
rations of Ger-
manicus.
A. D. 15.
A. U. 768.*

---

[1] Tacitus adds (*Ann.* i. 52.) that he was mortified by the glory
Germanicus acquired. It is possible that the young general's popularity at Rome caused his success to be magnified or extolled beyond
its deserts. It was evidently far too slender to cause in itself any
reasonable ground of jealousy.

the Gaulish province. The resistance opposed by the Chatti in the field was easily overcome. The Romans destroyed their stronghold, known by the name of Mattium; and having thus crippled their means of annoyance, returned to the Rhine, to co-operate in another direction with the expedition of Cæcina. The short interval which had elapsed since the defeat of Varus had sufficed to divide the victorious Cherusci into hostile parties. Segestes, the favourer of the Romans, besieged by his son-in-law Arminius, solicited their relief. He could offer, in return for their assistance, many spoils of the Varian disaster; and was able to deliver to them many noble women, the wives or children of the chiefs of his nation. Among these was Thusnelda, his own daughter, the consort of Arminius, a woman of high spirit, and more attached to the cause of her husband than that of her parent. These important hostages were transferred to the other side of the Rhine. The wife of Arminius was sent to Ravenna in Italy, where the child she bore him was bred in the fashions of his captors, and lived, we are told, to experience some sport of adverse fortune, the particulars of which have failed to descend to us.[1] The division to whom this easy success had fallen was recalled once more to the Roman quarters, and Tiberius himself conferred on Germanicus the title of imperator.

Arminius and his faithful Cheruscans were exasperated at this treachery of their old chief, which seems indeed to have disgusted even those among them who would have laboured for a compromise between the hostile powers. The defection of Inguiomerus, a kinsman

Germanicus revisits the scene of the slaughter of Varus.

---

[1] Tacitus related it in his Annals; and it must have found a place in one of the lost portions of that work, probably in the great lacuna in the fifth book, which refers to the date U. C. 784.: "Educatus Ravennæ puer quo mox ludibrio conflictatus sit in tempore memorabo." *Ann.* i. 58.

of Arminius, but one who had leant hitherto to the
Roman side, convinced Germanicus that there was
no longer room for craft and diplomacy, but that
the whole of north Germany must be thoroughly
subdued by the sword, or finally abandoned. The
temporizing policy of Augustus, who hoped gradually to sap the spirit of liberty by the charm of
Roman caresses, must now be regarded as a failure;
insult and injury had exasperated the German chiefs
beyond hope of reconciliation; arms alone could
decide whether the empire should be extended to
the Elbe, or restrained henceforth within the barrier
of the Rhine. This was the result to which the
young Cæsar's impetuosity had brought affairs on
the frontier: it remained to be seen whether the
same ardent spirit could effect the conquest of the
people whom it had so thoroughly alienated. Towards the summer his plans were matured for a
simultaneous attack in three directions on the Cherusci, as the head of a general confederacy. Cæcina
was ordered to lead his force through the country
of the Bructeri to the Ems; a body of cavalry was
despatched by a more northerly route along the
borders of the Frisii to the same destination; while
Germanicus himself embarked with four legions, to
coast the shores of the continent, and enter the river
at its mouth. The three corps effected their junction
with that precision to which the Romans had now
attained by repeated experiments, having swept away
all resistance throughout the region between the
Lippe and the ocean, which their eagles had before
scarcely penetrated. Cæcina had overthrown the
Bructeri in an engagement of some magnitude, and
had recovered the eagle of the nineteenth legion.
The division of Germanicus ascended the waters of
the Ems, or skirted its banks, till it reached the
forest of Teutoburg, where it explored the vestiges
of the great disaster after the lapse of six years, and

traced with mournful interest the remains of the camps of Varus, which showed by their diminished size and unfinished defences the failing strength and decreasing numbers of the flying force at each successive nightfall. The soldiers collected the bones of their slaughtered countrymen, still lying, some in heaps together, others scattered at unequal distances, and paid them funeral rites, erecting over the remains a monumental barrow, of which the Cæsar himself placed the first sod.[1] Advancing further, their excited feelings were relieved by an opportunity for action. Arminius had availed himself of the recesses of his forests to conceal a portion of his forces, and the Romans were too eager for the onset to take due precautions against surprise. The presence of mind of Germanicus saved them from a severe disaster ; but though the victory remained at last undecided, it became prudent to withdraw from the field and retire to the stations already fortified on the Ems. From hence, on the approach of the winter season, they were led back to the frontier by the same routes by which they had advanced. Cæcina making his way through woods and marshes to the head of the causeway of Domitius was attacked by Arminius and reduced to perilous straits. Enclosed within his lines by overpowering numbers, he owed his deliverance to the rashness of the Germans, who once repulsed were easily thrown into confusion by a dexterous manœuvre. A great slaughter ensued among them, from which Arminius made his escape with some loss of honour. The Romans thus relieved continued their homeward march, and arrived in safety at Vetera, where the rumour of their surprise and destruction had already preceded them. The

Marginal note: Funeral honours paid to the remains of the slaughtered Romans.

---

[1] Tac. *Ann.* i. 61, 62.: "Cupido Cæsarem invadit solvendi suprema militibus ducique . . . . primum exstruendo tumulo cespitem Cæsar posuit."

residents of the left bank, in their alarm, would have broken their communications, and abandoned the fugitives to their fate, had not Agrippina shown herself worthy of her husband's and her father's courage. Placing herself at the head of the bridge, from which she refused to move, she awaited the return of the remnant of the rout; and as the long train of four unbroken legions defiled, with ensigns displayed, before her, she addressed them with the warmest acknowledgment of their deserts, her heart swelling with wifelike pride and emotion.[1]

The return of Germanicus himself was subjected to perils of another kind, and clouded with serious disasters. He had descended the Ems on board his vessels; but when he put out to sea, among the shallows of the Frisian coast, he found it necessary to lighten them. For this purpose he disembarked two legions, charging them to conduct their march homeward within sight of the ocean. Obeying these directions, however, too closely, a great number of the men were lost in the equinoctial tides, which overflowed the level shores, and swept away a large portion of their stores and baggage.[2] The main strength of the legions was at last collected once more in winter quarters; but to recruit them to their proper footing, and supply their full complement of horses and equipments, it was necessary to put under requisition, not the Rhenish provinces only, but the whole extent of Gaul, and even Spain and Italy. The collection of means of transport for such forces as the Roman generals moved year by year in these regions, over wide tracts of uncultivated heath or woodland, from which every vehicle and beast of burden was swept by the retreat-

Disaster of Germanicus on his return by sea.

---

[1] Tac. *Ann.* i. 69. The writer obtained this anecdote from the elder Pliny, who wrote an account of the German campaigns. Vetera Castra is the modern Xanten, nearly opposite to Wesel. Mannert. *Georgr.* iii. 431.   [2] Tac. *Ann.* i. 70.

ing natives, must have taxed to the utmost the resources of all the provinces of the West.   The more
we study the history of these expensive though fruitless campaigns, the more shall we admire the powers
of the Roman government, the effective organization
of every branch of its service, and the well-trained
energies of all its officers, from the imperator to the
centurion and primipile.[1]

It appears from this narrative that the success of
Germanicus in these forays had been dubious at best.   He had left no more solid
monument of his prowess than the mound
erected over the Varian remains; and this

Tiberius mur-
murs at the
slender results
of these cam-
paigns.

the natives indignantly levelled as soon as his back
was turned.   No fortress had been established to check
the enemy's return into the tracts from which he had
been for a moment dislodged; no roads had been
formed to assist the advance of a future expedition;
the savage mode of warfare which the invader had
as usual permitted himself in ravaging the country
with fire and sword, had made it not less untenable
by Roman settlers than by its native possessors.
Tiberius was far from satisfied with these results; and
while he suffered the citizens to regard the surrender
of Segestes and the capture of Thusnelda, the sole
trophies of the campaign, as substantial tokens of
success, for which not Germanicus only, but his lieutenants also, might deserve the triumphal insignia,
he was at heart deeply vexed with the real failure of
the year's exertions.   His ill-humour vented itself
in murmurs against his nephew's conduct, who had
damped, he said, the courage of the legionaries by
showing them the bloody traces of a Roman defeat;
he even pretended that, in performing funeral rites,
Germanicus had profaned the sanctity of his Augural

---

[1] Tac. *Ann.* 71.: "Ad supplenda exercitus damna certavere Galliæ,
Hispaniæ, Italia; quod cuique promptum, arma, equos, aurum,
offerentes."

office. He cavilled at the spirited movement of
Agrippina, in which, he insinuated, she had over-
stepped the duties of her sex, to ingratiate herself
with his legions. What would be left, he asked, for
the imperators themselves to do, if their wives could
venture to pass along the lines of the maniples, to
approach the standards, and offer with their own
hands largesses to the soldiers. He complained that
the mutinous spirit of the army had been conjured by
the intrigues of a woman, when the name of the chief
of the commonwealth had failed to coerce it.[1]

The assumption of so ungracious an attitude towards the defenders of the national interests,
in the midst of foreign foes and domestic
sedition, was at best impolitic; the Romans
regarded it, moreover, as unjust and base, and unworthy of the descendant of their magnanimous
Cæsars. They ascribed it, however, less to the jealous
temper of their ruler himself, than to the sinister
influence of a low-born favourite, impatient of a
rival's successes, who now prompted his master's apprehensions, and suggested the recall of Germanicus
that he might no longer spend the blood and treasure
of the empire in schemes for his own advancement,
from which the nation derived no benefit.[2] This fatal
adviser will be brought more formally on the stage
at a later period : it is enough to say of him now that
Tiberius listened with complacency to his questionable counsel. But the hesitation now becoming habitual with him in all public affairs still prevented
him from acting upon it; while the young Cæsar,
burning for martial fame, and equally unconscious,
perhaps, both of the suspicions raised against him,
and of the failure of his recent enterprise, was re-

The Romans
offended at
this jealousy.

---

[1] Tac. *Ann.* i. 69.: "Compressam a muliere seditionem, cui nomen
Principis obsistere non quiverit."

[2] Tac. *l. c.*: " Accendebat hæc onerabatque Sejanus."

doubling his preparations for another campaign, and dreaming of more conclusive successes.[1]

The failure of the last expedition was ascribed at the Roman quarters to no defect in the valour of the soldiers, or the skill of their chiefs, but simply to the natural difficulties of the route they had chosen, which lay further to the north, and was more embarrassed by swamps, forests, and broad rivers, than the regions with which the invaders acquainted themselves in their earlier operations.   It may be supposed, moreover, that the inhospitable wilderness was exhausted of its scanty resources.   Accordingly, Germanicus prepared a naval armament on a larger scale than before, which he collected in the island of the Rhine and Wahal, and directed through the channel of the lake Flevus to the ocean.[2]   Before embarking, however, he sent his legate C. Silius, to make a demonstration against the Chatti in the south, and led himself a force of six legions along the valley of the Lippe, to secure the roads and strongholds, and provide for the defence and supply of his armies on their return.[3]   This done he transported the main strength of his armaments in a thousand vessels, to the mouth of the Ems, thus saving them a great amount of time and fatigue.   Leaving his ships at their anchorage under sufficient protection, he then directed his march towards the south-east, so as to strike the bank of the Weser at a spot where the Germans had assembled a large force.   In the ranks of the invading army there was a brother of Arminius entrusted with a command, whose fidelity to the Romans was attested by the loss of an eye in their service, and by the surname of Flavius, which

Third campaign of Germanicus. A.D. 16. A.U. 769.

He confronts the German forces on the Weser.

---

[1] Tac. *Ann.* ii. 5.

[2] He descended into this lake by the Fossa Drusiana, the channel which Drusus cut, as before mentioned, from the Rhine to the Yssel.

[3] Tac. *Ann.* ii. 6.

he had adopted as the client of a Roman officer. Arminius, we are told, demanded a parley with the renegade across the stream which divided the hostile arrays; and when, according to the agreement, they were left to converse alone, began by inquiring the occasion of his wound. Flavius specified the place and the engagement. *And what*, demanded the other, *was your reward?—Increase of pay, a gold chain and chaplet, with other military distinctions,* was the reply. And when the German freeman retorted with a sneer on these *vile badges of servitude,* the Romanized Flavius continued unabashed to urge on him the obvious inducements to submission, such as the magnitude of the Roman power, the clemency of the emperor, the kindness with which his wife and child had been treated, and, on the other hand, the sure penalty of resistance. Arminius replied by appealing with fervour to the love of their country, the memory of their fathers, and the venerable names of their ancestral divinities: he contrasted with pride his own position, as the chief of his own people, with the subaltern rank of his recreant brother. From argument the debate was presently swayed to rebukes and mutual invectives, until, exasperated as they were, they would have plunged into the stream and decided their controversy in its waves had not the comrades of Flavius interfered and carried him away, leaving Arminius vainly defying with uplifted voice and hands the adversaries whom he could not reach.[1]

The next morning the Romans effected the passage of the Weser in the face of the enemy, not unwilling perhaps to give way, and draw them further into the heart of a thick jungle with a broad river in the rear. In the depths of a sacred forest the Germans had collected the forces of many nations, and were preparing to assail the

Germanicus explores the courage of his soldiers.

---

[1] Tac. *Ann.* ii. 9, 10.

invaders' camp by night. The imagination of our
eloquent historian Tacitus kindles with the approaching catastrophe of the great epic of the German wars,
and from the Homeric dialogue of his Flavius and
Arminius, he proceeds to charm us with the night
adventure of his hero Germanicus. Not trusting
entirely to the reports of his brave but sanguine
officers—and the spirit of flattery, he thought, might
sway the representations of his personal attendants
—the imperator resolved to explore, disguised, and
at night, the real temper of the soldiers, and ascertain how far he might rely on the courage which had
never yet been fairly confronted with the victors of
the Teutoburg. Wrapt in his Gaulish bearskin, and
attended by a single companion, he traversed the lanes
of the camp and leant over the tent-ropes. The
soldiers he found everywhere vying with one another
in the praise of their young general: one boasted of
his noble descent, another of his manly beauty; his
patience, his kindness, his serene temper were in the
mouths of all. To-morrow, they said, in the ranks,
they would prove their gratitude and affection: they
would sacrifice to vengeance and glory the faithless
foe who had violated the peace of Rome. At this
moment an emissary of Arminius riding to the foot
of the rampart, proclaimed aloud in the Latin tongue
his leader's promise of wives, lands, and a daily
largess to all who would abandon the Roman service
and take refuge in the ranks of freedom. The offer
was received with shouts of indignant scorn. *Let
but the day break*, exclaimed the legionaries, *let but
battle be joined, and we will seize each for himself
on wives and lands and plunder*. Germanicus
withdrew well pleased with the result of his experiment, which was succeeded by a dream of favourable
omen. The harangue he addressed next morning to
his men contains a vivid description of the disadvantage under which the barbarian laboured, from

the size and weight of his weapons, his want of defensive armour, his slow and unwieldy motions, his ignorance of discipline, and impatience both of toil and pain. Everything that made him most terrible at first sight was found, when examined, an encumbrance and a defect. Encouraged and confirmed in their hopes and expectations, the Romans prepared cheerfully for the combat.[1] On the other hand, Arminius and his associates were not less prompt and energetic. Each at the head of his own

Arminius encourages the Germans. people described the Roman army as the mere remnant of the Varian legions, the swiftest of foot, who had saved themselves once by flight from German vengeance: they were no other than the recreants of the Rhenish camps, who would rather rise against their own officers than rally in the face of the enemy. These, they said, were the slaves who had been reduced by stripes, the wretches who had skulked from pursuit of the brave Cherusci to the furthest shores of the ocean. Nor were the Germans suffered to forget how cruel and rapacious these ruffians had shown themselves in their moments of success: the freedom of the patriot warriors was the last possession left them; let them now defend it with their lives.[2]

The position of the Germans occupied the declivity of the hills which bounded the valley of the

Great battle and victory of the Romans. Weser, extending into the broad plain at their foot and resting on a wood in the rear, which, from the absence of undergrowth, presented no obstacle to a retreat.[3] The Romans, however, having crossed the stream at various points,

---

[1] Tac. *Ann.* ii. 12, 13.   [2] Tac. *Ann.* ii. 14.

[3] Tacitus calls the spot "Campus cui Idistaviso nomen." There is no clue for identifying it. See the article on the word in Smith's *Dictionary of Geography*, in which Grimm is said to have shown that the plain was probably called Idisiaviso, that is, *the maiden's meadow*, from idisi, a maiden, and wiese, a meadow.

contrived by skilful movements to outflank their opponents; and while the cavalry gained the wood behind them, the main strength of the legions engaged
their attention in the plain. The front line of the
Germans, drawn up at the foot of the hills, was driven
back and sought refuge in the wood at the same
moment that the bodies kept in reserve behind,
assailed by the Roman horse, were dislodged from its
shelter, and driven headlong towards the plain. The
Cherusci, the bravest and steadiest of the native forces,
had occupied the centre of the declivity; but neither
their resolute courage, nor the skill and vigour of
their leader Arminius, availed to sustain them against
the overwhelming pressure of the conflicting tides of
fugitives on either side. Thus thrown into confusion,
the rout of the Germans was rapid and complete.
Arminius and Inguiomerus still maintained the
unequal contest with conspicuous gallantry; but,
hemmed in between the advancing forces of the
Romans, their destruction seemed inevitable, and they
owed their lives, as was suspected, to the treachery
of some German auxiliaries, who suffered them to
burst through their ranks, disfigured and wounded.
Broken in front and rear the remnant of their host
took flight at every point where they could find an
opening: great numbers were slain in attempting to
cross the river before, many more fell in the wood
behind them, where they climbed the trees for safety,
but were transfixed with arrows, or crushed by the
felling of the trees themselves: over an area of ten
miles in width the ground was thickly strewn with
the bodies of the slain; and if the combat itself had
been soon decided, the pursuit and slaughter continued without intermission till nightfall. At the
close of the day the victors reared a great mound of
earth, which they surmounted with the arms of their
slaughtered enemies, and the chains found ready in
their camp for binding their captives. On the

summit they raised a stone pillar inscribed with the
names of the conquered tribes ; and, finally, the army
saluted the absent Tiberius with the title of Imperator, ascribing the fortune of the day, with redoubled loyalty, to his sacred auspices.[1]

Yet no sooner had they completed these memorials
Renewed en- of their triumph than the worsted foe ral-
gagement, and
final success of lied, it seems, for another contest. Doubt-
the Romans. less the victory had been far less complete
than the flatterers of the empire or the panegyrist of
Germanicus had represented it. The barbarians, we
are assured, were about to fly beyond the Elbe, and
relinquish their territories for ever, when the report
of the erection of this insulting monument roused
them from their panic and despair. Once more
flinging all timid counsels to the winds, they seized
a spot surrounded by woods and morasses, and defended by an old native earthwork, and there collecting in a mass formidable alike from its numbers
and resolution, defied the advance of the conqueror.
Here invasion reached its limits. Germanicus indeed led his legions steadily to the foot of the well-
manned lines. He made skilful dispositions for
attacking them. He forced the barrier, entered the
narrow area within which the Germans were thronged
densely together, with a swamp behind, and incapable
of retreat. The struggle was furious and bloody.
Everything was against the Germans; the closeness
of the combat, in which their long swords and even
their unwieldy frames were a disadvantage; the recollection of their late defeat; and the consciousness
that their last stronghold was stormed before their
faces. Even Arminius had lost his gallant spirit;
broken by repeated defeats or the wounds he had
sustained, he was less decided in his orders, and less
conspicuous in the medley. Never, on the other

[1] Tac. *Ann.* ii. 16—18.

hand, did Germanicus more strenuously exert himself.   He strove to carry with his own hand the
victory his dispositions had brought within his grasp.
Throwing his helmet from his head, that no Roman
might fail to recognise him, he adjured his soldiers,
in the midst of their ranks, to redouble blow on
blow, and give no quarter : this, he cried, was no day
for making captives, but for utterly destroying the
German nation.   Multitudes of the barbarians were
slain, while the invaders acknowledged but a trifling
loss.   Nevertheless the legions, we are told, were
recalled from the scene of slaughter to their camp
for the night, while we hear nothing of the rout or
retreat of the enemy.   It is admitted that the engagement of the cavalry in another quarter was
indecisive.   No song of triumph arose on the dispersion of the great German confederacy, at the
abandonment of their country, or their flight behind
the Elbe; there is no word of their suing for peace
or pardon.   If Germanicus erected yet another
trophy, and emblazoned it with a flaunting inscription, proclaiming that he had subdued all the nations between the Rhine and Elbe, the narrator of his
exploits himself confesses that the boast was vain
and presumptuous.   Of all the native tribes the
Angrivarii alone offered to capitulate; but their
humble submission appeased, it is said, the vengeance of the conqueror, and he consented to accept
it as a national acknowledgment of defeat.[1]

· Nor was it from any anxiety about his own return
that Germanicus acquiesced so easily in
this pretended pacification.   The second
month of summer saw his legions withdraw

Return of Ger-
manicus again
unprosperous.

from their advanced posts in the Cheruscian territory, and retire, some by land, but a large force on
board the numerous flotilla which had wafted them

---

[1] Tac. *Ann.* ii. 19—22.

to the mouth of the Ems.[1] The vessels were assailed
by severe gales, and once more suffered terribly from
the violence of the winds and waves, though the fears
of the timid mariners may have magnified the loss
and danger. These disasters, however, sufficed to
raise the Germans again in arms, so little had they
been dispirited by the dubious success of the recent
invasion. Germanicus, always prompt and active,
however questionable we may think his skill in conducting, or forethought in planning, his expeditions,
collected his troops without delay, and by a rapid
incursion into the lands of the Marsi and Chatti,
checked at least the contagion of their revolt. The
recovery of the last of the Varian eagles
shed a final gleam of glory over the enterprises of Rome in this quarter. Once more
the legions were led back to their winter stations.
The young Cæsar was assured that the enemy had
never felt such consternation and despair, as when
they found him prepared to take the field at the
moment when his fleet was lying broken on their
shores. Never were they so much disposed to entertain counsels of submission, as during the winter
that followed. One more campaign, he was convinced, would complete the conquest of the North.
But while meditating on his future triumphs, he was
admonished by many letters from Tiberius, that it
was time to abandon projects which had reaped in
fact nothing but recurring disappointments. It was
time, the emperor suggested, to change the policy
which had hitherto reigned in the Roman quarters,
and relinquishing the employment of military force,
which had been attended with grave losses both by
sea and land, trust to the surer and safer method of
engaging the enemy in domestic dissensions. Closely
as the German confederates had been bound together.

Recovery of the last of the Varian eagles.

---

[1] Tac. *Ann.* ii. 23.: " Adulta jam æstate : " thus explained by
Servius on Virg. *Ecl.* x. 74.; *Georg.* i. 43.

under the pressure of foreign aggression, seeds of disunion were still rife among them, and the policy of intrigue, ever patient and watchful, could hardly fail in the end to undermine the nationality of the barbarians. If further laurels, he added, were yet to be gained by arms, it was fair to leave the harvest to be gleaned by the stripling Drusus, for whose maiden sword no other foe but the Germans was left.[1]

The reasoning of Tiberius was specious, and the course he suggested required only vigilance and perseverance to be fully successful. But in laying down a line of traditional policy, which might demand the care of many years, and of more than one or two generations to effect it, he could pledge neither himself nor his successors to persist in it. In fact, the central government ceased from this time to take any warm interest in the subjugation of the Germans; and the dissensions of their states and princes, which peace was not slow in developing, attracted no Roman emissaries to the barbarian camps, and rarely led the legions beyond the frontier, which was now allowed to recede finally to the Rhine.[2] The conquests indeed of Germanicus had been wholly visionary: the language of Tacitus

The frontiers of the empire finally bounded by the Rhine.

---

[1] Tac. *Ann.* ii. 26. Suetonius (*Tib.* 52.) adds that Tiberius was generally reputed to have disparaged the *glorious successes* of Germanicus as prejudicial to the public interests. It is vexatious, however, to observe how little reliance we can place on the panegyric of Tacitus. His story of the last campaign bears strong features of romance. The interview of the German brothers is an heroic episode. It is not usual with ordinary mortals to converse across a stream a hundred yards in width. The night watch of Germanicus, though not in itself improbable, is suspiciously in unison with the epic colour of the general narrative : and the splendid victories ascribed to him are evidently belied by the results. The account of the shipwreck of the flotilla is a clang of turgid extravagances, amplified perhaps from the statement which Pliny may have founded, with little discrimination, upon the fears and fancies of the survivors.

[2] We shall trace at a later period some further advances of the empire between the upper Rhine and Danube.

is equally extravagant both in vaunting his triumphs, and in blazoning his disasters; and the almost total silence of Dion, a far more sober authority, on the exploits of the popular hero, stamps his campaigns with merited insignificance. Nevertheless there seems no reason to doubt that the discipline of the legions, and the conduct of their officers, even without the genius of a Sulla or a Cæsar at their head, must gradually have broken the resistance of the northern freemen, and that little more of toil and patience was wanting to make the Elbe the permanent frontier of their conquests. This accession of territory would have materially abridged the long line of the national defences, and the garrisons of the Elbe and Danube might have afforded each other mutual support in the peril of a barbarian invasion. It is not impossible that the result of one or two more campaigns at this critical moment might have delayed for a hundred years the eventual overthrow of the Roman Empire. It would be too much to say that the failure of such a result is to be regretted; nor can we venture to lament, for the sake of the Germans themselves, that they were not at this period reduced to subjection to a power of higher and finer organization than their own. But while the gallantry with which the Germans defended their savage homes must always excite our admiration, while we applaud their courage and self-devotion, and thrill at the echoes of their shouts of defiance and songs of triumph, it will be well to guard against an unreflecting sympathy with that misnamed liberty for which they so bravely contended. The liberty of the Germans was at best only the licence of a few chiefs and warriors, backed by a dark and a bloody superstition, in which the mass of the people, the bravest and least corrupted part of the nation had no genuine share.[1]

[1] Tacitus, in his curious but fanciful picture of Teutonic life and manners, would make it appear that the whole body of freemen were

Notwithstanding the false colours he has aimed at throwing over it, the picture of Teutonic freedom which Tacitus gives us is gloomy and revolting, with its solitary caves or wigwams in the forest, its sexes undistinguished in dress, its women, cared for indeed, but not for their charms or virtues, but as beasts of burden and implements of labour. That it was powerless to effect any progress, or to rise of itself to a higher sphere of civilization, appears from the continued barbarism of the four succeeding centuries, during which it roamed its forests unassailed by Rome, and constrained by no foreign pressure. The instincts of Order and Devotion, which distinguished the northern conquerors of Europe, lay undeveloped in the germ, till, in the course of Providence, they met the forms of Law and of Religion which they were destined so happily to impregnate. As with their own lusty youths, to whom the commerce of the sexes was forbidden till they had reached the fulness of manly vigour, the long celibate of German intelligence may seem designed by a superior Wisdom to crown it with inexhaustible fertility.[1]

The offer of the consulship, which the emperor now tendered to his nephew, was equivalent to a command to abandon the camp; and Germanicus was compelled, with sore reluctance, to relinquish his visions of immortal glory for the empty pageant of municipal honours. It was natural that he should see, in this sudden

Germanicus is recalled to Rome.

---

equal and independent: but this is contrary to all experience, and is opposed to the usage of client or retainership, which seems to have been common in Germany as well as in Gaul. The slaves of the Germans, as our author himself remarks (*German.* 25.), were not domestic, like the Roman, but attached to the soil; they were in fact not slaves, but serfs, and as such we may be assured that they bore arms in their lords' following. The German polity was probably no other than clanship, under which a system of the grossest tyranny is upheld by a perverted sentiment of honour.

[1] Tac. *German.* 20.: "Sera juvenum Venus, eoque inexhausta pubertas."

abridgment of his triumphs, not the prudence but the jealousy of his chief; and such unquestionably was the general view of the army, delighted with his liberality and condescension, and of the people, not unwilling to form the most unfavourable judgment on the acts of a ruler so destitute of the genial graces which captivate an unreflecting populace. Yet it cannot in fairness be imputed as a crime to the emperor, if he desired to break the connexion between his kinsman and the distant legions of the Rhine, which had already expressed their readiness to carry him to Rome and place him on the throne of the Cæsars. Germanicus, with the generosity and perhaps carelessness which belonged to his character, had given some ground of umbrage by offering largesses to the soldiers from his own resources, such as, under a monarchical regime, can only proceed safely from the monarch himself; and Tiberius merely followed the policy of his predecessor in allowing no more than two or three successive campaigns to the same leader, beneath the same eagles, and in the same quarter of the empire.

With the close of the year 769, Germanicus quitted the scene of his high-spirited efforts, being summoned to celebrate the triumph which was offered him in lieu of victory.[1] Of this flattering distinction, indeed, the emperor took to himself the lion's share. The triumphal arch, which was erected on the slope of the Capitoline, was designated by the name, not of Germanicus, but of Tiberius.[2] The recovery of the eagles of Varus, and

Triumph of Germanicus.

---

[1] Tac. *Ann.* ii. 41.: " Bellumque, quia conficere prohibitus erat, pro confecto habebatur."

[2] Tac. *l. c.:* " Fine anni arcus propter ædem Saturni ob recepta signa cum Varo amissa, ductu Germanici, auspiciis Tiberii . . . . dicatur." This arch of Tiberius, as it is called, but I know not on what precise authority, stood on the slope of the Clivus Capitolinus. Dezobry supposes that it was small and plain, from its having apparently been erected and dedicated in the course of one year Another

the overthrow of the Germans, were together blazoned on the medals which commemorated the solemnity.[1]   As the victor approached the city, the
populace, full of enthusiasm, poured forth from the
gates to the twentieth milestone to meet him, and
the ardour of the prætorians, the body-guards of the
emperor himself, was not less conspicuous than if
they had served under his colours or partaken of his
benefactions.[2]   The triumph was celebrated on the
26th of May; the Cherusci, the Chatti, the Angrivarii,
and the nations generally between the Rhine and
Elbe, were specified as the vanquished enemy.[3]
Captives were forthcoming, of noble birth and distinction among their people, to adorn the ceremony;
and it was without remorse, without even compassion,
that the Romans beheld Thusnelda, the betrayed wife
of Arminius, led before them, with the infant child
whom she had borne in servitude and sorrow.[4]   The
spoils of war were also exhibited, and the mountains
and rivers of Germany, together with the battles
themselves, were represented in pictures or emblem-
atically designated.   But the citizens gazed at
none of these shows so intently as at the figure of
the young imperator himself, conspicuous for the
manly graces of his person, and surrounded in his
chariot by the five male descendants of his fruitful
union with Agrippina.   Surely there was no room,
behind so well-plenished an equipage, for the slave
who attended the happiest of heroes in the crisis of

arch of Tiberius was erected by the emperor Claudius near the
theatre of Pompeius. Suet. *Claud.* 11.

[1] See Eckhel, *Doctr. Numm.* vi. 209. : "Signis receptis devictis
Germanis."   Tiberius took the title of Germanicus (Dion, lvii. 8.),
but declined that of Pater Patriæ. Tac. *Ann.* i. 72.

[2] Suet. *Calig.* 4.

[3] Tac. *Ann.* ii. 41.: "C. Cæcilio, L. Pomponio, coss., Germanicus
Cæsar, A.D. vii. Kal. Junias, triumphavit de Cheruscis, Chattisque, et
Angrivariis."

[4] Strabo, vii. p. 291.: who gives the child the name of Thume-
licus.

his felicity, and whispered in his ear that he was
only mortal! Yet the spectators at least required
no such grisly memento. In the midst of their
brilliant jubilee they were smitten with a painful
misgiving: they remembered how their affection for
the father, Drusus, had been blighted by sudden disappointment; how Marcellus, the uncle, had been
snatched away in the glow of his youthful popularity:
brief and ill-starred, they murmured to themselves,
were the loves of the Roman people.[1]

---

[1] Tac. *Ann.* ii. 41.: "Breves et infaustos populi Romani amores."
The list of early bereavements of the same class might be enlarged
with the names of Caius and Lucius Cæsar, and even of Agrippa
Postumus: but I do not venture to step beyond the lines traced by
Tacitus, and attach to any of these the same painful reminiscences
he has specified in the case of the others.

CHAPTER XLIII.

Mission of Germanicus to the East, and of Drusus to Illyricum.— Retirement of Maroboduus, and death of Arminius.—Germanicus journeys through Greece and Asia Minor.—Intrigues of Piso and Plancina against him.—He settles the affairs of Armenia, and visits Egypt.—His sickness and death imputed to Piso.—Grief of the citizens.—Piso attempts to seize the government of Syria.— Is baffled and sent to Rome.—The friends of Germanicus accuse him before the senate.—His defence, suicide, and condemnation. —Tiberius free from suspicion of the murder of Germanicus.— Imposture of Clemens.—Intrigues of Libo Drusus.—Deterioration in the conduct of Tiberius.—Influence of Livia over him, and of Sejanus. (A. D. 17—20, A. U. 770—773.)

THE cloud which lowered on the countenance of the Roman people was dispelled by an act of opportune liberality. Tiberius now stepped forward in the name of his adopted son to bestow on the citizens a largess of three hundred sesterces a-piece, and they hailed with acclamations the announcement that the senate, at his desire, had chosen their favourite for the consulship of the ensuing year. It was considered as a special mark of honour that the emperor deigned to accept the same office in conjunction with him. But ere the period for his assuming it had arrived, a new duty had been found for him to discharge. The affairs of the East required to be set in order. The decease of Archelaus, the king of Cappadocia, who had lately died at Rome of distress and apprehension, under a charge preferred against him in the senate, had offered an opportunity for annexing that country to the empire, and its ample revenues had enabled Tiberius to reduce by one-half the tax of a hundredth on sales.[1] The organiza-

Mission of Germanicus to the East.

---

[1] Tac. *Ann.* ii. 42.: "Fructibus ejus levari posse centesimæ vectigal professus, ducentesimam in posterum statuit." But Cappadocia

tion of this new acquisition remained to be completed. At the same time the people of Commagene, and the still autonomous districts of Cilicia, were said to desire, on the recent death of their native princes, to be subjected to the direct dominion of the Romans, while the provincials of Judea and Syria, on their part, were exclaiming against the weight of the imperial burdens, and entreating to be partially relieved from them.[1] Nor was the peace which had reigned between Rome and Parthia since the interview of their chiefs on the Euphrates secure and satisfactory. After more than one court-revolution, Vonones, a son of the great Phraates, whom Augustus had retained as a hostage, perhaps at his father's desire, and had bred in Roman manners, had been called to the throne by the voice of his countrymen, and placed there with the consent of the imperial government. But his subjects soon manifested disgust at the foreign habits of their new ruler, and ventured to discard him. He took refuge, it appears, not among his old friends the Romans, but in the kindred land of Armenia, which not only offered him an asylum, but, in the actual vacancy of its own throne, accepted him precipitately as its sovereign. Hereupon Artabanus, chief of the neighbouring kingdom of Media, but himself of the royal race of the Arsacidæ, whom the Parthians had invited to rule over them, required the Armenians to surrender the fugitive; but Silanus, the proconsul of Syria, was instructed to anticipate this result, and had succeeded in getting possession of his person by artifice, to be kept in custody within the Roman frontiers, and employed on some future occasion. The Parthians were indignant at the loss of their victim, the Armenians mortified at the in-

---

was proverbially a poor country: "Mancipiis locuples eget æris Cappadocum rex:" perhaps some treasures were found accumulated in the royal strongholds.

[1] Tac. *l. c.*: "Provinciæ Syria atque Judæa, fessæ oneribns, diminutionem tributi orabant." For the annexation of Judea on the banishment of Archelaus, see vol. iv. chap. xxxvii.

sult to the object of their choice; but Silanus was
directed to amuse and negotiate with both powers,
and avoid an open rupture by all the arts of diplomacy.[1]   Tiberius might hope that the mission of a
chief of higher name and authority, attended by an
imposing force, and surrounded with the pomp of
imperial dignity, would awe, as on former occasions,
the murmurs of his rivals into silence.   Resolved not
himself to abandon the helm of government, and
deeming his own son Drusus too inexperienced for
the arduous office, he made choice of Germanicus to
represent the majesty of the empire in the East.
For this purpose he placed him in the same position
as Agrippa had held under Augustus, and required
the senate to confirm by a decree his appointment to
an extraordinary command over the provinces beyond
the Hellespont, with full powers for making war or
peace, for annexing provinces, enfranchising cities,
and modifying their burdens.   Tiberius would allow
no delay.   The young Cæsar was directed to cross
the sea the same autumn, and the consulship, which
he had been summoned from Germany to hold, he
was permitted to retain in Asia.[2]

In the course of the same year Drusus was sent
into Illyricum, with directions to watch
the movements of the Germans on their *Drusus at the same time sent to Illyricum.*
southern frontier.[3]   Of the two princes
Drusus was supposed to be the emperor's favourite,
and such, as his own child in blood and the child of
his cherished Vipsania, he might naturally be.   But
the citizens cast themselves on the opposite side,
and showered all their affection on Germanicus,
whose character was made to shine in popular nar-
ratives in contrast with that of his less fortunate
cousin.   A reason for this preference they dis-

---

[1] For the affairs of Parthia and Armenia in detail, see Tac. *Ann.*
ii. 1—4.

[2] Tac. *Ann.* ii. 43.   [3] Tac. *Ann.* ii 44.

covered in the fact of his higher maternal descent;
for Germanicus was the son of an Antonia; while the
mother of Drusus was a Vipsania only, and his grandsire, Pomponius Atticus, the friend of Cicero, was a
simple knight.[1] But the cousins, or brothers as they
were legally styled, were unconscious of these jealousies, or at least unaffected by them. Whatever
dissimilarity there might be in their tempers, they
lived in perfect amity. Tiberius was anxious that
Drusus should emulate the elder prince in the career
of public toils and honours. He was glad to remove
him from the dissipations of the capital; he was de-
sirous also of completing his military training; it was
surmised by some that he felt more secure in his own
elevation above the laws when each of his children
stood at the head of one of the chief armies of the
republic. But the state of affairs on the Danubian
frontier undoubtedly required the presence of a commander on whose loyalty and zeal the emperor could
fully rely, and the mission both of Germanicus and
Drusus seems to have been dictated by a legitimate
policy.

The withdrawal of the Roman forces from the soil
of Germany had restored peace to its northern districts; but no sooner were Arminius
and his Cheruscans relieved from their an-
nual aggressions, than they turned their
arms on their own brethren, the Suevi in the south.
The kingdom of Maroboduus, which he professed to
rule after the fashion he had learnt in the city of the
universal conquerors, gave umbrage to the national
spirit of the yet untamed barbarians. Even among
his own subjects there were many who viewed his
innovations with disgust. On the first onset of the
Cherusci, the Semnones and Langobardi, who were
numbered among the Suevic tribes went over to

War between the Marco-manni and the Cherusci.
A.D. 17—19.
A.C. 770—772.

[1] Tac. *Ann.* ii. 43.

them; and this defection was but partially balanced
by the caprice of Inguiomerus, the bravest of the
northern patriots, who, with a band of clients and
retainers, attached himself to the service of Maroboduus.   Nor indeed had the Cherusci been so long
confronted with the Roman legions without acquir-
ing some knowledge of their tactics.   When the two
native armies met in the field they were found to be
armed and marshalled alike, after the fashion of the
masters of the art of war.   Each of the rivals could
vaunt that they had learnt to baffle the terrible Romans with their own weapons : the Cherusci could
point to the spoils they had wrested from Varus ; the
Marcomanni boasted that they had kept Tiberius himself at bay and sent him back unlaurelled across the
Danube.   The battle which now ensued between them
resulted in the defeat of Maroboduus ; and upon this,
many of the tribes he had enlisted under his standards passed over to the other side : when he could no
longer make head against the triumphant Arminius,
he prostrated himself before the emperor and implored his succour.   Tiberius replied that he had no
right to look for assistance from the power from
which he had himself withheld aid in its contest with
the Cherusci : nevertheless the Romans were magnanimous as well as powerful, and would not refuse
to interfere to save their new client from destruction.
It was under these circumstances that Drusus was
despatched to the Danube, with directions ostensibly
to negotiate terms for Maroboduus : but he received,
it would seem, more private instructions, to raise fresh
enemies against him, and secretly effect his ruin from
another quarter.[1]   Shielded from the violence of Arminius, the king of the Marcomanni was overthrown
by the intrigues of Catualda, a chief of the Gothones,
who had suffered some injury at his hands.   Driven

[1] Tac. *Ann.* ii. 44—46.

across the Danube, he addressed a letter to Tiberius,
in which he solicited an asylum in the Roman territories, and his request was coldly
granted. Retained in honourable confinement at Ravenna, he was constantly amused
with the hope of being restored to power by the Roman armies: but the expected moment never came,
and after lingering in suspense and disappointment
through a period of eighteen years, he died at last an
object of scarcely merited contempt to the few who
yet remembered that he had been a king and the
founder of a kingdom.[1]

Maroboduus seeks shelter within the Roman dominions.

The success of the artifices of Tiberius against
German liberty was further exemplified in
the offer he is said to have received at
this period from a chief of the Chatti, to
effect the removal of Arminius privily. The barbarian demanded to be furnished with some subtle
poison, such as the Romans were but too skilful in
preparing. This nefarious proposal was recited to
the senators by the emperor's command, that they
might hear his generous reply to it. Their fathers,
he reminded them, had forbidden the employment
of poison against Pyrrhus, for the Romans were wont
to avenge themselves on their enemies, not by secret
machinations, but openly and with arms.[2] But the
empire, in fact, had no more now to fear, from the
influence of its ancient antagonist; for Arminius,
the bulwark of German independence, degenerated
in the hour of his triumph from the virtues of a
patriot chief, and himself affected the tyranny over
his countrymen which he had baffled in Germanicus,
and rebuked in Maroboduus. His people retorted
upon him the lessons of freedom with which he had

Death of Arminius. A.D. 21. A.U. 774.

---

[1] Tac. *Ann.* ii. 63.

[2] Tac. *Ann.* ii. 88.   See, for the generosity of Fabricius, Plutarch
in Pyrrh. 12.; Cic. *de Off.* iii. 22.; Val. *Max.* vi. 5. 1., and other
writers.

inspired them, and after a struggle of some length and many vicissitudes, he was slain by domestic treachery.   The liberator of Germany had achieved victory over the Romans, not in their youth and weakness, like Pontius or Porsena, but at the period of their highest power and most varied resources.   His life was extended through thirty-seven years only, during twelve of which he had enjoyed the chief place among his countrymen: his name, though its reputation was clouded at its close, continued long to be chanted in their households as the watchword of liberty and glory: but to the Greeks, whose view was limited to the world of Hellas, the fame of the German hero remained unknown; and even the Romans disregarded it in comparison with more ancient celebrities, till Tacitus rescued it from obscurity, and poured on it the full flood of his immortal eloquence.[1]

The operations which occurred at the same period on the southern frontier of the empire were of little political importance.   While the African provinces were numbered among *Career of Tacfarinas in Africa.* the most opulent of the Roman possessions, they were, from the character of the country, generally exempt from the barbarian warfare, by which so many other districts were harassed or alarmed.   The skirts of the long chain of the Atlas, indeed, always harboured tribes of unsubdued and predatory barbarians; but the strength of the African hordes was so feeble, their means and resources so limited, that their warfare was rather that of banditti than of hostile nations.   Only when marshalled by a chief of Roman origin or training could they become formidable either from

---

[1] Tac. *Ann. l. c.* If the twelve years of his authority are counted from the defeat of Varus (762), his death would take place in 774. Tacitus does not mark the date very distinctly. Dion only once mentions the name of Arminius, in connexion with Varus, and never alludes to him again.

their skill in fight or their powers of combination.
Thus in the wars of the first Cæsar, a knight named
Sittius had placed himself at the head of a disciplined
force, with which he had seemed for a moment to
hold the balance between the contending factions of
Rome itself. We now read of the exploits of a native
warrior named Tacfarinas, who turned the science
he had acquired in the Roman camp, as a captain of
Numidian auxiliaries, into an instrument of arrogance
and insult to the majesty of the empire.[1]   Having
deserted the service of the proconsul, he had gathered
round him the bands of roving robbers who infested
the mountains, and had divided them into troops
and companies.   Accepted as their chief by a tribe
called the Musulani, he had associated with them
the Moorish warriors on their borders, who owned
the sway of a leader named Mazippa: while the one
body, armed and trained after the manner of the
legions, formed the main strength of these confederate forces, the other, following the fashion of the
country, skirmished actively on its flanks, and carried fire and sword within sight of the Roman cantonments.   Disaffection was spreading among the
subject nations of the province itself, when the proconsul Furius Camillus advanced with the forces
under his command to repress it by a decisive blow.
The defence of the peaceful province had been entrusted to a single legion with its auxiliary cohorts,
and this little army well handled was sufficient to
overcome all resistance in the field.   Tacfarinas,
confident in the tactics he had learnt from his late
masters, ventured to give battle, and suffered a
speedy defeat.   The proconsul claimed the honours
of a conqueror; and Tiberius, it was surmised, was
the more willing to grant them on account of the
obscurity of his name, which, high as it once stood

---

[1] Tac. *Ann.* ii. 52.

in the fasti of the republic, had been illustrated by
no distinctions since the almost forgotten days of
the Gaulish invasion.[1] Camillus himself had had
no previous experience in arms; nor was he now
elated with success, or tempted, as the chastiser of a
horde of savages, to believe himself a mighty general.
He was not indeed aware of the fact, soon proved by
the event, that his success was illusory and indecisive.

Germanicus, after passing but a few months in
Rome, had departed by Ancona and the
Dalmatian coast, where he had had an interview with Drusus, to assume his ample
powers in the East. By the first day of
the new year, the commencement of his consulship.
he had arrived at Nicopolis, the city founded by
Augustus on the shores of the Ambracian Gulf. The
descendant in blood of Antonius, and in law of Octavius, might behold with mingled feelings the scene
of a battle so fortunate, and at the same time so
fatal, to his race.[2] From thence he shaped his course
through Athens, where he recommended himself to
the citizens by his studied moderation, in dismissing
all his lictors but one ; and received in return the
highest compliments the Athenians could confer,
which consisted, it would seem, in a studied panegyric on their own greatness.[3] From Athens he
crossed to Euboea, and thence to Lesbos, in the usual
track of the Roman proconsuls. From Lesbos, however, he took a wider sweep, visiting the Propontis
and the cities on both its shores, and entering the
Euxine Sea, partly to gratify his interest in scenes

(margin note: Tiberius III., Germanicus II., consuls. A. D. 18. A. U. 771.)

[1] Tac. *l. c.*: " Nam post reciperatorem Urbis, filiumque ejus Ca-
millum, penes alias familias imperatoria laus fuerat."
[2] Tac. *Ann.* ii. 53.: " Sacratas ab Augusto manubias (the beaks
suspended in the temple of Apollo) castraque Antonii, cum recorda-
tione majorum suorum adiit."
[3] Tac. *l. c.*: " Excepere Graeci quaesitissimis honoribus, vetera
suorum facta dictaque praeferentes, quo plus dignationis adulatio
haberet."

of historic celebrity, partly to console and encourage
by his presence the places which had suffered most
severely from the vicissitudes of war and the oppression of unjust rulers.[1]   Only the year before no less
than twelve cities of the interior had been overthrown
or damaged by a destructive earthquake: but steps
had been already taken through a special commission
of inquiry, and by the prompt remission of several
years' tribute, to repair the effects of this extraordinary visitation.[2]   Germanicus does not seem to have
made it part of his business to visit the sufferers.
His travels were prompted perhaps chiefly by curiosity of a character more or less enlightened.   Thus,
for instance, he steered for the coast of Samothracia,
in order to be admitted to the mysterious rites of
the Cabiric priesthood, but could not reach it from
adverse winds.   He landed, however, on the shore
of Ilium, again skirted the coast of Asia, and consulted the oracle of Apollo at Claros, where the priest
who revealed the answer of the divinity is said to
have given him an intimation of the early death
which awaited him.

The interests which Germanicus thus appears to
Piso Cnæus
Calpurnius
appointed pro-
consul of Syria. have indulged were scarcely worthy, perhaps, of the prince to whom public affairs
of so much importance were entrusted, at a
moment when every step he took was watched, as
he must have known, with jealous scrutiny, not only
by the emperor, but by at least one powerful rival
among the nobles.[3]   It is possible, indeed, that the

---

[1] Tac. *Ann.* ii. 54.

[2] Tac. *Ann.* ii. 47.: "Eodem anno (770) duodecim celebres Asiæ
urbes conlapsæ nocturno motu terræ . . . . mittique ex Senatu
placuit qui præsentia spectaret refoveretque."   A prætorian senator
was sent to obviate any jealousy on the part of the consular governor
of the province.   It is just possible that this might be the reason why
Germanicus omitted to visit the injured cities.

[3] Tacitus notices the antiquarian spirit of the Greeks rather contemptuously. *Hist.* ii. 4.: "Spectata opulentia donisque regum, quæ- .

innocent character of a traveller and a sightseer was purposely adopted to disarm suspicion : but in fact a wiser man than the young Cæsar would have felt that he was more concerned to guard by vigorous and decisive movements against the intrigues of a fellow-subject than the distrust of their ruler. On appointing Germanicus to the command in the Eastern provinces, Tiberius had taken the precaution, so his conduct was interpreted, of removing from the government of Syria the prince's friend and adherent Silanus, and placing there a man whose pride and personal pretensions might be used as an instrument for controlling his ambition.[1] Cnæus Piso, on whom this appointment was con-ferred, was a member of the Calpurnian gens, which claimed as high an antiquity as any of. the oldest families of Rome, and at least in the last century of the republic, had repeatedly filled the highest magistracies. The surname of Piso was common to more than one branch of this noble house, and the prænomen Cnæus had descended to the personage now before us from a father who had fought through the wars of Cæsar and Pompeius, had shared the disasters of Cassius and Brutus, and though pardoned by Octavius, had

Pride of the Calpurnian gens, and antagonism to the Cæsarean family.

que alia lætum antiquitatibus Græcorum genus incertæ vetustati affigit." But the Roman nobles showed their Hellenic culture by affecting a similar taste; thus Cæsar, the Cæsar at least of Lucan, spent a day in visiting the plain of Troy, under the guidance of a native cicerone: " Herceas, *monstrator* ait, non respicis aras? "· *Phars.* ix. 979. Comp. viii. 851.: " Nam quis ad exustam Cancro torrente Syenen Ibit, et imbrifera siccas sub Pleiade Thebas, Spectator Nili? " and the whole spirit of the description of the Nile in the tenth book. See also the address to Celer in Statius, *Sylv.* ii. 2. 197.:

" Te præside noscat
Unde paludosi fœcunda licentia Nili . . . .
Duc et ad Æmathios Manes ubi belliger urbis
Conditor Hyblæo perfusus nectare durat . . . . "

[1] Tac. *Ann.* ii. 43. The daughter of Silanus was betrothed to Nero, the eldest son of Germanicus, then a mere child. The marriage seems never to have taken place.

disdained to solicit employment under the new institutions.[1]   Only when spontaneously offered him by the emperor had he deigned to accept the consulship. Cnæus Piso, the son, was reputed a proud man among the proudest of circles, the magnates of the expiring free state and the rising empire ; a class whose intense self-assertion was inflamed by family names, family rites, family images and ensigns. The decline of their numbers after the slaughter of the Sullan wars had imparted still greater concentration to this feeling ; and claiming complete equality among themselves, they hesitated to acknowledge a superior even in the emperor himself. To an Æmilius or a Calpurnius, a Lepidus or a Piso, the son of an Octavius was still no more than a plebeian imperator, raised to power by a turbulent commonalty : a breath, they felt, had made him, and a breath, they fondly believed, might yet overthrow him. Whether as an emperor or a private senator, whatever might be his actual powers, his pretensions to legitimate right they haughtily despised and repudiated. They had marked, no doubt with peculiar jealousy, the alliance of the plebeian Octavius with one of their own houses, the Claudian, the nobility of which it was impossible to gainsay : but this served only to convert their disdain into jealousy, and impel them to a state of antagonism or rivalry, from which they had before held contemptuously aloof. When once invited to compare themselves with their ruler, it was easy to persuade them that each had individually a claim to empire, to the full as good as the man whom fortune had placed in the ascendant. Piso deemed himself the natural equal of Tiberius, or if he had

---

[1] Tac *Ann. l. c.*; comp. Smith's *Dict. of Class. Biography*, art. Piso, Nos. 22, 23.   There were also two Cnæus Pisos before the last-mentioned, one quæstor to Pompeius in the Piratic War, the other the associate of Catilina, murdered in Spain.   It is not clear from which of these the Pisos in the text descended.

any misgivings of his own, his consort Plancina, the daughter of Munatius Plancus, the chief who for a moment had trimmed the scales between the armed factions of the republic, was of a temper to dispel or overrule them.   This imperious woman had formed, moreover, an intimacy with the empress-mother, in whose plans for prolonging the tutelage of Tiberius she had probably borne a part.   She had learnt to despise the son in the cabinet of the mother.   Still more did the vainglorious pair look scornfully on the children of the man for whom they had so little respect himself.   Piso believed that he was appointed to the government of Syria in order to check the ambitious designs which it was so easy to impute to Germanicus, and Plancina may have been instructed by Livia to play the rival to Agrippina; for the people, at least, were easily persuaded that the imperial house was already a prey to domestic jealousies.   Conscious of their own preference for Germanicus, they were not less convinced of the partiality of Tiberius for Drusus, and they were persuaded that the fertility of Agrippina, the consort of the one, must be a source of mortification and dislike, when contrasted with the barrenness of Livilla, the wife of the other.[1]

The mission which Piso seems to have considered as covertly confided to him, that of thwarting his superior, and bringing his authority into contempt, he began to discharge with zeal, and even precipitate vehemence, from the moment he

Plancina, wife of Piso, a favourite of Livia.

Conduct of Piso in Syria.

[1] Tac. Ann. ii. 43. The name Livilla, the diminutive of Livia, was used frequently to distinguish the wife of Drusus from the empress mother.   Livilla was a daughter of the elder Drusus, and sister of Germanicus, married first to Caius Cæsar in very early youth, and, on his decease, to the son of Tiberius, her cousin.   She may have had one daughter Julia, afterwards united to Nero Drusus and Rubellius Blandus, in the first ten years of her second marriage; but it was not till 772 that she bore a son, one of twins, named Tiberius Gemellus.   See Ann. ii. 84.

quitted Italy. Following Germanicus to Athens, he
pretended to reflect on his unseemly derogation from
the majesty of the ruling people, in paying his tribute
of courteous admiration to the monuments of the
city of Minerva. The prince, though not uninformed
of this insolent behaviour, nevertheless treated his
subordinate with marked kindness: on one occasion
he even saved his life, by sending him assistance
when in danger from a storm at sea, and when his
death, if he had been overwhelmed in the waters,
might have been fairly ascribed to accident. From
Rhodes, where they met for the first time, Piso proceeded direct to the eastern provinces, while his chief
still lingered on his route ; and on reaching Syria and
the quarters of the legions, began without delay a
course of conduct which seems to point, not so much
to a studied hostility to Germanicus, as to a rash and
crude design of seizing supreme power for himself.
Not only did he adopt every method of corruption,
to make himself a party among the officers and
soldiers: he went so far as to dismiss both centurions
and tribunes of his own authority, and to remodel
the command of the troops to suit his own purposes.[1]
The men, debauched already by the general relaxation of discipline, seem to have been easily won over;
and even the provincials, unconscious, it would appear,

---

[1] The exact position of Piso towards Germanicus, which seems to
have allowed him considerable, but ill-defined authority, is marked
by the term *adjutor* applied to him by Tiberius at a later period, *Ann.*
iii. 12. It will be remembered that when the young Caius Cæsar
was sent by his grandfather Augustus to compose the affairs of the
East, a *rector* was provided him, to advise or even, inexperienced as
he was, to direct his public measures. His first *rector* was Quirinius
(*Ann.* iii. 48.), who, as A. Zumpt has shown in his *Comment. Epigraph.* ii., was probably proconsul of Syria at the time of his arrival.
The appointment of Piso seems to have been meant as an imitation of
the policy of Augustus. In the proconsul of Syria Germanicus received not a *rector*, but, as an older man, an *adjutor* only, whose
duties were less clearly defined; there is no reason to suppose that
Tiberius had any sinister view in giving him this honorary assistant.

of the true duties of a Roman imperator, applauded
his indecent indulgence, and entitled him the *Father
of the Legions.*[1]   In these artifices he was warmly
seconded by Plancina, who courted the soldiers by
appearing at their reviews and exercises, a practice
which the Romans pronounced unfeminine; and the
rumour was industriously spread that the conduct of
her husband, and her own constant abuse of Germanicus and Agrippina, were not displeasing to the
emperor himself.

Strange indeed it must appear, if these proceedings have been truly reported, and if, as *Germanicus
leaves it unno-*
we are assured, he was fully acquainted *ticed, and de-
votes himself*
with them, that Germanicus should have *to affairs.*
postponed their repression to any other object of
his mission whatever.   Such conduct could have no
other result, whatever the feeling which originally
prompted it, than military insubordination, and dis-
cord in camp and council; and it is difficult to conceive that the vicegerent of the emperor could have
any other duty so urgent as that of crushing the
first germs of civil commotion.   Germanicus, however, was advised otherwise.   The settlement of
the relations of the empire with Armenia was the
direct object of his mission, and to this he calmly
devoted his whole attention.   In order to give full
weight to the terms he was instructed to impose, he
marched in person within the Armenian frontiers at
the head of his forces.   Instead, however, of restor-
ing the fugitive Vonones, still retained in custody in
Syria, to the throne from which the jeal- *He crowns
Polemo with*
ousy of the Parthians had ejected him, he *the diadem of*
affected to consult the wishes now expressed *Armenia.*
by the capricious Armenians themselves, in appointing in his room a son of Polemo, king of Pontus,

---

[1] Tac. *Ann.* ii. 55.: "Ut sermone vulgi Parens Legionum ha-
beretur."   It is not clear perhaps whether the writer means by *vulgus*
the generality of the provincials, or the rank and file of the army
itself.

named Zeno, whose early training in their own customs gave him a nearer claim to their regard. In the royal city of Artaxata, and surrounded by the native nobility, the Roman Cæsar placed the diadem on his destined vassal's head, saluting him in the name of his new subjects with the title of Artaxias, signifying greatness or sovereignty. To the envoys of Artabanus, who professed an ardent wish to cultivate the friendship of Rome, and begged for their chief the honour of an interview on the Euphrates, he replied with the dignity which befitted his position, and the modesty, at the same time, which was peculiar to himself. He assented, moreover, to the request of the Parthians that he would at least remove Vonones further from the frontier, and assigned him a residence at Pompeiopolis, on the Cilician coast. Vonones, it seems, had been making interest with Piso and Plancina, and built on their influence his hopes of returning in triumph to Armenia or even to Parthia. It was surmised that the ease with which Germanicus yielded on this point to the desires of Artabanus was partly owing to the hostile relations subsisting between himself and the Syrian proconsul. Piso had offended him, as an imperator, beyond forgiveness in disobeying his commands respecting the movement of troops, and the meeting between them, which took place at their winter quarters at Cyrrhus, had been marked by coldness on the one side, and defiance hardly disguised on the other. Piso had taken on himself to check the customary adulation of an eastern prince, who had offered Germanicus a crown of gold, of much greater weight than that he tendered to his subordinate, rejecting the present to himself with pretended indignation, and exclaiming that the compliments addressed to his superior befitted the son, not of a Roman prince, but of a Parthian tyrant.[1]

[1] Tac. *Ann.* ii. 56—58.

The formal reduction of Commagene and Cappa- Germanicus
visits Egypt.
A.D. 19.
A.U. 772.
docia to the condition of provinces, com-
pleted the work of the year. In the following winter Germanicus made a tour in
Egypt, with the professed object of examining the
state of that province; but his ardour in the study
of antiquities was, it would appear, a more urgent
motive for his journey.[1] His behaviour to the natives there was as usual studiously moderate and
courteous: he not only appeared among them unat-
tended by soldiers, and in the peaceful garb of a
Greek philosopher, as Scipio had visited Sicily in
the heat of the Punic war, but opened the granaries
for the cheaper and more abundant supply of grain.
Tiberius is said to have addressed him with a gentle
reproof for a condescension which was deemed unworthy of his station; but the affairs of Egypt lay
beyond the sphere of his mission, and he was rebuked more pointedly for disregarding the rule
established by Augustus, that no senator nor even
a knight should enter Egypt at all, except with the
emperor's special permission. While, however, these
unfavourable remarks were yet unknown to Germanicus, he continued his progress, ascending the
Nile from Canopus, visiting the Pyramids and temples on its banks, and listening with awe and wonder
to the mysterious music which *breathed from the
face* of Memnon.[2] He consulted, moreover, the
oracle of the bull Apis, and received, it was said, an
ominous response.[3] Nor did he retrace his steps till
he had reached Elephantine and Syene, the furthest
limits of the empire.[4] The real objects of his mis-

---

[1] The motive which Suetonius alleges, to take measures for the
relief of an impending scarcity, is not mentioned by Tacitus, and
seems at least superfluous. Suet. *Tib.* 52.; Tac. *Ann.* ii. 59.

[2] Tac. *Ann.* ii. 60.

[3] Plin. *Hist. Nat.* viii. 71.

[4] Tac. ii. 61.: "Elephantinen ac Syenen, clanstra olim Romani
imperii; quod nunc (in the time of Trajan) rubrum ad mare pa-

sion to the East had been already accomplished, and
he might amuse his leisure with contemplating the
wonders of the land of mystery and fable; but the
notice which now reached him of the emperor's displeasure, hastened perhaps his departure from it.
The senate indeed, while it listened with silent deference to the murmurs of Tiberius, concurred in
voting an ovation to his nephew for his settlement
of the affairs of Armenia, and an ovation also to his
son for the capture of Maroboduus. The two princes
were invited to enter the city in solemn procession
together.[1] But Germanicus now shaped
his course from Egypt to Syria, where he
found that his regulations and appointments had been audaciously overruled by Piso.
The warmth to which he was at last excited by this
insolence seems to have determined the offender to
quit the province of his own accord. Piso had already made preparations for relinquishing his post,
when the feeble state of health into which the Cæsar
now fell induced him to defer his departure. Presently, however, the young prince seemed to revive,
and the provincials vied with one another
in courtly demonstrations, at which Piso
was so mortified as to break out into actual
violence against the astonished populace of Antioch.
Retiring, however, no further than Seleucia, he there
proposed to await the event of his chief's sickness,
which had again returned; while the attendants of

Germanicus returns to Syria.

His sickness imputed to poison admin- istered by Piso.

tescit;" meaning perhaps the Indian Ocean. Syene, the modern
Assouan, was supposed to lie under the Tropic of Cancer, a fact which
the ancients established from the direct rays of the sun being visible
there, as they affirmed, at the summer solstice at the bottom of a well.
This phenomenon, however, might be observed at any spot within a
quarter of a degree of the actual circle. Mannert. x. i. 322.; Malte-
brun, *Geogr.* i. 9. Its exact latitude, indeed, is 24° 5′ N., while
the tropical circle is 23° 28′, a difference of 37′. It is said, however,
that the inclination of the shadows is still not perceptible to the eye
there.

[1] Tac. *Ann.* ii 64.

Germanicus murmured their suspicions that he had administered poison to their patron. They pretended, moreover, that he had assailed his life with magical incantations, in proof of which they produced charms and amulets, with the remains of human bones, hidden under the floor of his apartment, and the name of Germanicus inscribed on leaden tablets buried amongst these implements of witchcraft. The Romans were fully persuaded of the pretended powers of sorcery, and they had ample experience perhaps of the actual effects of poison : yet it hardly occurred to them that the use of the one must be superfluous as an adjunct to the other. We may be allowed to think that in producing this secondary proof of Piso's criminality, they have weakened the credibility of the primary accusation.[1]

Meanwhile the messengers whom Piso sent to inquire after the prince's health were naturally regarded as spies, if not as assassins. Germanicus, it seems, was himself fully impressed with the idea that he was the victim of treachery, and he dictated from his bed a letter to the culprit, in which he formally renounced his insidious pretensions to friendship.[2] At the same time he commanded him to surrender the ensigns of authority, and, as some related, to quit the province, fearing to expose to his implacable hatred, on his own anticipated decease, the lives and fortunes of his defenceless family.[3] Whether commanded or only admonished, Piso sullenly submitted. He put himself on board a vessel, and sailed westward: nevertheless he continued to linger on his route, awaiting the moment of the prince's dissolution to return, and boldly seize again the proconsular power in Syria.

Death of Germanicus. A. D. 19. A. U. 772.

---

[1] Tac. *Ann.* ii. 69.; Dion, lvii. 18.
[2] Tac. *Ann.* ii. 70.: " Componit epistolas, queis amicitiam ei renuntiabat."
[3] Tac. *l. c.*: " Addunt plerique, jussum provincia decedere."

Germanicus grew rapidly worse. With his failing
breath he called his friends into his presence, and
adjured them to prosecute Piso and Plancina as the
real authors of his death, and charge the senate to
avenge his murder with a stern and righteous judgment.   Many brave and noble spirits were assembled
round his bed, devoted to the republic and the Cæsarean family, and this appeal to their affection was
not made in vain.   They promised to hold his last
wishes sacred ; nor did they fail in their promise.[1]
Finally the dying man turned to his faithful Agrippina, whose heart was ready to break with grief and
rage, and implored her to moderate her transports,
to check the fury of her indignation, and for the sake
of their children, so dear to both, abstain from any
show of pride which might give offence to personages
more powerful, as he said, than herself.   This covert
allusion was supposed to point at Tiberius himself ;
and the rumour was eagerly embraced by a licentious populace, that their favourite with his last
breath had warned his relict to beware the malice of
her natural guardian.[2]

The character of Germanicus, as I have already
intimated, is represented as one of the most
interesting of Roman history.   It is embel-
lished by the warmest and most graceful
touches of the greatest master of pathos among Roman writers, and invested with a gleam of mournful
splendour by the laments and acclamations of the
populace to whom he was endeared.   It is the more
difficult to form a just estimate of it, from the im-
possibility of distinguishing, in the pages of Tacitus,
the genuine statements of history from the gloss put
upon them by a sentimental admirer.   On the whole,
the impression we may most justly receive is, that
Germanicus was a man of warm and generous temper, but too soft, perhaps, and flexible in disposition

Reflections upon his character.

[1] Tac. *Ann.* ii. 71.   [2] Tac. *Ann.* ii. 72.

ever to have become a patriot or a hero. His condescension to the susceptibilities of the Athenians and
Alexandrians was rather puerile than statesmanlike.
It is a childish affectation in a ruler to pretend to be
an equal. The hard and self-controlling Tiberius
was right in reproving it. The emperor, the real
man of the world, trained in action and suffering,
knew better the painful requirements of the imperial
station. Nor, again, was the taste the young prince
exhibited for mere curiosities, and the excitement of
sight-seeing, quite worthy of his deep responsibilities.
His proceedings, indeed, are described by Tacitus in
the spirit of a dilettante, and some portion at least of
the frivolity which seems to attach to them may be
laid perhaps to the charge of the author rather than
of the actor himself. Such, nevertheless, under the
circumstances of the times, was not the stuff of which
the ruler of a hundred millions of men could auspi-
ciously be made. We shall meet, as we proceed, with
similar examples of well-disposed youths born in the
Roman purple, displaying in early life almost feminine graces of character, but degenerating under the
trials and burdens of maturer years into timid and
selfish tyrants. But it is futile perhaps and presumptuous to draw conclusions from such slight and
shadowy data as we possess : the remains of Germanicus have been embalmed in the fragrance of an
immortal history, and it seems a kind of desecration
to turn him in his tomb.

The decease of the illustrious Cæsar drew tears
from the provincials, and even from the
people of the neighbouring countries, while *Germanicus fondly com-*
allies and tributaries felt that they had lost *pared to Alexander the Great.*
in him a generous friend and protector.
Solemnized at a distance from the home of his race,
his funeral was not adorned with the images of his
ancestors, which occupied their niches along the walls
of the paternal mansion : but the place and circum-

stances of his death, cut off as he was by premature
disease far from his native soil, on the spot which
his virtues and genius had made his own, throw some
colour of excuse over the fond idea of a resemblance
between him and the great Alexander.[1] The character of the renowned Macedonian conqueror was indeed the type to which the Romans were constantly
turning. Pompeius had emulated it; even Crassus
had aspired to it; the flatterers of Octavius had confidently ascribed it to their patron. The claims of
Germanicus to such a comparison were slight indeed;
the only points of similitude that could be pleaded
for him were his youth and generosity, the first an
universal, the second a common attribute of early
manhood: yet such is the charm of these qualities
that they gained him more perhaps of his countrymen's admiration than if he had conquered a Mithridates, or avenged the defeat of Carrhæ. His body
was consumed in the forum at Antioch, after being
exposed to public view naked. Such as were already
Suspicions of   preoccupied with the conviction of his as-
poison.   sassination are said to have traced on it in-
dubitable marks of poison; while less prejudiced observers, it was admitted, perceived no indications to
justify the suspicion. The friends of Germanicus,
however, were intent on bringing the supposed culprits to justice. They seized a woman named Martina, a creature of Plancina, and one already obnoxious in popular estimation to the charge of a professed poisoner, and sent her to undergo examination
at Rome, while they concocted their formal accusations against both Piso and his wife. The lieutenants
of the deceased prince, and as many senators as were
present, took on themselves, in the absence of any
regular authority, to choose a proconsul for Syria, in
anticipation of the legitimate appointment of the em-

[1] Tac. *Ann.* ii. 73.

peror. It was important for their views against the
late proconsul to occupy the place he had so reluctantly vacated, and shut the doors of the province
against his unauthorized return. The imperium was
devolved, after some discussion among them and the
competition of more than one candidate, upon Cnæus
Sentius.[1] Agrippina herself made no longer stay in
Syria, but embarked with her children, and, bearing
the ashes of her husband, directed her course for
Rome.[2]

Piso meanwhile awaited the long-expected assurance of his enemy's removal at the island of Indecent exul-
Cos. His triumph was insolently avowed. tation of Piso.
He did not hesitate to offer vows and sacrifices on the
occasion; and his wife, it was remarked, chose that
moment for putting off the garb of mourning which
she had recently adopted for the death of a sister.[3]
Nor were there wanting among the adherents of the
disgraced proconsul advisers who counselled him to
return without delay to Syria, and claim the province
as his own. His dismissal, if such it really was, had
been irregular; it had been unauthorized either by
the emperor or the senate; the substitution of a successor might be represented as violent and indecent.
His son Marcus, however, would have dissuaded him
from so daring an act, so near akin to treason and
rebellion, and recommended rather his continuing on
his course to Rome, and seeking at the emperor's
hands restitution of the government of which he had
been, as was alleged, so arbitrarily deprived.[4] The
bolder advice prevailed. The more Tiberius actually
rejoiced in the death of the prince he so deeply dis-
trusted, the more, it was argued, would he, for appearance sake, steel himself against the appeal of that
prince's acknowledged enemy. At the same time the
pride of Piso revolted against the indignity of kneel-

---

[1] Tac. *Ann*. ii. 74.   [2] Tac. *Ann*. ii. 75.
[3] Tac. *l. c.*   [4] Tac. *Ann*. ii. 76.

ing even to the noblest of the Romans.   If terms were
to be made, he would make them sword in hand.
Without absolutely contemplating an armed insurrection against the imperial authority, he still rashly
fancied that his position would be more secure and
independent at the head of the Syrian legions, than
as a solitary suppliant at the door of the palace.   He

He claims the government of Syria. addressed a letter to the emperor, setting
forth his complaints against Germanicus,
and representing his claims to the government which had been abruptly taken from him.
Then summoning his guards and centurions, he retraced his steps towards Antioch.   Landing on the
coast, he intercepted some detachments which were
marching into Syria, while at the same time he required the petty chiefs of Cilicia to furnish him with
their stipendiary forces.[1]   The Mediterranean itself
was not wide enough to allow the foes of Agrippina
to pass her without meeting.[2]   An altercation ensued
between them, which nearly led to a desperate encounter ; but when Vibius Marcus, who conducted
the widow homeward, cited the assassin, as he freely
styled him, to purge himself at Rome, Piso abstained
from a hostile defiance, and replied that he would
not fail to appear at the legitimate summons of the
prætor.   At the outset of his daring enterprise his
courage seems to have already failed him.   His forces,
indeed, were altogether inadequate to the service
for which he had designed them, and his only hope

---

[1] Tac. *Ann.* ii. 78.   Cilicia Aspera, as has been shown by Zumpt
(*Comm. Epigr.* ii.), was annexed to the province of Syria after its
separation by Augustus from Cyprus, which was surrendered to the
senate.   Hence we infer that Quirinius, who gained the triumphal
ornaments for his victories over the Homonadenses, a Cilician tribe,
was actually governor of Syria.   Tac. *Ann.* iii. 48.   Accordingly the
bold act of Piso in arming the militia of this district was not an invasion of another governor's authority, but only the assertion of what
he pretended to be rightfully his own.

[2] Tac. *Ann.* ii. 79.

must have lain in the cowardice or want of faith of
the chiefs opposed to him.   But Sentius stood his
ground firmly.   He repelled Domitius, the officer
whom Piso had sent before him to secure a footing
in Syria ; and, when Piso himself took refuge in the
fortress of Celenderis in Cilicia, advanced with the
forces of the province against it, and sat down reso-
lutely to reduce it.   In vain did Piso try all the arts
of persuasion and corruption on both the men and
their leaders.   Baffled and reduced to despair he sued
for leave to remain unmolested in the place, on surrendering his arms, till the question of the Syrian
government should be decided by the emperor.   His
conditions were rejected, and no other indulgence
was accorded him than leave to quit his place of refuge, and take ship direct for Rome.[1]

Thus defeated in an adventure so questionable in
its character, Piso must have felt his posi- Sympathy of
tion, whether as a suppliant for the prince's the Romans
                                              for Ger-
favour or a claimant for his justice, far more manicus.
insecure than it had been before he rashly turned
back from Cos.   The temper of the citizens was inflamed violently against him.   In their breasts, at
least, there was no doubt of his guilt ; and the freedom with which, in the bitterness of their sorrow,
they coupled the names of Tiberius and Livia with
those of the detested Piso and Plancina was far more
likely to irritate the emperor against him than induce him to throw a shield over his misfortunes.   The
first news which arrived at Rome of the failing health
of Germanicus had excited popular suspicion against
his uncle : it was muttered that his reputed patriotism, and the desire ascribed to him to restore the republic, were the cause of the fatal hostility of the
head of his house.   On a premature announcement of
his death the whole city spontaneously assumed all

[1] Tac. Ann. ii. 79—81.

the outward marks of an appointed mourning; and
when again fresh arrivals from Syria proclaimed that
he was still living, the people passed to the opposite
extreme of frantic exultation, till the doors of the
temples were burst with the pressure of the crowd of
grateful worshippers.[1] But the fatal assurance of his
actual decease was not long delayed.   The usual
honours paid to the dead Cæsars were decreed him with more than usual genuine-
ness of feeling.   Triumphal arches were
erected to him, not in Rome only, but on the Rhine
and among the heights of the Amanus; and it was
recorded upon them that he had *died for the republic*.[2]   His statues were set up in various cities, and
sacrifices made before them ; finally his bust was
placed in the libraries and public galleries among the
masters of Roman eloquence.   The exhibition of this
feeling was directed personally to the hero : the rest
of the imperial house could claim no share in it.
When Livilla, the wife of Drusus, herself the sister of
the lamented prince, brought forth at this time a
twin-birth of sons, and Tiberius proudly boasted that
never before had such good fortune befallen a parent
so illustrious, the people took no part in his rejoic-
ings, but rather murmured at an event which seemed
to add weight and influence to a rival branch of the
Cæsarean family.[3]

*Demonstra-
tions of grief
on his death.*

The arrival of Agrippina and her mournful equipage, first at Brundisium, and presently in
the city, awoke the sorrows of the people
to a louder and if possible a more universal
explosion.   The funeral honours granted
by the emperor were not wanting in decent solemnity.
He ordered the magistrates of every district through

*Arrival of the
remains at
Rome.
A. D. 20.
A. U. 773*

---

[1] Suet. *Calig.* 5.; Tac. *Ann.* ii. 82.   [2] Tac. *Ann.* ii. 83.
[3] Tac. *Ann.* ii. 84.   Of these children one was Tiberius Gemellus,
whose name will appear again on these pages: the other seems to
have died in infancy.

which it passed to meet and attend it on its way; he
directed that tribunes and centurions should bear
the urn on their shoulders, and the altars of the Dii
Manes should smoke with propitiatory sacrifices.
Drusus, with the younger brother and children of
Germanicus, went forth as far as Tarracina to meet
it: the consuls, the senate, and a large concourse of
all ranks fell in with the procession as it drew nearer
to the city.[1] But one thing seemed still wanting to
complete these funeral honours. The emperor,
the chief of the house which had lost so *Funeral
honours paid*
distinguished a member, the chief of the *them by the*
state which mourned so cherished a hero, *people.*
was himself absent. Even within the city, and after
the dear remains had been consigned to the Cæsarean
mausoleum, Tiberius abstained from ap- *Reserved de-*
pearing in public, and letting his people *meanour of
Tiberius and*
behold him in the same garb of mourning *Livia.*
as themselves. Livia also maintained a similar reserve; nor less did Antonia herself, the mother of
the deceased. The suspicions already current against
Tiberius and the aged empress were confirmed by
this unaccountable coldness: it was rumoured that
they kept close within the palace lest the people
should discover that under the guise of sorrow their
eyes were really tearless; and Antonia, it was believed, was forbidden to attract attention to their
absence by showing herself to the citizens.[2] These
surmises were, perhaps, hardly fair. Tiberius may
have had no personal affection for his nephew: he
was probably jealous of him, and mortified at his
popularity: in the midst of the wailing citizens he,
at least, might have been no genuine mourner. Yet

[1] Other extraordinary signs of grief are recorded by Suetonius,
l. c. Even foreign princes laid aside their royal ornaments on the
day when this solemnity was reported to them; the king of the Parthians abstained from the state exercise of hunting.

[2] Tac. *Ann.* iii. 3.

it is difficult to suppose that one so long trained in
dissimulation would have found it hard to cast a decent cloud over his countenance, and a man so crafty
and politic as he is represented, would have affected
at least the feeling of the hour, however little he
may have really shared it.   The fact is, however,
that the breast of Tiberius was something very different from a mere calculating machine. He had strong
feelings, and even violent prejudices on certain points
of conduct.   He detested all outward expression of
sensibility from temper rather than policy.   The
lightness and frivolity of the Italian character, en-
feebled as it now was by moral and sensual indulgence, its vehement gesticulations, its ready laugh
or sigh, its varying smiles and tears, he despised
with cynical indignation. Self-sufficing himself, and
always self-controlled, he scorned the woe or the
pleasure which seeks relief or sympathy from any
outward demonstrations.   There was, moreover, a
dogged obstinacy about him which forbade him in
this case to yield to the wishes and expectations of
the people, just as on a former occasion he had held
out morosely against the reasonable inclinations of
Augustus.   He was in fact one of those very unami-
able men who subject their conduct to harsh inter-
pretations from mere perverseness of temper, and
the dislike and distrust they create in the breasts of
those around them.   In certain positions in life such
men are unavoidably thrust into crimes, and into
such we shall soon find Tiberius impelled without
the power of resistance.   But it is probable that at
this period at least he was much misconstrued, and
the time has not yet come to employ those sable
colours in which the brush of his delineator must
eventually be dipped.

The injustice, indeed, of the historians generally,
and even of a Tacitus or a Suetonius, could touch him
no further in his tomb; but it is not too much to say

that the injustice of the Romans of his own day went
far to confirm the vices, and exasperate the   Tiberius
hatred, they so impatiently proclaimed.   checks the flow
of popular
Such was the inconsistency of his char-   feeling.
acter that Tiberius was keenly alive to the popular
opinion which he allowed himself so wantonly to outrage. He had long felt soreness and resentment at
the distaste his countrymen had from an early period
evinced for him. Mortified at the disappointment
of his wish, if not his efforts, to conciliate them, not
the less was he piqued at the success of his predecessor in the same course, from whose artifices his own
pride revolted. The wound festered in silence and
concealment. Conscious of unpopularity himself, he
became jealous of every mark of popular favour towards others, and conceived by degrees a deadly fear
of the guileless multitude of dupes and drones around
him. Speaking of his position in relation to his
people, he is said to have used the expression *I hold
a wolf by the ears.*[1] The description was a totally
false one : it was the excuse of a coward to himself,
which he sought presently to justify by acts of spas-
modic ferocity ; but the populace, meanwhile, unconscious of its master's alarms, and alive only to his
infirmities, indulged in the luxury of woe with a
levity as frivolous as it proved eventually fatal. Not
content with maliciously comparing with this neglect
of Tiberius the warm feeling exhibited by Augustus
on the death of Drusus, his going forth two hundred
miles in the depth of winter to meet the bier, con-
veying it in person into the forum, and pronouncing
the funeral address from the rostra, they lavished all
their praises and acclamations on the widow of their
favourite, declaring her the true glory of Rome, the

---

[1] Suet. *Tib.* 25.: " Ut sæpe lupum se auribus tenere diceret." Donatus or Terence (*Phorm.* iii. 2. 21.) gives the Greek proverb: τῶν
ὠτῶν ἔχω τὸν λύκον οὔτ' ἔχειν οὔτ' ἀφεῖναι δύναμαι. Baumgarten
Crusius on Suet. *l. c.*

only genuine child of their late master, the last surviving specimen of ancient virtue.[1]   Their vows for
her safety were mingled with passionate adjurations
for the health and happiness of her offspring, and
their escape from the perils which surrounded them.
Tiberius chafed at these ebullitions of ill humour,
and was provoked to check them by an edict, in
which he gravely declared that many noble Romans
had died for the republic, but none had been be-
wailed with such an outburst of sensibility. It was
well, he said, that it should be so, well for himself
and for the people; but let some moderation be observed.   There was a certain dignity and reserve becoming a prince and an imperial people, which might
be disregarded by private persons and petty com-
monwealths.   Enough had been given to sorrow:
let them remember the example of the divine Julius
on the loss of his only daughter, of the divine Augustus on the death of his grandsons.   How often had
the Roman people borne with firmness the rout of
its legions, the slaughter of its generals, and the overthrow of its noblest families!   *Princes are mortal,
the state is eternal.   Let every one return to his
affairs: let every one,* he added,—for the season of
the Megalesian games was at hand,—*let every one
resume his amusements.*   And so the great tide of
life closed over the remains of Germanicus.[2]

While he was thus sowing the seeds of a long and
deep misunderstanding between himself and
his people, Tiberius was reflecting, with
gloomy misgivings, on the late proceedings
of Piso.   Though morbidly jealous of any encroachment on the paramount authority he claimed at home
and abroad, he was not the less fixed in his resolution not to obtrude it on general notice by a direct

*Piso refers his
cause to the
emperor.*

---

[1] Tac. *Ann.* iii. 4.: "Decus patriæ, solum Augusti sanguinem, uni-
cum antiquitatis specimen."
[2] Tac. *Ann.* iii. 6.

vindication. His aim was to throw on the senate the burden of defending the prerogatives it had, as he pretended, spontaneously conferred on him. Accordingly, while he watched the acts of the proconsul, scrutinized his motives, and strove to penetrate his designs, he was not less vigilant in observing the disposition of the nobles, and estimating the support they would tender to himself. Piso's daring attempt to recover a province from which he had been officially dismissed was an insult to the government: but would the senate regard it as an insult to itself? —did it identify the emperor's cause with its own? —might it not rather decline to interfere between the master and the instrument he had himself chosen, and lean, at least in inclination, to the side of a member of its own body, in opposition to the authority which rivalled and controlled it? Such considerations as these, which Piso himself fully understood, weighed forcibly on Tiberius, and made his measures appear uncertain and vacillating. The culprit relied on the boldness and decision of his attitude. When required by Sentius to refer his cause to the judgment of the emperor, he did not hesitate to accept the challenge. From the coast of Cilicia he had proceeded in the direction of Rome; nevertheless he did not care to betray by his haste any symptoms of anxiety. He travelled slowly from city to city, and instead of taking the direct route by Dyrrhachium and Brundisium, sent his son in advance with letters full of obsequious deference to the emperor, while he stepped himself aside into Dalmatia to obtain an interview with Drusus, who had returned there from attending the obsequies of Germanicus. Tiberius received the young man with courtesy and even favour. Drusus, on the other hand, whose demeanour was generally open even to bluntness, affected a reserve and caution, in which he had evidently been instructed by his father, but assured

Piso of his hope and trust that the rumours about the manner of the Cæsar's death would prove entirely groundless.[1]

The minds both of the citizens and the chiefs of the state being in a feverish state of excitement every step the culprit took became a matter of suspicion and misconstruction. If on landing at Ancona he fell in with a legion on its march to Rome, having been removed from Pannonia under orders for Africa, and accompanied it for some miles on its route, it was reported that he had unduly courted the favour of the officers and soldiers; if, again, he left it at Narnia, and betook himself to the easier transport of a vessel down the Tiber, it was suggested that his conscious guilt sought to avoid just suspicion, or that his treasonable plans were not yet fixed and mature. It was charged against him as a grave misdemeanour that he had allowed his bark to be fastened to the walls of the Cæsarean mausoleum on the margin of the Campus Martius. The pomp and even the affectation of cheerfulness with which he took his way into the city, attended by a retinue of clients, together with his wife Plancina, and a bevy of her female friends, gave umbrage to a populace bent on taking offence. They pointed with malicious spite, as their ancestors might have done two or three centuries before, to the mansion of the Pisos overhanging the forum, in proud defiance of the commons below, and resented, as tokens of guilty ambition, the laurels and flags with which it was decorated to receive its long absent master; nor less at the number of friends and courtiers, who repaired thither to salute him and partake of his hospitality.[2] The death of the poisoner Martina, which occurred suddenly on her passage to Rome, was regarded by many as a device of the accused himself, or was taken as an indication of collusion between him and his prosecutors.[3]

He reaches Rome.

[1] Tac. *Ann.* iii. 7, ᶜ.   [2] Tac. *Ann.* iii. 9.   [3] Tac. *Ann.* iii. 7.

Such being the temper of the public mind, and
so strong the appearances of Piso's double His accusers prepare their process against him.
guilt, there could be no lack of accusers to
spring up, and seize the occasion to make a
show of their eloquence, their zeal for law and justice,
their love for the Roman people and the family of
their ruler. It might rather be apprehended that the
ends of justice would be defeated by the precipitation
of intemperate assailants, or even by the false play
of pretended enemies.   Accordingly when Fulcinius
Trio, a young noble, ambitious of notoriety, came
forward, the day after Piso's arrival, to lodge an impeachment against him, the real friends of Germanicus, those to whom he had personally committed
the vindication of his cause, were alarmed for the
success of their maturer plans.   Two of these, Vitellius and Veranius, immediately entered the court,
and protested against Trio's right to prosecute at all,
declaring at the same time for themselves that they
were not come to declaim in behalf of Germanicus,
but to attest by their solemn evidence the fact of
Piso's criminality. These representations were judged
to have weight, and Trio was refused permission to
make his oration against the culprit, as regarded his
alleged misconduct in the East: he was indulged,
however, with an opportunity of uttering an harangue
on the early career of Piso, and of blackening his
character, to the extent of his ability, by a general
defamation. Such were the facilities the Roman procedure gave to the young and ambitious declaimer:
but attacks like these were mere empty displays of
rhetoric, and served no purpose but to amuse the idle
or gratify the malicious.   Meanwhile Piso's friends,
disregarding such frivolous demonstrations, and fixing
their attention on the real point of attack, were striv-
ing to secure the emperor himself as judge in the
case ; for the emperor's consular or tribunitian power
gave him formal jurisdiction in criminal trials, when-

ever he chose to exercise it.   Piso had every reason to shrink from an appeal to the people ; nor was he without grave apprehension of the bias of the senators against him.   His best chance of a favourable, or even of a fair hearing, lay before the tribunal of Tiberius himself, who had at least no partiality for Germanicus, and who, it was well known, was indisposed to parade himself as the author of strong measures against senators and nobles.   But Tiberius, on his part, shrank from the invidious position of a judge in a case so delicate.   Not directly refusing the onerous responsibility, he seated himself indeed on the bench with certain of his own intimates as his assessors ; but after listening for a time to the denunciations of the one party, and the obtestations of the other, he finally remitted the adjudication of the cause intact to the senate.[1]

Nothing now remained for the accused but to prepare his defence in the regular way.   He solicited the noblest and ablest men in the city to plead his cause.   L. Arruntius, Asinius Gallus, S. Pompeius, and others hardly less illustrious, refused on various pretences to defend him.   M. Lepidus, L. Piso, and Livineius Regulus, at length promised to stand by him ; and great was the admiration of the citizens at the confidence of the friends of Germanicus on the one hand, and the assurance of the culprit on the other ; while they anxiously asked one another what the conduct of Tiberius would be, and whether he would sternly repress all personal feeling, and leave free scope to the force of truth and the influence of eloquence and reason.[2]   The proceedings indeed were opened by the emperor in a speech of studied fairness and moderation.[3]   He represented that Piso had been a trusty officer of Augustus, and that he had himself, not

The trial of Piso before the senate.

The proceedings opened by a speech from Tiberius.

---

[1] Tac. *Ann* iii. 10.   [2] Tac. *Ann.* iii. 11.
[3] Tac. *Ann.* iii. 12.: " Die Senatus Cæsar orationem habuit meditato temperamento."

without the consent of the senate, attached him as a coadjutor to Germanicus.[1] Whether in that capacity he had exasperated his chief by contumacy and rivalry, whether he had betrayed satisfaction at his death, or even actually effected it, it was for the senate, he said, impartially to decide : if the former, he would himself resent it as a father, but he would not judicially punish it as a prince; if the latter, it would be the duty of the senators on their part to visit the murderer with a murderer's reward, and console the family of the deceased with the vengeance which the law prescribed. He recommended them to examine carefully the charges of seditious intrigues and irregular ambition; and whether the culprit had actually attempted to recover his province by arms, or his faults had been exaggerated by the malice of his accusers, whose over-zeal the emperor felt bound at the outset to stigmatize and repress.[2] *For what right had they*, he asked, *to expose the body to the public eye, and invite provincials and foreigners to examine the pretended tokens of poison which it was impossible to test, if after all the crime was still unproved and matter of judicial inquiry?* He went on to charge the judges not to allow his private sorrow, great as he assured them it was, to influence their decision; to exhort the accused to omit no topic suitable for his own defence, or, if necessary, for the inculpation of Germanicus himself; to encourage his advocates to exert their eloquence to the utmost in the cause of the unfortunate defendant; finally, he begged all parties to disregard any popular

[1] Tac. *l. c.*: " Adjutorem Germanico datum." For the force of this expression, see above.

[2] Tacitus says, " Armis repetita provincia;" that is, he claimed by force of arms possession of *his own* province. If he had occupied a post such as Celenderis in another province, and employed its native forces, there would have been no question of the gravity of his crime, and no excuse for neglecting to animadvert upon it. A. Zumpt, *Comment. Epigraph.* ii.

surmises that might be promulgated to his own personal discredit in the matter.

Thus encouraged, or possibly perplexed and frightened, the senators addressed themselves to the work before them. Two days were allowed to the managers of the prosecution for exhibiting their charges ; then after an interval of six days, three more were granted for the defence. Trio, who had thrust himself, as has been said, into the front, began with a long and desultory attack on the conduct of Piso when he formerly governed in Spain; an abuse of rhetoric only sanctioned by custom, but which could hardly produce even the petty result to which it was directed, of creating an unfavourable impression against the accused in the minds of his judges. An important part of the space allotted for the prosecution was wasted in this unprofitable skirmish. When, however, the genuine accusers stood forward with the decisive features of the case in hand, they found the tribunal, from whatever reason, so well disposed towards them, that they were not required to bring on every point the most conclusive evidence. Servæus, Veranius, and Vitellius followed one another in denouncing the culprit with equal fervour, and the last of the three with conspicuous eloquence, for his enmity to Germanicus, his intrigues with the soldiery, his attempts, only too successful, by poison and magic, against the life of his commander, and finally. his armed assault on the prerogatives of the republic. Had Piso not been first conquered as an enemy, argued Vitellius, he could not have been now prosecuted as a criminal. Then followed an interval for the judges to reflect, and for the accused to prepare his defence. On most points of attack neither refutation nor excuse was possible ; the political charges were too patent to be rebutted, too flagrant to be palliated. Here at least the replies of Piso were weak and vacillating. The charge of poison, however, he did not shrink

Speeches in accusation.

Piso defends himself.

from meeting with a stedfast denial ; and this, indeed, either from mismanagement on the part of the prosecution, or from the real absence of any reasonable grounds of proof, had completely broken down ; for it was founded not on any alleged connexion between Piso and the notorious Martina, nor on testimony extorted from his slaves, whom he freely tendered for examination on the rack, but on the monstrous and incredible story, that, at a banquet given by the prince, while reclining at his side, he had with his own hands communicated poison to the viands on the table.[1] The rumours of magical incantations were invented perhaps for the populace of Antioch and Rome : though repeated in the presence of the senators, we hear of no attempt either to substantiate or refute them. But the judges, some on one account, some on another, were implacable. Tiberius himself could not forgive the attempt upon the province, and the senators, for the most part, were obstinately convinced that the prince had met his death by unfair contrivance. There prevailed, however, among them a vague suspicion that there had been collusion of some sort between Piso and the emperor himself. It is possible that some of the judges or the accusers ventured to suggest that Piso's instructions should be produced, and that this was refused both by the one and the other.[2] Meanwhile the people had satisfied

---

[1] Slaves could not be questioned by torture against their own master, except, under the emperors, in cases of treason ; but he might offer them to be tortured as witnesses in his favour. Rein, *Criminal-Recht der Römer*, p. 542. Pliny mentions (*Hist. Nat.* xi. 71.) that Vitellius in his speech, still extant in the writer's day, argued that poison had been administered, from the fact he asserted that the heart of Germanicus would not burn. (Comp. Suet. *Calig.* 1.) The same, however, was believed to occur in the case of the morbus cardiacus (heartburn or cardialgia : v. Hardouin's note) ; and Piso pleaded that this was the malady of Germanicus.

[2] At this place there is an unfortunate lacuna in the MSS. of our authority Tacitus : the words, " scripsissent . . . . . expostulantes ; quod haud minus Tiberius quam Piso abnuere," seem to point obscurely to this supposition.

themselves of the full atrocity of the culprit's guilt.
They surrounded the tribunal with cries of vengeance,
threatening that if acquitted by his judges, they
would tear the murderer to pieces with their own
hands.   They would have broken the busts and
statues of Piso within their reach, and exposed them,
in default of his own mangled limbs, on the Gemonian
stairs, had not a military force arrived in time to
protect them.   The criminal was removed from the
bar in a closed litter, attended by a tribune of the
prætorians : some supposed that this was to shelter
him from the popular indignation, but others already
whispered that it was determined to sacrifice him.[1]

Thus ended the first day of the defence, and the
culprit reentered his house with a gloomy presentiment of defeat.   Thus far, however, his wife had affected to unite her cause with his, and had loudly
declared that she would share his fortune for good or
for evil.   If the general feeling was not less strong
against her than against her husband, she might indulge in warmer hopes of protection from the favour
of Livia; and as long as her interests were united
with his, he might trust to escape under the shelter
of her superior influence.   But while Piso was bat-
tling desperately for his life in the senate-house,
Plancina was soliciting the empress in the recesses
of the palace, keeping more aloof from him as the
charges seemed to press harder, urging excuses for
herself independent of him, and finally separating
Deserted by her cause from his altogether.   As soon
Plancina, Piso as Piso discovered this, his last hope was
commits
suicide. gone.   Hesitating to confront his accusers
again, he was with difficulty prevailed on by his sons
to nerve his resolution for a second appearance before his judges.   There he heard the charges once
more repeated, and underwent interrogations which

---

[1] Tac. *Ann.* iii. 13, 14.: " Vario rumore, custos salutis an mortis
exactor sequeretur."

seemed to wax more manifestly hostile: but when he looked towards Tiberius, and observed how cold and reserved was his demeanour, how studiously he repressed every mark either of compassion or anger, he felt that his doom was inevitable. Carried back once more to his own dwelling, he called for his tablets, as if to compose the peroration of his defence, wrote a few lines, which he sealed and delivered to a freedman, after which he bathed and dressed as usual for supper, and retired, after taking it, to his couch. At a late hour of the night, seizing the moment of his wife leaving his bedchamber, he ordered the doors to be closed. The first who entered at daybreak discovered him lying with his throat severed, and his sword on the ground beside him.[1]

Such an end at such a moment gave rise to many whispered surmises. The Romans, ever prone to suspect foul play and underhand contrivance, could easily be led to impute the catastrophe to the emperor himself; and it is worth while to notice that our historian

Rumour that Piso was put to death by the emperor's order, unfairly countenanced by Tacitus.

reveals to us on this occasion the questionable sources to which we seem to owe many of his gravest incriminations. *I have heard old people mention, he says, that Piso had often certain papers in his hand, the contents of which he did not publicly divulge; but that his friends used to affirm that they were the actual instructions addressed to him by Tiberius regarding the unfortunate Germanicus. These he had resolved to lay before the senators, and reveal the real guilt of the emperor, had not Sejanus, the confidant of Tiberius, dissuaded him by false hopes from his purpose. They added that he did not kill himself, but was, in point of fact, assassinated.*[2]

---

[1] Tac. *Ann.* iii. 15.

[2] Tac. *Ann.* iii. 16.: "Quorum neutrum asseveraverim: neque tamen occulere debui narratum ab iis qui nostram ad juventam duraverunt."

The writer concludes this narration, however, with cautioning the reader that he does not affirm this circumstance as an ascertained fact; and such, it must be remarked, is too frequently his habit, to be excused, perhaps, only from the paucity of trustworthy documents in his reach,—to insinuate the truth of popular rumours under pretence of merely recounting them. It is not too much to assert that he really means us to believe most of the stories he thus repeats, under the protest that he cannot vouch for them. With this caution against the seductive influence of the most eloquent of historians, I return to the narrative before us.

Tiberius expressed, it seems, his mortification at the death of the criminal: he might easily foresee and deplore the suspicions to which it would expose him. He allowed the son of the deceased to read to the senate the last words his father had written, which were now found to contain a vindication of his own children from the charge of treason from which he had failed to relieve himself, and an appeal to the emperor in their favour, by the five and forty years of his own faithful services, by the consulships accorded him by Augustus, and the friendship extended to him by Tiberius himself. Such, he said, was his last dying petition. Of the false Plancina he made no mention at all. The case for the defence being thus abruptly cut short, the accusers might still use their right to reply. But the senators were not unmoved at the spectacle of war still waged against a prostrate and insensible victim. They were satisfied with expunging Piso's name from the Fasti, and confiscating a portion of his estates, decreeing at the same time that his elder son Marcus should be banished for ten years, and Cnæus, the younger, renounce the prænomen he had derived from his father. Tiberius interfered to obtain some mitigation even of this sentence, protesting that it was too much to dis-

Sentence against Piso.

grace the name of Piso, when that of Marcus Antonius, who had fought against his country, and of Julus, who had dishonoured the imperial house, were
allowed to retain their place in the rolls of honour.
He spared also the property of the deceased, on this,
as on other occasions, displaying a laudable abstinence in this respect. But he had used his influence,
in deference to his mother, to screen Plancina from
prosecution; and so poignantly did he feel the disgrace of this interference, so much was he mortified
at the murmurs of the citizens, as to seek to repair
his credit by a show of lenity and moderation towards
her husband and family. At the same time, he restrained the adulation which would have decreed him
extraordinary honours for thus avenging the loss of
Germanicus. It was no matter, he protested, of public joy and thanksgiving; it was the last act of a
domestic calamity, fit only to be buried in the recesses of his own memory. Upon the accusers, however, he bestowed places in the priesthood, and promised to elevate Trio to civil distinctions, cautioning
him at the same time to use his powers of oratory
with temper and discretion in future.[1]

A calm review of the circumstances of this celebrated trial seems to leave no cloud of suspicion on the conduct of the emperor himself. It results clearly from the acknowledgments of the narrator, whose hostility to
Tiberius is strongly marked, as we shall see, throughout the course of his history, that the evidence in
proof of the murder was completely nugatory. Still less does there appear any reasonable ground to implicate Tiberius himself in the
schemes of Piso, even supposing Piso's guilt in this
respect to be still matter of question. The fault,
which gave rise to the most unfavourable surmises,
lay in his want of firmness and decision in conduct-

Tiberius free from all suspicion in regard to the death of Germanicus.

No proof of the murder.

---

[1] Tac. *Ann.* iii. 17–19.

ing the case. However deeply irritated at his proconsul's contumacy, he could not divest himself of
the jealous distrust of his too subservient nobles,
which impelled him constantly to throw on them the
responsibility of an inquiry, which, as chief of the
state, was legitimately his own. The position he held
was a source of unceasing alarm and anxiety to him.
Already he found himself beset by the first dangers
of an intruding dynasty, the repeated apparition of
rival claimants and pretenders. The first steps of his
illustrious predecessor had been dogged by the upstart
Amatius. At a later period Augustus had been perse-
cuted by a bold impostor, who declared himself the real
son of Octavia, for whom Marcellus had been substituted by fraud.[1] The death of the wretched Postumus
was speedily followed by the enterprise of
one of his slaves, named Clemens, who pretended to represent him. On the decease
of Augustus, this man, we are told, formed
the design of hastening to Planasia, and carrying off
his master to the legions on the Rhine. He might
have succeeded, but for the slowness of the merchant
vessel in which he sailed for the island. On arriving
there he found the prince already despatched. Conceiving at once a still more daring project, he secreted
or dispersed the ashes of the murdered man, to destroy the evidence of his death, and retired for a
time to Cosa, on the opposite coast of Etruria, till his
hair and beard were grown, to favour a certain like-
ness which he actually bore to him. Meanwhile,
taking a few intimates into his confidence, he spread
a report, which found ready listeners, that Agrippa
still lived. He glided from town to town, showing
himself by twilight, for a few minutes only at a time,
to men prepared for the sudden apparition, until it
became noised abroad that the gods had saved the
grandson of Augustus from the fate intended for him,

Enterprise of the Pretender Clemens.
A. D. 16.
A. C. 769.

---

[1] Val. Max. ix. 15. 2.

and that he was about to visit the city and claim his rightful inheritance. At Ostia, Clemens was received by a great concourse of people, and numbers repaired privily to him on his entrance into Rome. It was long, however, before Tiberius could resolve to act vigorously against him. He would rather have left the vulgar imposture to die a natural death, than interfere to check it with the bruit of arms. At last he determined to exert himself. The pretender was speedily entrapped, by two simulated believers, and brought bound to the palace. When asked by Tiberius what right he had to assume the name of Agrippa? *The same,* he replied, *that you have to that of Cæsar.* The names of no loftier accomplices could be extorted from him, and it is probable that the design was from first to last merely a wild conception of his own. Tiberius was glad to bury the whole matter in oblivion. He put the man to death in the recesses of the palace, and had the body secretly removed, nor did he cause inquiry to be made into any circumstances of the attempt, though some of his own family and many knights and senators were said to have privily favoured, and even given money to advance it. Such was the received account of the affair; as much, that is, as the emperor chose to reveal, or the people ventured to guess of it.[1]

But the sally of an obscure slave was far less formidable than the intrigues of illustrious nobles, equals of the emperor himself in birth and ancestral honours. It was a tradition of the party which Tiberius historically represented, that every scion of a consular house was a possible candidate for the empire; and if his own jealousy ever slept for a moment, officious advisers were not wanting to excite his fears, and urge him to renewed vigilance. A young noble named Libo Drusus, of the Scribonian gens, the same which had given consorts

Intrigues of Libo Drusus. A. D. 16. A. U. 769.

---

[1] Tac. *Ann.* ii. 39, 40.; Suet. *Tib.* 25.; Dion, lvii. 16.

to both Octavius and Sextus Pompeius, was suspected,
from the accession of Tiberius, of cherishing the project of supplanting him. His juvenile ambition had
been fostered by the artifices of a pretended friend,
who had tampered with the weakness of his character,
and led him into criminal relations with the soothsayers and diviners, who were casting the horoscopes
of the unwary, and flattering with dangerous dreams
every illicit aspiration. Libo admitted to his bosom
the wildest hopes of fulfilling the pretended destiny
of his illustrious ancestors. The sharer of his counsels betrayed them in due time to the emperor. Such,
however, was the apprehension Tiberius entertained
of the influence of a noble name, that he did not
venture at once to check him. On the contrary, he
continued for more than a year to load him with
honours; while such was his fear of personal violence,
that, when Libo assisted him at a sacrifice, he caused
him to be furnished with a knife of tin; and in con-
versing with him, pretended always to lean confiden-
tially on his arm, to prevent him from drawing forth
the weapon which he might carry beneath his girdle.[1]
It was not till he had obtained distinct proof that
Libo had consulted a magician, who pretended to
evoke the dead for unhallowed inquiries, that Tiberius ventured to convene the senate, *to deliberate,* as
the tenour of his summons ran, *upon a dreadful
and monstrous crime.* Libo was soon made aware
of his danger. He clothed himself in mourning, and
glided from house to house, suing in vain for the
advocacy of his illustrious friends. All shut their
doors, or turned their backs upon him. On the day of
the trial, he appeared in the senate without a patron,
and studied only to excite commiseration by real or
pretended sickness. Of accusers there was no lack.
Among them was Firmius, the false friend already
noticed, and Fulcinius Trio, the rabid declaimer. The

· Suet. *Tib.* 25.

charges produced embraced some of the wildest fictions.   One of the prosecutors asserted that he had been promised gold enough to pave the Appian Way to Brundisium.   On this and other testimonies scarcely less trivial, it was determined to examine his slaves; and as the law forbad the examination of a master's slaves against him in a capital case, Tiberius caused them to be enfranchised before subjecting them to the question.   Libo now felt that his fate was decided. Returning home, after the first day's investigation, for as yet the personal liberty of the noble Roman was never restricted, even under a capital charge, he sat down to table, but after some hesitation, accomplished his own destruction.[1]   The prosecution was carried on notwithstanding ; and when the culprit's guilt was finally declared to be proved, Tiberius asserted that he intended to pardon him, had he allowed him the opportunity.[2]

The readiness of the senators to combine against the presumed enemies of the prince, the zeal with which they vied with one another *Apprehensions of Tiberius.* in leading the prosecution against them, the eagerness with which they united in decreeing their death, and the confiscation of their property, all these tokens of devotion might have reassured even the fears of Tiberius, and made him feel secure of the submission of his courtiers.   But it seems to have had rather the contrary effect of alarming him.   He saw in it the most fatal evidence of the degradation of the Roman character, and he augured from it that the time would arrive when, every bond of religious feeling being broken, the loyalty with which Augustus had inspired his subjects would give way to selfish passions, and the man who should succeed in out-bidding

---

[1] Thus when Cicero assigned the Catilinarian conspirators to the custody of certain nobles, the legal fiction of their freedom was ostensibly respected.

[2] Tac. *Ann.* ii. 27—31.

him in popularity would become master of their venal
affections. These apprehensions were increased by
every expression of freedom hazarded by his anticipated rivals, which he presumed to be grounded on
the conviction that their time was coming, and that
there was in the community a large mass of feeling
which responded to their pretensions. Among the
nobles there was a certain class who affected to in-
demnify themselves for the loss of substantial liberty
by petty sallies of impatience, and scarce disguised
irony, and among these Piso had been eminently conspicuous. Thus, for instance, when Tiberius had announced, on a certain occasion, that, contrary to his
usual reserve, he would give his opinion on a particular charge in person, Piso ventured to ask, would
he speak first or last ?—*if first*, he added, *I shall have
a guide to follow; if last, I fear lest I may un-
wittingly dissent from you.* Such, says Tacitus,
were some of the last traces of expiring liberty.[1]
While, however, any such traces, however slight, still
remained, the shadowy phantom of the Republic
continued to flit before the eyes of the Cæsar. There
was still, he apprehended, a germ of sentiment existing, on which a scion of his own house, or even a
stranger, might boldly throw himself, and raise the
standard of patrician independence. The death of
Piso concurred with that of Germanicus
to relieve him from the terrors of this
hateful anticipation. From this time he
began really to reign. He was well aware, indeed,
that he had fastened on himself the hatred of the
citizens by the mere suspicion of his complicity in
deaths which had so manifestly served his interests;
he knew that all his acts and measures would henceforth be construed to his injury, and a dark cloud of
national distrust hang for ever on his memory. But,
on the other hand, these were the mere shadows of

Relieved by
the deaths of
Germanicus
and Piso.

---

[1] Tac. *Ann.* i. 74. Comp. ii. 35.

evil. To the loss of his good name he was becoming more and more hardened. The flattery of poets and historians, even the clamorous applause of the populace, he could buy again if he chose; but with his cynical contempt for his people, he did not think them worth the cost in shows and largesses. He now felt himself safe from the machinations of his nearest enemies, and free to exchange the disguised autocracy of his predecessor, which he wanted himself the tact and moderation to wield, for the direct and harsh exercise of uncontrolled dominion.

Nevertheless, while Tiberius was thus rising supreme over the laws of his country, and the lives and fortunes of the citizens, he was not himself exempt from certain concealed and mysterious influences, which continued almost insensibly to direct and control him. The first of these was the will of Livia, who seemed now, in extreme old age, to reap the full fruits of her ambition, the passion to which she had subjected every other inclination through her long career of intrigue. Her son had risen under her auspices, and mainly, perhaps, by her direct contrivance, to the summit of power which she had so deeply coveted for him, and her own influence over him had increased rather than diminished with his success. All Rome regarded the empress-mother with far more awe and obsequious submission than the empress-consort. If she had really been the mistress of the councils of Augustus, he at least had retained the ostensible power. But the habits of obedience she had early impressed on her son remained deeply stamped on his retentive disposition; nor, however much her yoke might sometimes gall him, had he the spirit to reject it when he became the master of all the world besides. The women whom she admitted to her intimacy presumed to defy the laws under her protection. On one occasion her favourite, Urgulania, being cited as a witness

before the senate, refused to appear, and the prætor
was complaisantly sent to take her examination iu
private, a privilege not accorded even to the sacred
character of the Vestals.[1]   On another, the same Urgulania was the cause of a struggle for supremacy
between Tiberius and his mother.   It was considered
a remarkable instance of firmness on his part, that
he insisted on her paying down the fine imposed on
her by a judicial sentence.   But the greatest triumph
of Livia's authority was seen in the acquittal of her
friend Plancina.   The emperor, consummate as was
his power of dissimulation, failed to disguise the disgust he felt at the part he was reduced to play in
deference to this love of power.

Another influence behind the throne has already
been glanced at, in accounting for the jealousy Tiberius felt of the martial aspirations
of Germanicus.   The most eloquent of the emperor's
flatterers, in concluding his brief survey of Roman
history which has come down to us, with a review
of the opening promise, such as he represents it, of
this ill-fated reign, after painting in flaunting colours
the virtues and successes of the third Cæsar, glides
into the reflection, that the good fortune of the
greatest men is generally to be traced in part to the
merits of their most cherished advisers.   Thus the
valour of the Scipios was supported by the genius
of the Lælii, and Augustus himself reclined on the
arms of an Agrippa and a Taurus.   In like manner,
he adds, did Tiberius rejoice in the powerful aid of
Lucius Sejanus, a man of rare ability, vigorous alike
in mind and body, a loyal servant, a cheerful companion, one whose natural modesty evinced his actual
desert, and smoothed the way for his well-merited
advancement.[2]   This and much more does Velleius

and of Sejanus.

---

[1] Tac. *Ann.* ii. 34.: "Tiberius hactenus indulgere matri. civile
ratus."

[2] Velleius Paterculus, ii. 127.

say in the praise of the favourite of Tiberius, the man whose name has become a by-word in history for all that is most fulsome in adulation, most base in dissimulation, most atrocious in crime. Sejanus belonged to the Ælian gens, perhaps by adoption, and his paternal family was only of equestrian rank.[1] On the mother's side he is said to have descended from a more illustrious ancestry. He was born at Vulsinii in Etruria. He seems to have first established his fortunes on the favours of a wealthy debauchee[2], but when he succeeded in attaching himself to the person of the young Caius Cæsar, the prospect of public eminence began to open upon him. On his second patron's premature decease he transferred himself to the service of Tiberius, over whom he soon acquired an influence, which it became the object of his life to confirm and extend. But the arts by which such influence is obtained over a timid and self-distrusting character, however sly and suspicious, do not always imply any great superiority of talent; and the enemies of Sejanus refused to allow the object of their abhorrence the praise even of eminent talents. They would only admit that he was active and hardy in frame, and was not deficient in boldness and enterprise: he had, they said, the address to conceal his own vices, while he was shrewd in unmasking the disguises of others. His pride and meanness were equal one to the other, and he could carry a pretence of moderation in his demeanour, while his lust of power and lucre was really unbounded.[3]

On his patron's succession to the empire, Sejanus was found useful, and retained the influence he had

---

[1] L. Ælius Sejanus was the son of Seius Strabo, a Roman knight.

[2] Tac. *Ann.* iv. 1.; Dion. lvii. 19. This was M. Apicius, the second of the three noted gourmands of the name, who are supposed to have flourished in succession from the time of Augustus.

[3] Tac. *l. c.*; Dion, *l. c.*

acquired by his skill in relieving him from the
weight of his burdens without seeming to
take them on himself. Tiberius sent him
on a confidential mission to advise the young
Drusus in Pannonia ; but he was speedily recalled
from this distant service, and appointed colleague
with his father in the command of the prætorian cohorts, quartered in the vicinity of the capital. This
charge placed him in a position of the strictest intimacy with the emperor, over whose personal safety
it was his duty to watch, while he provided for the
execution of his orders in Rome. Here he may have
suggested that distrust of Germanicus to which the
Romans ascribed the hero's recall from the Rhenish
frontier ; he may have prompted the mission of Piso,
as a check on the presumed ambition of the young
prince in Asia; he may have whispered to the proconsul of Syria an assurance that his opposition to his
chief would not be distasteful to the sovereign power at
home. However this may be, Tiberius required a staff
to lean upon, and Sejanus was strong enough and bold
enough to supply one. Anxious as the new emperor
was, from his first accession, to know everything, and
to do everything himself; impatient as he was of
leaving affairs to take their course under a wise but
distant superintendence, and jealous of all interference with his own control; yet, finding day by day
that the concerns of his vast administration were slip-
ping away beyond the sphere of his personal guidance, from the inability of any single mind to embrace
them all together, he was reduced to the necessity of
falling back on extraneous assistance; and he preferred, from the character of his mind, to draw irregular aid from a domestic favourite, rather than throw
irresponsible power into the hands of his remote vice-
gerents. He controlled the satraps in his provinces
by the agency of a vizier at home.

CHAPTER XLIV

The functions of the comitia: 1. Election of Magistrates; 2. Legislation; 3. Jurisdiction: transferred to the senate, and hence to the
emperor himself.—The emperor's control over the senate.—The
law of majestas: its origin, application, and extension under
Tiberius from acts to words and injurious language.—Cases of
constructive majestas.—Delation encouraged by Tiberius.—Consolidation of the Roman dominions under Tiberius.—Stations and
discipline of the legions.—The government and improved treatment of the provinces.—Government of Italy and the city.—Dissipation of the times.—Measures of Tiberius.—His own vices and
virtues.—His deference to the senate.—Defects of temper and
demeanour.

THE democracy, when roused to deadly struggle
against the aristocracy, generally gains the *General result
of the struggle*
victory; but the fruits of victory it has sel- *between democracy and*
dom the capacity to retain. The empire of *aristocracy.*
the Cæsars was founded, as we have seen, on the passions and just claims of the popular branch of the
Roman community; but while the show of power, its
trappings, and even its emoluments, fell again into
the hands of the nobility, the real substance eluded,
as usual in such cases, the grasp both of the one and
the other. We have already remarked the care of
Augustus to raise the dignity of the senatorial order,
while he repressed all free action in the commons,
and deprived them, one by one, of the prerogatives
they had acquired through so many revolutions.
Though the descendant and representative of Marius,
he was in fact, as regarded the relations of the two
rival orders of the state, no other than a second
Sulla.[1]

[1] See Hoeck's *Röm. Gesch.* i. 3. p. 50. foll. I have found the advantage of having before me this author's luminous view of the constitution of the empire under Tiberius.

But whatever remained to be done, to reduce the
The balance trimmed by the tact of Augustus. Roman plebs to utter insignificance, was speedily effected by the regulations of Tiberius. The balance between the conflicting powers of the state was only trimmed for the moment by the sagacity and fortune of Augustus, for whom all parties were content to waive the exaction of their legitimate or pretended rights. When a successor followed, with less personal authority and less delicacy in the management of it, the machine of government might have been in danger of collapsing. The appointment of magistrates, the enactment of laws, the constitution even of the judicial tribunals, had all been left unfixed in principle, and abandoned, as occasion arose, to the wisdom and moderation of the emperor, on which all equally relied. The Romans acquiesced in the fiction which was now palmed upon them of equal laws and a regular constitution : but in fact the limits of every department of government were normally undefined. This was a state of things which, however passive in temper the mass of the nation had now become, could not longer endure in More logical character of the polity of Tiberius. the face of a restless and sensitive nobility. Tiberius, moreover, from the character of his mind, required a more logical development of the polity he had undertaken to direct, and that polity had begun spontaneously to assume, as the condition of its existence, both outward form and internal organization.

The transfer of the business of the popular assemblies to the senate is announced, as we The threefold functions of the Comitia. have seen, by Tacitus with a coolness and indifference which may seem scarcely worthy of its apparent importance. Whatever the aspirations of the historian may have been for the so-called liberty of the old aristocracy, the traditions of which he has hallowed by his deep and melancholy regrets, it is probable that no Roman of his day, the second century from the loss of independence, really felt the value of the forms of the free-state, which had so long passed from degradation to oblivion. But in fact the change which he here announced was less important than at first sight it appears. On the other hand, the action of the Comitia had been already paralysed for half a century, and was now only quickened occasionally by the emperor himself to serve his own purposes, while, on the other, its presumed functions, though thus ostensibly abolished, were not in reality absolutely extinguished. The functions of the Comitia, whether the people met by tribes or centuries, were properly threefold, those of Election, of Legislation, and of Jurisdiction ; and it will be desirable to pause at this point of our narration, to review briefly the position in which the empire found these functions respectively.

I. The popular privilege of election, whether of the higher or the lower magistrates, had been limited by the first Cæsar, and after him by the triumvirs. In the plenitude of their confidence, the people had urged their patron, the Dictator, to assume the sole nomination to all civil offices; and it was by a mere act of grace on his part that the free choice of one-half of them was remitted to the popular assemblies, while of the other he accepted only the right to nominate and recommend, the latter act being of course virtually equivalent to a direct appointment.[1] The proceedings of the triumvirs were merely irregular and revolutionary.[2] They grasped the direct appointment of all: but it was among the first cares of Augustus, on succeeding to his parent's inheritance, to return to the principles set forth by Cæsar, and restrict himself to the nomination of one-half of the magistrates, leav-

I. The election of magistrates.

[1] With the exception of the consuls, the appointment of whom he reserved solely to himself. Dion, xliii. 45. See vol. ii. ch. xxi.
[2] Appian, iv. 2., v. 73.; Dion, xlvii. 15., xlviii. 35. 53.

ing to the assemblies of the tribes and centuries the
unfettered election of the rest. He claimed only a
veto on the nomination of unworthy candidates; but
while he reserved to himself the decision of what
should constitute merit or demerit, he reduced in
fact the succession to all places of trust and power to
a matter of personal favour. Such was the pretended
restoration of the prerogatives of the people, for which
Augustus obtained credit [1]: it was a part of the general system of dissimulation with which he deceived a
willing people, a system which could only succeed in
the hands of one whose personal merits were dearer
to them than any consistent theory of government.

Augustus
nominates
magistrates
to the Comitia.
It was with a peculiar feeling of complacency
that they beheld, year after year, the solemn mockery of the emperor's descent
into the Field of Mars, when he led his clients by
the hand, recommending their claims, and asking for
them the suffrages of all comers, till he finally registered his own vote in their behalf.[2] Such was the
practice of Augustus through the greater part of his
long reign. Towards its close, when he could less
easily bear the fatigue of this repeated exertion, he
contented himself with furnishing his nominees with
written credentials, and spared himself the trouble
of attending personally with them.[3] Even this was
not precisely a novelty; it was following the precedent of the Dictator, and it was accepted by the
people as a sufficient recognition of their ultimate
right of election. They continued to go through the
ancient forms of polling, with the bridge, the pen-
fold, and the urn; and with respect at least to those

[1] Suet. *Oct.* 40.: "Comitiorum pristinum jus reduxit." Dion, lvi.
46.: τὸ τε ἀξίωμα τῶν ἀρχαιρεσιῶν αὐτῷ ἐτήρησε.

[2] Suet. *Oct.* 56.: "Quoties magistratuum comitiis interesset, tribus
cum candidatis suis circumibat, supplicabatque more solemni. Fe-
rebat et ipse suffragium, ut unus e populo."

[3] Dion, lv. 34.: γράμματα τίνα ἐκτίθεις συνίστη τῷ τε πλήθει καὶ τῷ
δήμῳ ὅσους ἐσπούδαξε.

places to which the emperor abstained from nominating, a stranger only historically conversant with the system of the free-state might have found perhaps nothing in the methods of procedure to awaken him from his dream of the republic of the Scipios.

With an instrument of government so conveniently adjusted to his hand, so facile and flexible to every touch, it is not likely that Augustus ever thought of placing further restrictions on the pretended freedom of election. Tiberius, however, found it advisable to announce that the reform which he himself meditated had already been conceived and planned by his predecessor.[1] But the transfer of power, or rather of the show of power, which he made, did not extend to closing the assemblies either of the tribes or centuries for purposes of election. While he continued the system of nomination and recommendation, addressing it not to the Comitia but to the senate, he still allowed the people to meet in their accustomed places, and with the ancient forms, to accept and ratify the choice of the superior order.[2] Hence we find the term Comitia still occasionally employed, though not quite correctly, to represent the election of magistrates; and the meetings of the people in the booths or septa, and on the

Tiberius nominates to the senate.

The Comitia still meet to accept the appointments of the senate.

[1] Vell. ii. 124. : "Primum principalium ejus operum fuit ordinatio comitiorum quam manu sua scriptam D. Augustus reliquerat." The pretexts assigned may be surmised from the further remarks this author makes on the subject (c. 126.): "revocata in forum fides; submota foro seditio, ambitio campo, discordia curiæ; sepultæque ac situ obsitæ justitia, æquitas, industria civitati redditæ."

[2] Thus although in *Ann.* i. 15. Tacitus had said that the Comitia were now transferred from the Campus to the Senate-house, in the eighty-first chapter of the same book he describes the action of the Comitia as still continuing: "De comitiis consularibus quæ tum primum illo principe ac deinceps fuere vix quidquam firmare ausim: . . . ." Comp. Dion, lviii. 20. I have stated in the text what appears to have been the ordinary arrangement; but this, it must be understood, was subject to occasional irregularities.

plain of the Campus Martius, continued to take place periodically to a much later period of the imperial history.[1] The candidates, already assured of their appointment, waited on the steps of the neighbouring temples while the auspices were taken and other tedious solemnities, which had long lost their significance, performed ; and these were finally closed by the announcement of a herald that the election had fallen on the nominee of the emperor.[2] From henceforth, however, we are to consider not only that every consular appointment is made by the mere voice of the emperor, but that every other magistrate is chosen by the senate, partly on the imperial nomination, partly with a show of free selection, and, finally, that to these at least the popular sanction is also ostensibly given.[3] The effect of the reform, therefore, is after all not the transfer of any substantial power from the one assembly to the other, but simply an additional ray of pale and doubtful lustre cast on the laticlave of the senator.

II. The second function of the Comitia, that of legislation, stood on a somewhat different footing from that of election. The popular prerogative of choosing the officers of state had never been called in question throughout the career of the republic : it might be considered as absolutely in-

II. The power of legislation.

---

[1] The Comitia of the tribes under the empire met no longer in the forum, but in the Septa Julia of Agrippa in the Campus Martius. Dion, liii. 23.

[2] See the description of this ceremony in Pliny, *Paneg.* 63., and the passages from Suet. *Domit.* 10. and Senec. *Ep.* 118., which are brought to illustrate it.

[3] The practice of a later period, as described by Dion (lviii. 20.), was probably the same in substance as that of the Tiberian : τῶν δὲ δὴ καὶ τὰς ἄλλας ἀρχὰς αἰτούντων ἐξελέγετο ὅσους ἤθελε, καὶ σφᾶς ἐς τὸ συνέδριον ἐσέπεμπε, τοὺς μὲν συνιστὰς αὐτῷ, οἵπερ ὑπὸ πάντων ᾑροῦντο. τοὺς δὲ ἐπὶ τὲ τοῖς δικαιώμασι, καὶ ἐπὶ τῇ ὁμολογίᾳ, τῷ τὲ κλήρῳ ποιούμενος· καὶ μετὰ τοῦτο ἐς τὲ τὸν δῆμον καὶ ἐς τὸ πλῆθος (the centuries and the tribes) οἱ προσήκοντες αὐτῷ, τῆς ἀρχαίας ὁσίας ἕνεκα, καθάπερ καὶ νῦν ὥστε ἐν εἰκόνι δοκεῖν γίγνεσθαι, ἐσίοντες ἀπεδείκνυντο.

herent in the people and inalienable from them.
Jealous of its own rights, and disposed to encroach
upon all others, the senate notwithstanding had never
ventured to claim a share in the appointment of
magistrates who were to preside over the common
weal. But the limits of the popular authority in
the making of the laws, on the other hand, had been
a constant subject of dispute between the two great
powers of the state. Previous to the enactment of
the famous Lex Hortensia, one of the great charters
of the rights of the commons, the *Scita* of the Plebs
were not binding on citizens generally until they had
been ratified by the senate. The Comitia of the
tribes were now rendered completely independent
of the superior order: nevertheless it was some time
before they asserted the powers thus secured to them
in defiance of the senate, with which they had been
long accustomed to co-operate harmoniously. The
most flourishing period of the Roman free-state was
that in which the two co-ordinate bodies were aware
of their respective prerogatives, but each abstained
from pressing them against the interests of the other.
While the people were the real depositaries *Independent*
of legislative power, the senate enjoyed the *legislation of*
the tribes
right of nominating provincial governors, *balanced by*
the decrees
and through them of ruling the provinces: *of senate.*
its decrees regarded the general administration of
the empire, and these, as well as the appointments
it made, were honourably respected by the assemblies
of the commons. When, however, the Gracchi and
their successors on the tribunitian benches thought
fit violently to resent the advantages which the senate
drew to itself from this division of government, the
several prerogatives of the two orders, never accurately adjusted, were easily made to clash. The equilibrium of mutual forbearance once disturbed, it was
impossible to restore the balance. Though the popular right of legislation was admitted, the senate

had many ways of thwarting, as well as of influencing
it indirectly. The demagogues, to counteract this influence, resorted to the violent measure of requiring
the assent of the senators to their most obnoxious
propositions, under pain of judicial penalties.[1]   This
state of chronic hostility and defiance was only for a
moment suspended by the reforms of Sulla, who
compelled the tribes to submit the *Scita* to the ratification of their rivals the senate.[2]   But the time
had passed when the selfish and grasping measures
of the senatorial body could be reconciled with the
claims of the inferior order to its full share in the
general government, and all Sulla's legislation fell
with a crash together, under the pretended patronage
of Crassus and Pompeius. Henceforth the legislative
monopoly of the Comitia remained unquestioned : it
was only subject to the indirect checks still left in
the hands of the consuls and augurs. It was perhaps
from their consciousness of the existence of these
checks, however, that the leaders of the people generally contrived to secure the approval of a majority
of the senate for their measures, and maintained to
the last a show of concurrent legislation.[3]

Nor had the senate indeed refrained, on its part,
from encroaching on the legislative functions of its rivals, and snatching by various
devices a substantive power of legislation
for itself. It demanded that its *Consulta*
should have the same independent force as the *Scita*
of the Plebs. As far as regarded merely administrative regulations, there was nothing in this contrary
to ancient and legitimate usage; the *Senatuscon-
sultum Ultimum,* so often alluded to, by which the
senate gave full powers to the consuls in cases
of emergency, was only an extreme application of

Legislative power gradually assumed by the senate.

---

[1] Appian, *Bell. Civ.* i. 29.   [2] Appian, *Bell. Civ.* i. 59.
[3] See Dion, xxxvi. 7. 20., xxxviii. 7.; Appian, *Bell. Civ.* ii. 12.; -
Hoeck, *Röm. Gesch.* i. 3. p. 58.

its undoubted right to secure the efficiency of the executive in every act and movement. The senate pretended, however, still further to the right of annulling the resolutions of the comitia ; and here again an extreme instance of its exercise has been more than once noticed, in the special release it accorded from certain laws, if not from the whole cycle of the laws of the commonwealth. To such encroachments the tribes were forced to submit whenever one of their tribunes had been gained by the opposite faction, an event of no uncommon occurrence; but no legitimate right could be established on a series, however long, cf exceptional irregularities, against which the great body of the people had never failed to protest. Augustus, as the champion of the people, was careful to give full force to their legislative prerogative. Though he generally proposed his measures to the senate, and obtained its formal consent to the ordinances which emanated in fact from the small committee of its body which he took into intimate counsel, he seems to have always submitted them to the comitia of the centuries also, and obtained for his Julian legislation the sanction of every order of the state.[1] His long and busy reign sufficed to settle the principles of law ; it remained for his successor rather to regulate the details of government, than reconstruct its essential forms.   Hence Tiberius, averse by temper to the multiplication of legal enactments, had little occasion to call into play the full machinery of law-making.   With the wider diffusion of the franchise the resident citizens of Rome ceased to represent the interests of the conquering race ;

---

[1] Heineccius, *Antiq. Roman*, i. tit. 2. 44.   Projects of law which had been sanctioned by the senate were afterwards demanded (rogatæ) of the Comitia Centuriata, by which they were ratified as leges.   But the Scita of the Comitia Tributa were made equivalent to leges by the lex Hortensia.

while the provincials were assuming more real importance in the eyes of the ruler, and the administration of the provinces, which had always been the function of the senate, became more and more coordinate with the general administration of the empire. Accordingly, without any ostensible reform, or the direct abolition of the popular prerogative, we find the power of making laws practically withdrawn, under Tiberius, from the comitia of the tribes. Two instances only are known of *Leges* passed in the regular course under his administration, while the *Consulta* of the senate are sufficiently numerous.[1] But the rights of the people in this respect were never formally annulled ; and even through another century examples are cited of laws passed and ratified according to the usage of antiquity. The decrees of the senate, however, came, at least immediately after Tiberius, to be designated in many cases as laws, and to carry the full force of the more regular enactments.[2]

We have in this a second instance of the way in which an appearance of authority was given to the senate, which in fact was a mere idle show. The legislative powers of this assembly were restricted, just as the elective, by the real and substantial prerogative of the emperor, supreme alike over all. Much reliance,

Transferred to the emperor's senatorial cabinet and hence to the emperor himself.

---

[1] The lex Junia Norbana (Gai. i. 22., iii. 56.; Ulp. i. 10.) and the Lex Visellia (Ulp. iii. 5.; Hoeck, *Röm. Gesch.* i. 3. p. 59.). On the other hand, examples of senatusconsulta constantly occur in Tacitus and Dion. The whole series of the leges Juliæ is a monument of comitial legislation under Augustus.

[2] Thus Ulpian (early in the third century, A. D.) says, " Non ambigitur senatum jus facere posse." *Dig.* i. 3. § 9. Asconius had long before specified the cases in which the senate could control the legislative prerogative of the people : " Quatuor omnino genera sunt in quibus per senatum more majorum statuatur aliquid de legibus. Unum est ejusmodi, placere legem abrogari : alterum, quæ lex lata esse dicetur ea non videri populum teneri: tertium est de legum derogationibus." The fourth case, which Asconius omits, refers to the *legibus solvere*. Ascon. *in Cornel.* p. 67. ed. Orell. See Rein, *Criminal-Recht der Röm.* p. 62.

indeed, cannot be placed on the assertion of Dion that the senate formally invited Augustus to make what proposals he pleased, and proposed even to bind itself by an oath beforehand to accept them as laws; for in the beginning of the empire the senate could hardly have assumed any such power of dispensing with the concurrence of the popular assembly.[1] That it obsequiously placed its own suffrage at his disposal is credible enough; but even this is to be understood of an extraordinary and momentary abdication of its proper responsibility. Nor in fact did Augustus himself definitively accept it. When, however, he chose himself a cabinet, consisting of a select number of senators, including the consuls and princes of his own family, to confer with on affairs of state, the senate did undoubtedly transfer all its proper functions to this body, which was in fact a standing committee of its own order, and was considered to represent the wisdom of the whole. The measures which had been discussed and adopted by this conclave were still promulgated before the entire assembly, by which they were accepted with acclamation, and through this channel the prince of the senate acquired unlimited power of legislation. Tiberius, it seems, did not retain this select council. His measures emanated from his own breast alone, except when he chose to take a private counsellor, such as Sejanus, into his confidence. He convened the fathers to listen to an address from his own mouth, in which he explained the scope of his plans, and proposed them for the assembly's consideration; or he put up some private member to make the proposition when he chose to disguise his own inclinations. He introduced also the custom of sending a written despatch to be read to the assembly in his absence, in which his views on any project of law, pro-

---

[1] Dion, liv. 10.

posed by himself or by another, were declared or insinuated.[1] But in all these cases the senate was regarded as competent to discuss and amend, and even, if it had the courage, to reject, though the latter alternative may have never been actually assumed. Many instances, however, are recorded of individual senators arguing upon the imperial proposition, and even condemning it, and, at least at the commencement of the Tiberian principate, it was deemed a refinement of flattery to affect such freedom of discussion. This, perhaps, is the limit to which the imperial authority extended in the matter of legislation at this period : it was practically complete, but in outward show reached only to recommendation. It must be understood, however, that the senate, in its proneness to adulation, was constantly representing itself as the devoted slave of the prince, and the mere registrar of his decrees ; accepting, in short, the practice as if it were the law of the time, and satisfying its own pride and dignity by a mental reservation, to the effect that its concession to its chief was a mere voluntary cession of its undoubted prerogatives, which it might at any time resume, and which, in fact, on the death of each emperor, reverted *ipso facto* to itself, to be ceded to his successor or withheld from him at its own proper pleasure.[2]

III. The criminal jurisdiction of the people and of the senate.

III. In regard to criminal jurisdiction the loss of the popular assemblies was still more complete and signal, while the senate, at least in outward appearance, gained all that the people had lost. From early times there

---

[1] The epistola or libellus of the princeps was recited by one of the quæstors, who was called his candidatus. *Digest.* i. 13. § 4.: " Ex quæstoribus quidam sunt qui candidati Principis dicuntur, quique epistolas ejus in senatu legunt."

[2] It was not, I think, till the time of the Antonines, as we shall see hereafter, that the Oratio or Rescriptum of the emperor was referred to in the same terms as a Lex. Comp. *Digest.* xxiii. 2. §§ 57, 58. 60.

had been a certain rivalry between the two powers
in respect to jurisdiction, and the mutual limit of
their prerogatives on this point was not strictly defined. The people in their centuries,—the assembly
in which wealth and station were most fully represented, and not merely numbers, as in the tribes,—
claimed the ultimate right of deciding on the citizen's
caput, that is, his civil status, and, at least in political cases, it was before this assembly that the chief
magistrates were required to summon offenders. But,
on the one hand, the comitia of the tribes encroached
gradually on this prerogative; on the other, the
senate claimed exclusive jurisdiction over the acts
of the citizens in the provinces, and, by some irregular and unexplained usurpation, sometimes within
the bounds of Italy also.[1] The last remnant of the
supreme power originally inherent in the people, was
the right of appeal to it, which was always possessed
by the criminal in capital cases; though even here
too the senate presumed to evade the principle of the
law, by declaring in extreme cases the state in
danger, and thrusting extraordinary powers into the
hands of the consuls. Thus the accomplices of
Catilina were brought to trial before the senate,
condemned, and executed without appeal, much to
their own astonishment at the vigour of the proceeding, and not without great offence to the people, or
at least to their leaders. But throughout Overridden
the last century of the free state the juris- by the fixed
tribunals.
diction both of the comitia and the senate was
almost completely over-ridden by the institution
of the *Quæstiones perpetuæ*, the permanent or fixed
tribunals, and the old contest between the two poli-

---

[1] This jurisdiction of the senate in the provinces was a part of its
administrative competence therein through its officers. Polybius
asserts that in his time it had jurisdiction also within the bounds of
Italy in cases of treason, conspiracy, and murder. Polyb. vi. 13.;
Hœck, i. 3. p. 63.

tical bodies of the commonwealth was exchanged for
a competition among its leading classes for admission
to these tribunals, or a preponderance in them.

The appeal to the people was tacitly extinguished

The appeal
transferred
from the
people to
the emperor.
by Augustus, who reserved the right of
judgment in the last resort to himself
alone, in virtue perhaps of his tribunitian
power, by which he was the constituted
guardian, and in some sense the vicegerent of the
tribes.[1]   But both he and still more his next successor invited the senate to take cognisance of many
offences which had hitherto been subjected to the

Cognisance
of charges
against
senators.
jurisdiction of the fixed tribunals. Mæcenas,
we are told, advised that all charges against
senators, their wives and children, should
be referred to the senate alone; and it has been
supposed, no doubt too hastily, that the counsels
popularly ascribed to this minister indicate the actual
course pursued by his master.[2]   In this case, however, it would be too much to affirm that either the
first or the second princeps actually transferred from
the tribunals to the senate the cognisance of all
charges against members of its own body.   In Piso's
process, for instance, though the culprit was himself
a senator, the prosecutors commence their proceedings by invoking the emperor to investigate the affair
in person, and he declines the task as inconvenient
rather than irregular.   He goes on to say in his
reply that, in remitting the affair to the judgment of

---

[1] The comitia of the centuries, as has been before remarked, represented the Roman people in their military character, and, therefore,
were held, not in the Forum, but beyond the walls: the distinctive
meaning and rights of this assembly became extinguished as the
citizens ceased to constitute the military force of the republic.

[2] Dion, lii. 31. Hoeck relies on this passage as if it were an express statement of the law or practice under Augustus. It is, however, pretty well understood, as I have elsewhere remarked, that the
counsels the historian puts into the mouth of Mæcenas represent more
correctly the usage of his own time, i.e. the third century.

the senate, he evinces his regard to the rank of Germanicus; for in a less conspicuous case the appointed tribunal for murders would have been fully competent to undertake the process.[1] It would appear, however, that the Quæstiones, though still existing, were gradually degraded from the high position they held under the republic. The senate received jurisdiction in cases not only of *Majestas* and *Repetundæ*, that is, of Treason and Extortion, but of Murder, Poisoning, Bribery, and others: and this was not confined perhaps to charges against members of its own order. A less invidious and at the same time a more brilliant prerogative of this body, however, was that of deciding upon the offences of allies and dependent sovereigns against the interests of the Roman state and its chief. This was a function which the assembly had claimed from an early period, as the executive of the Roman people abroad; nor had it ever been wrested from the senate by the comitia, nor transferred to any special tribunal. On the whole, the senate, from the time of the Tiberian principate, may be described as a high Court of Criminal Jurisdiction of the most comprehensive kind.

The senate under the empire becomes the chief court of criminal jurisdiction.

The Romans, consistently with their inveterate jealousy of all that savoured of monarchical authority, refused to assign the highest judicial competence to any single judge, and when the unwieldy proportions and gross unfairness of such a tribunal as that of the people themselves, assembled in their comitia, became no

Paramount jurisdiction of the emperor himself.

[1] Tac. *Ann.* iii. 12.: "Id solum Germanico super leges præstiterimus, quod in curia potius quam in foro, apud senatum quam apud judices, de morte ejus anquiritur." An ordinary case of murder would have been tried by the quæstores homicidii in a basilica adjoining the Forum. The quæstiones perpetuæ were, by legal fiction, committees of the tribes, and the basilicas were the committee-rooms of the Forum, their place of assembly.

longer tolerable, they invented, in the Quæstiones
Perpetuæ, a sort of virtual representation of themselves by standing committees. The number of
members of each of these boards might vary from
three or four to twenty or thirty, or even more.
Charges of inferior gravity were referred to a commission, consisting nominally of a hundred members,
but sometimes in reality much exceeding that number. The vital principle of the most perfect systems
of modern procedure, which secures the responsibility
of the judge by isolating him from the rest of the
community, and bringing public opinion to bear on
him from the eminence of his character and position,
was abhorrent from the democratical spirit of the
Romans, and the fixed idea of their polity, that truth
was to be found in the decisions of a majority. These
views, however, were irreconcileable with the principles of monarchy; and the emperor had, in fact,
no alternative, but either to appoint special judges
of eminence enough to make their decisions respected,
or to become himself the controller of the decisions
of a more numerous and less responsible body. From
the moment that judicial competence was spread over
a body of six hundred members, the concentration of
actual jurisdiction in the hands of their chief became
inevitable. It is of little consequence, therefore, to
inquire from which of his special functions the princeps might most logically derive the judicial prerogative which was soon found to attach to him;
whether it proceeded from the sovereignty of the
people lodged virtually in his person; whether from
the military autocracy of the imperium; or whether
from the combination of the consular, the proconsular, and the tribunitian powers, each of which undoubtedly conferred jurisdiction in particular cases.
Of the first of these hypotheses, it may be remarked
that the sovereignty of the people was certainly not

at this period directly and legitimately transferred
to the emperor[1]; of the second, that the judicial
functions of the imperator were restricted to the
camp[2]; and of the last, that the jurisdiction of the
three magistracies above named was in each case
specifically limited; nor would the combination of
all together extend so far as to cover that claimed
and exercised by the emperor, which was, indeed,
practically unlimited. It may be admitted, however,
that it was the jurisdiction of the emperor in these
several capacities that gave him his ground of vantage for consolidating his more sweeping pretensions.
In proportion as these powers themselves became more
extensive, so did the judicial qualification they imparted become less strictly defined. The imperial
prerogative of Pardon was an extension or distortion
of the tribunitian right of Succour: that of revising
or annulling the decrees of the senate was an exaggeration of the privilege of Intercession; and we
can imagine how, when the emperor was thus raised
above all legitimate principle and usage, both accused and accusers might combine to cast themselves at the foot of the throne, and solicit the
arbitration of a judge from whose preeminence they
might expect impartiality. The Romans, it must
always be remembered, were to the full as impatient

---

[1] Even at a much later period the basis of the imperial power
assumed by Ulpian, after Gaius, is of course a mere legal fiction :
". Quod populus ei et in eum omnem suam potestatem conferat."

[2] Dion affirms (liii. 17.) that the emperor derived from his imperium the right of putting senators and knights to death within the
city. This is one of many passages of this writer of the third century
in which he puts the admitted usage of his own day on the footing
of earlier and legitimate principles. The practice employed, as we
shall see, by Tiberius himself, in the latter part of his reign, was a
mere usurpation of the sword, and bore no constitutional sanction.
It was precisely for such usurpations as this that the acts of certain
of the emperors were formally rescinded by the senate after their
deaths.

in thrusting irregular powers upon their ruler as he was in usurping them.[1]   From the combination of both these impulses, the jurisdiction of the senate had become, before the death of the second princeps, entirely dependent on his direction; and whenever his interests were at stake, the judicial sentence of the fathers was no other than the expression of his will inspired by himself.   In the same way, moreover, the decisions which he pronounced with his own mouth were generally merely the echoes of his private pleasure.[2]   Accordingly, except in certain outward show, and the popular estimation thereto attaching, the senate derived little or no advantage from its apparent triumph over the people in the matter of jurisdiction.   In this as in other respects it was the mere passive instrument of the emperor's will, and its character became insensibly degraded by the consciousness that all its magnificent pretensions were no better than empty shadows.   With a set of high-sounding formulas ever in its mouth, it was, in fact, only blowing bubbles for the amusement of a frivolous populace.

Such was the process by which the three sovereign rights of the Roman people were gradually taken from them and transferred in name to the rival body of the senate, but in fact to the emperor himself.   Henceforth it depended on the personal character of the chief whether the government of Rome assumed or not the appearance of that autocratic despotism which it really was, however the fact might be disguised.   As regarded

Supremacy of the emperor in election, legislation, and jurisdiction.

---

[1] Hence the memorable expression ascribed to Tiberius himself, with regard to the Roman people : " O homines ad servitutem paratos."   The sentiment was no doubt commonly in men's mouths. So Cæsar in Lucan : " Detrahimus dominos urbi servire paratæ." *Phars.* i. 351.

[2] See Hoeck, i. 3. 68.; citing Suet. *Tib.* 60. 62.; Tac. *Ann.* iii. 70.

the right of jurisdiction, Tiberius continued for the most part to maintain the principle of administration which he had asserted from the first, that of using the senate as the ostensible instrument of his government. He refrained generally, as in Piso's process, from assuming judicial powers himself, and referred all suitors for his decision to the great assembly of the state. This moderation sufficed to satisfy the mass of his subjects. The reform of the rights of election caused but a slight murmur among the people from whom they were finally withdrawn[1]; the abolition of their legislative and judicial competence was accepted without a sign of mortification. The populace of Rome had bidden farewell to all its political interests, and it is only from their connexion with politics that the rights of legislation and jurisdiction are ever interesting to the great body of a nation. The senate itself was flattered by the appearance of a victory over the rivals with whom it had waged such long and dubious warfare. It might amuse itself with the idea that it had found compensation for the disasters of Pharsalia and Philippi, and that the chiefs who had been borne to power on the shoulders of the popular party had been compelled, even in the moment of their elevation, to negotiate the support of the power which they had worsted in the field. But the princeps had in fact got the senate completely under his influence. The powers of the censure alone, the highest and most venerable perhaps of any functions of administration, gave him, under the fairest disguise, a direct means of controlling it. The sum of twelve hundred thousand sesterces being fixed as the qualification for a place in the assembly, the emperor encouraged men of birth,

The emperor's control over the senate through the powers of the censorship.

---

[1] Tac. *Ann.* i. 15.: "Neque populus ademptum jus questus est nisi inani rumore."

whose fortunes had fallen below this standard, to
apply to him for an increase of means; at the same
time he took care to let them feel, by an occasional
repulse, accompanied with harsh observations, how
mere a matter of favour such an indulgence would

Petition of a pauper senator. be. After aiding, as it was styled, the census of several of the body, his rejection of
the petition of a pauper senator named
Hortalus, a grandson of the illustrious Hortensius,
caused considerable dismay. How the wealth accumulated by that busy advocate had been dissipated,
does not appear; but already under the principate of
Augustus Hortalus had received a pecuniary gratification, to enable him to marry and rear a family,
and maintain the honours of his historic house. Still,
however, was he haunted by the demon of poverty.
Rising in his place in the senate-house, at the open
doors of which he had stationed his four sons, and
turning himself on the one hand to the bust of Hortensius, conspicuous among the images which adorned
the hall, on the other to that of Augustus, he addressed a speech to Tiberius, entreating him in the
names of both to afford him the succour he required.
But whether from a settled policy of degrading the
representative of a great republican name, or from
personal dislike, or, as Tacitus insinuates, merely from
a spirit of surly opposition to the inclination of the
senators around him, Tiberius not only rejected the
application, but rebuked it as presumptuous and importunate. *The divine Augustus,* he said, *gave you
money spontaneously, without solicitation, nor did
he mean to bind himself or me to repeat the same
liberality on all occasions.* He consented, however,
to gratify the senate by making a trifling present to
the children; after which he made no further effort
to save the rapid decline and degradation of their
house.[1]

[1] Tac. *Ann.* ii. 37, 38.

This control over the senate was still further assured by the right of its princeps to convene
it at his own pleasure on extraordinary
occasions, as well as to prorogue its ordinary
sittings.   If he could not legitimately require it to affirm every proposition he placed before
it, he was enabled at least to defeat at once any
motion that was disagreeable to himself, either by
dissolving the assembly, or even by putting his veto
upon the transaction.   The utmost liberty it continued to possess extended not to acts, but merely to
language, if the indistinct murmurs and interjectional
sarcasms which were occasionally heard within its
walls could be dignified with such an appellation.
But every such indication of independent opinion,
however disguised and smothered, was watched with a
jealousy which the substance of power never allowed
to slumber, and the law of Majestas or Treason,
which Tiberius brandished over the heads of his
counsellors, was an instrument of flexible and search-
ing application for unveiling their hidden sentiments,
no less than for controlling their conduct.

The emperor's control over the senate by the law of Majestas.

Majestas, according to the Ovidian apologue, was
the daughter of Dignity and Respect, who
first after the dispersion of primeval chaos
taught the rules of courtesy to the rude
and undisciplined divinities.[1]   Ages rolled away, and
when the Giants rose in arms to restore universal
anarchy, Jove overthrew them with his bolts, and
defended the majesty of the gods, never again to be
presumptuously assailed.   Hence, she ever sits beside him ; she cherishes and protects him ; the awe
inspired by her influence makes his sceptre to be

Origin of the law of Majestas.

---

[1] Ovid, *Fast.* v. 23. :

> " Donec Honos placidoque decens Reverentia vultu
>   Corpora legitimis imposuere toris."

Honos and Reverentia are correlatives : the one is the honourable
station or office, the other the respect due to it.

obeyed without force of arms. She has descended
also upon the earth. Romulus and Numa acknowledged and adored her; nor less did their successors,
each in his own generation. She it is that makes
our fathers and mothers to be respected; she attends
upon our youths; she protects our virgins; she commends to the consul his fasces and ivory chair; finally,
she rides aloft on the laurelled chariot of the imperator.[1]   Such was the language by which a flatterer
of Augustus might divert the imagination of his
countrymen from the idea of the abstract majesty
of law and constitutional principle, to that of the
glory which surrounded the person of the ruler;
from the recollection of kings and consuls to the
contemplation of the emperor himself, over whom
all the ensigns of office were suspended.   Under the
empire the law of majesty was the legal protection
thrown round the person of the chief of the state:
any attempt against the dignity or safety of the community became an attack on its glorified representative.   Nevertheless, it is remarkable that the first
legal enactment which received this title, half a century before the foundation of the empire, was actually
devised for the protection, not of the state itself, but
of a personage dear to the state, namely, the tribune
of the people.   Treason to the state indeed had long
before been known, and defined as *Perduellio*, the
levying of war against the commonwealth.   Laws on
this subject had existed from the time of the kings.

The lex
Apuleia,
A. U. 654.
But the crime of majesty was first specified
by the demagogue Apuleius, in an enactment of the year 654, for the purpose of
guarding or exalting the dignity of the champion of
the plebs.   Any attempt against the prerogatives of
this popular officer was declared to be an assault on

---

[1] Ovid, *l. c.*:

> " Illa datos fasces commendat, eburque curule;
>   Illa coronatis alta triumphat equis."

the greatness and dignity of the commonwealth itself: to detract from the majesty of the tribune was
an offence which the new law smote with the penalties
of treason.[1]

The law of Apuleius was followed by that of
another tribune, Varius, conceived in a
similar spirit.   But it was the object of
Sulla, in the ample and methodized scope

The lex Varia : the lex Cornelia.

of his Cornelian constitution, to withdraw the
definition of majesty from a mere offence against
public officers, to attempts on the general interests
of the commonwealth.   The dictator conceived and
embodied, in the spirit of a proud republican, the
noble sentiment of a patriot of our own, that *There
is on earth a far diviner thing, Veiled though it
be, than parliament or king.* He recalled men's
minds from the vulgar personifications to which democracy naturally inclines, to the higher abstractions
of an enlightened political wisdom.   The distinction
between Majestas and Perduellio henceforth vanishes:
the crime of Treason is specifically extended from acts
of violence to measures calculated to bring the state
into contempt.   It is made to include not only acts
of commission, but many cases of the neglect or imperfect performance of duty.[2]   It is now majestas in

---

[1] Among the numerous treatises upon this subject I have particularly referred to some chapters in the work of Rein on the Criminal
Law of the Romans.   He assigns the date of the lex Apuleia to 654
u. c., not 652.   The personal application of the law appears in a
passage of Cicero (*De Invent.* ii. 17.): "Majestatem minuisti quod
tribunum pl. de templo deduxisti ;" but the more general definition
of the crime is given in the *Ad Herenn.* ii. 12.: "Majestatem is
minuit, qui ea tollit, ex quibus civitatis amplitudo constat."   Again,
the two branches of the crime are combined in one view (*De Invent.*
ii. 17.): "Majestatem minuere est, de dignitate, aut amplitudine,
aut potestate populi, aut eorum quibus populus potestatem dedit,
aliquid derogare :" or once more, "Aliquid de re publica, quum
potestatem non habeas, administrare."   Rein, *Crim-Recht der Römer*,
p. 509.

[2] Thus, on the words of Cicero against Verres (2 *Verr.* i. 33.),
"Quid imminuisti jus legationis," the Pseudo-Asconius remarks

a public officer, not only if he wages war without
due authority from the state, or betrays his trust to
the enemy, or foments sedition among the citizens or
mutiny among the soldiers; but if he shrinks from
asserting to the full the prerogative of his office,
whether military or civil, or forbears to deliver his
prisoners to the proper authorities for punishment or
ransom.[1] To remove or overthrow a monument of
the glory of the commonwealth, such as a statue or a
trophy, might afford ground for a charge of this
nature, as wounding the pride of the nation or touching its honour.[2]

The motive for Cæsar's legislation on the subject
of majestas, in which he went further into details
than Sulla, but in no respect diverged from his principles, was no other perhaps than a determination to
obliterate every monument of the usurpation of the
senate, and its redoubted dictator. Cæsar was the
hereditary antagonist of Sulla, and, to complete the
full cycle of his rivalry, it was necessary that he
should emulate his predecessor in legislation as well
as in arms and administration. The chief
provisions of the lex Julia on this subject
have been preserved to us by the jurists of the later
empire; but we are not perhaps quite competent to
decide how far the law, as it came from Julius himself, was modified by his next successors. It is still
a disputed point whether Augustus promulgated any
distinct lex Julia of his own upon Majestas; though
there is no question that in some respects he ex-

The lex Julia de Majestate.

<hr>

(Orell. p. 182.): " Qui potestatem suam in administrando non defen-
derit, imminuti magistratus veluti majestatis læsæ reus est."

[1] Cæsar's juvenile act of audacity in punishing his captive pirates,
and refusing to deliver them to his superior officer, was a defiance of
the Cornelian law of Majestas. See vol. i., ch. iii.

[2] This is one of the charges Cicero brings against Verres (2 *Verr.*
iv. 41.), of which he affirms, " Est majestatis quod imperii nostri
gloriæ rerumque publicarum monumenta evertere atque asportare
ausus est."

tended the law of his predecessor, including in his
definition the publication of written pasquinades
against the emperor, as an indirect mode of bringing
the person of the ruler into contempt, and smooth-
ing the way for disaffection and resistance.   This is
perhaps the only trace of any desire on the part of
the two first emperors to give the law a special
application for their own protection; and even in
the Cornelian law some provision seems to have been
made to check the licence of railing against the
constituted authorities.[1]

It will be important for the just appreciation of
later usage in respect to this grave offence,
the highest, except sacrilege, known to   *Provisions of
the Roman law, to place before our eyes   the Julian Law
                                             of Majesty.*
a comprehensive sketch of the Julian enactments
regarding it.   Majestas, then, was defined to be
injury to the state :— 1., in respect of its public
enemies, as by the surrender of cities or persons,
the abetting or assisting them in their enterprises,
desertion to them, cowardice in action against them,
and the like: 2., in respect of its internal constitution, as by illicit combinations, clubs, and conspiracies,
or more openly by sedition and riot : 3., in respect
of its officers, as when one magistrate encroached on
the functions of another, or withheld from his successor the forces of his province, or released a criminal
from punishment, or made war without public authority ; or, again, where one compassed the death of a
public officer, or wrested from him his prerogatives :
4., from the falsification of the public documents.—
It was necessary to the establishment of the crime
to prove the criminal intention ; but the attempt was
held to be equally obnoxious to the law as the act
itself, and the accomplice by aid or counsel was

[1] Cic. *ad Div.* iii. 11.: "Et si Sulla voluit ne in quemvis impune
declamare liceret."

amenable to the same punishment as the principal.[1] This punishment was simple and uniform. It consisted in the interdiction of fire and water, which was practically equivalent to banishment, and was attended with confiscation of property, being the same penalty which attached to the more ancient crime of perduellio.[2] The trial of charges of this kind was regularly reserved for one of the special tribunals. During the brief period of Cæsar's power it does not appear that this tribunal was ever called into action. Trials for majesty were few even under the long principate of his successor. Augustus carefully abstained from the employment of an engine which he well knew must, from the nature of things, tend to fix in men's minds a sharp distinction between the chief of the state and the state itself. The sacredness which attached to the tribunitian office, now vested in himself, could not fail to raise the person of the ruler above the abstract ideas of constitutional principle; but he was anxious not to hasten the moment when the people of Rome should regard the law of treason merely as a device for their ruler's security. He felt himself protected by other and stronger safeguards; while the chief danger of his position actually lay in the risk of his disguise being torn too rudely from him.

Reserve of Augustus in its application.

It has been already shown how the natural policy of Tiberius pointed in another direction. The second princeps required special guarantees for his security. Accordingly from the very commencement of his reign

Under Tiberius protection demanded for the person of the emperor.

---

[1] See Rein (*Criminal-Recht*, pp. 518—525.), chiefly from the writings of the jurists. Tacitus (*Ann.* i. 72.) states the principle of the law : "Si quis proditione exercitum aut plebem seditionibus, denique male gesta re publica majestatem populi Romani minuisset : facta arguebantur, dicta impune erant."

[2] Tac. *Ann.* iii. 50.: "Bonis amissis aqua et igni arceatur : quod perinde censeo ac si lege majestatis teneretur." Comp. iii. 38. 68., iv. 42.; Paulus, v. 29. 1.

we mark a change in popular opinion, which he fostered and encouraged. The person of the emperor begins now to be the great subject of the law of treason : though not formally so pronounced, the idea that the emperor is himself the state begins to predominate in the national feeling over every other. The emperor is now in the world what the gods are in Olympus, a being to be reverenced and feared simply for himself, without regard to his attributes, or the qualities he may be supposed to embody. Attempts on his life become heinous deeds, only to be compared with sacrilege against the blessed divinities. Not only such overt acts, however, but any conduct or language which could be construed into the compassing of his death, became involved in the crime and penalties of treason. Rome was full of soothsayers or magicians, who pretended, by casting horoscopes or evoking dead men's spirits, to communicate a knowledge of future events. By playing on the credulous cupidity of heirs or fortune-hunters, these impostors acquired wealth and consideration. In the age of Catullus, a wicked parent might *wish* for the death of his son, or the son disclaim all sorrow for the loss of his parent : but in the next generation Ovid could represent the guilty spendthrift as *inquiring into the years* of the sire who stands between himself and fortune.[1] To inquire thus into the years of the emperor, to explore, that is, the secret of his destined term of life, was now reputed treasonable : there must be, it was argued, some stronger motive for such an inquiry than mere indecent curiosity : the man who sought to ascertain beforehand the day of the emperor's

---

[1] Compare, among the signs of human degeneracy in Catullus, liv. 401.:

　　" Destitit extinctos natus lugere parentes:
　　　Optavit genitor primævi funera nati . . . . ."

with Ovid, *Metam.* i. 148.:

　　" Filius ante diem patrios inquirit in annos."

doom must have some illicit interest in the dire event ;
he must cherish the hopes of a traitor in his heart.[1]
Not only pasquinades and injurious publications of
every kind directed against the emperor were now comprehended in the qualification of majestas, but also
abusive and insulting language, which Augustus had
so magnanimously tolerated. The two first Cæsars,
and generally the best and wisest of their successors,
allowed ample licence to the tongue, in the freedom
of which the Romans continued to demand indulgence
long after they had surrendered all independence of
action.[2] This licence of language was fostered by
the manner of their education. We have seen how

Licence of
language in
use among
the Romans.

they were brought up from childhood as
gladiators in the arena of debate and
declamation : fence of tongue was the weapon with which they were to maintain against every
assailant their honour, their fortunes, and their lives.
Readiness of speech and ease in the handling of the
weapons of retort and sarcasm were carried from the
schools of rhetoric to the tribunals or the forum, and
again from the places of their public exercise to the
private assembly or banquet. Scurrility of language
was indeed characteristic of the Italians, and was

---

[1] Paulus, v. 21. 3.: "Qui de salute principis vel de summa rei-
publicæ mathematicos . . . . consulit, cum eo qui responderit capite
punitur." Tertull. *Apol.* 35.: "Cui opus est perscrutari super
Cæsaris salute, nisi a quo aliquid adversus illum cogitatur vel optatur
aut post illum speratur et sustinetur ?"

[2] The laws of the twelve tables had specified defamatory writings,
or publication generally, as one kind of Injuria ; but the excessive
severity of the penalty, which was no less than death, seems to show
that the crime was not practically visited at all. The disuse of this
process gave occasion for the prætors to issue notices against libel in
their edicts, and one or two cases occur, under the free state, of
actions for slander, for satirical writings, or misrepresentations on the
stage. Fines and civil infamy were the penalties now attached to
this offence. Sulla, and after him Augustus, legislated specifically
upon the subject of the famosi libelli : confining themselves, however, to writings only, and allowing full licence to merely oral
abuse. For the proceedings of Augustus, see Suet. *Oct.* 51.; Tac.
Ann. i. 72. See this subject fully discussed by Rein, pp. 354—385.

common to all classes: it extended from the senators
and knights to the lowest of the populace; it startled
alike the decorum of patrician nuptials and enlivened
the humours of the Saturnalia.   The coarse ribaldry
of the Fescennine farces embodied the same spirit of
unbounded personality which glows in the polished
sentences of Cicero, or flashes from the point of an
epigram of Catullus.   According to Roman habits of
thought, and agreeably perhaps to the theory of the
Roman polity, the private life and habits of the
citizen were as much the property of his fellow-
countrymen as his conduct in public affairs.   His
domestic vices were charged as crimes against
society, and an accusation of bribery or extortion
was habitually introduced by a pretended exposure
of sins of lewdness or intemperance.   This licence of
defamation was the birthright of the free Roman, of
which he was often more jealous than of his independence in thought and action.   He might subject
himself to the arbitrary authority of a tribune or a
dictator without a murmur, as long as he was permitted to retort upon them with jests and scandalous
anecdotes.   No government could maintain itself on
the basis of popular opinion without repressing these
extravagant excesses.   When the chief of the state
was raised to an eminence from which he could
not descend into the arena of personal controversy,
it became a necessary act of policy to restrain the
licence of attack by measures of adequate severity.[1]

Two accounts are given us of the provo-   Conduct of
cation which induced Augustus to extend or   Augustus and
Tiberius with
restore the laws against defamatory writings.   respect to
injurious
On the one hand, we are told that he was   language.
offended by the licentiousness of a writer named

---

[1] On one occasion Augustus threatened to retort : "Faciam sciat
Ælianus et me linguam habere ; plura enim de eo loquar:" but he
abstained nevertheless from committing himself to the unequal
encounter. Suet. Oct. 51.

Cassius Severus, who lashed the most illustrious of
the citizens of both sexes indiscriminately.[1]   We
may infer, therefore, from this statement, that the
emperor now afforded the protection of the law to
women as well as to men, which was probably a
novelty; at least, the principle of the original laws
of libel was founded on the civil dignity of the
citizen, to which a woman could lay no claim.[2]   On
the other hand, it is stated that he was moved to
this course by an attack made on himself by Junius
Novatus, a partisan of the unfortunate Agrippa.   If
this be true, the confirmation of the law must have
been among the latest acts of the aged emperor's
reign.[3]   In either case, it does not appear that the
first princeps gave himself any other protection in
this particular than what he allowed to every citizen.
As regarded himself, he is said to have been very mild
in prosecuting or punishing this offence, and to have
refused to inquire at all into mere oral invectives.[4]
Very different, however, was the conduct in this respect of his uneasy successor.   The awkward and ungenial manners of Tiberius had been an early subject
of ill-natured remark : he was already accused of
gross intemperance, against which many pungent epi-
grams were directed.[5]   But as he rose in eminence

[1] Tac. *Ann.* i. 72.: "Commotus Cassii Severi libidine qui viros
fœminasque illustres procacibus scriptis diffamaverat."

[2] Injuria was anything which unfavourably affected the public
estimation of a citizen, and consequently his power of serving the
state.   But Augustus treated Defamation not as Injuria, but as
Majestas, the greater scope of which enabled him to throw the shield
of the law over illustrious women also.

[3] Suet. *Oct. l. c.*

[4] Suet. *Oct.* 55.   He contented himself, according to this writer,
with contradicting by proclamation some of these attacks, and forbade
the senate to prohibit by a decree the introduction of posthumous
abuse of the emperor in wills.   But Dion (lvi. 27.) says that
he caused some libels against him to be burnt, and punished the
writers.

[5] Suet. *Tib.* 42.   The supposed fragment quoted by Burmann is
in fact this passage of Suetonius versified:

and power, the attacks on him assumed a more serious form, impugning his character as a ruler, im-
puting to him cruelty beyond the law, and a pride
indecent even in the first of the citizens.   The free
insinuation of disagreement between the prince and
his mother might lead to inconvenient revelations of
his domestic privacy.[1]   When on his first accession
to power his pleasure was taken by the prætor about
the appointment of the special commission for Majestas, he evaded the question with a general reply.
He did not intend to allow these cases to fall under
the jurisdiction of an independent tribunal, but to
reserve them for the cognisance of his own instrument,
the senate; or perhaps at this time he had not really
determined what course he should pursue.   At first he
met such accusations with a magnanimity worthy of
a great monarch: *Let them hate me,* he was heard to
say, *as long as in their hearts they respect me; . . . .
in a free state,* he added, *both mind and tongue
should be free:* but unfortunately he could not
maintain this elevation of sentiment, and the bitterness with which he presently revenged himself on his
detractors was supposed to prove that the charges

> " Exinde plebs Quiritium vocavit
> Non Claudium Tiberium Neronem
> Sed Caldium Biberium Meronem."

Comp. Suet. *Tib.* 59.:

> " Fastidit vinum quia jam sitit iste cruorem;
> Tam bibit hunc avide quam bibit ante merum."

[1] Tac. *Ann.* i. 72.: " Hunc quoque asperavere carmina, incertis
auctoribus vulgata, in sævitiam superbiamque ejus, et discordem cum
matre animum "   We may conceive the effect on prince and people
of such an epigram as the following placarded on the walls of a
modern European capital: Suet. *l. c.*:

> " Aspice felicem sibi non tibi, Romule, Sullam:
>   Et Marium si vis aspice, sed reducem:
> Nec non Antoni civilia bella moventis,
>   Nec semel infectas aspice crede manus:
> Et dic, Roma perit: regnabit sanguine multo
>   Ad regnum quisquis venit ab exsilio."

against him were pointed with the fatal sting of truth.[1]

When, however, it once became known that the new princeps was jealous of his estimation in the minds of the citizens, and would not suffer himself or his position to be disparaged by railing defamation, there were many to urge him forwards, and impel him beyond the bounds he may have originally prescribed to himself. It was impossible to maintain any clear distinction between the guilt of written and merely spoken libels. It might be said, indeed, that the one admitted of direct proof, while the other could only be prosecuted on the precarious ground of hearsay evidence; or that the one argued deliberate intention, the other might be a momentary ebullition of thoughtless spleen; or, lastly, that the one was a crime recognised by the ancient laws, the other was not less expressly countenanced by them as a privilege of the Roman freeman. But all these considerations gave way, and not unjustly, to the conviction that the malice might be the same, the injury equal in either case, and that common sense and equity demanded that they should both be brought under the same category of crime. Tiberius was encouraged, not by courtiers only, but by jurists and philosophers, in extending the definition of majesty from writings to words; and in so doing, he only carried out a sound and reasonable principle. But this was not all. It was easy to see that there might be many other ways of bringing the person of the sovereign into contempt, besides either writings or words. The same jurists who could not blind themselves to the logical sequence from one of these to the other, were at a loss

Crime of Majesty extended from writings to words.

---

[1] Suet. *Tib.* 42.: "Oderint dum probent : dein'vera certaque esse ipse fecit fidem." 28.: "In civitate libera linguam mentemque liberas esse debere."

to distinguish from them a variety of actions, some monstrous and many merely ridiculous. Thus Falanius, a knight of obscure position, was accused of disrespect to the princeps, amounting to the guilt of treason, inasmuch as he had admitted a low

and profligate actor to assist in celebrating the rites of the deified Augustus. Another of the same class, named Rubrius, was charged with having forsworn himself in the name of that illustrious divinity, and again, of allowing, at the sale of a villa, the sacred image to be sold along with it. It was pretended that disrespect towards the deceased Cæsar was an injury to his living successor. But Tiberius refused to subscribe to this doctrine. He wrote a letter to the consuls in favour of the accused, asserting that Livia herself, in exhibiting games in her husband's honour, had not deemed it requisite to inquire into the life and manners of all the professional people she employed; adding that perjury in the name of Augustus was no more a subject for human laws than the violation of an oath to Jupiter; and ending with the memorable aphorism, profane perhaps in the mouth of any one not himself next of kin to divinity, that the gods should be left to mind their own honour.[1] About the same time a man of higher rank and character, named Granius Marcellus, apparently a connexion

of the imperial house, then prætor of Bithynia, was accused by an officer of his own staff of having uttered in conversation some reflections on the emperor's personal habits; a charge which, we are assured, it was impossible to refute, so strong was the presumption against any man of having remarked on the profligacy which was notorious to all the world.

---

[1] Tac. *Ann.* i. 73.: "Jusjurandum perinde æstimandum quam si Jovem fefellisset : Deorum injuriæ Dis curæ."

But a more specific charge against the prætor was
that of having placed his own effigy in a higher and
more conspicuous place than those of the Cæsars,
which, as remotely connected with his family, adorned
the hall of his mansion : it was even suggested, as an
impious flattery at which the emperor's modesty would
revolt, that he had removed the head from an image
of Augustus, and replaced it with that of his living
successor.   In this case also Tiberius rebuked the
officious zeal of the prosecutor.   The culprit was
acquitted of the charge of treason ; but he happened
to lie at the time under a charge of extortion in
his province, and on this the senate was permitted
to condemn him.[1]

But of all the charges of this nature now preferred, none was more extravagant than
that against Lutorius Priscus, a knight
who had obtained great success with some
verses he had composed on the death of Germanicus.
Tiberius himself, relaxing from his usual reserve and
parsimony, had rewarded the well-timed compliment
with an imperial largess.   On the occasion of an illness which occurred to Drusus, the poet was tempted
to try the fortune of his muse again, and prepared a
second dirge, in anticipation of a second decease in
the Cæsarean family.   Drusus recovered ; but the
author's vanity prevailed over prudence and propriety, and he recited his verses before a fashionable
audience.   The matter became noised abroad, an information was laid against the culprit, and on the
motion of Haterius, a consul designate, the senate
condemned to death as guilty of speculating on a
Cæsar's death, and therefore, by an easy inference, of
compassing it by wishes and prayers.   Of the senators
two only ventured to excuse him on the ground of
thoughtlessness and levity : exile they would have

Case of
Lutorius
Priscus.

_____
[1] Tac. *Ann.* i. 74.

regarded as sufficient punishment for a fault which could hardly be expected to find imitators. But their representations were unavailing. The wretched man was dragged to prison and immediately strangled. Tiberius, who was absent from Rome at the time, was mortified at this sanguinary proceeding, and still more, perhaps, at the indecent haste with which it had been conducted. Refraining from any direct censure of Haterius, or the senate generally, he contented himself with praising the sentiments of the more merciful minority, and decreed that henceforth an interval of ten days should always elapse between sentence and execution, to leave room for the exercise of pardon. This considerate provision continued in force not only during the government of Tiberius, but under his successors also.[1]

But the senate pretended, in its servile adulation, to grieve at the restraint which the emperor thus imposed on its headlong zeal in defence of his dignity. A knight named Ennius was soon afterwards denounced for having melted down an image of the emperor, and converted it into plate for the service of the table. On this occasion Tiberius peremptorily forbade proceedings to be instituted. Thereupon, Ateius Capito, now grown grey in reputation as the most eminent jurist of his times, assumed the tone of injured liberty, and complained that the fathers should be debarred from the free exercise of their undoubted right of judgment: the crime, he declared, was a grave one, and however mild he might be in avenging a private wrong, he for one could not suffer the majesty of the republic to be assailed

Case of Ennius. A. D. 22. A. U. 775.

---

[1] For the story of Lutorius Priscus, see Tac. *Ann.* iii. 49—51., under the date A. U. 774, A. D. 21. Dion (in lvii. 15.) relates that a certain Vibius Rufus prided himself on possessing two great curiosities, the relict of Cicero, and the chair in which Cæsar was slain, as if the one could make him an orator, and the other an emperor ; and seems to think it showed great moderation in Tiberius to overlook such a treasonable imagination.

with impunity.   Tiberius knew the man, the hoary apologist for the Cæsarean usurpation, and could appreciate at its proper value this empty show of zeal for independence.   He paid no regard to the objection, but persisted in his interference; not displeased at the jealousy with which the jurist was henceforth more generally regarded, who thus disgraced his own name, and degraded in the eyes of the citizens the dignity of his science.[1]

Such, indeed, was the proneness of the senate to this mode of flattery, that no public charge against an illustrious citizen seems to have been thought complete, unless coupled with the imputation of disrespect towards the emperor.[2] Thus about the same time we hear of Silanus, proconsul of Asia, being accused of extortion; but no sooner was the impeachment set forth, than a consular, an ædile, and a prætor started up with some other vague charges against him, as that he had *profaned the divinity of Augustus, and disparaged the majesty of Tiberius*.   In the trial which followed the emperor seems to have disdained to take notice of these accessory incriminations.   The case against Silanus was sufficiently clear.   He had not the courage or the eloquence to defend himself, but threw himself despairingly on the imperial clemency, and the dignity of his own family, for protection.   Tiberius, however, fortified by the conduct of Augustus in a case of similar guilt, and glad to gratify the popular sentiment by making an example of so noble a culprit, encouraged the senate to proceed to sentence against him; and when it decreed the punishment of relegation to an island, interfered only to mitigate the penalty by naming Cythera as the place of con-

Case of
Silanus.
A. D. 22.
A. U. 775.

----

[1] Tac. *Ann.* iii. 70.

[2] Tac. *Ann.* iii. 38.: " Postulaverat repetundis, addito majestatis crimine, quod tum omnium accusationum complementum erat."

finement, instead of the more inhospitable rock of
Gyarus.[1]

Tiberius had exhibited similar magnanimity in two
previous cases, which are reserved to be
mentioned together, because they relate to
women; for political charges against women
were a new feature in Roman procedure.
Apuleia Varilia was a connexion of the imperial
family, being a granddaughter of Octavia; as such,
the crime of adultery, with which she was charged,
became an offence against the law of Majesty.   But
to enhance her guilt, expressions of disrespect towards
Augustus and Tiberius, and even against Livia, were
imputed to her.   Upon the first and principal charge
the emperor was satisfied with referring the prosecutors to the Julian law of adultery : he refused to
listen to the charge of disrespect towards himself and
his mother ; the insinuation of an offence against the
sanctity of Augustus he would alone permit to be
made the subject of inquiry.   This last charge speedily
fell to the ground ; but the licentiousness of an illustrious matron, which was amply proved, was punished
with removal beyond the two hundredth milestone.[2]
Nearly similar to this was the case of Lepida, who
combined with her Æmilian ancestry a connexion
with the Sullan and Pompeian houses, and who was
esteemed of sufficient political importance to be subjected to charges of adultery and poisoning, aggravated by inquiries through the soothsayers into the
destinies of the imperial family.   In this instance,
also, we find Tiberius exercising great moderation in
regard to the charges which affected himself, first
desiring the senate to dismiss them altogether, and
when it persisted, forbidding the examination of the
culprit's slaves against her.   She was ultimately convicted on the other accusations, and interdicted fire

(marginal note:) Case of Apuleia and Lepida, A. D. 17. A. D. 20.

---

[1] Tac. *Ann.* iii. 66—69.   [2] Tac. *Ann.* ii. 50.

and water; but even then, the confiscation of her estates, which should properly have followed, was remitted.[1]

Such was the moderation of Tiberius for several years from the commencement of his reign,

The injustice
Tiberius has
done to his
own repu-
tation.

in the defence of his own person and position; such was the difficulty in which he was placed by the overweening zeal of flatterers, and still more by the ambition or cupidity of senators, who sought distinction or profit from the trade of criminal accusation. Tiberius himself, besides the desire he manifested for the attainment of substantial justice, was admitted on all hands to be free from the sordid vices so common among his countrymen. He was, to use the strong but rough expression of Tacitus, *firm enough against money*.[2] But if he has failed in other respects to obtain from history all the justice he sought to obtain for his people, the cause lay partly in himself, and in the peculiar infirmity into which his excess of zeal betrayed him. The mind of Tiberius was characterized by a certain painful preciseness: he was possessed with the litigious spirit which insists on its presumed rights, in spite of every inconvenience. He was deficient in breadth of view, and sought in vain to compensate for it by subtlety and acuteness. Accordingly, we are not surprised to find that the general and statesman, the chief of innumerable armies, and the head of a confederacy of nations, was moreover a purist in his use of language, and fond of disputing with the grammarians on the exact meaning of words, full of notes and queries on the most trifling and puerile subjects of literary curiosity, in which certainly truth could not be attained, and as certainly was not worth attaining.[3]

[1] Tac. *Ann.* iii. 22, 23.
[2] Tac. *Ann.* iii. 18.: " Satis firmus adversum pecuniam."
[3] Suet. *Tib.* 70.: " Affectatione et morositate nimia obscarabat

Tiberius carried in short to the throne the temper of a pedant, and a pedant on the throne is in danger of becoming a tyrant. Hence the encouragement he unfortunately gave to the criminal informers, or delators; His encour-
agement of
the delators
or criminal
informers. an encouragement which he soon acknowledged to be pernicious, and withdrew in dismay, till the distrust and apprehensions of increasing years drove him again into the same fatal course. The delator was properly one who gave notice to the fiscal officers of moneys that had become due to the treasury of the state, or more strictly to the emperor's fiscus.[1] The title was first extended from this narrow sphere to persons who lodged information in case of any offences punishable by fine; and when Augustus undertook to legislate comprehensively on the subject of marriage, its obligations and its violations, he was induced, by the great difficulty of executing the provisions of an unpopular enactment, to subsidize by pecuniary rewards informers against its transgressors.[2] It was the aim of Augustus to attach every citizen to some peculiar branch of industry: wherever he could he gave direct occupation; in many other cases he indirectly pointed out where it might be found. He now called into existence a new employment, though he did not himself live to see its progress and development. Many were the knights and senators who now learnt to make a traffic of their eloquence and accomplishments, in the service of the emperor, by the vindica-

stylum . . . . monopolium nominaturus prius veniam postulavit." Dion (lvii. 15.) says that he suffered a project of law to drop rather than use a Greek word for which there was no Latin equivalent. Comp. also, the story of Capito, in lvii. 17., and Suet. *de Illustr. Gramm.* 22.

[1] See Rein, *Criminal-Recht*, p. 814, note.

[2] Tac. *Ann.* iii. 28.: " Inditi custodes, et lege Papia Poppæa præmiis inducti."

tion of his unpopular laws. They reaped their reward not in money only,—though a portion of the pecuniary mulct fell regularly to their share, and the senate not rarely decreed them a special remuneration,—but in political distinction also, and even in a notoriety akin to fame. Their love of power was amply gratified, when they saw the criminal, a man perhaps of the noblest birth and highest position, quail before their well-known energy and audacity, and desist from a hopeless contest with their acknowledged powers of persuasion. Feared by the great, they became the patrons and champions of the people, who were always ready to behold in the attack on noble offenders a vindication of popular rights and principles. They acquired in the forum some portion of the consideration which attached of old to the sturdy independence of the tribunes, while they were thrust into the favour and confidence of the princeps, or at least of his nearest advisers, in the palace. The trade of the delator became thus, under bad emperors, the broad and beaten track of a crafty ambition.[1]

But this infamous practice became so marked a feature in Roman society, and affected so painfully the imaginations of the people, that it will be well to spend a few moments here in depicting to ourselves its action more widely. We must trace it back, like every other pest of the imperial times, to its first origin under the republic, when the evil inherent in its principle was disguised or even ennobled by loftier aims, and by the freshness of its growth in an atmosphere of freedom. The liberty of the Roman citizen, the prime jewel of his existence, was to be maintained at any price.

Passion of the Romans for accusation.

---

[1] On the rewards of the delators, see Suet. *Tib.* 61.; Dion, lviii. 14.; Tac. *Ann.* ii. 32., iv. 30., vi. 47.

It was maintained by a system of universal terrorism. Every citizen was invited to watch over the conduct of his compatriots, and to menace every deviation from the path of civil virtue with a public accusation. Every young noble was trained in the art of pleading, partly to enable him, when his own turn came, to defend himself, but primarily to furnish him with weapons of offence, and thereby with the means of self-advancement. Rhetoric was an instrument of power, by which he might expect to make himself admired by the people, and feared by competitors of his own class. He fought his way to public honours on the floor of the law courts, dragging successively from their benches the tribunes, the prætors, and the consuls, before whom he first began his career of eloquence. The intrigues and treasons of the men in power did not always suffice to furnish victims for this mania of impeachment: it was necessary to extend the inquisition into the provinces, and summon before the bar of Roman opinion the governors who had sinned, if not against the laws of the republic, against those at least of humanity and justice. To interest the citizens, to inflame their passions, to bias their judgments on the subject of crimes thus perpetrated on remote provincials, required great exertion of art and eloquence; but the genius and industry of the young advocates and their teachers kept pace with every demand upon them. Feelings of party were appealed to in the place of genuine patriotism. The truth of the accusation became of little importance; it was the great triumph of the rhetorician, not unfrequently gained, to baffle the interests of a political faction, without regard to the intrinsic merits of the case. The young orator, who at the age of nineteen or twenty could sway the votes of a bench of judges against some veteran proconsul grown grey in the service of the state, was marked as sure to rise to the highest political eminence.[1]   The energy and aggressive spirit of the Romans was ever conspicuous in the toga no less than in the sagum ; they preferred the attack to the defence, in the forum as well as in the field.

It was the glory of Cicero that he abstained in his early career, while yet his fame was to be acquired, from this common routine of prosecution, and sought the less dazzling career of a pleader for the accused.   Yet in the most glowing of his effusions, both in public and private causes, he appears as the assailant ; and neither humanity nor policy prevent him from declaring himself the enemy of the man against whom he seeks to enlist his hearers' prejudices.[2] The Romans made no scruple of avowing their personal animosities ; the spirit of revenge with them was a virtue which a man would affect if he had it not.[3]   In the heart of the Roman friendship occupied the place of love ; it was invested with a sanctity and solemnity of obligation which approached almost to chivalry : but the reaction from it was an enmity not less deeply felt nor less solemnly pronounced : the foe was not less devoted than the friend.[4]   Neither

The want, under the empire, of great and interesting topics for eloquence.

---

[1] Thus Crassus maintained an accusation at nineteen years. Cæsar at twenty-one, Pollio at twenty-two.   Tac. *de Orat.* 34.; Quintil. *Inst.* xii. 6.

[2] There are some curious passages in the speech *de Provinciis Consularibus,* in which Cicero excuses himself for seeming to waive his notorious hostility to Cæsar : "8. Me communis utilitatis habere rationem, non doloris mei."   "18. Accepi injuriam ; inimicus esse debui ; non nego."   "20. Hoc tempore rei publicæ consulere, inimicitias in aliud tempus reservare deberem."

[3] Tac. *de Orat.* 36.; "Assignatæ domibus inimicitiæ.   40. Jus potentissimum quemque vexandi, atque ipsa inimicitiarum gloria." *Hist.* ii. 53.: "Ut novus adhuc, et in senatum nuper ascitus, magnis inimicitiis claresceret."   Champagny, *Césars,* i. p. 237.

[4] The Duel, the legitimate descendant of private warfare, could have no place in Roman society, which regarded man as the citizen only, an unit in the body corporate.   Personal violence was prohibited by law, and even carrying arms was interdicted.   The *Cut,* the resource of sullenness and shyness, is, I believe, a strictly English

shame therefore nor humanity interfered to check this passion for accusation, in which the Romans were to the full as unscrupulous and unfeeling, though dealing with their own countrymen, as they were in invading the lands of the foreigner. This fearful vice was gilded under the free state by the splendour of the objects to which it was directed, the magnitude of the interests involved, and the abilities and powers of the giants it summoned to the contest.[1] In the atmosphere of liberty it called many corresponding virtues into action; it produced on the whole one of the highest manifestations of human nature, and taking the good with the evil, we may not perhaps be entitled to regret the existence which was permitted to it. But for the same vice, as it appeared under the empire, no such excuse can be offered. Then too, as soon as the young patrician had quitted the schools of the declaimers, he longed to make a trial of his accomplishments, and sought an object on which to flesh the maiden sword of his eloquence. There were no longer party interests into which to throw himself; the class of intriguing politicians no longer existed, whose attempts against the liberties of the commonwealth demanded his vigilance and invited his exposure; the provinces, administered at last on settled principles, and kept under the eye of the central government, afforded still some, but much rarer, cases of public wrong to denounce and avenge. What remained then for the

institution ; and the formal renunciation of friendship was the last resource of outraged feeling among the Romans. Thus Germanicus sends Piso a solemn declaration that their friendship is at an end. Tiberius forbids Labeo his house. Tac. *Ann.* vi. 29.: " Morem fuisse majoribus, quoties dirimerent amicitias, interdicere domo, eumque finem gratiæ ponere." In reply to the common apology for the duel, that it prevents assassination, it may be remarked that assassination was almost unknown to a late period among the Romans.

[1] The reader should refer to the passage of Tacitus *de Orat.*, 34—37., one of the most interesting in ancient literature.

young aspirant? how exercise the gifts he had so
long been fostering in private, and ventilate abroad
the talents to which schools and saloons had accorded
such inspiriting acclamations? The progress of
special legislation, diverted as it was from the public
to the private career of the Roman, entering into his
dwelling and penetrating the recesses of his home
life, gave birth to manifold modes of transgression
and evasion, such as the prying eyes of a domestic
spy alone could track. The government, which
might despair of vindicating its authority by the
exertions of its own officers, was grateful to the
passion for forensic distinction, which now urged
the aspirant for fame to drag to light every petty
violation of every frivolous enactment. According to
the spirit of Roman criminal procedure, the informer
and the pleader were one and the same person.
There was no public accuser to manage the prosecution for the government on information from whatever sources derived; but the spy who discovered
the delinquency was himself the man to demand of
the senate, the prætor, or the judge, an opportunity
of proving it by his own eloquence and ingenuity.
The odium of prosecution was thus removed from
the government to the private delator; an immense
advantage to a rule of force which pretended to be
popular. The common right of accusation, the birthright of the Roman citizen, the palladium, so esteemed, of Roman freedom, became thus the most
convenient instrument of despotism. But however
odious such a profession might generally make itself,
whatever the infamy to which it would be consigned
by posterity, those who practised it reaped the reward
they sought in money and celebrity, in influence and
authority, in the favour of the prince, and not rarely
in the applause of the multitude. They could wreak
their malice on their private enemies under the
guise of zeal for the public service; they might

gratify the worst of passions, and exult, under the shadow of the imperial tyranny, in the exercise of a tyranny hardly less omnipotent of their own. The social corruption such a state of things produced grew fast and rankly, and is marked by the swift progress of the contagion from the first raw and ignoble professors to men of real distinction in the state. Beginning with youths fresh from school, or the teachers of rhetoric themselves, it soon spread to magistrates and consulars, and many of the most illustrious statesmen of the early empire were notorious for their addiction to this meanest and most debasing of vices.

As for Tiberius himself, the fanaticism with which he strove to execute in detail the laws bequeathed him by his predecessors, induced him early to stoop to the degradation of countenancing the practice of delation. Refusing to bend under the enormous burden of public affairs, and disdaining or fearing to associate with himself any assistant, as Augustus had wisely done from the first, he strove pertinaciously to make himself familiar with the whole machinery of government, and to take a personal share in all its procedure. He was constant in attendance on the judicial trials of the senate, but only to secure the impartiality of its decisions; he assisted also at the tribunals of the magistrates, taking his seat at the extremity of the bench, to avert the suspicion of unfairly influencing them.[1] Delation he prized as the machinery by which the true ends of justice could, as he imagined, most readily be obtained. When he discovered the vile uses to which it was put, and felt its impolicy

Encouragement of delation by Tiberius.

---

[1] Suet. *Tib.* 33.: "Ac primo catenus interveniebat ne quid perperam fieret . . . . assidebatque juxtim vel ex adverso in parte prin.ori." Comp. Tac. *Ann.* i. 75.: "In cornu tribunalis." Dion, lvii. 7. But, as Tacitus remarks, "Dum veritati consulitur, libertas corrumpebatur."

and unpopularity, he did not refuse to check and
discourage it; and he established a new tribunal of
fifteen senators, by the weight of whose character he
may have hoped to moderate it, and afford, as was
said, some alleviation to the peril and terror of the
citizens.[1]   Certain it is that the records of the earlier
years of the Tiberian despotism abound in evidence
of the emperor's solicitude for the pure administration of justice, and the constant struggle in which he
was engaged with the reckless spirit of violence and
cruelty, of which accusers and judges equally partook.   Ultimately his own steadfastness and constancy gave way. He yielded to the torrent he could
no longer stem alone. He resigned himself to the
sedulous attentions of an evil counsellor, who relieved
him by consummate artifice, without his consciousness, of great part of his burden, and persuaded him
to neglect the rest, and leave the corruption of society to take its course. Tiberius was induced to
acquiesce in the necessity of vices he had originally
striven to resist, and to wrap himself in the selfish
conviction that his own safety was the highest object
of government.   Then came the full development of
the occult principles of the law of treason; then
came the fierce and fanatical stimulus which was
given to the appetite for delation; the conflagration
raged over Rome and Italy, involving every noble
mansion in its blaze, and overthrowing many to
their foundations.[2] It was ruled to be criminal to
perform before an emperor's effigy on a coin or ring
any act which would be indecent in the presence of
the emperor himself, such as to strip a slave for
chastisement, or even to strip oneself for the bath;

[1] Tac. *Ann.* iii. 28.

[2] Tac. *l. c.*: "Urbemque et Italiam et quod usquam civium corri-
puerant, multorumque excisi status."   Comp. *Ann.* i. 73.: "Quibus
initiis, quanta Tiberii arte, gravissimum exitium irrepserit, dein re-
pressum sit, postremo arserit, cunctaque corripuerit."

finally, a citizen was condemned for entering a brothel with a piece of money on which the imperial countenance was stamped.[1] While the fountain of justice was polluted by founding inquiry into these offences on no express laws, but only on perverse and extravagant deductions from them, the legitimate forms of procedure were no longer carefully preserved. Though in cases of majestas the senate alone was the authorized tribunal, the prince gradually claimed to take cognisance of them himself. Tiberius ceased to abide by the ordinary rules of evidence. Augustus himself had evaded the principle of law, that a slave might not be examined by torture against his master, by causing him to be seized and sold to a public officer, and then stretched as the slave of another on the rack.[2] But even this formality was no longer observed. The penalty of death was frequently substituted for banishment, and the worst precedent of the Sullan proscriptions was sometimes followed, in subjecting the criminal's children to the same fate as himself. The property of the condemned was confiscated : if his life was spared, he might be disqualified from making a will; and if he perished before sentence by his own hand, baffled justice might avenge herself by the infliction of posthumous infamy.[3] On the case of Ælius Saturninus, who was flung from the Tarpeian rock for a libel on the em-

Extravagances of the Law of Majesty.

A. D. 22.
A. U. 775.

---

[1] Suet. *Tib.* 59. It must be remembered that the emperor's was not the only head still stamped upon the current coins. Other members of the Cæsarean family partook of that honour. The gold and silver coinage was imperial, but Augustus allowed the senate to issue the copper currency. The names, however, of the triumviri monetales do not occur on medals after the year 740, according to Eckhel, *Doctr. Numm.* v. 64.

[2] Dion, lv. 5.; Tac. *Ann.* iii. 67.

[3] Tac, *Ann.* ii. 31. This was called "damnatio memoriæ." Suetonius crowns this confusion of law and justice by saying, "Omne crimen pro capitali receptum."

peror, an historian remarks that this was one only of
many instances of the infliction of death for reflections on the life and habits of Tiberius; upon which
he adds, that the Romans marvelled at the impolitic jealousy which thus exposed by public processes
details which, whether true or false, acquired from
these processes only their general notoriety and acceptance.   People, he says, imagined Tiberius must
be mad to insist, often against the explicit denial of
the accused, that crimes and vices had been imputed
to him, which a man of sense would have willingly
left unnoticed.   But for the wisdom and policy of
his general administration, which was still patent to
the world, this hypothesis of insanity would have received general assent : as it was, his conduct in this
respect could only be viewed as a strange example
of human inconsistency.   The particulars, however,
of these charges, thus scrupulously and minutely
detailed in the language of legal procedure, were
preserved in the public records, which thus became
an official repository for every calumny against the
emperor which floated on the impure surface of common conversation.   We cannot but suspect that this
was the storehouse to which Tacitus and Suetonius,
or the obscurer writers from whom they drew, resorted for the reputed details of a prince's habits,
whom it was the pleasure and interest of many parties to blacken to the utmost.   The foulest stories
current against Tiberius were probably the very
charges advanced against him by libellers such as
Saturninus, which he openly contradicted and denounced at the time, and which would have sunk
into oblivion with the mass of contemporary slander,
but for the restless and suicidal jealousy with which
he himself registered and labelled them in the
archives of indignant justice.[1]

[1] Dion, lvii. 22, 23.

The subjects of Tiberius, we are assured, conceived a high opinion of the wisdom and policy of his general administration. Even Tacitus, not a favourable nor even a just critic of his character, admits that his conduct in regard to the law of majesty was the only blot on a government distinguished, at least for many years, by prudence, equity, and mildness.[1] But Tacitus, as we shall presently see, is far from consistent with himself in this, as in other expressions of opinion. The first and most urgent duty of the chief of the empire, following the traditions of the consular administration, was to maintain the honour and security of her possessions abroad, and against the foreigner on the frontiers. The law of empire, in the popular view, was continual progress and aggression. To extend the limits of his own province was the business of every proconsul, and to extend the limits of every province was still reputed the paramount duty of the imperator, himself the universal proconsul. The first idea of Cæsar, on attaining sovereignty in the city, was to effect the annexation of Parthia. Augustus had no such wild ambition, no such blind instinct of conquest: he sedulously abstained in many quarters from sending forward the conquering eagles, feeling as he did that the extent of his possessions was already quite as great as one arm could control, too great indeed, as had been amply demonstrated, for the jealous co-rule of consuls and senators. Nevertheless Augustus had never wholly desisted from aggressive warfare beyond the limits of Terminus. In Egypt and Arabia, as well as still later in Germany, he had maintained views of conquest, though he had refrained from putting out in any quarter the whole strength of his armies.

Consolidation of the Roman dominion under Tiberius.

---

[1] Tac. *Ann.* iv. 6.: "Leges, si majestatis quæstio eximeretur, bono in usu." By this we are not to understand merely the judicial procedure, but the handling of the broad principles of administration.

During his reign the empire had been increased with
solid additions; and it had been no vain boast of his
courtiers that he had advanced its frontiers into new
zones and under unknown constellations.[1]   Yet Augustus, it was well known, had left to his successor,
as a legacy of political wisdom, the counsel not to
extend the limits of Roman sovereignty.   This advice
Tiberius frankly accepted.   He withdrew his legions,
as soon as the ambition of Germanicus would permit
him, within the Rhine; and if he allowed campaigns
to be still waged in the valleys of the Atlas, these
were strictly for security and not for conquest.   His
abstaining from the plantation of military colonies
in the provinces, was a pledge of the sincerity of his
peaceful policy.[2]   Instead of extending the frontiers,
he was intent on consolidating his possessions within
them, converting tributary kingdoms into taxable provinces, and reducing restless barbarians to something
more than a nominal subjection.   It was under this
reign, accordingly, that the far regions of Africa, so
long exposed to plunder and disturbance from the
nomade hordes in the recesses of their mountains,
were placed in a state of security, which continued
unassailed for centuries; that the authority of Rome
was first established permanently throughout the wild
district of Thrace, so important for connecting the
conquest of Rome on the Danube with the sources
of her wealth in the Lesser Asia; that Cyzicus and
Cappadocia were incorporated in the universal empire,
and made to contribute from their wealth or poverty
to relieve the pampered impatience of taxation in
Rome and Italy.   All these were in fact substantial
conquests, though they might not be known by such
a title, in which the emperor spared no artifice nor
even fraud, while he cautiously abstained, as far as

---

[1] Virg. Æn. vi. 795.:   "Jacet ultra sidera tellus,
              Extra anni Solisque vices . . . ."

[2] See A. Zumpt. *Comment. Epigraph.* i. 381.

possible, from the use of arms.[1]   The reign of Tiberius deserves, accordingly, to be marked as an era
of no trifling moment in the consolidation of the
Roman power.   It is probable that his own contemporaries were by no means unaware of this, and
abundantly satisfied with a policy which threw many
of their burdens on their subjects and auxiliaries.
Victories and triumphs could have done no more.
But a hundred years later, as we shall see, another
emperor arose, who added wide provinces to the unwieldy bulk of his dominions, and performed martial
exploits which recalled the days of the Pompeius and
of Cæsar; and transient and fruitless as his successes
proved, they served to point an unfavourable and
unjust comparison with the bloodless gains of his
predecessor.   Tacitus, who wrote under the inspiration of the glories of Trajan, though admitting the
general wisdom of the third Cæsar's policy, conde-
scends to sneer at his abstinence from conquest, as
something pusillanimous and unworthy of the Roman
name.[2]

While, however, Augustus had been obliged to
entrust the conduct of his campaigns to *Stations of
the legions
under Ti-
berius.* princes raised almost to an equal rank and
power with himself, his successor, by refraining from aggressive warfare, with the vast combinations it required, could keep all his lieutenants in the modest position befitting their vocation,
and spare the empire the perils which might flow
from an excited and pampered ambition.   The
legions were maintained in the same stations as

---

[1] Suet. *Tib.* 37.: " Hostiles motus per legatos compescuit ; nec
per eos nisi cunctanter et necessario. Reges suspectosque commina-
tionibus magis et querelis quam vi repressit."

[2] Tac. *Ann.* iv. 32.: " Princeps proferendi imperii incuriosus erat."
Compare iv. 4. with a direct allusion to the conquests of Trajan,
" Quanto sit angustius imperitatum."   Here again, as in the case of
delation, we see how Tacitus's estimate of the policy of Tiberius is
coloured by his glowing conceptions of his own master's glory.

under Augustus. The bank of the Rhine was still
guarded, as we have seen, by eight, four in the
Upper, and as many in the Lower Germania. The
Iberian provinces were secured by three only; for
their reduction, though recent, was now justly deemed
complete. Mauretania, which Augustus had at one
time incorporated with the empire, had been again
erected into a tributary kingdom, and given to Juba,
as a present from the Roman people. The African
provinces were held by two legions, and two more
were stationed in Egypt. Four were assigned for the
protection of the East; they were quartered prin-
cipally at Berytus or the Mediterranean, at Antioch
and Cæsarea, or in scattered detachments on the
heights of the Taurus and Libanus: they showed a
front to the Parthians on the Euphrates, and supported the trembling thrones of the petty chiefs of
the Caucasus, who were maintained as a check on the
more powerful sovereigns of the plains. Thrace was
consigned to the defence of kings of its own nation,
under Roman superintendence; while two legions
were posted on the Danube in Pannonia, and as
many on the same stream, after it took the name
of Ister, in the lower regions of Mœsia. Two more
divisions, making a total complement of five-and-
twenty, were quartered in Dalmatia, and formed a
reserve for the armies of the East, while at the same
time they were near enough to awe the submissive
populations of Greece and Lesser Asia. Their position at Apollonia, Dyrrhachium, or Nicopolis was
more important from its proximity to Italy, of which,
in fact, they constituted virtually the garrison; for
the empire still preserved the tradition of the republic, that the legions were the instruments of foreign
domination, not of domestic authority; and no legionary force was allowed to pitch its tents within
the sacred limits of the land, all the free inhabitants
of which were now Roman citizens. The police of

Italy was entrusted to a force of the name of which she had not yet learnt to be jealous. Three Urban and three Prætorian cohorts, the city guards and the life-guards, kept watch over the security of the metropolis and the person of the ruler ; but these it was thought necessary to levy exclusively from the most central districts of the peninsula, from Latium itself or from Umbria and Etruria, and the ancient colonies of the Latin franchise.[1] Slender as these forces appear for the defence of so vast a territory, we are to remember that the auxiliary troops dispersed in the provinces where they were most needed are not included in the list; and these, we are assured, in general terms, may have equalled the number of the legionaries.[2]

It might be easier to maintain the fidelity and discipline of these numerous armies in the excitement of warfare than under the dull monotony of the camp in time of peace. Tiberius's success in this respect,—for after the first commencement of his reign there was no mutiny, nor even the seditious attempt of a discontented officer,—arose no doubt from his firmness in refusing concession to demands for relaxation and indulgence. The complaints which startled him on his accession to power were put down partly by the vigour of his envoys,

The discipline of the legions strenuously maintained.

[1] In giving this list of the legions, Tacitus (*Ann.* iv. 5.) refers particularly to the ninth year of Tiberius (A. U. 776, A.D. 23). He does not mention, and seems indeed not to know of any German guards at Rome. Augustus, we have seen, had such a body-guard ; but he dismissed them after the defeat of Varus, and it is probable that they were not re-embodied by his successor.

[2] Tacitus points out this difference between the legions and the auxiliary cohorts, that the latter were constantly moved from place to place, while the former were kept stationary. The exact proportion of auxiliaries was uncertain, and no doubt varied. Dion, lv. 24. That they were generally about equal to the legionaries may be deduced from Tacitus, *Ann.* iv. 5. Suet. *Tib.* 16. and from the arrangements of the Hyginian camp. See Marquardt in Becker's *Röm. Alterth.* iii. 2. p. 365.

the princes of his own family, but partly also by vague assurances of redress, extorted from his first alarm; these however he retracted or evaded on recovering his presence of mind. The crisis, it may be allowed, was one at which any actual concession might probably have broken down the whole system of iron discipline on which the obedience of the legions rested. Nor would Tiberius encourage the soldiers to look for extraordinary gratuities by occasional largesses, such as Augustus and Cæsar before him had so liberally dispensed. After paying them the sum bequeathed them by his predecessor, which indeed he thought it became him to double, he made no further appeal to their favour and gratitude, except on one important occasion, at a late period of his reign, in requital for a particular service.[1] He trusted, for securing their devotion, solely to the regard they entertained for his title of Imperator, and the deserts by which he had attained it.

Not only the respect in which the commonwealth was held by foreign potentates, but the submission and awe of the provincial populations depended mainly on the firmness of the hand which kept her soldiers to their standards.[2] The tranquillity and contentment of the provinces under Tiberius bear witness to his merits as commander of the Roman armies. While writers with whom we are the most familiar depict the character of this Cæsar in the most hideous colours, and only with manifest reluctance admit any circumstances which bespeak the moderation and equity of his rule, it is remarkable that the independent testimony of two provincial authorities combines to assure

The governors of provinces kept for several years in office.

---

[1] Tac. *Ann.* i. 36.; Dion, lvii. 5.; Suet. *Tib.* 48.

[2] Vell. ii. 126.: " Diffusa in orientis occidentisque tractus, et quidquid meridiano aut septentrione finitur, pax augusta per omnes terrarum orbis angulos a latrociniorum metu servat immunes."

us that in the provinces at least his administration
was beneficent, and his memory held in honour.
Thus Philo of Judæa speaks in glowing terms of the
wisdom and mildness of the government of Alexandria under the auspices of Tiberius, and exalts still
more eloquently the happy condition of the world
at the moment of his decease.[1]   Again, the Jewish
historian Josephus confirms the statement of others,
that this emperor departed widely from the ordinary principle of provincial administration, in prolonging the stay of the proconsuls from its usual
brief term to a longer and ultimately to an inde-
finite period.[2]   This novel usage, he assures us,
though allowing that it coincided with the emperor's habits of procrastination, and a certain infirmity of purpose which grew upon him in age,
was conceived in a spirit of equity, and intended to
remove the main cause of the sufferings of the provinces, in the ardour with which each new governor
had hastened to make his fortune.   Tiberius was
wont to justify his policy by an appropriate apologue:
—*A number of flies had settled on a soldier's wound,
and a compassionate passer-by was about to scare
them away.   The sufferer begged him to refrain.
These flies, he said, have nearly sucked their full,
and are beginning to be tolerable: if you drive them
off, they will be immediately succeeded by fresh
comers with keener appetites.*   The progress indeed
of regular government seemed to demand a change
on this point, which should enable the affairs of the
empire to be conducted by fixed and uniform procedure, while it spared the people the fluctuations as
well as the expenses incident to a continual change

---

[1] Philo *in Flacc.* 1, 2.; *Legat. in Cai.* 2.: τίς γὰρ ἰδὼν . . . . οὐκ
ἐθαύμασε καὶ κατεπλάγη τῆς ὑπερφύους καὶ πάντος λόγου κρείττονος
εὐπραγίας.   This curious passage will deserve to be noticed more
particularly at a later period.

[2] Joseph. *Antiq. Jud.* xviii. 7. § 5.

of governors. It serves to mark the transition now in progress in the government of the provinces, from the sway of an encamped proconsul to that of an established viceroy. There seems no reason to doubt that the conduct of Tiberius in this particular, stripped of all unfair interpretation, was part of a settled and well-meant policy, however much it may have indulged the personal indolence, to which alone his detractors have chosen to ascribe it, or agreed with his jealous indisposition to multiply the number of distinguished and confidential coadjutors.[1] But it caused, we may suppose, great dissatisfaction among the candidates for place and emolument, and may be ranked among the motives of the hatred of the nobility towards him.

This change in the view in which the provinces were to be regarded, no longer as prostrate enemies, but as common children of the state with the citizens themselves, appears in the acknowledgment first made by Tiberius of the duty of extending the public liberality to the wants of the national dependents. A great step was gained in the cause of humanity and civilization, a great advance towards the overthrow of the selfish prejudices of conquest, when the subjects were admitted to have claims on the state as well as obligations towards it. It marks the commencement of what has been called the reaction of the provinces upon Rome, when, on the occasion of an earthquake, which overthrew not less than twelve cities of Lesser Asia, the prince proclaimed aloud that it was an imperial

Improved treatment of the provinces.

---

[1] Suet. *Tib.* 41. 63.; Tac. *Ann.* i. 80., vi. 27. Dion (lviii. 23.) accounts for it differently : τοσοῦτον πλῆθος τῶν τε ἄλλων καὶ τῶν βουλευτῶν ἀπώλετο ὥστε τοὺς ἄρχοντας τοὺς κληρωτοὺς, τοὺς μὲν ἐστρατηγηκότας ἐπὶ τρία, τοὺς δ' ὑπατευκότας ἐπὶ ἓξ ἔτη τὰς ἡγεμονείας τῶν ἐθνῶν, ἀπορίᾳ τῶν διαδεξομένων αὐτούς σχεῖν. But whatever be the merits of the system, it was introduced in fact not by Tiberius, but by Augustus. See Dion, lv. 28.

calamity and merited relief from imperial resources.[1] The control of the provincial governors was no longer left to the casual and interested activity of self-constituted accusers, or to the jealousy of political partisans: never before had the officials been kept in the path of moderation and purity by the restraints of a systematic procedure; and the many instances in which they were still accused and convicted of rapacity and injustice may be accepted in proof, not of the increased frequency of their guilt, but of greater vigilance in detecting it. It will be remarked, also, on examining the cases of this kind recorded, that they refer more commonly to the senatorial, such as Asia and Africa, than to the imperial provinces.[2] In the latter the officials were appointed more directly by the emperor himself, and their duties and prerogatives more definitely prescribed. Good conduct, whether in the highest posts or the lowest, secured them undisturbed enjoyment of their places for many years or even for their lives. The happier lot of these provinces is attested by the fact that, to be removed from the rule of the senate and placed under that of the emperor, was regarded as a boon by the provincials themselves.[3] The old plan, indeed, of farming the revenues of the provinces by the publicani, now as heretofore generally Roman knights, still continued in force : the time had not yet arrived, perhaps, when this system, which recommended itself

---

[1] Tac. *Ann.* ii. 47. (A.U. 770, A.D. 17), alluded to also by Pliny, *Hist. Nat.* ii. 86.: "Eodem anno xii. celebres Asiæ urbes collapsæ nocturno motu terræ." Their taxes were remitted for a term of years, large sums were granted them in ready money, and a special commissioner was sent by the senate to superintend its application. See above, chap. xliii. The twelve cities all lay in the district of Lydia. This earthquake is perhaps the most destructive of any on record. Comp. Von Hoff, *Erdoberfläch.* iv. 169. But even while I write the city of Broussa is trembling to its foundation with another.

[2] See Hoeck, *Röm. Gesch.* i. 3. 98.

[3] Comp. Tac. *Ann.* i. 76.: "Achaiam et Macedoniam onera deprecantes levari in præsens proconsulari imperio tradique Cæsari placuit."

quite as much for its simplicity and convenience as for the means it afforded of enriching the ruling class, could be dispensed with. The corporation of publicani, which engaged for the revenues of a district, required the heads of towns and cantons to assess the proportions of houses and families; and probably the levy was thus on the whole more equitably as well as more economically made, with the aid of local knowledge, than it would have been by processes more familiar to ourselves, and adapted to more homogeneous populations. But Tiberius deserves credit for the firmness with which he resisted the temptations which commonly beset a government under this method of taxation. He refused to apply the screw to his financial agents, and require the larger return which he was assured might easily be extracted from them. *A good shepherd*, he was wont to say, *must shear his sheep and not flay them.*[1] Among his wholesome regulations for the protection of the provincials against the rapacity of their rulers was a decree, by which the officers, however guiltless they might be themselves, were made responsible for the misconduct of their consorts in this particular: for the women, it was found, were more prone to take bribes and sell the favours of the government than the men. He ruled, however, after a debate, the details of which are curious and not uninstructive, that the attendance of the wives upon their husbands abroad was a less evil than such as might flow from forbidding them that indulgence.[2]

But the care of Tiberius was not confined to the provinces. He devoted himself with untiring industry to the reform of abuses in the government of Italy, to assuring general security and tranquillity, and alleviating distress.

Government of Italy and the city.

---

[1] Suet. *Tib.* 32.: "Boni pastoris esse tondere pecus non deglubere." Comp. Tac. *Ann.* iv. 6.; Dion, lvii. 10.　　　[2] Tac. *Ann.* iv. 20. foll.

He protected the inhabitants from robbers and banditti by military posts in various places, and stimulated the diligence of the city police. His measures for maintaining order in the capital were temperate and well considered. Instead of treating the players, whose over-ardent admirers were constantly fighting and rioting about them, as mere servants of the government, and subjecting them again, as before the time of Augustus, to the rods of the prætor, he was satisfied with reducing the public grants for their encouragement, and forbidding the senators from entering their dwellings, and the knights from trooping round them in the streets: the theatre alone, he declared, was appropriated to visiting them. At the same time, they were no longer held re- Control over sponsible for the peace of the city; but the the players. penalty of banishment was denounced against the spectators who should cause disturbances there.[1] On occasion, however, of a riot which occurred in the year 776, we find that both the players themselves, and the leaders of the theatrical factions, were expelled together from the city, nor was the emperor prevailed on, by the most pressing instances, to recall the offenders.[2]

This interference with their amusements was a grave offence to the populace. When Tiberius limited the number of gladiators in the arena, the citizens complained with bitterness that he took no genial pleasure in the old Roman recreations. They were indignant at having their draught of blood The sooth-measured to them by drops. Though all sayers expelled from classes were equally addicted to the crime Italy. or folly of consulting conjurors and diviners, the measures which Tiberius enforced, after the example

[1] Tac. *Ann.* i. 75.; Suet. *Tib.* 34.　Comp. *Digest.* xlviii. 19. 28. § 3.; Vell. ii 126.: " Compressa theatralis seditio."
[2] Suet. *Tib.* 37.; Tac. *Ann.* iv. 15.

of Augustus, Agrippa, and the legislators of the free state before them, for expelling the astrologers from Italy, caused far less dissatisfaction. This latter prohibition, indeed, was easily evaded.[1] The emperor himself, the most superstitious of his nation, could not resolve to rid his own palace of the herd of soothsayers, who so well knew how to play upon his fears and hopes. While he indulged himself in prying into his own future fates, he could not prevent the inquiries of friends or enemies, flatterers and intriguers: to cast the imperial horoscope became the dangerous amusement from which few courtiers or politicians had the firmness to abstain. The *Mathematici*, said Tacitus, are a class who mislead the ambitious and disappoint the powerful; who will always be forbidden a place among us, yet will always be retained here.[2]

These measures against the astrologers were not more ineffectual than those which Tiberius also took for the suppression of Egyptian and Jewish rites. He was not led, however, to these regulations by the principles which animated his predecessor. He did not regard himself as the defender, or restorer of the ancient cult, as the patron of Roman observances in opposition to novel and extraneous usages. He looked merely to the practical evils which might result from any heterodox movement, and his zeal against these Oriental innovations was roused by the mystery in which they were for the

Suppression of the Egyptian and Jewish rites.

---

[1] Tac. *Ann*. ii. 32.   One of these people was thrown from the Tarpeian rock, another was beaten to death with the stick, the ancient military punishment.   Tacitus says, " Consules extra portam Esquilinam, cum classicum canere jussissent, more prisco advertere." This is explained by Suetonius, *Ner*. 49.: " Nudi hominis cervicem inserere furcæ et corpus virgis ad necem cædere."

[2] Tac. *Hist*. i. 22.: " Genus hominum potentibus infidum, sperantibus fallax, quod in civitate nostra et vetabitur semper, et retinebitur."

most part shrouded, by the nocturnal ceremonies which they generally affected, and by the connexion with the dreaded inquiry into the future generally ascribed to them. A single case of gross scandal imputed to the priests of Isis at Rome was sufficient perhaps to give colour to the emperor's strong proceedings against that cult and its followers. The statue of the goddess was precipitated into the Tiber, and her rites forbidden in the capital.[1] Similar measures were taken against the religious observances of the Jews at Rome. When required to enlist in the Roman armies, this people pleaded their ancient national prejudice against military service, and the indulgence it had enjoyed from earlier Cæsars. But this refusal was now made a pretext for accusing them of disloyalty, for the prohibition of their worship, the demolition of their sacred instruments and vestments, and finally their expulsion from Italy. Four thousand freedmen, of Jewish origin or tenets, were drafted from Rome into Sardinia, to repress the brigandage of that wild region.[2] It would seem, however, that at a later period Tiberius relaxed in his severity towards this people, and adopted means of conciliating them. They were fain to believe that the harshness of his earlier legislation was due to the malignant influence of the detested Sejanus.[3]

---

[1] See in Josephus (*Antiq.* xviii. 3.) the story of Mundus, whose licentious passion was gratified by the priests of Anubis.

[2] Tac. *Ann.* ii. 85.: " Quatuor millia libertini generis ea superstitione infecta : et si ob gravitatem cœli interissent, vile damnum." I infer from the construction that the writer here expresses the sentiment of the decree itself, rather than his own. Suet. *Tib.* 36.: " Judæorum juventutem per speciem sacramenti in provincias gravioris cœli distribuit." Comp. Senec. *Ep.* 108. The incident has been already referred to in chap. xxxiv. The victims, as I suppose, were partly Jews by extraction, but perhaps more generally proselytes of Greek or Asiatic origin.

[3] Philo, *Legat. ad Cai.* 24. On the statement of Tertullian (*Apol.* 5.), regarding the favour, as he pretends, of Tiberius towards Christianity, I shall speak on a future occasion.

The establishment of a regular system of legal protection for subjects of every degree went
hand in hand with the abolition or limitation of such irregular substitutes for it as
the right of asylum, with which religious feeling had
stepped in where human law failed to perform its
duty. It was chiefly in the eastern provinces that
this right of asylum was recognised and sanctioned
by long usage and favour. The multiplication of
these places of refuge, fostered by the cupidity of
the priests, had extended a dangerous impunity to
all manner of crimes, and increased the number of
offenders. Such, however, was the influence of the
priests on the superstition of the vulgar, that every
attempt to check this encouragement to disorder had
been vehemently resented, and had led in many cases
to disturbances and riots. Tiberius undertook to
abate the nuisance, and acted with good sense and
decision. He required the cities which exercised this
right of protection in their cherished fanes, to produce just grounds, by prescription or legal ordinance,
for the claims they advanced. He limited the extent
of territory to which the privilege should apply, for
it was claimed not for the sacred walls only, or the
outer inclosure of the temple, but often for large
tracts of land around them; he defined, perhaps with
greater strictness, the character of the offences to
which protection should be granted; and thus, without
abolishing the institution itself, he set some bounds to
its licence, with the approbation, no doubt, of the
wisest of his subjects.[1] In Rome, the centre of law
and rights well understood, the privilege of asylum
had never flourished as in the more disturbed regions

Limitation of the right of asylum.

---

[1] Suet. *Tib.* 37. : " Abolevit et vim moremque asylorum quæ
usquam erant ;" but Tacitus (*Ann.* iii. 60.) modifies this statement:
" Crebrescebat Græcas per urbes licentia atque impunitas asyla sta-
tuendi . . . . facta senatusconsulta quis, magno cum honore, modus
tamen præscribebatur."

of the East. Nevertheless the tribunitian sanctity of
the emperor became gradually extended to his statues,
and culprits or fugitive slaves, on touching an image
or picture of the august personage, were allowed to
defy the law, and the privileges, otherwise unbounded,
of their masters. This means of protection was soon
turned to a weapon of offence ; holding up an imperial coin between his thumb and finger, any ruffian
might stand in the public streets and rail with impunity against the honourable and noble : the client
might abuse and threaten his patron, the slave might
even raise his hand against his master. This flagrant
abuse was not checked, for none ventured to brave
the delators, who might easily frame on the attempt
a process of majestas, until a senator having been
pelted with opprobrious language by a woman, a notorious delinquent, whom he was bringing to justice,
Drusus himself, at the request of the per-   A. D. 21.
plexed fathers, interposed and threw the   A. C. 774.
offender into prison, in spite of the emperor's image
which she eloquently brandished in his face.[1]

   This insolent defiance of public opinion and the
general sense of morality was an ominous   Flagrant dis-
sign of the times. No sumptuary laws,   sipation of
the times.
though sanctioned by the wisest politicians, and in-
voked by the uneasy consciences of the citizens themselves, availed to stem the dissipation and extravagance, which increased with every restriction upon
nobler aims and occupations. The vast sums no-
toriously expended on the dainties of the table, the
profusion of table ornaments, plate, and jewellery,
and the extravagant prices given for articles of mere
fashion, such as vases of mixed Corinthian metal, and
boards of Numidian citron-wood, provoked the indignation of the morose Tiberius.[2] He urged the

---

[1] Tac. *Ann.* iii. 36.

[2] Tertull. *de Pallio*, 5.: "M. Tullius quingentis millibus orbem
citri emit, qua bis tantum Asinius Gallus pro mensa ejusdem Maure-

senate to repression. But his counsellors were indisposed to strong measures, and the emperor himself soon wearied of the hopeless struggle. Contenting himself with some trifling regulations for appearance sake, he acknowledged with a sigh that the times were not fit for a censorship of manners. When the ædiles represented that the sumptuary laws of Augustus, fixing the prices for certain articles

Tiberius despairs of checking it by sumptuary laws. A. D. 22. A. U. 775. of luxury, were habitually disregarded, he replied that those after all were but trifling matters compared with the real dangers accruing to the commonwealth from the demands of selfish cupidity and the accumulation of great estates. *Italy,* he exclaimed, *yea, Rome herself depends for her daily food on foreign harvests, on the vicissitudes of the weather, and the uncertain humours of the Ocean. Unless our provinces come to our support, will our farms maintain us, or our forests feed us?* He alluded to the neglect of cultivation throughout the peninsula, which was now generally remarked, and to the complaints which had grown in force for a hundred and fifty years, of the decline of the ancient strength of the country, the population of free labourers. This, he said, was a graver concern than the price of plates and dishes; the latter might be a fitting matter for the ædiles to care for, as consuls, prætors, and every other magistrate had each their proper sphere of vigilance; but something of higher and more general interest was demanded of the princeps. While therefore he maintained the peace and credit of the empire, and quelled the turbulence or corruption of the assemblies, and the faction of the senate,—while he provided for the wants of the day before him, and supplied an abundance of grain to the city,—he cast on the ædiles

taniæ numerat." Comp. Lucan, ix. 426., x. 144.; Petronius *Satyr.* 119.; Martial, ix. 60. Plin. *Nat. Hist.* v. 15.

the care of the sumptuary enactments which were vainly expected to train the age to economy, but which the age rejected with insolent contempt.[1]

As regarded public morality, Tiberius marched in the steps of his predecessor, not indeed in the spirit of an enthusiast, or with any ardent aspirations for the purity of the Roman blood or honour of the Roman name, but as a matter of duty and discipline. He resented the insensibility to shame of many of the young citizens even of knightly or senatorial families, who, in their passion for displaying their accomplishments as singers or dancers on the stage, a degradation strictly forbidden to their class, contrived to get themselves legally degraded, to enable them thus to present themselves with impunity. Against this ignoble evasion new and more stringent edicts were levelled. In making the licentiousness of a Roman matron a public offence, Augustus had overshot his mark. Among other impediments which arose to the enforcement of the Julian legislation on this delicate subject, it was found difficult to induce disinterested persons to prosecute as public accusers. Possibly it was with the view of obviating the scandal of open procedure in such lamentable cases, that Tiberius revived the primitive usage, and delivered the culprits to be tried and punished by their own kinsmen, *after the manner of the ancients.* In the olden time, these domestic tribunals had inflicted even death for trifling indecorums. But the law allowed the defenceless frail ones a method of escape, which some women did not scruple to embrace. The penalties of irregularity were strict and severe; but from these professed prostitution was exempted, and immunity might be purchased by exchanging the

Shamelessness of both sexes.

---

[1] Tac. *Ann.* iii. 53, 54.; Vell. ii. 126.: " Revocata in forum fides, summota e foro seditio, ambitio campo, discordia curia . . . . quando annona moderatior?"

decent stole of matronhood for the toga of the avowed courtesan.[1]   While resort to this disgraceful refuge was confined to a few plebeian cases it attracted little notice; when, however, wives of men of the highest class were found to inscribe themselves on the ædile's list, to escape the loss of dowry, confiscation, and banishment, the penalties of the Julian law, the princeps determined to close this last means of retreat, by a new and sweeping edict.[2]

The Roman legislators had never been famous for adhering in their own persons to the rules they enforced on their fellow-citizens. What then, it may be asked, was the private character of the man who showed himself thus harsh and prudish in his public capacity?   His amusements and relaxations, no mean element in the character of every Roman, were frivolous rather than corrupt; nor yet, at least, can he fairly be charged with habits of excessive indulgence.   In regard to women, there is no evidence against the morals of Tiberius up to the period we are now considering: towards the wife of his choice he had shown strong affection, while as to the worthless consort who was imposed upon him, however sternly he may have resented her profligacy, we know not that it was provoked by similar profligacy on his part.   The prejudices of the Romans were early excited against him, and no reliance can be placed on their malicious assertions that his natural reserve was a mask assumed to conceal the grossest improprieties.   On this score, neither history nor anecdote has any story at this time against him: the charge of habitual intemperance rests

Immorality ascribed to Tiberius.

---

[1] Hor. *Sat.* i. 2. 63.: "Quid interest in matrona, ancilla, peccesve togata?"

[2] Tac. *Ann.* ii. 85.; Suet. *Tib.* 35.   The enactment on this subject, cited by Papinian (*Dig.* xlviii. 5. 10.), is probably that of Tiberius : " Mulier quæ evitandæ pœnæ adulterii gratia lenocinium fecerit aut operas suas scenæ locaverit, adulterii accusari damnarique ex senatus-consulto potest "

chiefly upon a ribald epigram, which may have
originated in the licence of the camp[1]; while the
saying ascribed to him that a man must be a fool
who required a physician after thirty, seems to show
that he enjoyed robust and equal health, such as was
never maintained through a long life by a confirmed
drunkard.[2]   Nor can we doubt the untiring perseverance with which Tiberius devoted himself through
at least the greater part of his principate to the en-
grossing cares of his station, cares which above all
others demanded a clear head and a sound body.
For several years he never quitted the dust and din
of Rome for a single day, and his time was given
without intermission to the discussions of the senate,
to the procedure of the tribunals, to conferences with
foreign envoys, and every other detail of his world-
wide administration.   The charge of profligacy, up
to this period, but slightly supported by external
testimony, falls to the ground before such strong
internal evidence of its falsehood.

But the morality of Tiberius was not confined
to abstinence from gross vice, or refrain-   His simplicity
ing from luxuries and indulgences which   and frugality
might have been less unsuitable to his position.   He

---

[1] Pliny asserts indeed that Tiberius was intemperate in his youth,
but admits that no such charge could be laid against him in his latter
years.   Plin. *Hist. Nat.* xiv. 28.: " In senecta jam severus ; sed ipsa
juventa ad merum pronior fuerat."   He tells an anecdote, or rather
a popular surmise, which must be taken for what it is worth, that
he selected Lucius Piso for the post of prefect of the city on account
of his admirable qualities as a boon companion; as, for instance, that
he could drink for two days and nights without intermission.   Plin.
l. c.   Comp. Senec. *Epist.* 83.

[2] The holding of this paradox, attributed to the great Napoleon
and others, always indicates exuberant health and spirits.   Suetonius
says of Tiberius on this point (*Tib.* 69.): " Valetudine prospera usus
est, tempore quidem principatus pæne toto prope illæsa, quamvis a
tricesimo ætatis anno arbitratu eam suo rexerit, sine adjumento con-
silioque medicorum."   Tacitus (*Ann.* vi. 46.): " Solitus eludere medicorum artes, atque eos qui post tricesimum ætatis annum ad
internoscenda corpori suo utilia vel noxia alieni consilii indigerent."

was anxious to exhibit the ancient ideal of the
Roman statesman in practising the household virtues
of simplicity and frugality.   His domestic economy,
formed on the pattern of Augustus, received additional hardness and severity from the habits of the
camp, with which he had been so long familiar.
The number of his slaves was limited; the freedmen
who managed his private concerns were kept strictly
within the bounds of modesty and propriety.   Their
services were rewarded with exactness, but at the
same time parsimoniously; nor did their employer
ever surrender to them any portion of his real
authority, or allow them undue influence over himself.[1]   The carefulness he exhibited in the government of his household was an earnest of the economy
of his public administration ; and as such the citizens might, at least, have admired it, however few
imitators it could find among them.   But Augustus
had had the art of combining personal simplicity
with a wise liberality in public matters, which was
beyond the conception of his more narrow-minded
successor.   The people were piqued at the cessation
of the largesses which used to flow to them from
the coffers of their inimitable favourite.   Tiberius,
who took no pleasure in the sports of the theatre
or circus, and could not, like Augustus, good-
humouredly affect it, reduced the salaries of the
mimes and the numbers of the gladiators. He
lavished no treasures on the decoration of the city,
content to execute with scrupulous fidelity the
designs his predecessor had left uncompleted. Yet
he too could, on worthy occasions, exhibit munificence on an imperial scale.   His relief to the ruined

---

[1] Tac. *Ann.* iv. 7.: "Rari per Italiam Cæsaris agri, modesta ser-
vitia, intra paucos libertos domus: ac si quando cum privatis discep-
taret, forum ac jus." But a darker colour is presently dashed into
the modest drab: "quæ cuncta non quidem comi via sed horridus ac
plerumque formidatus, retinebat tamen, donec," &c.

cities of Asia was conceived in the spirit of an
Augustus or a Julius, and the aid he extended to
the decayed scions of noble houses at home showed
that he could be generous from policy, as well as
sparing from temper.[1] In times of scarcity he did
not fail to check the rise of prices, according to the
best lights of his day, by compensating the dealers
in grain from his own means ; and from the same
well-managed resources he indemnified the citizens
for their losses by the great fire which ravaged the
quarters of the Cælius and Aventine.[2] The whole
empire reaped abundant fruits from this prudent
considerateness, in the undiminished supply of all
sources of public revenue, and the opening of new
ones. The government was enabled to fulfil every
engagement with punctuality: its civil officers, regularly and adequately paid, had no excuse for extortion, its soldiers were kept within the bounds of
discipline, and, receiving punctually their daily dole,
submitted without a murmur to the labours of the
camp and the threats of the centurion.

At the same time, with all his frugality, Tiberius
obtained the rare praise of personal indifference to money, and forbearance in claiming
even his legitimate dues.[3] In many cases *His moderation in regard
to money.*
in which the law enriched the emperor with the
property of a condemned criminal he waived his
right, and allowed it to descend to the heir. He
frequently refused to accept inheritances bequeathed
him by persons not actually related to him, and
checked the base subservience of a death-bed

[1] Vell. ii. 126 : "Fortuita non civium tantummodo sed urbium
damna principis munificentia vindicat."

[2] Comp. Tac. *Ann.* ii. 87., iv. 64., vi. 45.; Vell. ii. 130.; Suet. *Tib.*
48.; Dion, lviii. 26.

[3] Tacitus (*Ann.* iii. 18.) says of him, as before quoted, "Satis
firmus, ut sæpe memoravi, adversus pecuniam." Comp. Dion. lvii.
10. 17.

flattery. With all these genuine merits towards the commonwealth, he was not blind to the advantage he might derive from pretending to another virtue, which ranked high in the estimation of the Romans, but to which he had no real claim. From the com-mencement of his principate he affected the most obsequious deference to the state,

His show of
deference to
the senate.

as represented by the senate, the presumed exponent of its will. His first care was to make it appear to the world that his own preeminence was thrust on him by that body, which alone could lawfully confer it. We have seen under what dis-guises, and by what circuitous processes, he had gradually drawn into his own hands the powers, by which he seemed only seeking to enrich the senate at the expense of every other order. The prompt-ness of its adulation, the proneness of its servility, he strove to check sometimes with grave dignity, at others with disdainful irony. When it proposed to call the month of November, in which he was born, after his name, as July and August had de-rived their titles from his predecessors, *What*, he asked, *will you do if there should be thirteen Cæsars?*[1] He would not allow himself to be called, in the addresses of its members, *Dominus* or *Lord*, as the style of a slave towards his master, nor his employments *Sacred*, as belonging only to divinity; nor again would he have it said that he *required* its attendance at his summons. He never entered the Curia with an escort of guards, or even of unarmed dependents, and rebuked provincial governors for addressing their despatches to himself, and not always to the senate.[2] His own communications to the august order were conceived in a tone of the deepest respect and even subservience. *I now say,* he would declare, *as I have often said before, that a*

---

[1] Dion, lvii. 18.   [2] Suet. *Tib.* 27. 30. 32.

good and useful prince should be the servant of the senate, and the people generally, sometimes of individual magistrates. Such was his demeanour throughout the first years of his government; it was only late, and by degrees, that he drew forth the arm of power from the folds of this specious disguise, and exhibited the princeps to the citizens in the fulness of his now established authority. But even to the last, though capricious and irregular in his behaviour, we are assured that his manner was most commonly marked by this air of deference, and the public weal continued still to be manifestly the ruling object of his measures.[1]

We have here before us the picture of a good sovereign but not of an amiable man. *The promise of his reign marred by defects of temper and demeanour.* Had Tiberius been so fortunate as to have died at the close of a ten years' principate, he would have left an honourable though not an attractive name in the annals of Rome: he would have represented the Cato Censor of the empire, by the side of the Scipio of Augustus and the Camillus of Cæsar. The sternness and even cruelty he had so often exhibited would have gained him no discredit with the Romans, so long as they were exerted against public offenders for the common weal, and for no selfish objects. Even the suspicion which from the first attached to him of having procured the death of Agrippa was probably little regarded: the exile of Augustus was already branded as a monstrous production of nature which ought never to have been reared, and might with little blame be got rid of. But as the fine and interesting features of his person were marred by a constrained and unpleasing mien and expression, so the patience, industry, and discretion of Tiberius were disparaged

---

[1] Suet. *Tib.* 29. 33.: " Paulatim Principem exseruit, præstitit me, et si varium diu, commodiorem tamen sæpius et ad utilitates publicas proniorem."

by a perverse temper, a crooked policy, and an uneasy sensibility.   The manners of the man, a mar-
tinet in the camp, a clerk in the closet, a pedant in
the senate-house, carried with them no charm, and
emitted no spark of genius to kindle the sympathies
of the nation.   The princeps, from his invidious and
questionable position, if once he failed to attract,
could only repel the inclinations of his subjects.   If
they ceased to ascribe to him their blessings, they
would begin without delay to lay to his charge all
their misfortunes.   The mystery of the death of
Germanicus threw a blight on the fame of Tiberius
from which he never again recovered.   From that
moment his countrymen judged him without discrimination, and sentenced him without compunction.
The suspicion of his machinations against Germanicus, unproved and improbable as they really were,
kindled their imaginations to feelings of disgust and
horror, which neither personal debauchery, nor the
persecution of knights and nobles, would alone have
sufficed to engender.[1]

[1] Tacitus, we have seen, had special inducements to do less than
justice to Tiberius ; nevertheless, his account of the tyrant is not on
the whole inconsistent.   But there is no part of Dion's history in
which he fails so much as in his delineation of this Cæsar's character.
It is a mere jumble of good and bad actions, for which the writer
sometimes apologizes, and insinuates as his excuse that the author of
them was mad.   The stories, however, themselves are often extravagant and puerile.   Such, for instance, is that of the architect, who,
being sentenced to banishment by Tiberius from mere spite, because
he had performed the wonderful feat of straightening an inclined
wall, in order to ingratiate himself with the tyrant, threw a glass
vessel to the ground, picked up the fragments, and set them together
again, whereupon he was immediately put to death, as too clever to
be suffered to live.   (Dion, lvii. 21.; comp. Petronius, *Satyr.* 51.   The
origin of the story may be traced perhaps to a statement in Pliny,
Hist. Nat. xxxvi. 66.)   There is something Oriental in the turn
which the fancy of Dion not unfrequently takes.

CHAPTER XLV

Comparison between Augustus and Tiberius.—Sejanus useful without being formidable.—Disturbances in Africa and revolt in Gaul.—Overthrow of Sacrovir (A. U. 774).—The tribunitian power conferred upon Drusus (A. U. 775).—Intrigues of Sejanus: establishment of the Prætorian camp.—Drusus poisoned by Sejanus (A. U. 776).—Deterioration of the principate of Tiberius.—Death of Cremutius Cordus and others.—Sejanus demands the hand of Livilla, and is refused by Tiberius.—He conceives the project of withdrawing Tiberius from Rome.—Retirement of Tiberius to Capreæ (A.U. 780).—His manner of life there.—Further deterioration of his government.—Death of the younger Julia and of the empress Livia (A. U. 782). (A. U. 774—782, A. D. 21—29.)

I HAVE described the rise and progress of Tiberius to a distinguished eminence among Roman statesmen : I have now to introduce the reader to the decline and fall of his well-earned reputation. The ruin of so fair a character, and the frustration of such respectable abilities and virtues was not the work of a day, nor the effect of any single crime or failure. The temper of the times and the circumstances of his position presented the most formidable obstacles to a sustained good government, which the Romans had not perhaps the patriotism to appreciate or support. But the honourable ambition of the second princeps to see everything with his own eyes, and execute everything with his own hands, was in fact itself suicidal. Augustus, with the Roman world exhausted and prostrate at his feet, craving only to be moulded by his policy and informed with inspiration from his mouth, had accustomed himself from the first to act by able and trusty ministers. He was wisely con-

Comparison between Augustus and Tiberius : the man of genius and the man of ability. A. D. 21. A. U. 774.

tent to see many things with the eyes of a Mæcenas,
to act in many things with the hands of an Agrippa.
His bravest auxiliary he ventured generously to connect with himself by the bonds of a family alliance.
At a later period he educated the members of his own
house to relieve him, one after another, of some of
the functions of his station. Tiberius he associated
with himself on terms of almost complete equality.
But Augustus was a man of genius : he was the soul
of the Roman empire : fame, fortune, and conscious
ability had inspired him with unwavering self-reliance. It was impossible for his successor, bred in
the sphere of an adjutant or an official, to have the
same lofty confidence in himself, and to discard with
a smile the suggestions of every vulgar jealousy.
Tiberius, thoroughly trained in the routine of business, might believe himself competent to the task of
government; he might devote himself with intense
and restless application to every detail of the public
service, and struggle against his overwhelming anxieties with desperate and even gallant perseverance.
But he was animated by no inward consciousness
of power, and when he felt himself baffled by the
odds against him, he could not look round serenely
for the help he needed. Those of his own household he repelled from him as enemies, and instead of
choosing the ablest counsellor in the fittest quarter,
allowed himself to fall under the influence of the
nearest and least scrupulous intriguer. Even Sejanus he did not formally appoint as his minister, nor
avowedly surrender to him any definite share in
his affairs ; but he yielded him his own mind and
will in all things, let the conduct of the empire slip
insensibly out of his own hands, and allowed the
world to despise him as the puppet of his own minion.
 It has been already represented that Tiberius,
from the character of his mind, preferred the ser-

vices of an obscure and humble client to those of an associate of lofty rank and corresponding pretensions. Accordingly, in giving his confidence to Sejanus, he never contemplated raising him to a position of independent authority: on the contrary, he conceived that the meanness of his origin, the subordinate office he filled, and above all, perhaps, the mediocrity of his talents, were a sufficient guarantee against his rising into rivalry with himself. The imperial family still flourished with numerous scions: among these his own son occupied the first place; and this prince, since the death of his cousin Germanicus, united every claim of birth, years, and ability to share with his father the toils and honours of administration. In the year 774, accordingly, Tiberius appointed himself consul in conjunction with Drusus, an union, however, of which the citizens, it is said, augured unfavourably: for all the previous colleagues of Tiberius — namely, Varus, Piso, and Germanicus—had perished by violent and shocking deaths.[1] Both in this instance, and in a fifth, which afterwards followed, these forebodings, it will appear, were destined to be fatally fulfilled. A deep gloom was settling on the imperial palace, from whence no light gleamed to cheer the Roman people, and dispel with the prospect of future prosperity the misgivings which now assailed them. The emperor began to betray a disposition for retirement and solitude. The moments he could abstract from the ceaseless pressure of business he devoted to consultation with astrologers and diviners, listening to their interpretation of his dreams, and requiring an exposition of the occult meaning of every sound that reached him, or

The jealousy of Tiberius not alarmed by the inferior origin and talents of Sejanus.

The imperial family.

Tiberius and Drusus, consuls.

---

[1] Tac. *Ann.* iii. 31.; Dion, lvii. 20.

vision that flashed upon his sight. In order perhaps
to secure himself from observation in pursuits which
he had interdicted to the citizens, he was now anxious
to escape from the city, where his residence had been
for many years unbroken, so painful was the assiduity
he had bestowed on the details of his vast administration. For this purpose he withdrew to the pleasant
coast of Campania, professing that his health required
change of scene and alleviation of labour, leaving the
conduct of the executive in the hands of Drusus, though
he retained a vigilant supervision of affairs, and constantly explained his views and wishes in despatches
addressed to the senate. The behaviour of
the young consul, thus watched and guided,
seems to have been temperate and judicious. He
smoothed the differences between the proudest and
most turbulent of the nobles; and his interference
was the more graceful as it was employed to enforce
an act of submission on the part of a Lucius Sulla, a
contemporary of his own, towards Domitius Corbulo,
a man of greater age and political experience.[1] He
checked, as we have seen, the licentious appeal to
the imperial majesty as a protection for calumnious
railing, and evaded rather than opposed the unseasonable rigour of the reformers, who asked the senate to
prohibit the governors of provinces from taking their
consorts with them. He had himself, he said, derived much comfort from the society of his own
partner in his various military missions, and Livia,
still the mirror of Roman matrons, had marched by
the side of Augustus from Rome to every frontier of
the empire. Drusus at this time was thirty years of
age. From his earliest adolescence he had been em-

Character of Drusus.

---

[1] Tac. *Ann.* iii. 31. This Corbulo must be distinguished from
another of the same name, whose exploits and melancholy fate will
occupy some of our future pages. He had already filled the office of
prætor, and is represented as an elderly personage. The younger
Corbulo died nearly fifty years later.

ployed in the career of arms, and he had already
been distinguished by a previous consulship in the
year 768.[1]   He was well known therefore both to the
soldiers and the people; and though neither the one
nor the other bestowed on him the regard they had
lavished on his cousin, he was not on the whole unpopular with either.   Even his vices were favourably
contrasted with those of his father.   He might be
cruel and sanguinary in his enjoyment of the sports
of the circus; the sharpest of the gladiator's swords
received from him the name of Drusian: but this
was better, in the popular view, than the moroseness of Tiberius, who evinced no satisfaction in such
spectacles at all.   He might be too much addicted
to revelry and carousing: but this again was a fault
which a few years might correct, and which showed
at least some geniality of temper, more amiable than
his father's reserve.[2]   We have a surer evidence of his
merits in the affection in which he had lived with his
more popular cousin, and the tenderness he displayed
for the bereaved children. Of these the eldest, known
by the name of Nero, was now sixteen; the second,
Drusus, was younger by a single year; while Caius,
the third, was only eleven.   The family of Germanicus had consisted altogether of nine, a number apparently very unusual in a Roman household.[3]

Some fresh incursions of Tacfarinas at this period
within the borders of the African province induced the emperor to address a missive
to the senate, to whom the government attached,

Renewed dis-
turbances
in Africa.

---

[1] Tac. *Ann.* i. 55.: "Druso Cæsare, C. Norbano Coss. A. U. 768."

[2] Tac. *Ann.* ii. 44., iii. 37.; Dion, lvii. 13, 14.; Plin. *Hist. Nat.*
xiv. 28.: "Nec alio magis Drusus Cæsar regenerasse patrem Tiberium
ferebatur."

[3] The horrid practice of exposure and infanticide—"Numerum
liberorum finire," as Tacitus gently qualifies it (*Germ.* 19.)—has
been already referred to.   The fact that women bore no distinctive
prænomen, is terribly significant. It seems to show how few daughters in a family were reared.

requiring it to appoint an efficient proconsul without
delay, to undertake the task of finally reducing him.
The provinces allotted to the senate were precisely
those in which there was least apprehension of serious hostilities, or prospect of the active employment
of their governors in the camp.   To equip an army
for actual service, to select an experienced commander, and send him forth to reap laurels, and perhaps to earn a triumph, was to trench upon the imperial prerogative; the submissive senators shrank
from exercising a right which accident had thus put
into their hands, and begged to refer the choice to
the emperor. With his usual dissimulation, Tiberius
affected some displeasure at the duties of the fathers
being thus thrown on himself; for he already bore,
as he declared, a heavier burden than one man could
well sustain. He refused to do more than nominate
two candidates, M. Lepidus and Junius Blæsus, between whom he required the senate to make the final

**Blæsus ap-
pointed
proconsul.**
selection.   Both disclaimed the honour;
but Blæsus was uncle to Sejanus, and for
him, as was well known, the appointment
was actually reserved.   The excuses of Lepidus were
accordingly accepted; those of his rival, probably
less sincere, were courteously waived; and the favourite was gratified by the elevation of a kinsman,
of no previous distinction, to a place of power, which
he might employ perhaps, at some future period, for
the advancement of his own fortunes.[1]

**Revolt in
Gaul.**
The consulship of Drusus was distinguished, however, by commotions of far greater importance in another quarter.   The success
with which the Germans had defended their liberties
against the invaders, had not been unobserved by
the nations, pacified though they were, and bowed to
the yoke for three quarters of a century, within the

---

[1] Tac. *Ann.* iii. **35.**

Rhine. For their advantage the discovery seemed
to be made that the legions were not invincible;
perhaps they read the secret of this decline of their
efficiency in the mutinous spirit which had been
manifested in their encampments. The panic which
had recently pervaded Italy, the alarm Augustus
had himself exhibited, and the violent measure of
expelling the dreaded Germans from the city, were
taken as a confession of weakness. At the same time
the exactions of the fiscal officers were continued and
perhaps redoubled; the demands made for military
supplies had become intolerably grievous: at last
some chiefs of the native tribes, men who had been
distinguished with the franchise of the city, and admitted to the name and clientele of the imperial
house, were roused by the general discontent, or their
own ambitious hopes, to intrigue against the power
of the conquerors. The ramifications of their conspiracy extended, it was said, through every tribe in
the country; its chief centres were among the Belgæ
in the north, and the Ædui in the interior; the most
prominent of its leaders in the one quarter bore the
Roman appellation of Julius Florus, in the other that
of Julius Sacrovir, a name which seems to mark him as
a man of priestly family, and armed, therefore, with
all the influence of his proscribed caste. But the
measures of the patriot chiefs were disconcerted by
the premature outbreak of the Andi and Turones.
Sacrovir himself, in order to save appearances, was
compelled to head his auxiliary cohorts by the side
of the legionaries, and assist in coercing his own im-
prudent allies. Nevertheless his real sentiments did
not escape suspicion; and when he threw off his helmet on the field of battle, in the exuberance, as he
protested, of his courage and resolution, some of the
rebel captives did not hesitate to declare that he had
made himself known to his friends to divert their

missiles in other directions. Tiberius was informed
of this presumed treachery, but he thought fit to take
no notice of it.[1]

The speedy reduction of the Turones and Andi did
not suppress the meditated revolt. When

Insurrection of the Belgæ suppressed.
the moment arrived the Belgæ were not
unfaithful to their engagements, notwithstanding this discouragement. Florus gained a few
Treviran auxiliaries, and gave the signal for revolt
by the massacre of some Roman traders. His ranks
were soon swelled by followers of his own clan, and
by the needy and oppressed of the surrounding
tribes; but unable to make head against the Romans
in the field they were driven to seek a refuge in the
dense forests of the Ardennes. Here they were surrounded, captured, and disarmed, chiefly by the efforts
of a personal enemy of Florus, a Gaul who himself
bore the name of Julius Indus. Florus now threw
himself on his own sword, and the Belgian insurrec-

Resistance of the Ædui under Sacrovir.
tion was at once suppressed. The resistance
of the Ædui under Sacrovir, who flew at
the same time to arms, was more resolute
and proved more formidable. The vigour of this
tribe was greater, its resources and alliances more
considerable, and the forces of the Romans were
stationed at a greater distance from it. The rumour
of the disaffection was even greater than the reality.
It was reported at Rome that no less than sixty-four
Gaulish states had revolted in a body, that the German tribes had united their forces with them, that
the obedience of either Spain was trembling in the
balance. The flower of the youth of the entire province was collected in the imperial university at
Augustodunum. Arms had been purchased or fabri-
cated in secret, and there were many brave young

---

[1] Tac. *Ann.* iii. 40.: " Eodem anno Galliarum civitates ob magnitudinem æris alieni rebellionem cœptavere." *Ibid.* 41.: " Tiberius
. . . . aluit dubitatione bellum."

hands to wield them. The chiefs of every clan were followed to the field by hosts of slaves and clients, very imperfectly equipped; but considerable reliance was placed on the native gladiators, of whom some troops were maintained in the Romanized capital, who were clad in complete chain or scale armour, and were expected to form a firm and impenetrable phalanx.[1] It required a pitched battle, with numerous armies arrayed on both sides, to bring this last revolt to an issue. Nevertheless, when Silius, the Roman general, was at leisure to direct two legions, with their auxiliaries, from their quarters in Belgica, against the centre of this insurrection, its power of resistance was found to be far below the alarm it had created. The Roman soldiers were animated with the most determined spirit; the hope of plunder among the opulent cities of the long pacified province nerved their discipline and courage, while the approach of the successors of the Cæsarean conquerors spread dismay among the raw levies of the Gauls. At the twelfth milestone from Augustodunum the insurgents awaited the advance of the Romans.[2] Their main body, consisting chiefly of the naked or light-armed, was speedily broken and put to flight; the mail-clad stood their ground, because they were unable to shift it; but poles, axes, and pitchforks completed the work of the sword, and once overthrown the iron masses could rise no more.

Crushed by Silius.

Sacrovir the Druid, the leader and soul of the rebellion, had effected his escape from the field; but his associates, now cowed and spiritless, refused to defend Augustodunum,

Death of Sacrovir and completion of the war.

---

[1] Tac. *Ann.* iii. 43.: "Crupellarios vocant." Thierry derives the word from the Gaelic "crup," "resserrer et aussi rendre impotent; crupach et crioplach, perclus, manchot." Thierry, *Gaulois,* iii. 275.

[2] The site of this battle must, in all probability, have been to the north of Augustodunum, on the road into Belgica, from whence the Romans were advancing. It would, therefore, be almost on the spot where Cæsar routed the Helvetii in his first campaign.

and threatened to deliver him into the hands of the victors. Flying from thence to a neighbouring homestead, he engaged his few faithful companions to sacrifice themselves over his body in mutual combat, having first fired the house, and involved the scene of blood in a general conflagration. It was not till this catastrophe was accomplished that Tiberius could proclaim, in a letter to the senate, the origin, and at the same time the completion of the war.[1] He could now afford, without exciting too much apprehension, to give a full and fair account of the recent danger, and to apportion their due meed of praise to his commanders, while he claimed for himself the merit of having directed their movements from a distance. He condescended to excuse himself and Drusus for having allowed an affair of so much moment to be transacted in the field without their own active participation. It was, he felt, something new in the military annals of the republic, that the imperator, the commander of her armies and the minister of her policy, and the consul, the executive instrument of her will, should entrust her vital interests to the hands of tribunes and lieutenants: but the capital was becoming, under the regimen of a single man, of far more importance than the frontiers, and any cause of alarm from abroad must redound with double force on the centre of the empire. Now that the alarm was removed, he added, he might venture himself to quit Rome, and visit the districts so recently disturbed. The senate applauded his sagacity, and decreed a Supplication for the return he promised from his sojourn in a suburban pleasure house, such

---

[1] Tac. *Ann.* iii. 47.: "Tum demum Tiberius ortum patratumque bellum senatui scripsit." Velleius (ii. 129.) turns this into a compliment: "Quantæ molis bellum . . . . mira celeritate compressit, ut ante P. R. vicisse quam bellare cognosceret, nuntiosque periculi victoriæ præcederet nuntius!"

as had often been tendered for Augustus, after distant and perilous expeditions. The proposal of an
individual flatterer, that he should be invited to
enter the city from Campania with the honours of
an ovation, he declined, not perhaps without some
resentment at an excess of officious adulation, which
seemed to savour of mockery.

Probably the emperor had no real intention of
quitting Italy. His years and increasing *The tribuni-*
infirmities might furnish a colourable ex- *tian power*
conferred
cuse; the constant pressure of business close *upon Drusus,*
in conjunction
at home was in fact an adequate reason. *with Tiberius.*
From day to day the obsequious senators continued
to urge him to regulate by his mere word every
public concern, and as regularly did he reply with
formal and diffuse epistles, reproving them for their
indolence or timidity, and then proceeding to discuss, balance, and decide the questions submitted to
his attention. In the year 775, on the completion
of his son's consulship, he desired the senate to confer on him the tribunitian power in conjunction with
himself, as Agrippa had been joined with Augustus,
and afterwards himself, in the highest of all honorary titles. It was as a mere title indeed rather than
a substantive office and function that the jealous
emperor meant this dignity to be imparted. As such
it might suffice to answer the murmurs he anticipated
on the avowal of his own debility. Nevertheless,
amidst every outward demonstration of subservience
and respect, the new appointment was canvassed in
some quarters with freedom, and received with ill-
disguised dissatisfaction. The pride, it is said, of
the presumptive emperor made him unpopular in
the senate; and he was not reputed to have yet
fairly earned, though indeed he had served the republic at home and abroad for eight years, a claim
to be thus designated as the future autocrat of Rome.
The loyalty of the Romans, at least of the proud

and querulous nobles, bore still a skin of soft and
delicate texture, which might be wounded by the
slightest shifting of the trappings in which it had
arrayed itself.[1]

But this discontent at the elevation of Drusus,
and the complaints that he, at least, had
no excuse from age or infirmity for declining the hardships of distant service, to
which nevertheless his father did not choose to dismiss him, were prompted or fostered, we may believe,
by the artifices of Sejanus. The unparalleled indulgence this man had obtained from his patron
only inspired him with the ambition of supplanting
the more legitimate object of imperial favour. His
influence had acquired the government of Africa
for his uncle, and with it the command of an army,
and the conduct of an important war. On the successful issue of the campaigns in which Blæsus was
now engaged, and on the final defeat, as he vaunted,
of the daring foe, who, though regarded by the Romans
as no better than a deserter and a bandit, had presumed to offer terms of accommodation with the
emperor on the footing of a rival potentate, Sejanus
succeeded in getting him leave to accept the impe-
ratorial title from his soldiers; a military distinction
now rarely and reluctantly accorded, treading, as it
apparently did, too closely on the imperial designation
of the chief of the state himself. Even Augustus
had discountenanced the licence earned and claimed
by the legions at the close of a well-fought day.
Blæsus was the last Roman officer in whose case this
military salutation was formally sanctioned by the
emperor. It was only as the proconsul of a senatorial
province that he could have any pretence for hearkening to it; and it was authorized this last time out of

Ambition and intrigues of Sejanus.

---

[1] Tac. *Ann.* iii. 56. 59.

regard only for Sejanus, Tiberius resolving, we may believe, never again to place a nominee of the senate in a position to merit it.[1]   It was fitting that the last surviving witness of the glories of the ancient Republic should expire with this final flicker of its military independence.   At the close of this year, the commencement of the sixty-fourth since the fatal era of Philippi, Junia Tertulla, the niece of Cato, the wife of Cassius, the sister of Brutus, was carried to the resting place of her illustrious house.[2]   In her had centred the revenues as well as the traditions of many noble families, and she gratified a just pride by distributing her riches by will among the most distinguished personages of the city, omitting only the emperor himself.   Tiberius bore the slight without remark, and permitted the virtues of the deceased to be celebrated in a speech from the rostra, which could not fail to revive the memory of a thousand republican glories.   But the leaders of the funeral procession, when they carried before the bier the images of the Manlii, the Quinctii, the Servilii, and the Junii, and of twenty in all of the noblest houses of Rome, were instructed to forbear from exhibiting the busts of Cassius and Brutus, who, in the pithy words of the historian, were in fact the more conspicuous for the absence of their illustrious effigies.[3]

Death and obsequies of Junia Tertulla.

---

[1] Tac. *Ann.* iii. 74.   De la Bleterie remarks (*Mem. Acad. Inscr.* xxi.) that Cornelius Balbus, the last private citizen who triumphed, and Blæsus, the last who was saluted imperator, were both proconsuls of a senatorial province, the only one in which military operations might be anticipated.   The next emperor withdrew the legion of Africa from the command of the senatorial proconsul, and placed it, as we shall see, under an officer of his own appointment.

[2] The battle of Philippi was fought in the autumn of 712.

[3] Tac. *Ann.* iii. 76.: " Sed præfulgebant Cassius atque Brutus eo ipso quod effigies eorum non visebantur."

The success which had thus far attended the in-
Sejanus
establishes
the Prætorian camp.
A. D. 23.
A. U. 776. trigues of Sejanus, had inspired him with
hopes the most unbounded. The prefecture
of the city, with which he had been invested,
was the immediate instrument of the imperial will, and though it had been held before him
by Messala, Taurus, and Piso, among the most
honoured names in Rome, it was not of a nature to
confer either power or dignity itself. But the new
adventurer conceived a design of using it to advance
an inordinate ambition. Hitherto the soldiers of the
prætorian guard, who were placed under his orders,
were quartered, nine or ten thousand in number, in
small barracks at various points throughout the city,
or in the neighbouring towns.[1] Dispersed in these
numerous cantonments, they were the less available
on a sudden emergency : their discipline was lax,
and scattered up and down among the citizens, they
were liable to be tampered with by the turbulent or
disloyal. Yet Augustus had never ventured on a
step so bold and novel as to bring them all together
into a camp, and let the citizens see and number the
garrison by which they really were enthralled. He
had kept no more than three cohorts or eighteen
hundred men in the city or at its gates. It was left
for the days of confirmed and all but acknowledged
royalty, and the private ambition of a minister, to
achieve this regal consummation. Perhaps the terror of the Varian disaster, when the city itself was
supposed for a moment to be defenceless against a
foreign foe, gave the first excuse for the change
which was speedily introduced. Beyond the north-
Its site and
dimensions. eastern angle of the city, and between the
roads which sprang from the Viminal and
Colline gates, the prefect marked out a regular en-
campment for the quarters of these household troops.

---

[1] Tac. *Ann.* iv. 2. Dion, 10,000, Tacitus and Suetonius, 9000.

The line of the existing enclosure, which was traced about two centuries later, exhibits a rectangular projection, by which the limits of the spot and its dimensions are still ascertained. An oblong space, the sides of which are five hundred and four hundred yards respectively, embracing an area of two hundred thousand square yards, was arranged like a permanent camp for the lodgment of this numerous force.[1] Having collected his myrmidons together, the prefect began to ply them with flatteries and indulgences: he appointed all their officers, their tribunes and centurions, and at the same time found means, through the agency of the senate, of advancing his creatures to employment in the provinces. It was strange to see how Tiberius shut his eyes to the manœuvres thus practised before his face. On the most public occasions he loudly proclaimed that Sejanus was *the associate of his own labours:* he permitted his busts and statues to be set up in the theatres and forums, and even to receive the salutation of the soldiers.[2]

Still, notwithstanding these unprecedented marks of favour, and the symptoms they revealed of the emperor's infirmity, Sejanus could not fail to see, in the recent elevation of Drusus, how far his master yet was from contemplating the transfer of empire from his son to a stranger. To remove the rival whom he despaired of supplanting was become necessary for his own se-

Machinations of Sejanus against Drusus.

---

[1] The dimensions of the prætorian camp are given in Bunsen's *Rome*, iii. 2. 359. The ordinary camp, according to the arrangement of Polybius, was a square of 2077½ English feet for a consular army of two legions, or including allies, 19,200 men. This area would contain 480,000 square yards. See General Roy's *Military Antiquities of the Romans in Britain.* According to the system of Hyginus, in the time of Trajan, the soldiers were packed much more closely.

[2] Tac. iv. 2.: "Facili Tiberio atque ita prono, ut socium laborum non modo in sermonibus, sed apud Patres et Populum celebraret ; colique per theatra et fora effigies ejus, interque principia legionum sineret."

curity; for Drusus was instinctively hostile to him; he had murmured at his pretensions, unveiled his intrigues, and in the petulance of power had even raised his hand against him.[1] The prince had complained that his father, though having a son of his own, had in fact devolved no small portion of the government on a mere alien. Sejanus, he muttered, was regarded by the people as the emperor's actual colleague: the camp of the prætorians was the creation of his caprice for the advancement of his authority; the soldiers had transferred to him their military allegiance, and his image had been openly exhibited as an object of popular interest in the theatre of Pompeius.[2] Moreover he had already contracted an alliance with the family of the Cæsars by the betrothal of his daughter to a son of Claudius, the surviving brother of Germanicus.[3] But Drusus was married to a weak and vain woman, whom Sejanus, by affecting a violent passion for her, had succeeded in seducing and attaching vehemently to his interests. Divorcing, as the first step in his designs, his own consort, Apicata, he had extended to Livilla the prospect of marriage with himself, and therewith of a share in the empire to which she encouraged him to aspire. Such at least was the story which was long afterwards revealed by the confessions of their slaves under torture; a story of little value, perhaps, except as displaying the current of popular opinion; for the wife of Drusus, it might be supposed, was already nearer to the throne than the paramour of Sejanus. Probably the unfortunate woman consulted no other

---

[1] Tac. *Ann.* iv. 3.   [2] Tac. *Ann.* iv. 7.

[3] Tac. *Ann.* iii. 29.: " Adversis animis acceptum quod filio Claudii soccr Sejanus destinaretur."   This marriage did not take effect, Drusus, the son of Claudius, dying by a singular accident while yet a child, a few days after the betrothal. Suet. *Claud.* 27.: " Drusum Pompeiis impuberem amisit piro, per lusum in sublime jacto et hiatu oris excepto, strangulatum ; cui et ante paucos dies filiam Sejani despondisset." Dion, lx. 32.

tempter than her own passion, and was persuaded to
listen to his solicitations for the removal of the obstacle between them.[1]   With the help of a confidential physician and a corrupt slave, they contrived,
after many delays, to administer poison to the prince,
of which he lingered long enough to give his decline
the appearance of a casual sickness, brought on, as
some imagined, by intemperance.[2]

The loss of the unfortunate son of Tiberius seems
to have been attended with none of those
passionate regrets which have thrown a
mournful interest over the decease of his
nephew.   The family of the popular favourite seemed, on the contrary, to gain fresh lustre
from the disaster which thus befell the rival branch
of the imperial house.   No suspicion was aroused, no
inquiry at least was made into the cause of the young
Cæsar's death.   The image of antique fortitude which
Tiberius pretended to present caused some curious
remarks, but little admiration, among the soft impul-
sive people, who had long cast aside the iron mask of
their ancient discipline.   Entering the senate, where
the consuls, in sign of public mourning, had relinquished their place of honour, and were sitting
promiscuously on the common benches of the senators,

_Firmness,
real or af-
fected, of
Tiberius at
this loss._

[1] Tac. *Ann.* iv. 8.: "Sejanus, maturandum ratus, deligit venenum,
quo paulatim irrepente, fortuitus morbus adsimularetur: id Druso
datum per Lygdum spadonem, ut octo post annos cognitum est."
Another version of the story, which Tacitus cannot refrain from
repeating, though he acknowledges how little it deserved credit, was,
that Sejanus contrived to poison the cup which Drusus was about to
present to his father, and warned Tiberius not to accept it : whereupon Drusus, having no suspicion of the fraud, and anxious in his
innocence to avert suspicion, himself swallowed the draught.   Tiberius, however, was persuaded that he committed the suicide in
despair of being discovered.   Tac. *Ann.* iv. 10.   Such were the
fantastic horrors which obtained credence among the citizens, and
such wild credulity is perhaps the strongest evidence of their fears
and sufferings.

[2] This was the cause, according to Suetonius (*Tib.* 62.), to which
Tiberius himself was induced to attribute it.

he bade them resume their curule chairs, and declared that for himself, he found his only consolation
in the performance, more strict than ever, of his
public duties. Tearing himself from the corpse of
his child and the embraces of his family, he rushed,
with redoubled devotion, into the affairs of the republic. He lamented the extreme age of his mother
Livia, his own declining years, now deprived of the
support of sons and nephews, and asked leave to recommend to the fathers the last survivors of his
hopes, the youthful children of Germanicus. The
consuls sprang to their feet, and left the room to
conduct the young Nero and Drusus into the assembly. They placed them before the emperor, who
taking them by the hand exclaimed : *These orphans
I placed under the protection of their uncle, entreating him to regard them as his own. Now that
he too is dead, I turn to you, fathers, and adjure
you by the gods of our country to receive, cherish,
and direct these great grand-children of Augustus.*
Then turning to the young men he added: *Nero
and Drusus, behold your parents : in the station to
which you have been born, your good and evil are
the good and evil of the state.*[1]

 In betraying the hollowness of his conduct to a
generation keenly alive to an overacted
hypocrisy, Tiberius showed how little he
comprehended the character of the times.
Augustus might repeat the farce of pretending to restore the Republic; but when the second
princeps now proposed, in the fulness of his simulated affliction, to imitate this magnanimity, every
feeling of compassion for the loss he deplored and of
admiration for his fortitude was overwhelmed by a
sense of ridicule. It was a relief to both parties to

*The Romans
ridicule Tibe-
rius's pre-
tended offer
to restore
the republic.*

---

[1] Tac. *Ann.* iv. 8. : " Ita nati estis ut bona malaque vestra ad rem
publicam pertineant."

divert their thoughts with the splendid pageant of a
funeral, in which the long line of heroes of the Julian
and Claudian houses, from Æneas and the Alban
kings on the one side, from Clausus, the Sabine chief-
tain, on the other, was represented by their genuine
or imaginary effigies.   Even while Tiberius was pronouncing the expected eulogy on the virtues of the
deceased, Sejanus, attending at his side, might be
emboldened, by the coolness with which the citizens
received it, to plan the completion of his
schemes by a series of fresh atrocities.   The   The mascu-
                                                         line virtues
                                                         of Agrippina.
brave Agrippina was not of a character to
be corrupted like the weak Livilla : her virtue was
invincible, and her vigilance never slept in guarding
her children from the perils that environed them.
But the circumstances of her bereavement, and the
favour which had been extended to her enemy Plancina, had left a fatal impression on her mind.   With
a rooted distrust of the emperor she joined a bold
and no doubt a fierce and violent spirit.   Like a true
Roman she exercised without fear or shame the
national licence of the tongue, and in a court where
no whisper was not repeated, proclaimed aloud to
every listener the wrongs of which she deemed herself the victim.[1]   The fertility with which her marriage had been blest had been long a source of
jealousy to the morbid self-love of the empress-mother,
which even in extreme age, and though her son had
reached the summit of her wishes, was piqued by the
maternal taunts of this Niobe of the palace.[2]   The
court was filled with spies and intriguers, encouraged
by Sejanus, with the assurance of favour from the
emperor himself, to place the worst construction on
her words and actions, and to entice her by insidious
artifices to utter every sentiment of pride and impatience.   To the suspicion that he was hostile at

---

[1] Tertull. *Apol.* 25.: " Illa lingua Romana."   [2] Tac. *Ann.* iv. 12.

heart to his nephew's family, Tiberius gave perhaps some colour by the moroseness with which he repelled the compliment to them, by which some of his least wary courtiers now sought to gratify him. When the priests directed that vows should be offered for the health of the princeps himself, conjoining therewith the names of Nero and Drusus, he rebuked them impatiently for their unseasonable officiousness. But with his usual maladroitness, the terms he used were such as seemed to imply a feeling of jealousy towards the young men. He complained that to join them with himself in this prayer for the imperial family was to make as much of their health, young and vigorous as they were, as of the grave infirmity of years under which he felt himself to labour. *Did you this*, he peevishly added, *at the request of Agrippina, or were you moved to it by her menaces?* When they protested warmly against either imputation, he recollected himself, and confined himself to a moderate rebuke, at the same time desiring the senate to abstain henceforth from exciting a giddy ambition by premature distinctions.[1] Sejanus followed in his master's key, and declared his alarm lest the state should be split into factions by the partisans of Agrippina and her children. He even recommended measures for reducing the influence of certain nobles who had shown most alacrity in serving them. Tiberius, sore and vexed with himself and all about him, acquiesced in every counsel his only favourite administered to him : he showed his ill-humour by a captiousness which could never refrain from bitter speeches even on the most trifling occasions. Disregard and sympathy seemed to be equally distasteful to him. When the citizens of Ilium sent envoys to condole with him on the death of Drusus, a deputation which could not

Marginal note: Tiberius apparently jealous of the family of Germanicus.

---

[1] Tac. *Ann.* iv. 17.

reach him till some months after the event, he con-
doled with them in return for the loss of their excellent townsman Hector.[1]

The year 776, the ninth of Tiberius, is marked by
Tacitus as the turning point in the cha-
racter of the second principate. Up to this   Deterioration
of the prin-
time the government, he affirms, had been   cipate of Tiberius from
conducted with honour and advantage to   the year 776.
the commonwealth; and thus far the emperor, he
adds, might fairly plume himself on his domestic
felicity, *for the death of Germanicus he reckoned
among his blessings, rather than his afflictions.*
From that period, however, fortune began to waver:
sorrows and disappointments harassed him and soured
his temper; he became cruel himself, and he stimulated cruelty in others.[2]   The mover and contriver of
the atrocities which followed, it was allowed on all
hands, was the wretched Sejanus.   Their instruments
were the corrupt and profligate courtiers, who pressed
forward to earn the rewards of delation, and soon
outstripped by their assiduity even the ardour of
Sejanus himself.   While the intrigues of the aspiring
favourite were directed against the friends and allies
of the family of Germanicus, Tiberius was perhaps
unconscious, in his retirement, of the secret machinations of the prefect, and seemed to wonder more
and more at the zeal of his subjects in hunting down
all whom they presumed to be his enemies, and
bringing them to condign justice.   His personal fears,
and by this time the selfishness of his character had
degenerated into excessive timidity, were constantly
excited by the pretended discovery of plots   Fate of
C. Silius.
against him.   The wife of Silius, the paci-   A. D. 24.
A. U. 777.
fier of Gaul, was a friend of Agrippina:
her husband accordingly was marked out for the first

---

[1] Suet. *Tib.* 25.

[2] Tac. *Ann.* iv. 1.: "Cum repente turbare fortuna cœpit ; sævire
ipse aut sævientibus vires præbere."

victim, and accused of the gravest crimes against the state.[1] It was affirmed that he had connived at the ripening projects of Sacrovir, instead of crushing the conspiracy in the germ : even when victorious, his triumph, it was insinuated, was sullied by selfish cupidity, and the faithful subjects of the empire had been made to groan under exactions which should have been confined to those who had joined in the rebellion. Such, it was said, were the vehemence and pertinacity with which these charges were pressed upon him, that despairing of his defence, he anticipated the inevitable sentence by a voluntary death.[2] He was not perhaps wholly innocent. But his wife, moreover, was driven into banishment; and the emperor's appetite for prosecution was at length whetted, to the great satisfaction of the delators, by the rich plunder which he was persuaded to taste. The treasures which Silius was convicted of having extorted from the provincials were in no case restored to them. Among the throng of courtiers who sought to gratify the government by enhancing the penalties of the condemned, the only course which remained for the best and wisest senators was to mitigate indirectly the dangers of the accused, by restricting the rewards of delation. M. Lepidus earned distinction in this small but honourable band by

A. D. 25.
A. C. 778.
the proposal, which was, however, probably ineffectual, that the profits of the accusers should be limited to one-fourth of the culprit's fortune, while the remainder was to be restored to

---

[1] Tac. *Ann.* iv. 19.

[2] The object of this suicide, a course to which we shall find the accused not unfrequently resort, was the hope of preventing the confiscation of property which would follow upon a judicial sentence. Silius, whatever gains he had acquired in his province, had been enriched by the liberality of Augustus, and in seizing upon his fortune for the fiscus, Tiberius for the first time showed an appetite for personal lucre : " Prima erga pecuniam alienam diligentia." Tac. *Ann.* iv. 20.

'his guiltless children. It was deemed worthy of remark, amidst so many instances of servility in the
nobles and jealousy in their masters, that such a
proposal should have been made at all, and made
without being resented.   Tacitus, as a disciple of the
school of the fatalists, of which the language at least
was fashionable in his day, is constrained on this occasion to inquire whether the favour or hostility of
princes is a matter of mere chance and destiny,
or whether there may not still be room for prudent
counsel and good sense in the conduct of human
affairs; whether a secure path of life, however hard
to trace, might not still be discovered amidst the
perils of the times, between the extremes of rude independence and base servility.[1] The great defect of
the Romans at this period lay in their want of the
true self-respect which is engendered by the consciousness of sober consistency.   Bred in the speculative maxims of Greek and Roman republicanism,
they passed their manhood either in unlearning the
lessons of the schools, or in exaggerating them in a
spirit of senseless defiance.

Silius, it would seem, had laid himself open to the
attacks of the informers, and there were Prosecution
others against whom the favourite's in- and suicide
of Cremutius
trigues were directed, whose public crimes Cordus.
or personal vices had alienated from them the compassion of the citizens. Nevertheless another of his
victims seems to have been a man of real merit,
though not of such a description as to engage for him
a great amount of popular sympathy. Cremutius Cordus, a follower of the Stoic philosophy, had composed
the Annals of the Roman Commonwealth during the
period of the Civil Wars. He had praised the pa-

[1] Tac. *Ann.* iv. 20.: "Unde dubitare cogor fato et sorte nascendi,
ut cætera, ita Principum inclinatio in hos, offensio in illos: an sit
aliquid in nostris consiliis, liceatque inter abruptam contumaciam et
deforme obsequium pergere iter periculis et metu vacuum."

triotism of Brutus, and had called Cassius *the last of*
the Romans, a phrase which, under the circumstances
of the time, was not a mere speculative inquiry, but
a pungent incentive to violence. Augustus, indeed,
had actually perused the volume, and though he
found in it no panegyric on himself, did not complain of it as disloyal or dangerous. But Augustus
was strong in the affections of his people, and could
afford to disregard the sophisms of the most vehement
of declaimers. Tiberius was far from sharing the confidence of his predecessor. He felt or fancied every
moment that he felt his throne tottering; but this
very sense of weakness induced him to abstain from
any act which might arouse the people from the
lethargy into which they had fallen. It was not till
the conduct of affairs came into the hands of a minister with personal ends to serve, that such experiments were made on the general patience, as the
prosecution of a respectable citizen, like Cremutius,
for the expression of a political opinion. The accusers
were clients of Sejanus, and though we know not
what was the special object of the favourite's hostility,
we may suppose that the philosopher was known as a
partisan of Agrippina. Whatever, however, was his
real crime, the charge against him was that of exciting the citizens to rebellion; a charge which no
judge in modern times could deem to be rebutted by
the reply that the ostensible objects of his praise had
been dead seventy years. To urge as an argument
that Augustus had tolerated his language a little
while before was merely trifling; every government
must judge of the licence that may be granted to
hostile criticism, and the circumstances of the later
period were essentially different from those of the
earlier. But the victim of Sejanus had no security
for a fair trial, a reasonable hearing, or a temperate
sentence. He provoked his judges and aggravated
his offence by anticipating injustice by violence.

Cremutius, now an old man, having delivered himself of a speech, such perhaps as Tacitus ascribes to him, full of bitter invective against the government and the times, went home without awaiting the proceedings with which he was threatened, and put an end to his own life by starvation. His books were ordered to be burnt; but some copies of them were preserved, and all the more diligently studied by the few who had secreted them.[1]

It must be remembered that in the peculiar position of Tiberius, policy required him to give wide scope to individual action in matters that did not immediately concern his own power and security. For the persecution of citizens by citizens he was not at least legally responsible: and it was one of those shadows of liberty which he was careful in conceding, to allow his subjects the gratification of their private enmities before the ordinary tribunals. The peculiar constitution of the Roman legal procedure, which permitted and indeed urged every citizen to assume the character of a public prosecutor, served to exonerate the chief of the state, in the view of his own countrymen, from a large portion of the odium which later ages have cast upon him. At the same time the firmness he occasionally exhibited, in spontaneously interposing to check the licentiousness of his people, was regarded by the citizens as a token of extraordinary consideration, and continued to secure him, among so many motives they had for disliking him, no small share of their respect and even favour. Thus, when Plautius Sylvanus, a prætor, was hurried before him, on the charge of having murdered his wife, and pleaded that she had, unknown to him, laid violent hands on herself, he marched direct to the chamber

Tiberius interferes to check the delators.

---

[1] Tac. *Ann.* iv. 34, 35. Comp. Suet. *Tib.* 61.; *Calig.* 16 ; Dion, lvii. 24.; Senec. *Consol. ad Marc.* 1. 22.

of the accused, and satisfied himself by personal examination of the unquestionable signs it exhibited of a struggle and murder. Such vigour and presence of mind could not fail to make a favourable impression on the multitude.[1] When Salvianus brought a charge against a noble citizen on the day of the Latin Feriæ, he resented the desecration of that holy season, and caused the intemperate accuser to be himself banished.[2] Again, when Serenus was condemned for seditious intrigues, on the accusation of his unnatural son, and the senate proceeded without hesitation to sentence him to death, Tiberius interposed to annul the decree, and desired his precipitate judges to pass a second vote. Hereupon Asinius Gallus proposed that, instead of death, the criminal should be relegated to the isle of Gyarus or Donusa; and again Tiberius, observing that those barren rocks were destitute even of water, declared that where life was conceded the necessaries of life ought not to be withheld.[3] In the case of a knight named Cominius, who had been condemned for the publication of libellous verses against himself, he extended to the convicted criminal a free pardon.[4] Such instances of lenity might contrast favourably with the relentless ferocity of the nobles towards one another; they allowed the citizens still to believe that in the dangerous times on which they had fallen, their best protection lay in the chief of the commonwealth, elevated by his station above the ordinary passions of the envious

---

[1] Tac. *Ann.* iv. 22., A.U. 777.

[2] Tac. *Ann.* iv. 36., A.U. 778.

[3] Tac. *Ann.* iv. 30. The treatment of the exiles seems generally to have been sufficiently mild. They seem to have been allowed to a great extent the choice of their island ; and when Augustus forbade them to settle at any spot within fifty miles of the continent, he excepted the pleasant retreats of Cos, Rhodes, and Lesbos. He also confined them to a single vessel of a thousand amphoræ and two pinnaces for the voyage and conveyance of their families, which further were limited to twenty slaves or freedmen. Dion, lvi. 27.

[4] Tac. *Ann.* iv. 31., A.U. 777.

and malignant among themselves. They were full of gratitude to him also for the good fortune which seemed to attend on his public administration. He had been enabled to suppress, by a happy accident, an alarming insurrection of slaves in Apulia, the nurse of servile seditions.[1] The year 777 had witnessed the final pacification of Africa.[2] While the emperor, out of compliment perhaps to the success attributed to Blæsus, had imprudently withdrawn a large part of the forces in the province, and encouraged the restless Tacfarinas to renew his attempts in that quarter, the gallantry of the new proconsul Dolabella had sufficed to bring the enemy to bay, to overpower and reduce him to self-destruction. The citizens rejoiced at this consummation of a tedious and expensive warfare, which had sometimes threatened their supplies, and were proud at beholding an embassy from the remote Garamantes, which came to solicit their clemency. Such, however, was the influence of Sejanus that Tiberius refused the triumphal ornaments to the victor, in order not to dim the lustre of the honours already accorded to the favourite's uncle.[3] But in the provinces, where the genuine merits of the emperor were known without those drawbacks which were but too notorious at Rome, his popularity was perhaps unalloyed. When he insisted on referring to the senate the charge of malversation, which the people of Asia brought against his procurator, and the fathers, thus encouraged, ventured to condemn the culprit, the grateful provincials decreed a temple to Tiberius in conjunction with Livia and the Senate of Rome. This example was about to be followed by the people of

The Romans acknowledge the good fortune of his administration.

---

[1] Tac. *Ann.* iv. 27., A.U. 777.

[2] Tac. *Ann.* iv. 23 : "Is demum annus populum Romanum longo adversum Numidam Tacfarinatem bello absolvit."

[3] Tac. *Ann* iv. 26.

Further Spain : but on this occasion the emperor declined the honour ; an act of modesty for which he acquired little credit, at least among his own countrymen, who regarded it as pusillanimous and mean. *The best of mortals,* they complacently urged, *had ever aspired to the highest distinctions; thus Hercules and Bacchus among the Greeks, and Quirinus among the Romans, had sought and gained a place among the gods of Olympus: Augustus had lived a hero's life in the hopes of such an apotheosis. Princes,* they said, *may command the present, but it should be their dearest ambition thus to take pledges for the future; indifference to fame is in fact a disregard of virtue.*[1]

At the extraordinary elevation to which he had now arrived, the head of the favourite began to whirl, and to his fevered imagination the utmost objects of his ambition seemed almost within reach. Once admitted within the pale of the Cæsarean family, there would be no distinction, divine or human, which he might not expect to fall on him. The last and most arduous step yet to be effected by his own happy boldness, was to secure his entrance therein by marriage with the widow of Drusus. If he had any hesitation at the last moment in taking the plunge which must mar his fortunes, if it failed to make them, the instances of Livilla herself, the partner of his guilt and the depositary of his secret, could not safely be disregarded ; the impatience of the woman overcame the last lingering scruples of his discretion. Sejanus composed an address to the emperor ; for Tiberius, shy and ever fearful of committing himself, had now adopted the custom, most foreign to the free-spoken habits of the Roman nobles, of requiring every suit to be made to him in writing. *The favour of Au-*

Margin note: Sejanus demands of Tiberius the hand of Livilla.

----

[1] Tac. *Ann.* iv. 38.: "Contemptu famæ contemni virtutes."

gustus, urged the suitor, *in the first instance, and latterly the many tokens of approbation he had received from his successor, had taught him ever to confide his wishes to the ears of the prince, even before disclosing them to the immortal gods. For splendid honours he had never sued; to watch and toil in the ranks for the safety of his imperator was his privilege and pleasure. Nevertheless he had attained the fairest of all distinctions, in being associated in many public functions with the Cæsar himself.* This *was the foundation of his present hopes. Augustus, he had heard, in seeking to establish his daughter, had deigned to review the order of Roman knighthood. Were a husband now required for Livilla, would not Tiberius cast his eye upon a friend, one pledged to be content with the glory of such a connexion, and never to renounce the laborious duties already laid upon him. For his own part, he should be amply satisfied with the security he should thus obtain against the malice of Agrippina, and that for his children's sake, not for his own: for himself it was enough, and more than enough, to have lived so long in the intimacy of a prince so illustrious.*

Tiberius, on receiving this application, which appears to have been wholly unlooked for, penned a hasty answer at the moment, in *His suit is rejected.* which he praised the regard Sejanus had ever shown him and referred slightly to the favours with which he had, on his own part, requited it. *He desired,* he said, *a short time to consider the matter more fully;* and finally replied, *that, while other men were permitted to look solely to their own advantage, princes in all affairs of moment must have regard to the opinion of the world. Accordingly,* he continued, *he would not resort to the answer which lay easiest and nearest at hand—namely, that it was for Livilla herself to determine whether, after Drusus, she*

*would wed another, or continue to bear her adverse
fortune under the roof of her father-in-law; further,
that she had a mother and a grandmother, advisers
nearer than himself; — no, he would act more
straightforwardly, and represent in person to his
friend the objections which really militated against
his suit.   The passions of Agrippina, he would remind him, would unquestionably break out more
vehemently than ever, if the marriage of Livilla
should sever the imperial family; the rivalry of the
women of Cæsar's house would undermine the fortunes of his children.   Sejanus, he added, was deceived if he imagined that it was possible for him
to remain in his present modest rank.   Once wedded
to a Caius Cæsar, and again to a Drusus, his new
wife would never deign to end her career in alliance
with a simple knight.   Could the emperor himself
permit it, did he think that the Roman people would
endure it, who had witnessed her brother, her father,
and their noble ancestors all crowned successively
with the highest honours of the state?   Was it true
that Augustus had for a moment contemplated the
union of his daughter with the knight Proculeius,
yet to whom did he actually espouse her?—first, to
the illustrious Agrippa, and secondly, to Tiberius
himself, to the man, in short, whom he had destined
for his successor.*   But in saying this the emperor
felt that he touched on delicate ground.   Sejanus
was too useful to be discarded, too formidable to be
driven to despair, and he dared not directly cut off
from him even the audacious hope of association in
the empire, or of succession to it.   Accordingly he
concluded with fair words, hinting that he had yet
more important confidences in store for the friend of
his bosom, and that no distinction was in fact too
great for his transcendent merits, when the proper
time should arrive for worthily acknowledging them.[1]

---

[1] Tac. *Ann.* iv. 39, 40.

If such was the language Tiberius really held, I see no reason to doubt its sincerity.   It was his habit to provide for present exigencies by any artifice that offered, but to leave the more distant future to circumstances.   I do not imagine that he had formed at this period any deliberate intention of thwarting the ambitious views of his favourite, or had destined any one of his own kindred to the succession.   But he shrank with a selfish instinct from encouraging in any quarter hopes which might get beyond his control, and again, he was alarmed at the consequences of too abruptly quashing them; so that between the one apprehension and the other, his whole study was to keep the presumptions of those around him in a state of perpetual suspense. This was the Tiberian scheme of policy.   Let those who describe Tiberius as a man of consummate ability and penetrating genius, represent it, if they can, as something eminently deep and subtle: to me it seems to bear the impress of great moral infirmity, while its execution was as clumsy as its conception was feeble.   It may be questioned, however, whether this occurrence, the account of which I have taken, with all other historians, from Tacitus, is after all correctly represented.   Sejanus, we are given to understand, was too well versed in courts, and familiar with the forms of an official refusal, to retain after receiving this answer any portion of his hopes: he regarded it, further, as the token of a settled enmity and design for disgracing him.   Yet it would seem, in point of fact, that even after this rebuff he was not forbidden to cherish still his brilliant anticipations, and that at a later period Livilla was suffered to enter at least into betrothal with him.[1]   Nor, accord-

---

[1] Dion (lviii. 7.) calls her afterwards his μελλόνυμφος, which seems to imply her being actually betrothed; and we can put no less definite meaning certainly on the phrase gener, which is applied to him in the fragment, obscure and corrupt it is true, of Tac. *Ann.* v. 6.   I am

ing to the statements of Tacitus himself, did he exhibit at the time any signs of despair. He proceeded
without a pause to repair the broken meshes of his
intrigues ; and while he postponed, at least for the
moment, his views of an imperial alliance, he revolved
new plans for making doubly sure the impending ruin
of his rival Agrippina. But he was anxious to remove
the emperor from the constant sight of the pomp with
which he continued to surround himself, of the crowds
that haunted his levees, and proclaimed aloud that
he was the real fountain of all imperial favour : on
the one hand he feared the jealousy of his master ; on
the other, it was hardly less dangerous for the
favourite to waive the importunate admiration of
sycophants and courtiers. To divert the one and yet
retain the other, one means only presented itself,
namely, to induce the emperor to quit the arena of
public life, and bury himself in a distant retreat,
whence all his orders would pass through the hands
of the minister.[1] The immediate attendants of the
imperator were properly his centurions and tribunes ;
these were the sentinels at his chamber-door, the
companions of his daily exercises ; by their hands
every letter to the consuls or senators would be conveyed : and Sejanus, as captain of the prætorians, and
the source of favour and promotion among them,
could thus keep close watch upon the correspondence
of his chief, as soon as he should have debarred him
from personal intercourse with the citizens.

The repeated excursions Tiberius had now made
from Rome, and his long-continued cessations from
the irksome routine of residence in the city, had confirmed his inclination for indolence and retirement ;

compelled to suspect that Tacitus has sacrificed the truth to introduce
this interesting dramatic interlude.

[1] Tac. *Ann.* iv. 41.: " Sejanus non jam de matrimonio, sed altius
metuens . . . . huc flexit ut Tiberium ad vitam procul Roma amœnis
locis degendam impelleret. Multa quippe providebat . . . ."

nor was there any difficulty in persuading him that his increasing infirmities demanded repose, Quarrel between Tiberius and Agrippina. A.D. 26. A.U. 779. after so many years of labour. But before he betook himself to the retreat he had perhaps long contemplated for his old age, some striking scenes of anger and recrimination occurred between him and Agrippina, which confirmed and exasperated whatever ill feelings subsisted between them. Among the attacks and insults which were hazarded against the wretched princess by the suitors for the favour of Sejanus, was the prosecution of her cousin Claudia Pulchra by a noble delator, on a charge of adultery combined with majesty.[1] It was affirmed that she had sought to employ poison against the emperor's life, as well as the more subtle influence of charms and incantations. When the trial came on, Agrippina rushed into the emperor's presence, at a moment when he was in the act of sacrificing to his father's divinity. *Should the same man*, she exclaimed, *offer victims to Augustus, and also persecute his children?* To this blunt address she added a shower of invectives against him, together with vehement protestations of her kinswoman's innocence. Forgetting for once, under this unexpected attack, the pertinacious reserve in which he was wont to wrap himself, Tiberius at last broke silence with a Greek quotation, implying, *Must I be denounced as a tyrant because you are not a queen?*[2] Rebuffed by this cold sarcasm, Agrippina retired hastily to her chamber, and flung herself on

---

[1] Lipsius cannot trace the origin of this Claudia, or her affinity with Agrippina. She is called her *sobrina*, i. e. cousin by the mother's side ; and from her name I conceive that she was descended from the Claudia, daughter of P. Clodius Pulcher, to whom Augustus was originally affianced, and whose husband is not known. Her only real connexion with the imperial family lay in the union of her son Quintilius Varus with a daughter of Agrippina and Germanicus.

[2] Tac. *Ann.* iv. 52.: "Correptamque Græco versu admonuit : non ideo lædi quia non regnaret."

her couch, where rage and mortification, combined
with the news of Claudia's condemnation, threw her
into a dangerous fever. When Tiberius visited her
sick-room, the poor creature's spirit was so much
broken, that she burst into tears, and implored him
to take pity on her solitary state by giving her a
husband to support and defend her. She was still
young, she said, and might become again a mother,
and brought up in all the dignity of Roman matronhood, she could find no solace except in a lawful
husband. There were many nobles, she remarked,
who would proudly assume the right of protecting
the widow and children of Germanicus. Tiberius,
thus abruptly solicited on a point which deeply concerned his policy, might have replied in nearly the
same terms as those he had addressed to Sejanus:
his duty to the state, as Tacitus himself allows, would
not suffer him to countenance a request which must
issue in fresh jealousies and enmities between the
members of the imperial family. But he did not
choose to reveal to an impatient woman the apprehensions to which the accomplishment of her wishes
would subject him, or make the humiliating confession that he could not venture in all respects to follow the exalted policy of Augustus: lest he should
give an opening for inconvenient discussion, he left
her, in his awkward way, without speaking a word.
The scene which thus passed in the recesses of the
palace was not generally disclosed, but was recorded
in her private memoirs by the daughter of Agrippina
herself, a personage of whom I shall have much to
relate hereafter.[1]

---

[1] Tac. *Ann.* iv. 53.: " Quæ Neronis principis mater vitam suam et
casus suorum posteris memoravit." It is natural to surmise that the
revelations of the palace which our historians relate, are derived in
a great measure from these family memoirs, and it is impossible to
overlook the probability that the conduct both of Tiberius and Sejanus
would be seriously misrepresented by an hereditary enemy to both.

In the height of her distress, and when the vexations of her position had thrown her more than ever off her guard, Sejanus contrived to instil fresh and yet more shocking suspicions into the mind of the unfortunate *Suspicions against Tiberius instilled into the mind of Agrippina.* princess, which served only to complete the disgust and alienation of Tiberius. The minister's creatures ventured, under the guise of friendly care for her, to insinuate that her uncle was seeking an opportunity of poisoning her, and enjoined her to avoid partaking of food at his table. The widow of Germanicus was residing under the roof of the head of the Cæsarean family: there were no separate establishments for princes or princesses of the blood imperial; but it was only on special occasions, perhaps, that the emperor invited the females of his house to sup in company with him. Agrippina had neither the temper nor the art to dissemble. Reclining by the side of her host, she rejected every dish presented to her with cold and impassive mien, and without excuse or observation. Tiberius could not fail to remark her behaviour, nor to guess its motive. To assure himself, he offered her some apples with his own hand, recommending their flavour; but she, all the more confirmed in her suspicions, handed them untasted to the attendants. Hereupon Tiberius turned to his mother on the other side, and muttered that none could wonder at any show of harshness in his conduct towards one who scrupled not to intimate her apprehensions of his intent to poison her. The incident was speedily noised abroad, and the rumour prevailed that he was actually meditating her destruction, and, not daring to effect it by public process before the face of the citizens, was contriving secret means of assassination.[1]

At a later period I shall have occasion to show more particularly how another history appears to have been vitiated by the same writer's unscrupulous malice.   [1] Tac. *Ann.* iv. 54.

Informed by his spies of the whispers thus circu-
lating among his subjects, Tiberius was an-
noyed, if not seriously alarmed. He tried
to give another current to men's thoughts,
and directed their attention to the curious
rivalry now presented by eleven chief
communities of the province of Asia, each of which
sought to approve itself the worthiest claimant for ·
the honour of erecting a temple to Rome and her
glorious imperator. The pretensions they severally
advanced were all nearly similar, appealing to the
splendour of their mythological origin, as founded
by some Jove-descended hero, to their connexion
with Troy, the reputed parent of Rome herself, or to
their well-attested fidelity to their conquerors. The
claims of Hypæpe, Tralles, Laodicea, Magnesia, Pergamus, Ephesus, Sardis, and others, were heard successively; but all were finally postponed to those of
Smyrna, whose people had crowned their merits towards the Republic by stripping the raiment from
their own backs to supply the necessities of Sulla's
army. Tiberius attended in the senate throughout
these discussions, which were protracted for several
days, and showed himself more busy and active in
public matters than had been usual with him for
some time past.[1] Nevertheless, he had been long
meditating a final retirement from Rome; and the
increasing suspicions and even offensive remarks of
the citizens tended no doubt to ripen this resolution.
Five years before he had allowed himself to be absent for a whole twelvemonth in Campania: he now
sought the same retreat once more; but this time he
probably determined in his own mind never again to
return. The motives of this determination were variously assigned by the ancients, and it is probable

Eleven cities of Asia con-tend for the honour of making Tibe-rius their tutelar divi-nity.

---

[1] Tac. *Ann.* iv. 55, 56. That the temple was to be specially dedicated to Tiberius, though not mentioned in this place, appears by
comparing it with cc. 15. 37.

that more than one combined to produce a resolution
so important.   We may believe that it was Tiberius
at least partly owing to the influence of meditates retiring from
Sejanus, who desired, as has been before the city.
observed, to withdraw his jealous master from the
daily sight of his favourite's undue preeminence.
It is possible also that Tiberius may have been
anxious to escape from the dominion his mother still
continued to exercise over him; for he was conscious
that he owed the empire to her influence over Augustus, or so at least she was herself firmly persuaded,
and never allowed him to forget it.   It seems probable, however, that he was thus driven into solitude
by the infirmity of his own temper; by his dislike
of the show and trappings of public life; by the
shyness which was natural to him, and which had
been undoubtedly increased to a morbid degree by
the long and painful solitude of his banishment at
Rhodes.   As he grew older he seemed more to lose
his presence of mind in public; and if sometimes a
senator broke out into invectives against him, or
assailed him with unseasonable questions, he became
confused and agitated.   His temper was exasperated
by the imputations made or insinuated against him,
and the charge of severity in his judgment on criminals piqued him to actual ferocity, which afterwards all the more distressed and alarmed him.[1]
For this retirement he had been, as we have seen, a
long time preparing, and the motives which now
impelled him to it were, we may suppose, the same
which had long been familiar to his thoughts, to
which increasing years had given strength Motives
and poignancy.   The bitterest of his ene- ascribed to him.
mies, however, declared that he had no
other wish than to exercise in secret the cruelty and

---

[1] Compare particularly the story in Tac. Ann. iv. 42.: " Cæsar
objectam sibi adversus reos inclementiam eo pervicacius amplexus."

atrocious lewdness to which, they asserted, he was
utterly abandoned ; or that he was ashamed of exhibiting to the public gaze the ungraceful leanness of
his bent and shrivelled figure, the baldness of his
forehead, and a face deformed by spots and pimples,
or the patches with which he concealed them.[1] We
have already seen reason for questioning the habitual
intemperance and dissoluteness of Tiberius, to which
such disfigurements as these were popularly imputed;
but the prejudice against him was deeply rooted in
the minds of the Romans, and was confirmed by repeated stories of the blackest colour, and the disgust
at the horrid monster expressed, it was said, by every
woman to whom he made his loathsome advances.

The immediate pretext for quitting Rome was the
object of dedicating temples recently erected to Jupiter at Capua, and to Augustus
at Nola, the spot from whence the late emperor had
ascended into the heavens.[2] It was in the year 779
that Tiberius slunk, as it were, out of the city, with
only a single senator, named Cocceius Nerva, in attendance upon him, nor, besides Sejanus himself,
more than one knight.[3] The rest of his retinue was
composed of a few men of learning, chiefly Greeks,
and some of them, no doubt, astrologers. The departure of the chief of the state from the centre of
government, except to command armies abroad, or
during the recess of business allowed in the summer
heats, had been so unusual, that, while the emperor's
real intentions were still confined to his own bosom,
the vulgar were busy in conjecturing the result, and
the searchers of the heavens, ever faithful interpreters
of the popular instinct, whispered that their art revealed to them that he was destined never to return.

Tiberius quits Rome.

---

[1] Tac. *Ann.* iv. 57.: "Erant qui crederent in senectute corporis
quoque habitum pudori fuisse." He was now (A. U. 779) in his sixty-
seventh year. "Traditur etiam matris impotentia extrusum."
[2] Suet. *Tib.* 45.   [3] Tac. *l. c.*

It was dangerous to give publicity to such surmises, which the sanguine and impatient shaped readily into the assurance that his death was at hand, and so brought many into trouble on the charge of anticipating the prince's decease.[1] The conjecture, indeed, proved literally correct, though not in the way that was anticipated. Tiberius never again entered Rome: but no man, says Tacitus, could have imagined that a Roman would voluntarily abandon his country for a period of eleven years.

Harsh, indeed, and unreal the historian's phrase may appear to our notions, *to abandon one's country*, or, more strongly still, *to exist without a country*, thus applied to a citizen quitting the walls of Rome to reside in a suburban retreat on the coast of Campania.[2] Doubtless we may trace in it something of an affectation of antique sentiment, from which Tacitus is by no means always exempt, not strictly in accordance with the genuine feelings of the time. We have seen, indeed, how deeply Cicero was moved at the thought of quitting the neighbourhood of his beloved city. His sensibility was more acute than other men's, but it only pointed in the same direction as theirs. The levity of Milo on the occasion of his banishment caused, perhaps, some revulsion in the sympathy of his party with him. Even in the camp of Pompeius the fugitive patriots could scarcely retain their assurance that they were still genuine Romans.[3] But we have seen how desperate was

What the Romans meant by "patria carere," abandoning one's country.

---

[1] Tac. *Ann.* iv. 58.: " Ferebant periti coelestium, iis motibus siderum excessisse Roma Tiberium ut reditus illi negaretur ; unde exitii causa multis fuit, properum finem vitæ conjectantibus vulgantibusque."

[2] Tac. *Ann.* iv. 58.: " Ut libens patria careret."

[3] The arguments of Lucan against this sentiment are not uninstructive. *Pharsal.* v. 26.: " Rerum nos summa sequetur
 Imperiumque comes . . . . non unquam perdidit ordo
 Mutato sua jura solo . . . .
 Ordine de tanto quisquis non exsulat, hic est."

Cicero's affliction at being exiled beyond the seas; how loath he was to follow the self-expatriated consuls; how anxious at the first moment to make his peace with the conqueror and return; how, in the last crisis of his fortunes, the imminent perils of his post at Rome could not induce him finally to desert it. Cicero would have been hardly less unhappy in a Campanian retirement than in Greece or Macedonia, if doomed irrevocably to sojourn among its foreign associations; for in this respect the change from Rome to Naples was hardly less complete than that to Rhodes or Athens. The Greek cities of Campania were, as we have seen before, in almost every particular, accurate and vivid copies of those beyond the sea : their foreign manners and habits, attractive as they were to the world-worn seeker for amusement and relaxation, were reputed by every true Roman altogether unworthy of his constant adoption. Rome was the proper sphere of his business and duty, the shrine of the gods, the sacred soil of the auspices, the tribunal of the laws, the stative camp of the warrior nation. There the Roman girded himself for the work of his great moral mission, to spare the subject, but beat down the proud; elsewhere he might loose his robes and put off his sandals, and indulge in recreations, which his conscience, strictly questioned, could scarcely distinguish from vices.[1] *To play the Greek*, for which his vocabulary furnished him with a short expressive term, was in his view pleasant but

---

[1] Thus Cæsar was reproached as " puer male præcinctus." The loose trailing of his toga in the forum was objected to Mæcenas. Such a want of etiquette was reputed a token of dissoluteness of morals. Suet. *Ner.* 51.: "Adeo pudendus ut . . . . prodierit in publicum sine cinctu et discalceatus." Horat. *Sat.* ii. 1. 71..

> " Quin ubi se *a vulgo et scena* in secreta remôrant
> Virtus Scipiadæ et mitis sapientia Læli,
> Nugari cum illo et discincti ludere, donec
> Decoqueretur olus, soliti."

wrong [1]: it might be excused in the overwrought statesman, in the exhausted soldier, in the mere thoughtless youth; but only as an exception to the common rule of life and conduct, as a rare holiday breaking the stern routine of daily practice, to which his birth and breeding devoted him.   The Roman must live and die in harness.   An Atticus renounced with the forms and duties of Roman life most of the rights and privileges of a Roman citizen.   As an Athenian burgher he forfeited the franchise of the conquering state; and the exemption he enjoyed from the calamities of the civil war was, in another view, the penalty he paid for the loss of the name of Roman.   But assuredly such were not the sentiments of the citizens of the age of Tiberius, still less those of a century later.   Life at Rome, while it still retained most of the outward forms of antiquity, the harsh restrictions upon freedom of action and conversation which had been endured by the Scipios and Catos, had lost the charms of political independence, for which alone they had been content to endure them.   The Roman noble now chafed at the stiff etiquette of his ancestors; he shrank from the importunate observation of his clients; he loathed the obeisances of his subjects, conscious that he deserved them neither by personal merits, nor substantial power; he rejoiced to escape from a multitude of jealous critics to companions who had no claim to watch or control him, who considered his countenance as a favour, and never paused to reflect whether it was unworthy in him to give, or in themselves to accept it.   Still the actual abandonment of the pre-

---

[1] Hor. *Sat.* ii. 2. 11.:

> "Si quem Romana fatigat
> Militia assuetum Græcari."

Hence also "græcatus," "græcanicus," applied to the manners of Romans imitated from the Greek.   "Græcanicus miles," a dissolute or luxurious soldier.   See Facciolati in voc.

scriptive post of duty was rare and remarkable. It
was affirmed, for instance, of Lucius Piso, one of the
chief magnates of the Tiberian senate, that in his
disgust at the proceedings of the delators, he had
expressed among his compeers, a determination to
withdraw from the city, and therewith from public
life altogether. It had been well for him had he
actually executed this threat : he had the courage to
bring the favourite of the empress to justice, but not
to quit the scene of his dangerous activity, and only
avoided by the opportuneness of his death the penalty
of charges of which he was speedily convicted.[1]

The retirement of Tiberius himself from the public
stage was however in no respect a real re-
linquishment of public occupation. No one
supposed that he would cease thereupon
from retaining the supreme oversight of the affairs of
the commonwealth; nor, in the existing state of political usage, was there any real impediment to his ruling
the empire from his quiet retreat. The undefined
character of the supreme authority had this advantage for its possessor, that it bound him to no stated
functions, requiring his presence at certain times, at
certain places. The consul must take the auspices,
and these could be taken only at Rome ; a dictator
must perform the rites of the Latin Feriæ on the
Alban hill ; a tribune must not absent himself from
the city during the period of his office : but none of
these restrictions applied to one who retained the
power of all these officers, but was exempt from their
restrictions. Even though in theory the safety of
the state might be regarded as entwined with the
performance of certain religious ceremonies by the
chief pontiff, yet from the time at least of Julius

Tiberius does not abandon public affairs.

---

[1] Tac. *Ann.* ii. 34.: " Inter quæ L. Piso ambitum fori, sævitiam
oratorum accusationes minitantium, increpans abire se et cedere
Urbe, victurum in aliquo abdito et longinquo rure testabatur." Comp.
.iv. 21. This was not the L. Piso, prefect of the city.

Cæsar, the presence of that august official had been for many years dispensed with, and there was nothing new at least in Tiberius delegating to others, or altogether omitting, duties which his imperial predecessors, and Lepidus in his retreat at Circeii, had been permitted to waive. Nevertheless this act was not without grave significance. Whenever Augustus had withdrawn from the heart of the empire, it was only to impart fresh vigour to the action of its extremities: never for a moment had he resigned his ostensible place as the prime mover of the whole machine, or let his subjects imagine that the wheels of government could continue to revolve by the mere impulse once communicated to them. The retreat to Campania was thus a great step in the development of despotism, the greatest step perhaps of all, inasmuch as it made it at once apparent that the institution of monarchy was an accomplished fact, and no longer the creature of variable popular caprice.

The retirement of Tiberius did not fail, however, to be followed by a succession of public calamities, and these were generally ascribed to so strange and inauspicious a proceeding. A private speculator had undertaken, *Disastrous occurrences ascribed to the retirement of Tiberius.* as a matter of profit, one of the magnificent works which in better times it was the privilege of the chief magistrates or candidates for the highest offices to construct for the sake of glory or influence. In erecting a vast wooden amphitheatre in the suburban city of Fidenæ, he had omitted the necessary precaution of securing a solid foundation; and when the populace of Rome, unaccustomed, from the parsimony of Tiberius, to their favourite spectacles at home, were invited to the diversions of the opening day, which they attended in immense numbers, the mighty mass gave way *Fall of the amphitheatre at Fidenæ.* under the pressure, and covered them in its ruins.

Fifty thousand persons, or according to a lower computation not less than twenty thousand, men and
women of all ranks, were killed or injured by this
catastrophe, which called forth an edict from the
senate, forbidding any one henceforth to exhibit a
gladiatorial show, unless his means were independent
and ample, while the rash projector was driven into
exile; a mild punishment, perhaps, if it was right
to punish him at all. The care and attention lavished
on the sufferers by the wealthiest people at Rome,
the spontaneous offering of medical care and attendance, served at least to remind the citizens of the
best days of the republic, in seasons of public
calamity. But this sorrow had not been forgotten
when it was redoubled by the disaster of a
great fire, which ravaged the whole of the
Cælian hill and a considerable area of the
city besides, occupied with dwellings of every class.
This catastrophe, however, gave Tiberius occasion
to exhibit a munificence and consideration for his
people, for which he had not yet acquired credit.[1]
The senate decreed that the hill should henceforth
bear the name of Augustus, in memory of this imperial liberality, and more particularly because, in
the midst of the general destruction, an image of the
emperor, it was reported, had alone been left standing
and unscathed. A similar prodigy had occurred in
the case of another personage of the imperial house,
the famous Claudia Quinta, whose effigy had twice
escaped the flames, and been placed thereupon as a
sacred relic in the temple of the Mother of the gods.[2]

Conflagration on the Cælian hill.

But to more intelligent observers these calamities
were far less alarming than the steady advance of the toils which were gradually
surrounding the family of Germanicus. Though the

Progress of delation.

---

[1] Vellius, ii. 130.

[2] Tac. *Ann.* iv. 62—64. It is hardly necessary to observe that
the new name of the Cælian soon fell into disuse.

charges urged against its members were managed by private delators, none could doubt that Sejanus himself was the mover of the horrid conspiracy. The first approaches against this illustrious house were made cautiously from a distance; it was deemed advisable to sap the outworks of the family in the persons of its remoter connexions, before assailing the citadel, and attacking the mother of the princes and the princes themselves. Domitius Afer, the same who had prosecuted Claudia Pulchra to condemnation, proceeded to advance charges of treason or licentiousness against her son, Quintilius Varus, the husband of one of the daughters of Germanicus.[1] In this odious prosecution he was joined by Dolabella, a kinsman of the unfortunate youth. The conduct of the first caused at least no surprise, for he was poor and delation was his trade; but Dolabella had no such excuse; and when he, highborn and wealthy as he was, stood forward to shed noble blood, the same which flowed in his own veins, the citizens were astonished and indignant. For once the senators ventured to stem the torrent of delation, which Sejanus was evidently directing to his own guilty purposes. They resolved before pronouncing sentence to await the decision of the emperor himself.[2] Such was the state of affairs, under the sway of the favourite and his creatures, that Tiberius was regarded as the last hope and refuge of the oppressed. Possibly, for we hear no more of the result, his interference saved the victim on this occasion. Nevertheless the power of Sejanus, whatever shock his recent rebuff may have given it, was now completely

---

[1] This Quintilius Varus was the son by Claudia Pulchra of the Varus who perished in Germany. His marriage to a daughter of Agrippina, whose name is not known, is mentioned by M. Seneca, *Controv.* i. 1. 3. It is strange that Tacitus should have omitted to mention this connexion; but we have seen that he was not well informed as to the position of Claudia.

[2] Tac. *Ann.* iv. 66.

re-established. A fortunate accident had enabled
him to prove his devotion to the emperor by saving
his life at the risk of his own. In the course of an
entertainment which Tiberius had held in the cool
recess of a grotto in Campania, the roof of the
cavern had suddenly given away, and covered the
tables and the guests themselves. Sejanus, in the
midst of the confusion, had thrown himself across
the prostrate body of his master, and bending in the
form of an arch, with a great exertion of his her-
culean strength, had shielded him from the falling
fragments.[1] This act of courage had made a great
impression on Tiberius, and seemed at least to have
obliterated the unfavourable feelings which the late
affair between them might have excited.

Renewed favour of Sejanus. The minister, to whom a double share of
the cares of government were now confided,
could easily persuade the senators that his influence
with his master was quite unbounded, and that no
cloud had ever passed over the sunshine in which he
basked. He set spies to watch every word and
movement of Nero, the eldest child of Agrippina,
and suborned the wife and brother of the luckless
youth to urge him to indiscretions, and aggravate
them by misrepresentation. Such, however, were
the young prince's admirable sense and conduct that
no handle could be found for framing an accusation
against him; while the rash and thoughtless Drusus
too often laid himself open to the machinations of
the common enemy of their family.[2]

Having performed the dedication of the temples
Tiberius retires to the island of Capreæ. in Campania, which had furnished the
immediate pretext for his removal from
Rome, Tiberius, in the year 780, crossed
the bay of Naples in quest of the spot which he had
already destined for his final retreat.[3] In vain had

[1] Tac. *Ann.* iv. 59.; Suet. *Tib.* 39.
[2] Tac. *Ann.* iv. 60.　　　　　　　　[3] Tac. *Ann.* iv. 67.

he issued orders, while traversing the dense populations of the continent, that no man should presume
to disturb his sullen meditations, and had even lined
his route with soldiers to keep his importunate
admirers at a distance. The concourse of idle and
gaping multitudes whom his arrival brought everywhere together became more and more odious to
him, and the sullenness with which he spurned
observation gave colour to the notion that he
shunned exhibiting to strangers the deformity of a
diseased and bloated countenance. He hastened to
bury himself in the pleasant solitudes of the little
island of Capreæ. While yet in the maturity of his
powers Augustus had been attracted by the charms
of this sequestered retreat; he had been struck particularly with the omen of a blighted ilex reviving
here during a visit he paid to the spot. Its genial
climate, he conceived, might conduce to the maintenance of his own health in more advanced age, and
with this view he obtained the cession of it from the
Neapolitans, to whose city it belonged, in exchange
for the more important nor, as reputed, less Description
salubrious island of Ænaria.[1]　Capreæ at of Capreæ.
this time indeed was little better than a barren rock,
the resort of wild goats, from which it derived its
name, about eleven miles in circuit; but it lay
within two hours' row of Misenum, the great naval
station of the Lower Sea. Easily accessible from the
mainland at one point, which it required little

---

[1] Ænaria or Inarime was famous for its medicinal springs: "Æna-
riæque lacus medicos." Stat. *Sylv.* iii. 5. 104. Augustus got possession of Capreæ in the year 725. Dion, lii. 43. Comp. Suet. *Oct.* 92.
Virgil, on his return from Greece in 735, devoted the remaining
months of his life to the revision of the Æneid at Naples, and some
passages even in the earlier books bear marks of interpolation at this
period. Possibly the reference to Capreæ (*Æn.* vii. 735.) is meant
as a compliment to Augustus: "Teleboum Capreas cum regna teneret
Jam senior." Augustus, then just completing his forty-fifth year,
was on the verge of Roman seniority.

vigilance to secure, the island is singularly difficult
of approach at every other. Its shores consist of
limestone cliffs, sheer precipices in most parts plunging directly into the deep sea. They are furrowed
here and there by those caverns celebrated for the
play of coloured light in their recesses, which, after
having amused and astonished the curious of our time
as recent discoveries, are now ascertained to have
been the forgotten haunts of Roman luxury. In the
interior, an uneven but cultivable surface rises at
either end of the island to the height of one thousand
and two thousand feet respectively; the eastern or
lower promontory having been, according to tradition, the favourite sojourn of Tiberius, and its dizzy
cliff the scene of his savage executions. We have
before noticed the channel, six miles wide, which
separated it from the coast of Campania, whence it
seems to have been divorced by a convulsion of
nature, and the two famous sea-marks which faced
each other on opposing summits, the pharos of
Capreæ and the temple of Surrentum. But while
few other spots could have combined the requisites
of solitude and difficult approach with such actual
proximity to the seat of government, Tiberius was
not insensible to the charms of its climate, and even
the attractions of its scenery; to the freshness of
its evening breeze, the coolness of its summers, and
the pleasing mildness of its winters.[1] The villas he
erected on the fairest sites within these narrow limits,
twelve in number and named after the greater gods
of the Olympian consistory, enjoyed, we may suppose, every variety of prospect, commanded every
breath of air, and caught the rays of the sun at every

---

[1] Statius (*Sylv.* iii. 5.) invites his wife to the shores of his native Parthenope;

> " Quas et mollis hyems et frigida temperat æstas ;
>   Quas imbelle fretum torpentibus alluit und s."

Could the lady resist so sweet an invitation to so sweet a place ?

point of his diurnal progress.[1]   From the heights of
Capreæ the eye comprehended at one glance the
whole range of the Italian coast from the promontory
of Circe to the temples of Pæstum, clearly visible
through that transparent atmosphere.   The Faler-
nian and Gauran ridges, teeming with the *noblest*
vineyards of Italy, the long ranges of the Samnite
Apennines, even to the distant Lucanian mountains,
formed the framework of the picture, while Vesuvius
reared its then level crest, yet unscarred by lava,
directly in the centre.   Facing the south, the spectator gazed on the expanse of the Sicilian Sea.   So
wide is the horizon that it is, perhaps, no fiction
that at some favourable moments the outlines of the
fiery isles of Æolus, and even of Sicily itself, are
within the range of vision.   The legends of Circe and
Ulysses, of Cimmerian darkness and Phlegræan fires,
of the wars of the Giants with Jupiter, and the
graceful omens which attracted the first settlers to
these shores from Greece, had perhaps a strange
fascination for the worn-out soldier and politician.[2]
Reclining on the slopes of Capreæ, and gazing on the

---

[1] Tac. *l. c.*   In his charming description of the villa of Pollius on
the Surrentine promontory, Statius specifies the various objects in
view from the spot, which are nearly the same as those commanded
by Capreæ.   The spacious residence of his friend comprised all the
advantages which could be sought for in the divers localities of the
Tiberian pleasure-houses :

> " Quæ rerum turba ! iocine
> Ingenium an domini mirer prius ? hæc domus ortus
> Prospicit, et Phœbi tenerum jubar ; illa cadentem
> Detinet, exactamque negat dimittere lucem . . . .
> Hæc pelagi clamore fremunt ; hæc tecta sonoros
> Ignorant fluctus, terræque silentia malunt . . . .
> . . . . Quid mille revolvam
> Culmina, visendique vices ? sua cuique voluptas
> Atque omni proprium thalamo mare, transque jacentem
> Nerea diversis servit sua terra fenestris . . . . "
> Stat. *Sylv.* ii. 2. 44.

[2] Stat. *Sylv.* iii. 5. 79.:

> " Parthenope, cui mite solum trans æquora vectæ
> Ipse Dionæa monstravit Apollo columba."

glorious landscape before him, Tiberius might dream
of a fairyland of the poet's creation, and seek some
moments of repose from the hard realities of his
eternal task, to perplex his attendants with insoluble
questions on the subjects of the Sirens' songs and the
name of Hecuba's mother.[1]   Nor could be be unmoved, though dallying with these fanciful shadows,
by the deep interest which the records of actual
history had thrown over the fateful scene.   There
lay the battle-fields of the still youthful republic :
there the rugged Roman was first broken by the
culture of Hellas : there captive Greece first captured her conqueror. There were the plains in which
the strength of Hannibal had wasted in ignoble
luxury ; and the dark crater of Vesuvius, from
whence had issued the torrent of servile insurrection, when the empire of the world was for a
moment shaken by the rage of a Thracian bondman.
The great Italian volcano had slumbered since the
dawn of history.   Tokens indeed were not wanting
on the surface of the fires still seething beneath
the plains of Campania ; the sulphureous exhala-
tions of Baiæ and Puteoli still attested the truth
of legends of more violent igneous action on which
the local mythology was built.   But even these
legends pointed to no irruption of Vesuvius : no cone
of ashes rose then as now from its bosom ; and
cities and villages clustered at its foot or hung
upon its flanks, unconscious of the elements of convulsion hushed in grim repose beside them.[2]

---

[1] Suet. *Tib.* 70. " Maxime tamen curavit notitiam historiæ fabularis,
usque ad ineptias atque derisum. Nam et grammaticos, quod genus
hominum, ut diximus, maxime appetebat, ejusmodi fere quæstionibus
experiebatur: quæ mater Hecubæ: quod Achilli nomen inter virgines
fuisset : quid Sirenes cantare sint solitæ."

[2] Tac. *l. c.*: " Prospectabatque pulcherrimum sinum, antequam
Vesuvius mons ardescens faciem loci verteret." This was written
about thirty years after the destruction of Herculaneum and Pompeii.

During his protracted sojourn in this pleasant locality the imperial hermit crossed but rarely to the continent, and twice only made as if he would revisit the city.[1] The seclusion of his lonely rock was guarded with the strictest vigilance, and the chastisement he was said to have inflicted on the unwary fishermen who landed on the forbidden coast increased the mysterious horror with which it came soon to be regarded.[2] But day by day a regular service of couriers brought despatches to him from the continent; nor did he ever relax from the scrupulous attention, in which he had so long been trained, to the details of business sent him by his ministers, which must have employed his mind and tasked his patience for many hours. He was surrounded moreover in the recesses of his privacy by a number of literary men, professors of Greek and other foreign extraction, among whom he diverted himself with abstruse inquiries, such as have been already noticed, into the most unprofitable questions of mythology or grammar. Distraction of mind was the object of his literary recreations; but like the generality of his busy and restless countrymen, he had no taste for matters of really interesting inquiry, and his studies, if not pernicious, were at best merely curious. He was peculiarly addicted to conversation with the soothsayers, of whom he entertained a troop about his person, making constant experiments of their skill in the examination of the lives and fortunes of his associates. Such was the account which reached the city of the life of the imperial misanthrope: it was coloured no doubt and distorted, inflamed and exaggerated: nevertheless it did not suffice to satisfy the prurient curiosity of

Occupation of Tiberius at Capreæ.

---

[1] Suet. *Tib.* 72 : "Bis omnino toto secessus tempore Romam redire conatus," scil. ann. 786. 788. Comp. Tac. *Ann.* vi. 1.; Dion, lviii. 21. 25.

[2] Suet. *Tib.* 60.

the citizens, stimulated beyond its wont by the extraordinary circumstance of his retirement from public observation. They filled the hours they supposed to be vacant from business with amusements of a far less innocent character, with debaucheries of the deepest dye, and cruelties the most refined and sanguinary: they accused the Roman Cæsar of the crimes of a Median or Assyrian; as if their perverted imaginations delighted in contrasting the most exquisite charms of nature with the grossest depravation of humanity: and all these charges, whether or not they were in his case really true, of which we have little means of judging, found easy credence from the notorious vices of their own degraded aristocracy.[1]

The retirement of Tiberius to Capreæ has been *Further deteri-* justly regarded as an important turning-*oration in the* point in his career; inasmuch as, having *government of Tiberius.* thereby screened himself from the hated gaze of his subjects, he could from thenceforth give the rein, without shame or remorse, to the worst propensities of his nature. From this time undoubtedly we find him less anxious to moderate the excessive flatteries of the senate, or to mediate between its servile ferocity and the wretched victims of the delators. Even on the calends of January, the strictest holiday of the Roman year, he could turn his solemn missive of vows and congratulations to a demand for the blood of Titius Sabinus, of distinguished equestrian family, who had been betrayed by a base intrigue.[2] *What a commencement for the new year is this!* exclaimed the affrighted citizens. *What victims are these with which Sejanus requires to be appeased! What day from henceforth will pass*

---

[1] Suet. *Tib.* 43—45.

[2] Tac. *Ann.* iv. 68.: "Junio Silano et Silio Nerva coss. (A.U. 781), fœdum anni principium incessit."

without an execution, if a season so holy and festive must be profaned with the chain and cord! But the emperor had attained a position in which he could despise these murmurs. The complaints he urged upon the senate of the peril in which he fancied himself to stand, as the mark of so many secret conspiracies and machinations, were interpreted into dark insinuations against his own nearest kindred: every member of the imperial family, cut off by age or accident, was supposed to relieve him either from the fear of intrigues, or the mortification of being observed and thwarted. Presently the Romans imagined that the cares of empire were neglected: an outbreak of the Frisii, which seems in fact to have been speedily repressed, was exaggerated by their undue apprehensions; and it was believed that Tiberius disguised the real extent of the disaster to avoid the necessity of sending a special legate to retrieve it.[1] Nevertheless the senate, we are told, was not so much concerned for a frontier injury, as for the perils by which it seemed itself environed at home; and against these it could devise no other precaution than the most lavish adulation of the emperor. It decreed an altar to Clemency and another to Friendship, by the side of which images of Tiberius and Sejanus were to be erected, and at the same time importuned its prince with fresh entreaties for the happiness of once more beholding him. But neither Tiberius nor his favourite vouchsafed a visit to the city or its vicinity. They contented themselves with leaving the island, and exhibiting their august presence at the nearest point of the Campanian coast. Thither flocked the senators, the knights, and numbers of the inferior citizens, more apprehensive of their reception by Sejanus than

---

[1] Tac. *Ann.* iv. 72.

even by Tiberius himself: nor did the minister's
conduct belie the dread they had conceived of him,
since the retirement of his master had served to
exalt him to a higher pinnacle than ever. Amidst
the various avocations of life in the city, the trooping
of flatterers and courtiers to his levees might be less
open to remark; but in the country, where there
was no other occupation and no other diversion, every
one's eyes intently watched all the rest, and the
Romans were shocked at the evidence they presented
to one another of the extent of their own servility.
At last Sejanus, in his arrogance, as they said, forbade
them even to throng his doors or crowd around him
on the sea-shore: he was afraid no doubt of the
jealousy of his master; and they returned in dismay
and dejection to their homes, to expiate hereafter as
a crime the intimacy they had so blindly pressed
upon him.[1]

The year 781, the first of Tiberius's sojourn at
Capreæ, beheld the death of the unfortunate
Julia, the grand-daughter of Augustus, in
the barren island of Trimerus, off the coast
of Apulia; a woman whose amours had
once threatened to raise up candidates for the throne,
but who in her disgrace had been so completely
abandoned by her friends and family that she owed,
it was said, the protraction of her miserable existence
for years to the ostentatious compassion of Livia.[2]
She was speedily followed to the grave by this hateful
protectress. The mother of the emperor, having
held in her own hands for seventy years the largest
share, it may be, of actual power of any personage
in the state, paid at last the debt of nature, at the
moment when her son had effected his escape from

Death of Julia the younger, the grand-daughter of Augustus.

---

[1] Tac. *Ann.* iv. 74.

[2] Tac. *Ann.* iv. 71.: " Augustæ ope sustentata, quæ florentis pri-
vignos cum per occultum subvertisset, misericordiam erga adflictos
palam ostentaba* "

her oversight, and had perhaps for the first time
defied her influence. She died in the year
782, at the advanced age of eighty-six, a Death of the empress Livia.
memorable example of successful artifice,
having attained in succession, by craft if not by
crime, every object she could desire in the career of
female ambition.[1]   But she had long survived every
genuine attachment she may at any time have inspired, nor has a single voice been raised by posterity
to supply the want of honest eulogists in her own
day.   Her obsequies gave occasion for the first public appearance of Caius, the youngest of the sons of
Germanicus, at this time in his seventeenth year, to
pronounce her funeral oration; for Tiberius excused
himself from attending, while he persisted in making
no change in the usual disposition of his day, and
forbade the senate, pretending that such was her own
desire, to decree divine honours to the deceased.[2]   At
the same time he took occasion to show his sense of
the liberty he had recovered by his mother's death,
by some pointed remarks on the servile flattery of
the *woman's friends,* her associates.   These remarks
were directed, it was believed, more particularly
against the consul Fufius, who had ventured, under
the powerful protection of the empress, to indulge
in unseemly sneers against the emperor himself.[3]
While such was the demeanour of Tiberius, it was
evident that he felt no personal regret for the loss he
had sustained, and the funeral passed over with little
ceremony or magnificence.   Even the will of Livia
remained for a long time unexecuted.[4]

[1] Tac. *Ann.* v. 1.; Dion, lviii. 2. Pliny makes her eighty-two: but
as Tiberius was now in his seventieth year, the earlier date assigned
for her birth is undoubtedly the true one.   Plin. *Hist. Nat.* xiv. 8.
[2] Tac. *Ann.* v. 1, 2.; Dion, lviii. 2.
[3] Tac. *l. c.*: "Dicax idem, et Tiberium acerbis facetiis irridere
solitus."
[4] Suet. *Tib.* 51.   In this and the preceding chapter instances are

The obsequies of the consort of Octavius were cele-
Her character.   brated under the name she had long borne
in public of Julia Augusta. By admission
into the Cæsarean family she had become invested with
the undefinable charm of far descended glory common to the children of Venus and Iulus, which might
seem to extend to her a rightful claim to apotheosis
hereafter, together with her husband and his divine
· parent. But her union with Octavius had in the
meantime entitled her to a share in the high and
expressive designation of August, which was scarcely
distinguished in the popular apprehension from that
of mistress or sovereign. She glided gracefully from
the wheel and the women's chamber to the chair of
council and even to the throne of state: the first of
Roman matrons she had been suffered, if not to assume a public capacity, at least to be addressed as a
public character.[1] Though little scrupulous, we may
believe, in the pursuit of her personal objects, she
was not without a right royal sense of the true dignity of her unexampled position. To the sterner
counsels of her husband she brought the feminine
elements of softness and placability. The policy of
Augustus in his later years was impressed with the
mildness and serene confidence of his consort; and
even under the gloomier tyranny of his successor
her chamber was the asylum of many trembling
victims of persecution, her extended arm bade defiance to the arts of an Afer and the power of a

---

given of the impatience with which Tiberius latterly bore the domination of his mother ; his harsh language towards her and about her,
and the indifference he manifested at her decease.

[1] Thus we find her addressed in the *Consolatio de morte Drusi* as
Princeps. The senate upon her death decreed her an arch, and the
title of Mater Patriæ, which Tiberius refused to ratify : nevertheless
medals exist on which such a legend appears, and it is a question
whether these were not struck in her honour even during the lifetime
of Augustus. See Eckhel, vi. 154, 155. Livia ultimately obtained
deification under the principate of her grandson Claudius.

Sejanus.[1]   Nor was her private benevolence less conspicuously exerted in behalf of noble indigence.   She
caused many poor but well-born children to be educated at her own expense, and gave portions to many
marriageable maidens.[2]   Her fidelity to her husband
may have been the result of prudence, her devotion
to her son a calculation of ambition; but it is impossible not to read in the monuments of her innumerable household, the tirers of her person, the attendants at her repasts, the ministers of her charities,
whom she survived to bury in one family mausoleum,
tokens of kindness and generosity, however mingled
with pride, which appeal forcibly to our admiration.[3]
But a later generation could never forgive her for
being the mother of Tiberius; and every step by
which the tyrant, the patron of the informers, the
decimater of the senate, advanced to the sovereignty
of the Roman people was ascribed to the ambition,
the arts, and the crimes of the unfortunate Livia.
The proscriptions were forgotten in fifty years, the
delations never.

---

[1] Dion, *l. c.*: καὶ ἀψῖδα αὐτῇ, ὃ μηδεμίᾳ ἄλλῃ γυναικὶ, ἐψηφίσαντο,
ὅτι τε οὐκ ὀλίγους σφῶν ἐσεσώκει, καὶ ὅτι παῖδας πολλῶν ἐτετρόφει.
Comp. Vell. ii. 130.: " Per omnia diis quam hominibus similior
fœmina, cujus potentiam nemo sensit nisi aut levatione periculi aut
accessione dignitatis."

[2] The Roman Juno was as merciful as she was modest, if we may
believe a fantastic story of Dion's : γυμνούς ποτε ἄνδρας ἀπαντήσαντας
αὐτῇ καὶ μέλλοντας διὰ τοῦτο θανατωθήσεσθαι ἔσωσεν, εἰποῦσα ὅτι ο᾽δὲν
ἀνδριάντων ταῖς σωφρονούσαις οἱ τοιοῦτοι διαφέρουσι.   Dion, *l. c.*

[3] The single columbarium of Livia which has been discovered, and
probably there were more, contains the ashes of above a thousand of
her slaves and freedmen : the diversity of their employments, all of
which are carefully recorded, is, as may be supposed, almost infinite
See Wallon, *Esclavage*, ii. 145., foll. after Gori.

CHAPTER XLVI.

The fate of the family of Germanicus.—Banishment of Agrippina and her son Nero.—Disgrace and imprisonment of her son Drusus.—Persecution of her friends.—Fate of Asinius Gallus.—Culmination of the fortunes of Sejanus.—His alliance with the imperial family and consulship (A. U. 784).—Alarmed at the jealousy of Tiberius, he conspires against him.—Tiberius determines, with the assistance of Macro, to overthrow him.—His arrest in the senate-house, and execution.—Proscription of his adherents.—Vengeance for the murder of Drusus.—Savage cruelty of Tiberius.—Horrible death of the younger Drusus.—Agrippina starves herself.—Infatuation of Tiberius.—His mortification at the despondency of the nobles.—Voluntary deaths of Nerva and Arruntius.—Prospects of the succession.—Caius Caligula and the young Tiberius.—Ascendancy of Macro.—Last days and death of Tiberius (A. U. 790).— Effects of the reign of terror: alarm of the nobles; thoughtless dissipation of the populace.—The provinces generally well cared for and prosperous.—Example from the state of Judea. (A. D. 29—37, A. U. 782—790.)

THE first incident which marked the withdrawal of Livia's protecting wing from the afflicted, was the appearance of a harsh despatch from Tiberius to the senate, directed against Agrippina and her son Nero. This letter, it was believed, had been written some time earlier, but withheld through the influence of the empress, who, while she was gratified by the depression of the family of Germanicus, had nevertheless exerted herself, not without success, to shield it from ruin. The emperor now complained in bitter terms of the alleged misconduct of his grand-nephew; not, indeed, of any political intrigues to his own prejudice, but of personal vices and dissoluteness; against the chaste matron, his mother, he had not ventured

Tiberius complains to the senate of Agrippina and Nero.

to utter even such imputations as these, but had confined himself to reproving once more the vehemence so often remarked in her language and demeanour.   The senators were in great perplexity : ready as they were to carry out the commands of their master, however atrocious, they dared not act on murmurs which conveyed no express order, and made no demand on their active interference.   While they deliberated, however, warned by one of their own body to take no hasty step in so delicate a matter, the people assembled before the doors, and bearing aloft the effigies of their favourites, shouted aloud that the letter was an abominable forgery, and the lives of the emperor's nearest kindred were menaced without his knowledge, and in defiance of his inclinations.   These cries evidently pointed at Sejanus as the contriver of a foul conspiracy ; but the favourite, perceiving his danger, played dexterously on his master's fears, representing the movement as an act of rebellion, the images of Nero and Agrippina as the standards of a civil war, till he wrung from him a second proclamation, in which the impetuosity of the citizens was sternly rebuked, the tardiness of the senate reproved more mildly, and the charges against the culprits repeated, with a distinct injunction to proceed at once to consider them with due formality.[1]

Thus encouraged and stimulated to take their part, the senators declared that they had only been withheld from a more zealous defence of the imperial majesty by the want of definite instructions.   Sejanus triumphed; accusers sprang up at his beck; the process was carried through, we may believe, with all the disregard of decency and justice for which the tribunal of the fathers had long been infamous ; and though we

They are banished to islands.

---

[1] Tac. *Ann.* v. 5., A.U. 782.   From this point there is a lacuna of two years in the annals of Tacitus.

have lost the details of it, we know that its result
was fatal to its unfortunate victims, and that both
the mother and son were banished to barren islands,
the one to Pandateria, the other to Pontia. True to
the indomitable ferocity of her character, the she-
wolf Agrippina resisted the atrocious mandate with
violence, and in her struggle with the centurion in
whose charge she was placed, such was the horrid
story which obtained credence with the citizens, one
of her eyes was actually struck from her head.[1]
Sejanus now urged his success with redoubled energy.
He had removed his two most conspicuous rivals to
an exile from which the members of the imperial

Sejanus
obtains the
disgrace of
the younger
Drusus.

family were never known to return. Drusus
still remained, of an age and character to
compete with him in the career of his ambition. Tiberius retained this prince, together
with his younger brother Caius, about his own person
at Capreæ: there was the more reason to fear the
favour he might acquire with his aged relative ; nor
were there the same opportunities for misrepresent-
ing his conduct, or urging him by insidious advisers
into political intrigues. But Sejanus, in seducing the
affections of his consort Lepida, found the means of
undermining his credit with the emperor. The faithless spouse was engaged, by the promise perhaps of
marriage with Sejanus, as the wife of another Drusus
before her, to excite the jealousy of Tiberius against
her husband; and thus even the recesses of the imperial retreat, in which the old man had sought to
bury himself from the crimes and follies of the world
he hated, were opened to the machinations of his
most intimate friends and relatives. Drusus was dismissed from Capreæ, and ordered to repair in disgrace to Rome. But Sejanus was not satisfied with
this indication of the sovereign's anger : fearing lest

[1] Suet. *Tib.* 53.

his master might change his mind, he induced the consul Cassius Longinus to make a motion in the senate on the prince's presumed misconduct; and the fathers hastened to respond to it by declaring him a public enemy. Drusus was immediately placed under arrest; but the privileges of noble rank still exempted him from confinement in the Mamertine dungeons, and he was thrust, in mockery of the free custody which was his legal right, into a subterranean chamber of the palace.[1]

Livia, as we have seen, had been surrounded in her later years by a little court of her own favourites, and among them were many grumblers and captious enemies of the emperor, who obtained leave, by flattering the vanity of their mistress, to vent even in her ears their ill-feeling towards the chief of the state. In vain had Tiberius chafed under the jeers of this licensed coterie; the influence of his mother had protected it, and he had been compelled to brood in secret over mortifications which he had not the spirit to resent. But he had not forgotten a murmur or a smile; and as soon as the patroness of the group was removed, he made his long-checked vengeance felt by its members in succession. The friends of Agrippina and her children he regarded in a still more serious light. They constituted in his view, not a private clique of dissatisfied scoffers, but a political faction; they were not discontented with his conduct or government, but, as he thought, and others doubtless thought the same, prepared as foes and rivals to substitute another government, the government at least of another, in its room. In the councils of this faction lay, as he conceived, the germs of a revolution of the palace and even of civil war. Among its chiefs were men of the

Tiberius persecutes the friends of Livia.

---

[1] Suet. *Tib.* 54.; Dion, lviii. 3., A.U. 783. At this point there is a short break in the remains of Dion's history.

highest birth and character. None was more dis-
Cruel fate of
Asinius Gallus,
a friend of
Agrippina. tinguished than Asinius Gallus, now an old
man, and a veteran dissembler, whose pre-
tensions have already been noticed. This
man had presumed to take to wife the unfortunate
Vipsania, the same from whom Tiberius had been
compelled to separate himself; and besides the personal feelings which this marriage had caused him,
Tiberius beheld in it a covert aspiration to a share in
the imperial inheritance. At the commencement of
his principate he had been openly treated by Asinius
as an equal in an assembly of equals. In consequence he had never ceased to regard him with
jealousy; and when latterly he observed him paying
marked court to Sejanus, he resented it perhaps as
an attempt to disguise increasing hostility to himself.[1] When Asinius came at last to Capreæ, as the
bearer of a vote of fresh honours to the favourite,
Tiberius received him indeed with the utmost apparent cordiality, but at the same time clandestinely
despatched an accusation against him to the senate,
and the senate proceeded to pass sentence upon him
without a hearing, at the very moment that he was
being entertained at the emperor's table. The consuls sent a prætor to Capreæ to arrest him before the
eyes of his host, who affected surprise and sympathy,
and desired that he might be kept in honourable custody till he should come in person to take cognisance
of so lamentable a case.[2] This period, however, never
arrived; and it was not till after three years of close
and cruel imprisonment that Tiberius consented at
last to give the word, not for his release, but for his

---

[1] Of Asinius, Augustus, as we have seen, had said that he was
ambitious but incapable. The conceit and captiousness of his feeble
character appears in the presumption with which, like his father
Pollio, he criticized the language and genius of Cicero. Quintil. xii.
1. 22.; Gell. *Noct. Att.* xvii. 1.; Suet. *Claud.* 41.; Plin. *Epist.* vii. 4.

[2] Dion, lviii. 3

execution, accompanied, it was said, with the savage remark, *Now at last I have taken him back to favour.*[1]

The base dissimulation of Tiberius, which he now seemed, from long habit, to practise almost unconsciously, and where for his own purposes it was least required, may serve to aggravate our disgust at his callous insensibility. We need not suppose, however, that it was from any wanton cruelty that so long a punishment was inflicted on the sufferer Among the infirmities which grew on Tiberius with advancing age were irresolution and procrastination, and neither in giving audience to an embassy, nor in deciding the fate of a criminal, could he determine to act with the promptness which befitted his position.[2] His jealousy once aroused with regard to Sejanus, he could not nerve himself to any definite course of action. The clamours even of the insensate populace had not been lost upon him; though every demand for the punishment of his relatives had come to him direct from the senators, he could not but perceive that the favourite might have moved them to it. From the objects of suspicion thus indicated to him, every suspicion rebounded on the head of the favourite himself. While he sought to disguise his doubts and anxieties, yielding in every point, more readily than ever, to the counsels of his insidious adviser, and consenting at his instance to the disgrace of his kinsmen or courtiers, he shrank day by day from issuing the order which should deprive him irrecoverably of their services. Thus while he kept Asinius and Drusus in confinement to gratify Sejanus, he could not yet resolve to

Procrastination and irresolution of Tiberius.

---

[1] Dion, lviii. 23.: who repeats, however, the same expression on another occasion. Comp. also Suet. *Tib.* 61.: " Et in recognoscendis custodiis precanti cuidam pœnæ maturitatem respondit : nondum tecum in gratiam redii."

[2] Joseph. *Antiq. Jud.* xviii. 7. 5.

deliver them to the executioner. Meanwhile he continued to heap fresh honours on his minister with a restless profusion, which itself implied distrust. Though the hopes Sejanus had conceived of entrance into the Julian house through an union with Livilla had been discouraged and deferred, it appears that the emperor relaxed after a time in his opposition to them, and that they were crowned, as has been said, at least with the ceremony of a betrothal. The marriage indeed may never have taken effect, though so completely was the connexion of Sejanus with his master secured by the mere act of affiance, that he receives from Tacitus the title of his son-in-law.[1] But the loss of the greater part of the fifth book of Tacitus's Annals deprives us of our surest guide to the machinations of the emperor and his minister. It would seem probable, however, that Tiberius, soon after the confinement of Drusus, became alarmed at the formidable attitude his favourite had assumed; and we may believe that, in conferring upon him the last marks of confidence he was really meditating his overthrow. Nevertheless when, on the first day of 784, Sejanus entered with Tiberius on the consulship, the worshippers of his uprisen star were disturbed by no presentiment of its impending decline. The origin of Sejanus was not such as to entitle him to an honour from which Mæcenas had modestly shrunk; but his flatterers, ascending higher in the annals of the republic, compared his rise with that of a Coruncanius, a Carvilius, a Marius, or a Pollio. It was no novel principle, they declared, for the senate or people to choose the

Sejanus becomes affianced to Livilla.

He is advanced to the consulship, A. U 'S4.

---

[1] Tac. *Ann.* v. 6., vi. 8. See above. Zonaras (xi. 2.) says expressly that he was married to Julia, daughter of Drusus; but Julia, the only daughter of Drusus we know of, was married to Nero. Tac. *Ann.* iii. 29., iv. 60., vi. 27. See Ritter on *Ann.* vi. 8., Suet. *Tib.* 65.: " Spe affinitatis deceptum."

best men for distinction regardless of their birth ;
and it was now left for Tiberius to show that the
wisdom of the emperor was not inferior to that of
the citizens.[1]   While, however, all orders vied with
one another in the respect they paid to Sejanus,
while the petitioners who had flocked to the minister
in Campania had been more numerous than those
who courted the prince himself, while games and
holidays were voted in his honour, and before his
images or pictures altars were raised, vows conceived, and sacrifices offered, an excess of flattery
which the emperor had personally spurned, Tiberius
trembled more and more for his own safety, and was
anxious at least to remove their idol from
his presence.   Accordingly, when he asso-   Tiberius and
                                            Sejanus
ciated Sejanus with himself in the consul-   consuls.
ship, he deputed him to perform alone the actual
functions of both in the city ; and now Sejanus, it
was remarked, was emperor of Rome, while Tiberius
was merely lord of an island.[2]   The senators received
the leader of their debates with acclamations, and
Sejanus, though not unconscious of the workings of
jealousy in his master's mind, persuaded himself that
he had reached an eminence from which he could
control or even defy them.   The attachment of the
citizens towards him was now, he conceived, amply
demonstrated : the alacrity with which they hailed him
as the emperor's colleague betokened their full consent to his seizing the undivided empire.   The decree
of the senate, which now conferred on him jointly
with Tiberius the consulate for five years, sounded in
his ears like the entire surrender of the government
to his hands, as it had formerly been surrendered to
Augustus ; and if any material resources were yet
required to secure his usurpation, he could wield, as

[1] Vell. ii. 128.
[2] Dion, lviii. 5.: ὥστε συνελόντι εἰπεῖν, αὐτὸν μὲν αὐτοκράτορα, τὸν δὲ
Τιβέριον νησίαρχόν τινα εἶναι δοκεῖν.

he conceived, in his faithful prætorians the final arbitrament of the sword.

Since his accession, however, to the principate, it had been the custom of Tiberius to retain his consulships only for a short period. In 771 he had abdicated office after a few days; in 774 after three months.[1] Now also, far from accepting the proffered five years, he resigned the consulship in the fifth month; and Sejanus, it seems, was required at the same time to give way to a consul suffect.[2] Faustus Cornelius Sulla was supplied in the place of the one, Sextidius Catullinus received the fasces from the other. Sejanus possibly now felt for the first time that he was treading a downward path. The flattering decree by which his consulship was held up to the imitation of all future magistrates, the offer of the proconsular power which was at the same time made to him, and his elevation by the emperor to the dignity of the priesthood, would all fail to reassure him; for at the same time Caius Cæsar was advanced to the priesthood also, and the favour with which the young prince was mentioned in an imperial rescript had been accepted by the citizens as a token that he was actually destined for the succession. Uneasy and irresolute in the midst of his success, Sejanus bethought himself of the resource which had hitherto never failed him, of a personal interview with his patron. He asked permission to visit his affianced bride, who was retained beneath the roof of her father-in-law at Capreæ, under the pretext of a sickness from which she was suffering. But to this demand Tiberius returned a refusal, though softened by the excuse that he was himself prepar-

Tiberius and Sejanus resign the consulship.

Tiberius refuses to see Sejanus,

---

[1] The consulship of 784 was Tiberius's fifth. See Tac. *Ann.* iii. 31. Suetonius, in calling it his third, is speaking only of his principate.

[2] Hoeck, *Röm. Gesch.* i. 3. p. 153., from Noris. *Epist. Cons.* in Græv. *Thes.* xi. 404.

ing speedily to remove with his family to Rome[1]
This repulse was followed by a decree forbidding divine honours to be paid to any mere mortal, and
fatal significance was attached to a letter, throughout
which the bare name of Sejanus was mentioned,
without the addition of any of his titles. At the
same time some of his personal enemies, it was observed, received unusual favours; all which things
were not overlooked by an anxious and vigilant herd
of courtiers, as ominous of impending disgrace. Already the crowd of senators and freedmen began to
waver in their devotion to the upstart. But, on the
other hand, his spirits were sometimes raised by the
hints the emperor took care to drop of his own failing health; by the death of Nero in his confinement,
starved, as was reported, by his unnatural uncle's
commands[2]; and by the appointment of his creature
Fulcinius Trio to the consulship for the latter part
of the year. He was most concerned, however, by
the manifest failure of the hopes he had entertained
of the good will of the people, whose predilection for
Caius, the youngest of the beloved family of Germanicus, had recently been warmly expressed. Re-
gretting that he had wanted courage to strike openly
while armed with the authority of the fasces, he
began now to concert with his nearest in- *who concerts*
timates the means of assassination. The *measures against his*
arrival of Tiberius at Rome would furnish *life.*
ample opportunity to a friend, a kinsman, and a
minister. Several of the senators had engaged in
the enterprise, the guards had been tampered with
and, it was hoped, secured; but the plot was soon

---

[1] This seems to be the meaning of Dion, lviii.7.: ὁ δ' οὖν Τιβέριος
ταῖς μὲν ἰσοψύναις ἐτίμησεν αὐτόν, οὐ μὴν καὶ μετεπέμψατο, ἀλλὰ καὶ
αἰτησαμένῳ οἱ ὅπως ἐς τὴν Καμπανίαν, ἐπὶ προφάσει τῆς μελλονύμφου
νοσησάσης, ἔλθῃ, κατὰ χώραν μεῖναι προσέταξεν.

[2] The death of Nero, which falls within the period for which we
have lost the narration of Tacitus, is learnt from Suetonius, *Tib.* 5.

extended beyond the limits of safety. One of the conspirators, named Satrius Secundus, already
infamous as a delator, revealed it to An-

The con-
spiracy is
divulged.

tonia, the aged mother of Germanicus, a
woman of noble character, who preferred, of the two
persecutors of her race, to save Tiberius and destroy
Sejanus.[1]

The emperor, possessed of all the proofs he required, hesitated, as usual, to act. He

Measures of
Tiberius to
circumvent
Sejanus.

shrank from openly denouncing the traitor,
and demanding his head of the senate;
and against a covert surprise Sejanus had sufficiently guarded himself. The stroke of Tiberius
was prepared with infinite cunning, and executed
with consummate dexterity and boldness. He entrusted it to Sertorius Macro, an officer of the body-
guard, on whom, in the absence of Sejanus, he had,
perhaps, relied for his personal security at Capreæ.
To this man he gave a commission to take the command of the prætorians at Rome, and even empowered
him, in the last necessity, to lead forth Drusus from
his dungeon, and place him at the head of affairs.[2]
It might not be safe, however, to assume authority
over a jealous soldiery, devoted, apparently, to their
familiar chief, and estranged from an emperor whose
person they had almost forgotten. But Macro, resolute and crafty, was not daunted. He aspired to fill
himself the place of Sejanus, and so lofty an ambition was to be deterred by no ordinary peril. Reaching Rome at midnight, the 17th of October, he sought
an interview with Memmius Regulus, now the colleague of Trio in the consulship, and known for his

---

[1] Joseph. *Antiq.* xviii. 7. 6. This conspiracy is unknown to
Dion apparently, but alluded to by Tacitus, Suetonius, and Josephus.
The loss of this portion of the Annals has deprived us of distinct
proof of it, but it was mentioned no doubt in the Memoirs of Agrippina.

[2] Tac. *Ann.* vi. 23.; Suet. *Tib.* 65.

steadfast loyalty. Opening to him the purport of
his mission, he required him to convene the senate
early in the temple of Apollo, which adjoined the
imperial residence on the Palatine. The spot was
somewhat removed from the common thoroughfares
of the city, and the approach to it by three narrow
gates might be easily guarded against a sudden attack. Another recommendation might be its proximity to the place where Drusus was confined, should
it become necessary to produce him. Macro next
repaired to Græcinus Laco, the captain of the Urban
police, and with him concerted measures for occupying the avenues to the temple with his armed
force, while he should himself amuse the dreaded
prætorians, and keep them close in their distant
quarters. Thus prepared, he threw himself in the
way of Sejanus, as the minister, wondering at the
hasty summons, and foreboding no good to himself
from it, was proceeding to the meeting escorted by
an armed retinue. To him Macro blandly intimated
that the occasion for which the fathers were convened
was in fact no other than the gracious appointment,
now about to be announced, of Sejanus himself to
the tribunitian power, an appointment equivalent,
as generally understood, to formal association in the
empire. Intoxicated with the prospect of the consummation, at the moment when he had rashly
resolved to hazard every thing on a daring treason,
Sejanus was thrown completely off his guard. Shaking off at the temple door the attendance of his
clients and soldiers, he entered with a light step and
smiling countenance; while Macro, hastily commu-
nicating to the prætorians without that he was appointed their prefect, and promising them an ample
largess on his installation, induced them to return
with him to their camp, and attend while he announced the circumstance to their comrades. He
only waited to present the emperor's letter to the

consuls, and then withdrew quietly in the tumult of
applause which greeted it, leaving Laco to watch the
proceedings. He required a little time to compose
the temper of the guards, of whose ready acceptance
of his appointment he could not feel secure. With
this object the letter of Tiberius had been made
more than usually diffuse. The consuls handed it
in due form to the quæstor, and as soon as the
buzz of expectation, and the compliments already
passing between Sejanus and his flatterers, who comprehended the great body of the senate, were hushed,
it was deliberately recited.

    Sejanus composed himself to endure the long pre-
His dispatch
to the senate. amble of the imperial missive, such as had
before often taxed his patience, but never
so much as on this fatal occasion.[1] It commenced
with a passing reference to various affairs of state;
then diverged to a gentle reproof of Sejanus himself
for some trifling neglect; thence wandered again to
more general subjects, mixed with strange, and as it
seemed fantastic, complaints of the solitude of the
poor old man, and his precarious position. It required one of the consuls to come with a military
force to Capreæ, and escort the princeps into the city,
that in the midst of his faithful citizens he might
securely unbosom his griefs. From these desultory
complaints, however, the letter descended gradually
to particulars, and proceeded to demand the punishment of certain personages well known as adherents
of Sejanus. For some time the senators had been
growing uneasy, not knowing what upshot to anticipate to a missive, the tone of which waxed less and
less in harmony with the addresses to which they had
been accustomed. One by one they slunk away from
the minister's side, and left him wondering and irresolute, still clinging to the hope that all would end

---

[1] Juvenal, x. 71.: "Verbosa et grandis epistola venit A Capreis."

as he wished, and shrinking to the last from the appeal to force which must irrevocably compromise him. The agitation of the assembly became more marked. Sejanus looked anxiously around. Suddenly, before the whole letter was yet unrolled, he found himself closely thronged by the chiefs of the senate, and precluded from shifting his position, while the sentence with which the long missive terminated denounced him by name as a traitor, and required the consuls to place him under arrest. Regulus called on him to surrender. Unaccustomed to hear the voice of authority, or bewildered with the sense of danger, he paused, and on a second summons demanded in confusion whether he was actually called? Once more the summons was repeated, and as he rose, Laco confronted him sword in hand, the senators sprang in a body to their feet, and heaped insults and reproaches upon him; while Regulus, fearing the risks of delay, staid not to put the question to the vote, but on the first voice given for his arrest, bade the lictors seize his hands, and hurried him off under an escort of guards _{Sejanus is arrested,} and magistrates. Rapidly as he was transported from the Palatine to the Mamertine dungeon, for no measures of law or etiquette were kept at a crisis of such peril, the populace was already apprised of his disgrace, and as he was led across the forum he might behold with his own eyes the consummation of his fall, in the overthrow of his statues with ropes and hatchets. The effigies of public men, conspicuous in the Sacred Way, or enshrined in halls and theatres, served often to divert from more important objects the fury of an enraged populace. To crush the marble image of an enemy to powder, to break the gold or brass for the melting-pot, and condemn to ignoble uses the hated limbs and lineaments, was the first impulse of scorn and passion, and might sometimes save his palace from destruction and his family from

outrage.[1] Macro in the meantime had not been less
successful in the camp. By boldly advancing his
offers to an immense amount, he had appeased the
first outbreak of sedition among the soldiers, and
when the senators ascertained that they were secure
on that side, they met again the same day in the
temple of Concord, as the spot nearest to the prison.
Here, encouraged by the acclamations of the people
and the indifference of the prætorians, they proceeded
to anticipate the well-perceived wish of the sovereign,
and put to   by decreeing death to the traitor. Sejanus
death.   was immediately strangled in the depths of
his prison, and his body dragged to the foot of the
Gemonian stairs for exposure. His death was followed
without delay by the arrest of his family, his kinsmen
and friends, the accomplices of his cherished schemes,
or the instruments of his fraud and cruelty; while
every one who hated the favourite or professed to love
the emperor hurried to the spot where his remains
were lying, and trampled with contumely on the ruins
of power.[2]

The first days which followed this catastrophe at
Confusion at   Rome were filled with scenes of confusion
Rome among
all orders of   and slaughter. The populace rushing from
the citizens.   one extreme to the other, now denounced
the fallen minister as the perverter of the emperor's
well-known generosity, and wreaked on his friends
and creatures their vengeance for every wrong inflicted by Tiberius on the children and adherents
of Germanicus. The prætorians were offended at
the superior reliance the emperor had placed on the
police, and vented their unreasonable indignation
in acts of riot and plunder. The senators, one and

---

[1] See the well-known lines of Juvenal, x. 61. foll.:

"Ex facie toto orbe secunda
Fiunt urceoli, pelves, sartago, patellæ."

[2] Dion, lviii. 9—11.; Seneca, *de Tranqu. Anim.* ii. 9.: "Quo die
illum senatus deduxerat populus in frusta divisit." Juvenal, *l. c.*

all, apprehensive of the jealousy both of the emperor and the populace, rushed headlong to condemn every act of flattery they had so lately committed.   They decreed that none should wear mourning for the traitor, that a statue of Liberty should be erected in the forum, that a day of rejoicing should be held, and finally that the anniversary of the happy event should be sanctified by extraordinary shows and solemnities.   Excessive honours, they proclaimed, should never again be paid to a subject : and no vow should be conceived in the name of any mortal man, save of the emperor only.[1]   Yet, so inconsistent is servility, they heaped in the same breath distinctions almost equal to those of Sejanus upon both Macro and Laco, which only the good sense of those fortunate officers induced them to decline.   They urged Tiberius to accept the title of Father of his Country, an assumption he had ever modestly declined, and now again rejected with becoming resolution, as well as the proposal that the senate should swear to all his acts. His rugged nature was softened by the sense of his deliverance.   The iron tears glistened on his cheek. *Steadfast as I feel myself,* he said, *in good and patriotic principles, yet all things human are liable to change; and never, so may the gods help me, will I bind the fathers to respect all the future acts of one who, even by falling from his right senses, may at any time fall from virtue.*"[2]

Tiberius, however, on his solitary rock had suffered hours of intense and restless anxiety.   The desperate resolution to which he had braced himself for the destruction of Sejanus had given a shock to his whole system, and during the

Intense anxiety of Tiberius.

---

[1] The few existing coins of Sejanus have been purposely defaced, Eckhel, *Doctr. Numm.* vi. 196.   We have busts ascribed to Brutus, Cicero, and Antonius, but none, I believe, of the disgraced minion of Tiberius.

[2] Suet. *Tib.* 67.

interval of suspense he seemed altogether unnerved.
He had disposed a system of telegraphic communications to reach from Rome to Capreæ; and while,
planted on the highest pinnacle of his island, he
watched for the concerted signal of success or failure,
a squadron of the swiftest triremes lay ready below
to waft him, if required, without delay to the legions
of Gaul or Syria.[1] When at last the news of the
arrest and execution reached him, though relieved
from an intolerable anxiety, he was yet so far from
recovering his equanimity that he refused admittance
to the deputation of senators, knights, and citizens
sent in haste to congratulate him; nor would he even
grant an interview to Regulus, his well-tried adherent, when he came, as the letter had directed him,
to escort the emperor to Rome with a military equipage.

That the fall of a discarded favourite should be
followed by the disgrace of his family, and
perhaps of his intimate associates, would
not be extraordinary under any monarchical
regime; but the wide and sanguinary proscription
which now descended on the nobility of Rome may
confirm our surmise of the actual guilt of Sejanus,
and of the discovery of a real plot against the ruler.
Had indeed the long gathering discontent of the
citizens come at last to a head? were the murmurs
which, whether waking or sleeping, ever pressed on
the ears of Tiberius, actually about to explode in
revolt or assassination? was the long day-dream of
his life, that he *held a wolf by the ears,* on the point
of being realized in a fatal catastrophe? Such at
least was the conviction under which his courage and
even his reason staggered. Tormented as he was by
these miserable alarms, we can be little surprised at

*Proscription
of the friends
of Sejanus.*

---

[1] Dion, lviii. 13.; Suet. *Tib.* 65.: "Speculabundus ex altissima
rupe."

the bloodshed in which he sought to drown his apprehensions. Yet in the midst of his frenzy, he was
not unmindful of his accustomed policy. The culprits whom he demanded for punishment were, at
least at first, a few only of the most conspicuous;
and these, with perhaps one or two exceptions, he
was content to reserve for a future sentence. The
choice as well as the condemnation of the majority of
these victims fell to the senate itself, which partly
from hatred of the fallen minister, partly to ingratiate itself with its terrified master, lent a ready ear
to the delators, or impelled the course of justice with
encouragements and rewards. Among the first to
follow the fortunes of Sejanus was his uncle Blæsus,
the object but recently of such special honours. Yet
the sons of Blæsus were spared; and even a brother
of the great criminal was suffered to escape, though,
if we may believe a strange anecdote which has been
reported to us, he had ventured to hold up the emperor to unseemly ridicule.[1]   One of his nearest
associates, named Terentius, was suffered to plead
that, in giving his confidence to the favourite in the
height of his influence, he had done no more than
follow the example of Tiberius himself. A horrid
story indeed is related of the execution of the young
children of Sejanus, who were hurried off to death,
with circumstances perhaps of more than ordinary
atrocity, in the first frenzy of the proscription.[2]   It

---

[1] The voluntary deaths of two Blæsi, evidently near relations and
probably sons of Blæsus the uncle, are mentioned on a latter occasion.
Tac. *Ann.* vi. 40. Lucius Sejanus, as prætor, had taken the fancy
of ridiculing Tiberius, who was bald, by collecting a set of bald performers for the Floralia. The 5000 link boys, who were appointed
to light the populace on their return from the theatre, were all closely
shaven. Tiberius pretended not to notice the insult. Bald men,
adds the historian, were from that time called Sejani, one does not
well see why. Dion. lviii. 19.

[2] The story can only be told in the words of Tacitus himself: "Por-
tantur in carcerem filius imminentium intelligens, puella adeo nescia,
ut crebro interrogaret, quod ob delictum, et quo traheretur? neque

has been imagined that the historian Velleius Paterculus, whose brief but spirited sketch of Roman affairs terminates with the sixteenth year of Tiberius,
and who is notorious for his flattery of Sejanus, was
involved in the general wreck of the fallen minister's
adherents: but there seems no reason to suppose this,
the work itself having evidently reached its destined
termination.[1]   On the whole, it would appear that
Tiberius, hardly less afraid to follow up his blow than
in the first instance to strike it, was satisfied with
watching from his retreat, which for several months
he did not venture to quit, the proceedings of the
senate against all who could be deemed his enemies.
Nor was it only fear for himself that alternately exasperated and unnerved him.   A terrible disaster
recurred to his memory.   The death of his son had
been unexpected and premature.   Sejanus had solicited the widow in marriage.   Suspicion worked
fiercely in the tyrant's brain.   Had Drusus perished
by poison, and was Sejanus the murderer?   The
surmise was speedily verified.   Apicata, the divorced
wife of Sejanus, had been spared in the search after
the accomplices of his recent crimes.   Her hatred to
the husband who had so deeply injured her was a
sufficient guarantee perhaps for her innocence of all
concert with him now.   But when she saw her children involved in the fate of their father she was
distracted with conflicting feelings.   As the last re-

facturam ultra: et posse se puerili verbere moneri. Tradunt temporis
ejus auctores, quia triumvirali supplicio adfici virginem inauditum
habebatur, a carnifice laqueum juxta compressam: exin oblisis fau-
cibus, id ætatis corpora iu Gemonias abjecta." *Ann.* v. 9. By the
salvo, "tradunt," &c., I conceive the writer to intimate that the story
was not detailed in all its horrors by accredited histories, but was
one of the flying anecdotes of the day (comp. *Ann.* i. 1.: "Recentibus
odiis compositæ"), which he found too piquant to omit from his
tableau. Compare the reference to it in Suetonius, who carelessly
generalizes the particular story into an ordinary occurrence. *Tib.* 61.
Dion (lviii. 11.) merely copies from the above.
[1] Vell. ii. 131.: " Voto finiendum volumen sit."

venge she could take on the cause of all her misery, she revealed every circumstance connected with the death of Drusus, with which she appears to have made herself well ac-

Vengeance on the murderers of Drusus.

quainted, the amours of Sejanus and Livilla, their guilty hopes and machinations, and the means by which they effected the destruction of their victim. Having made this disclosure, and excited the horror and dismay of the emperor to a pitch of frenzy, she put an end to her own life.   Eight years had elapsed since the crime had been committed; but means for investigating the circumstances were still at hand, nor were objects wanting on whom the thirst for vengeance might be wreaked.   The slaves and other agents employed were sought out and questioned in the presence of Tiberius at Capreæ, and the guilt of Livilla established beyond a doubt.[1]   The public execution of a daughter of the imperial house was still an act from which the emperor would shrink; but he had other means not less sure for punishing her, and the report that, spared the cord or the falchion, she was starved to death in the custody of Antonia seems not unworthy of belief.[2]

Early in the year 785 Tiberius crossed the narrow strait which separates Capreæ from Sur-

Tiberius quits Capreæ and approaches Rome.

rentum, and made a progress along the Campanian coast, as if about to revisit his capital.   The citizens, still willing to deceive themselves as to his character and motives, were exulting in the assurance that with the fall of Sejanus a marked and happy change would appear in his behaviour.   To the blighting influence of an unworthy favourite they fondly ascribed the reserve, the mo-

---

[1] The stories of the tortures which used to be enacted in the presence of Tiberius at Capreæ for his amusement, of the bodies thrown over the cliffs, &c. (Suet. *Tib.* 62.), originated probably in the report of the proceedings of this domestic tribunal.

[2] Comp. Suet. *Tib.* 62. with Dion, lviii. 11.

roseness, and hardness of their master's temper, forgetting how the germs of these vices had been already
manifested in his early youth, and that they were
such as advancing years could not fail to confirm and
aggravate.   But as they had lately clapped their
hands with savage delight over every fresh victim
offered to the emperor's safety, so they were now
prepared to welcome the emperor himself, as one
restored from an unjust exile, and to exchange with
him smiles of mutual love and reviving confidence.
From Rhodes he had returned to the cold embrace
of a haughty father; from Capreæ he would be wel-
comed by the acclamations of a humble and self-
reproachful people.   But the ardent greeting they
reserved for him was destined never to be tendered.
They were surprised. perhaps, to hear that his excessive timidity had induced him to quit the land, and
take refuge on board a trireme, which bore him up
the Tiber, while guards attended on his progress, and
rudely cleared away the spectators from either bank.
Such was the strange fashion in which he ascended
the river as far as the Cæsarean Gardens and the
Naumachia of Augustus; but on reaching this spot,
and coming once more beneath the hills of Rome,
he suddenly turned his prow without landing, and
glided rapidly down the stream, nor did he pause
again till he had regained his island.[1]   This extraordinary proceeding, the effect of fear or disgust,
caused no doubt deep mortification among the populace.   It was followed by indignant murmurs, and
petulantly ascribed to the foulest motives.   Such, it
was muttered, was the caprice, not of a princeps or
an imperator, the child of law and organized government, but of a king: such a king as ruled with de-
spotic sway over the slaves of Asia; such a king as,
guarded in the citadel of Ctesiphon or Artaxata, de-

---

[1] Tac. *Ann.* vi. 1.

spised all human feelings, and trampled on all principles, sporting, for his selfish pleasure, with not the
lives only, but the honour of his miserable subjects;
such as tore from them their children to mutilate or
deflower, and stimulated his brutal passions by the
nobility of his victims.   All this and worse   Atrocious
was now freely ascribed to the recluse of licentiousness ascribed to
Capreæ; he slunk, it was asserted, from the him.
sight of the good and pure, to the obscurity of his
detestable orgies; he was the patron of panders, the
sport of minions; he was drunk with wine, and drunk
with blood; the details which were freely circulated
of his cruelty and licentiousness were coloured from
the most loathsome scenes of the stews and the slave-
market.

Such, unfortunately, was the open and flagrant
character of Roman vice, that even the best This licen-
and purest of the citizens were too much tiousness the common vice
familiarized with its worst features to shrink of his class.
from describing it with hideous minuteness.   We
may be permitted to cast a veil over a picture which
called up no blush on the face of that generation,
the fidelity of which, as regards Tiberius himself, we
have no right either to affirm or deny.   The excessive sensuality of the Roman nobles, pampered by
all the appliances of art and luxury, was in fact the
frenzy of a class deprived of the healthy stimulus of
public action, and raised above the restraints of decency and self-respect.   The worst iniquities ascribed
to Tiberius may be paralleled in the conduct of private individuals, the accounts of which may have
been coloured by a prurient imagination, but at least
have not been distorted by malice.[1]   The senators,

---

[1] If I accept the charges of Tacitus and Suetonius against Tiberius,
it is from my persuasion of the general character of vice in high
places, as pourtrayed by Juvenal, Pliny, Seneca, Petronius, and in
fact almost every writer of these times.   Gems, mosaics, and other
objects have been found in modern times at Capri, representing, it is

however, evinced no shame at the degradation into which their chief had fallen. They hastened to vote that the estates of Sejanus should be confiscated, not to the treasury of the state, but to the private purse of the emperor; and then, apprehending perhaps that his late hasty retreat had been caused by distrust of his subjects, ordained that whenever he vouchsafed to visit the Curia a special guard of their own body should attend upon him, A similar honour had been tendered to Julius Cæsar, and even Augustus, on a certain occasion, had availed himself of such a protection; it is not easy, therefore, to understand why it should have been left in this case to one of the least considerable of the order to propose, or be discussed and sanctioned with a smile of ridicule.[1] Tiberius, however, declined the equivocal compliment, which, indeed, would have little served to calm his fears had he really entertained the intention of again entering the senate-house; for it was among his proposed guards themselves, of whom few were not related to or associated with some of his victims, that his most dangerous enemies were numbered. At this moment his breast was torn by conflicting alarms. When his first fury against Sejanus was satiated, or his first blind apprehensions removed, he showed an inclination to desist from the proscription, and allowed himself in more than one instance to be swayed to mercy; not from compassion or clemency perhaps, but through fear of irritating too many families, and

said, the very monstrosities indicated by the historians, and have been considered as conclusive proofs of the facts charged against him.   It is quite possible, however, that these objects were suggested by the descriptions themselves.   At all events it must be remembered that the island was occupied by many successive proprietors after Tiberius, and among them by the virtuous M. Aurelius, all of whom must have had these indecent figures constantly in their sight.   The age and the class must bear their share of the common guilt: "factum defendite vestrum, consensistis enim."

[1] Tac. Ann. vi. 2.; Dion, lviii. 17.

aggravating the perils against which he was guarding. But, on the other hand, the spirit of delation which he had evoked was now too potent to be laid. It had become the ambition, the glory, the livelihood of many; and to deprive them of it was to sow the seeds of perilous dissatisfaction among the cleverest, the boldest, and the most desperate class of citizens. While trimming the vessel of his fortunes between this Scylla and Charybdis, another rock soon appeared ahead. News was brought to Rome that a pretender to the name of the unfortunate Drusus, still a prisoner in the palace, had appeared in Achaia and Asia, and had deceived many by the similarity of his person, and the devotion to him of some of the freedmen of the emperor himself. As the reputed son of Germanicus he was received in various quarters with open arms. The Greeks were easily moved by anything strange and novel; the legions of Egypt and Syria, to which he was making his way, had loved and admired the man he claimed for his father. But the vigour of the imperial commanders speedily checked his enterprise. He was pursued across the Ægean and the Isthmus of Corinth to Nicopolis in Epirus, where, it appeared, having been more strictly interrogated, he had retracted his first assertion, and represented himself as of noble but inferior and less invidious parentage. From Epirus he had taken ship as if for Italy, while the emperor was duly apprised by his lieutenants that he might be expected to arrive there. This, according to some accounts, was the last that was publicly heard of him: other writers, however, pretended to know for certain that he fell into the hands of the emperor, and was promptly destroyed.[1]

An impostor arrested and put to death.

[1] Tacitus (*Ann.* v. 10.) relates this occurrence towards the end of the year 784, while Dion (lviii. 25.) places it as late as 787, supposing, perhaps, that it could not have occurred before the death of the real Drusus.

The miserable ends of Drusus and Agrippina, which

followed at no long interval, were possibly determined and hastened by this untoward event. When Tiberius perceived how easily even a false Drusus might lead a movement against him, he might be impelled at last to make his decision regarding the fate of the real one. What that decision would be could not be for a moment doubtful. The poor youth had been too fearfully wronged to be again trusted with liberty. Yet Tiberius must have regretted the step he had taken, at the suggestion of Sejanus, of alienating his innocent kinsman from him. It was not that he wished to clear the field of promotion for a grandson by the removal of his grand-nephews. To Caius, the youngest son of Germanicus, he was at the moment displaying the highest favour, while he kept his mother and brother in such cruel durance. To the stripling Caius he seemed already to hold out the prospect of succession: he bred him under his own eye at Capreæ; he kept him in close attendance on his person, and gave him in marriage one of the noblest maidens of the city, the daughter of M. Junius Silanus.[1] It was rumoured, not unnaturally, that he was about to reconcile himself to the surviving members of his nephew's family, to atone for the death of Nero by the release and reinstatement in their proper honours of Drusus and Agrippina. But the relentless monster had determined far otherwise. Not only had he destined Drusus, after three years' confinement, to death, but he allowed him to perish in lingering torment by withholding from him necessary food. On the subject of death by starvation the Romans seem to have had a peculiar feeling which we can

---

[1] Suet. *Calig.* 12.; Tac. *Ann.* vi. 20. M. Junius Silanus was the brother of Decimus Silanus, the paramour of the younger Julia.

hardly understand.   In many cases of suicide which
occurred about this period, we find the sufferer choosing rather to perish miserably by inanition than to
give himself a blow.   More particularly we may
observe in the imperial murders which have been
recorded, that the victim was often left to die of
mere want, and untouched by the sword.   A superstitious notion may have been current that death by
famine was a kind of divine infliction; it might seem
like simply leaving nature to take its appointed
course.   The Romans were so familiar with the practice of exposing infants, and even the infirm and old
among their slaves, that they may have regarded with
some lenity the crime of murder in this, as they
deemed it, extenuated form.   It was merely, for-
sooth, leaving to the care of the gods those whom it
was inconvenient or impolitic to care for oneself.
Tiberius, with a bluntness of perception which seems
almost inconceivable, addressed a letter to the senate,
detailing in the minutest way the circumstances of
this miserable death, showing how the poor wretch
had prolonged his existence for nine days by gnaw-
ing the stuffing of his pallet, and recording every
sigh and groan he had uttered, even to the last desperate imprecations he had heaped on his tormentor.
Every syllable was duly vouched by the testimony of
slaves, who had been set to watch his last moments.
It is impossible to believe that this was a mere wanton
piece of unnatural cruelty.   It must have had a
political purpose; and we may conjecture that it was
meant, first, to establish on unquestionable testimony
the actual decease of Drusus; and, secondly, to prove
that no drop of the Julian blood had been shed, no
spark of his divine spirit extinguished, by the hand
of the executioner.[1]

[1] Tac. *Ann.* vi. 24.; Suet. *Tib.* 65.; Dion, lviii. 13. (A.U. 786,
A.D. 33).

The senate shuddered, we are assured, with horror
Agrippina starves herself. at the recital of this abominable epistle;
but the persecution of the house of Germanicus had not yet reached its climax. After the
downfall of Sejanus, in whom she recognised her
fiercest enemy, Agrippina may have allowed herself
to indulge fresh hopes. But it soon became only
too manifest that the crimes of Sejanus, by which
she had herself so grievously suffered, were made a
pretext for cruelties with which they had no connexion, and that the exasperation of the emperor
against his old minister would bring no alleviation to
the lot of that minister's victims. She continued to
linger in cheerless exile: whether in that solitude
she was afflicted with the intelligence of her two
elder sons' miserable end, or suffered to learn the
favour with which her youngest was at the same time
entertained, she seems in either case to have soon
despaired for herself, and to have resolved to escape
by her own deed from miseries which were now past
relief. It was reported that she put an end to her
own existence by pertinacious abstinence from food,
in spite of the emperor's command that nourishment
should be forced upon her; an act of fortitude not
unworthy of her determined and vigorous character.
Even after her death Tiberius was base enough to
insult her memory, by charging her with a criminal
amour, and insinuating that she had abandoned life
in disgust and mortification at the execution of her
lover Asinius. The common voice of her fellow-
citizens, not too prone to believe in virtue, absolved
her from this foul accusation; her faults were not
those at least of feminine weakness, and had her
chastity been assailable, it would not perhaps have
withstood the artifices of Sejanus.[1] Nevertheless,

---

[1] I will not dwell upon the faults of Agrippina; but it must be
observed that even Tacitus represents them in very strong language:

that her memory might be branded with ignominy, Tiberius required the senate to pronounce the anniversary of her birth a day of evil omen, and to note in the calendar as a providential coincidence that her death had occurred on the day of the punishment of Sejanus. He claimed credit for himself that he had not taken her life by violent means, and had forborne from exposing her body in the Gemoniæ. The senate acquiesced and applauded as it was required, and decreed solemn thanks to the emperor for his clemency; moreover, that a yearly festival should be celebrated on the auspicious eighteenth of October. The remains of Agrippina and her children were excluded from the mausoleum of the Cæsars, until Caius at a later period caused them to be exhumed from their ignoble sepulchres and removed to the resting-place which became them.[1]

The prosecution meanwhile of the friends of Sejanus had continued unabated, the emperor vying with his own creatures and flatterers in discovering matter of accusation against every one who could be proved or credibly suspected of participation in his guilt. But Tiberius had actually shed the blood of a few only: his victims were quartered as captives on the magistrates and nobles, or confined, perhaps, in stricter durance within his own palace. Some of them had been plundered and reduced to beggary; some, perhaps, had been tortured; some were guilty, but their lives protected by their powerful connexions; others, unquestionably innocent, might be personally obnoxious. Tiberius was harassed by the anxiety of determining how to ap-

Massacre of the proscribed friends of Sejanus.

" Æqui impatiens, dominandi avida, virilibus curis fœminarum vitia exuerat."

[1] Tac. *Ann.* vi. 25. Agrippina died on the 18th of October, 786, two years after Sejanus. Comp. Suet. *Tib.* 33, 54.; *Calig.* 15.; Dion, lviii. 22, lix. 3. The bones of Drusus only were dispersed and could not be recovered.

portion their punishments; whom it might be safe
to pardon, and whom it would be invidious to destroy. Suddenly the tyrant was seized with a horrid
caprice, a fit, it may be, of madness, on the verge of
which his unquiet brain was ever trembling, and he
conceived the idea of relieving himself from his perplexity by a single stroke of the pen. He issued an
order, such as there was no parallel for in his previous
policy, and such as, in one so little wont to initiate a
novelty either in counsel or in act, can hardly be
ascribed to anything but uncontrollable frenzy, that
all the captives of the Sejanian conspiracy should at
once be put to death as traitors. The order was
executed without compunction. Not men only, but
women ; not adults only, but children, were involved
in the frightful massacre : some were noble, many of
baser birth ; in some places they perished singly, in
others they fell in promiscuous slaughter one upon
another. The mangled bodies were exposed in the
Gemoniæ, and guards were placed around to drive
away their mourning relatives, or to watch and report
their lamentations. After some days' exposure the
remains were dragged to the river bank and flung
into the stream, and even those which were cast back
upon the land were forbidden the rites of sepulture.
The common duties of humanity, says Tacitus, were
abandoned in the general terror ; and all natural
compassion cowered in silence beneath the tyranny
that reigned rampant in every quarter.[1]

[1] Tac. Ann. vi. 19. Comp. Suet. (Tib. 61.), who, however, specifies
twenty as the greatest number that fell, at least on any one day, and
the massacre probably passed off in a single paroxysm. The language
of Tacitus, it may be presumed, is considerably exaggerated. But
Lucan's tableau of the proscriptions is not improbably coloured from
the account he had himself heard from the witnesses of this dreadful
sacrifice (ii. 101.):
      " Nobilitas cum plebe perit, lateque vagatur
      Ensis, et a nullo revocatum est pectore ferrum . . . .
            . . . . nec jam alveus amnem,
      Nec retinent ripæ, redeuntque cadavera campo."

It has been suggested that there may have been a touch of insanity in the conduct of Ti- *Despair and apparent insanity of Tiberius.* berius at this period, and certainly there is something more than the mere atrocity of the acts themselves to countenance a supposition which may afford, perhaps, a slight relief to the mind of the reader. The blood of the Claudii, as we have before noticed, was tainted, apparently through many generations, with an hereditary vice, sometimes manifesting itself in extravagant pride and insolence, at others in ungovernable violence; and the whole career of Tiberius from his youth upwards, in its abrupt alternations of control and indulgence, of labour and dissipation, had been such in fact as might naturally lead to the unsettlement of his mental powers. This inward disturbance showed itself in a very marked manner in the startling inconsistency which became now more and more apparent in his conduct. While at this period Tacitus denounces in the most glowing terms the vehemence and recklessness of his cruelty, the particular anecdotes he relates of his behaviour are generally indicative of transient fits of leniency. He was extremely sensitive, says Suetonius, to the pasquinades which circulated against him in the capital, to the imputation freely cast on him of degrading and secret enormities, and to the furious invectives of his perishing victims. The king of the Parthians had the audacity to address him a letter, in which he noted with disgust his indolence and shameless indulgences, and urged him to satisfy by a voluntary death the sentiment of universal execration. Yet these charges and insults Tiberius himself freely published to the world at the very time that he complained so bitterly of them : no man could say worse things of him than he spontaneously and consciously admitted of himself in the extraordinary revelations he made of his own feelings. At last, we are told, he fell into a state of disgust and des-

peration. A letter he addressed to the senate has
been in part preserved to us by his awe-stricken contemporaries, whom it deeply impressed, breathing as
it does the very spirit of incipient madness in the
terrors of a distressed conscience, unable to fasten on
the precise and proper object of its perturbation.
What to write to you, Fathers, at this juncture, he
said, *or how not to write, or what to forbear from
writing, the Gods confound me worse than I feel
day by day confounded, if I know.*[1] So had his
crimes and abominations, says Tacitus, redounded to
his own punishment. *Nor in vain,* the historian
goes on to moralize, *was the wisest of philosophers
wont to maintain that, could the hearts of tyrants
be opened to our gaze, we should behold there the
direst wounds and ulcers; for the mind is torn
with cruelty, lust, and evil inclinations, not less
truly than the body by blows.*[2]

The despair of the now miserable tyrant is hardly
less strongly marked in his distress at the
circumstances of the death of an attached
adviser and servant, Cocceius Nerva, a man
held in high repute as a legal authority, and
one whose character and attainments were among
the most respectable supports of the Cæsarean government. The fortunes of Nerva were flourishing
in the full sunshine of his master's favour; his health
of body was unimpaired, and his mind mature and
vigorous: he had no outward cause of chagrin, none
of apprehension for the future. Yet this man, it
was announced, had formed the resolution of termi-
nating his own existence; for it had become the
fashion to make an avowal to one's friends and

His mortification at the suicide of Cocceius Nerva.

---

[1] Tac. *Ann.* vi. 6. under the date 785: "His verbis exorsus est,
Quid scribam vobis, P.C., aut quomodo scribam, aut quid omnino non
scribam hoc tempore, Di me Deæque pejus perdant quam perire me
quotidie sentio, si sciam."

[2] Tac. *Ann. l. c.* from Plato, *de Republ.* p. 575.; Ritter *in loc.*

family of such an intention. Tiberius sought the
suicide's chamber, where he was calmly awaiting, in
discourse with his friends and relations, with resolute
refusal of all sustenance, a slow and painful death.
Tiberius entreated him to explain the motive of
this desperate determination, to which, however, the
sufferer could not be persuaded to return a distinct
answer. With friendly zeal he solicited him to desist
from it, but again without success. Lastly, he urged
how injurious it would be to his own reputation as
emperor, if one of his nearest intimates should thus
make, as it were, his escape from life without even
assigning a motive to allay the agitation of the public
mind. Nerva calmly waived all discussion upon the
subject, and the all-powerful ruler found himself
repulsed and impotent in the presence of one who
had sentenced himself to death. Those who were
best acquainted with the real sentiments of the
suicide averred that the melancholy state of affairs
had filled the sage's mind with alarm and indignation,
and that he had deliberately resolved to shun the
future with honour, while still uninjured and unassailed.[1]

Nor, it may be believed, did the example of Nerva
remain without imitators. None of them,
however, was so illustrious as L. Arruntius, *Voluntary death of Arruntius.*
a noble, as we have seen, so distinguished
in character and position that Augustus had not
omitted to note him among those chiefs of the senate
who might, as he said, have contended with his own
heir for the empire. This man, however, notwithstanding this invidious distinction, and in spite of
the crabbed humour with which he had ventured to
gibe at the emperor himself, had escaped unharmed
almost to the last year of Tiberius. Yet from the
fortitude of his crowning act we may believe that he

[1] Tac. *Ann.* vi. 26.

had merited this escape by no unworthy compliances: he had merely abstained from irritating his master's jealousy by measuring himself with him in overt opposition.   On the occurrence of a disastrous inundation, it was to Arruntius that the task was assigned of providing for the future security of the city, which involved perhaps some arbitrary interference with the rights of property, of which the Romans, however great the necessity for it might be, were always excessively jealous.   At one period Tiberius proposed to remove him from Rome by the honourable appointment of a government in Spain; but again, unable to prevail on himself to entrust a possible rival with so much power, he had kept him by his own side in the capital, requiring him to execute his office by the hands of legates.   The delators had been eager to fasten a charge upon one who stood so exposed to their aim; but he had defeated at least one accusation, and secured the punishment of his assailants.   At last, however, he was more fatally involved in a charge brought against a certain Albucilla, the wife of Satrius, the denouncer of Sejanus.   Treasonable practices, impiety, as it was phrased, against the emperor, had been alleged against her; and as the looseness of her conduct was notorious, the known or supposed partners of her debauchery were presumed from that circumstance to be concerned also in her disloyalty.   Among these was Arruntius; but so little could be really advanced against him, or so adverse or indifferent was Tiberius to the prosecution, that the accused were permitted to remain at large with only a vague charge hanging over them. Some of them by merely keeping quiet escaped all further animadversion.   The friends of Arruntius would have persuaded him to rely on the emperor's clemency, and make no movement on his own part. But he proudly refused to owe his safety to an evasion.

The same conduct, he declared, *does not become all men alike. I have lived long enough. I have nothing to regret but having endured life so long amidst so many insults and dangers, exposed as I have been to the arrogance formerly of Sejanus, and now of Macro:*—for Macro had by this time become almost as obnoxious as his predecessor.— *True, I might perhaps still secure myself for the brief period which yet remains to the aged emperor: but how could I hope to escape intact through the reign of his successor?* With these words he caused his veins to be opened, and allowed himself to bleed to death. He foresaw a more intolerable servitude impending, and resolved to flee alike from the recollection of the past, and the prospect of the future. Though Arruntius himself might have escaped on this occasion, Albucilla was eventually condemned and executed; while those of her accomplices were selected for banishment or disgrace who were most obnoxious for their crimes, and particularly for that of delation.[1]

In the midst of his terrors and his cruelties Tiberius was distressed and perhaps amazed at the evidence these deeds afforded of the horror in which his government was now held. If *Reflections on the policy of Tiberius.* in the proscription of all, even of his nearest kin, who had seemed to menace his power, he had shown himself sanguinary and relentless, yet these were but few in number; they belonged, moreover, as he might presume, to a class too far exalted above the mass even of the nobles of Rome to excite much general sympathy. Why, he might ask, should the Romans interest themselves in mere family quarrels, and the bootless question, which candidate for the tyranny should actually climb the throne? But, on the other hand, he may have flattered himself that in the

---

[1] Tac. *Ann.* vi. 47, 48. under the year 790.

punishment of many bad citizens, by which his reign had been distinguished, he had shown a sense of equity and public spirit. Every Roman was concerned in his overthrow of an upstart like Sejanus; in the just retribution he had launched at the detestable delators, the foes not of the prince but of the people themselves; in the high moral feeling he had displayed in chastising the vices of women of quality; in pronouncing sentence on an Albucilla, a Claudia, an Urgulania, and recently on Plancina: for the wife of Cnæus Piso, though long protected, first by the favour of Livia, and still later by the disinclination of Tiberius to give a triumph to Agrippina, had at last been sacrificed to the unappeased enmity of the citizens. He might affect to plead for himself, as his successor afterwards pleaded for him, that it was not he that had warred against the senate, but the senators against one another. Of the four great nobles indeed whom Augustus specified as not unfit to compete with him for empire, three had since perished by violent deaths. Nor can Tiberius himself be relieved from the guilt of effecting the death of Asinius Gallus. Of neither Piso, however, nor Arruntius could it be said that he had devised and compassed his destruction; and the consideration in which Lepidus continued to be held shows that the highest rank and position were not necessarily fatal to their possessor.[1] M. Æmilius Lepidus, the son of Æmilius Paulus and a Fausta Cornelia, who thus combined in his origin descent from the most illustrious of the Roman houses, might have considered himself a far

---

[1] These four nobles are here mentioned together, because Tacitus leaves it uncertain whether Cnæus Piso or Arruntius was one of the three especially designated by Augustus. " De prioribus (*i.e.* Gallus and Lepidus) consentitur: pro Arruntio quidam Cn. Pisonem tradidere." He adds, untruly as we have seen: " Omnesque præter Lepidum, variis mox criminibus, struente Tiberio, circumventi sunt." *Ann.* i. 13.

greater man than any Octavius or Antonius, and
have looked down with complacent superiority upon
even a Julius or a Claudius.   But this distinguished
noble had acquiesced in the choice, if such we may
call it, of the Roman people; taught by the insignificance into which his kinsman the triumvir had
fallen, that the day of great names had passed, that
the nobles were unworthy to bear rule and the people incompetent, he had suffered the chief of the
Claudii to take precedence of him in the senate :
and while occupying himself the second place, he
had used his influence discreetly and liberally, and
had succeeded more than once in tempering the
severity of his colleagues.[1]   Another of the notabilities of the preceding reign, who had also retained his
honours under Tiberius, was Lucius Piso, chief pontiff and prefect of the city, a man of ability without
ambition, who had discharged the functions of a
difficult post with tact and considerateness, while in
the senate his voice had always been given on the
side of justice, and when that was defeated, had at
least recommended moderation.[2]   Such were the
men who, without despairing of their position, and
flying to death or retirement, could find a sphere
for their virtues even under the strong constraint of
the imperial government; and from more than one
passage of Tacitus, severe as he is in judging the
crimes and policy of Tiberius, it appears to have been
well understood among the nobles, that *even under
bad princes there is still a sphere for great men;*

[1] For instances of the influence of Lepidus, see Tac. *Ann.* iii. 50.,
iv. 20.

[2] Vell. ii. 98.; Tac. *Ann.* vi. 10.: "L. Piso pontifex, rarum in tanta
claritudine. facto obiit" (ann. 785): "nullius servilis sententiæ sponte
auctor, et quotiens necessitas ingrueret, cupienter moderans . . .
Ætas ad octogesimum annum processit . . . . præcipua ex eo gloria
quod præfectus urbi recens continuam potestatem, et insolentia
parendi graviorem, mire temperavit." For the scandalous charges
against the prefect Piso, see above, chap. xliv.

*that loyalty and moderation combined with indus-
try and vigour obtain the more genuine honour,
from the proneness of the proud and turbulent to
rush on certain ruin without advantage to any.*[1]

It may be true that Tiberius, in one of his gloomiest
moods, dissatisfied with himself yet indignant at the dissatisfaction of his people,
actually gave vent to his vexation in the
memorable quotation from a tragic writer, *After my
death perish the world in fire.*[2]   But the same sentiment has been ascribed to other tyrants in later times,
and may be regarded as expressive merely of the
judgment mankind in general have formed of their
extravagant selfishness.   As regards Tiberius, indeed,
it may have been put into his mouth by a later
generation which had suffered under the sway of successors even worse than himself, and believed that in
consigning them to such ruthless rulers he had evinced
a wanton indifference to their misery, if not rather a
fiendish exultation in it.   But our estimate of the
conduct of Tiberius in this particular must be founded
on a fair consideration of the circumstances in which
he was placed.   We must not suffer ourselves to be
biassed by the notions of a later age, to which the
principle of direct appointments had become familiar.
After weighing the statements of different writers, we
shall see reason probably to accede to that of Tacitus
in preference to others, according to whom Tiberius
made no appointment, designation, or recommendation of a successor to the imperial prerogatives.   He
could not have done so without directly violating the
settled principle of his government, which he pre-

Marginal note: Question of succession to the empire.

---

[1] Tac. *Ann.* iv. 20.; *Agric.* i2.

[2] Dion, lviii. 23.: τοῦτο τὸ ἀρχαῖον ἐμοῦ θανόντος γαῖα μιχθήτω πυρί.
See the allusions to the sentiment in the ancients, Cic. *de Fin.* i. 19.;
Senec. *de Clem.* ii. 2.; Suet. *Ner* 38.; Claudian *in Rufin.* ii. 19. in
Reimar's note.   Comp. Suet. *Tib.* 62.: " Identidem felicem Priamum
vocabat, quod superstes omnium suorum exstitisset."

tended to found on the spontaneous concession of the
people. The establishment of monarchy was not
even yet recognised as a constitutional fact. The
chief of the Julii might appoint, like any private
citizen, the heir to the domestic rites and honours of
his house; but this inheritance conveyed no title to
the Imperium or Principate, the Consular or the Tribunitian power. Herein lay, as Tiberius was well
aware, the secret of the new government's weakness:
this uncertainty as to the future was the main cause
of the tyranny into which he had himself insensibly
lapsed. No greater blessing could have been bestowed
on the Romans by a wise and honest ruler than the
transmutation of their polity from a pretended commonwealth to an acknowledged monarchy. But dire
experience had not yet perhaps taught them to acquiesce in the assumption by their dying chief of a
power over their political future. Would they respect
his disposition of their indefeasible prerogatives after
his decease? Would they not, on the contrary, resent
it? This was a question which Augustus had not
ventured to ask. Yet the founder of the empire had
been too deeply interested in the success of his work
to leave its prospects to blind chance. He had shown
himself anxious, during his own term of government,
to pave the way for the recognition of his intended
successor, by gradually investing the proposed heir of
his private fortunes with public honours and titles
akin to his own : so that Tiberius had been able, on
his father's decease, to glide, almost unobserved, into
the sovereign power. Such undoubtedly was the
generous policy which became a ruler to whom the
interests of the state were really dear, and who sought
to found the greatness of his own house on the prosperity of the people. But to such a policy the spirit
of Tiberius was not perhaps equal. A cruel misfortune
had deprived him of Germanicus; but so had Augustus
also lost his Agrippa. Drusus was removed from him

by the treachery of an unworthy favourite; but in like manner his predecessor had had to mourn the early and ill-omened loss of Caius and Lucius. Here, however, the parallel ceased. While the first princeps continued after every disappointment to repeat his genuine efforts to secure the principles of family succession, and called Tiberius himself, in default of still nearer kinsmen, into alliance and partnership in the empire; the second sacrificed all to an unworthy jealousy, and chose rather to murder his nephews than to risk being supplanted by them.

Accordingly, towards the end of his career, Tiberius found himself supported by only three surviving males of the lineage of Cæsar, and none of these had received any training in public life. Tiberius Claudius Drusus, born in the year 744, was the last of the sons of the eldest Drusus, and the nephew of the reigning emperor, by whom he had been adopted on his father's death, at the desire of Augustus. But Claudius (to give him the name by which he will become familiarly known to us) was reputed to be infirm both in health and understanding. Like Agrippa Postumus, he was destined from early youth to be excluded from public affairs, and all political instruction had been purposely withheld from him. Yet he was not perhaps destitute of talents; he devoted himself to the study of books, and possibly he appreciated them, while the weakness of his bodily frame contributed to keep him from the ruder and coarser diversions, to which the want of practical employment might have driven a bolder and more vigorous man. His character and attainments, however, we shall have a future occasion to estimate more precisely: for the present it is enough to say that he had probably owed his life, amidst the fall of so many of his relations, to the general conviction that he was unfit to rule, and therefore not to be feared as a candidate for the suffrages of the people.

Surviving members of the imperial family.

Upon him the emperor scarcely deigned to bestow a thought at this crisis. Two others, however, there were, both much younger than Claudius, between whom the hopes of the Julian house were divided; Caius, the youngest son of Germanicus, and Tiberius, surnamed Gemellus, the child of the second Drusus; the one grand-nephew, the other grandson, of the emperor, but both equally reputed his sons or grandsons by adoption.[1]   Of these Caius was born in the year 765, Tiberius in 772.[2]   The former had been enrolled at an early age among the augurs and pontiffs, and had since been advanced to the quæstorship, the first step in the legitimate career of honours; the latter had not yet been introduced into public life, his tender years hardly permitting it.   From neither of these striplings certainly could the emperor anticipate any rivalry with himself; but untried and almost unknown as they still were, he shrank from insulting even his subservient senate by claiming for them the highest prerogatives.   The daughters of Germanicus he had married to citizens of distinction.   Julia was united to Vinicius, whose municipal and equestrian extraction had been recently illustrated by the rise of both his father and grandfather to the consulship.[3]   Drusilla had wedded a Cassius, whose family was plebeian, though it vied with the noblest of Rome in antiquity and reputation, besides the peculiar lustre which had been shed upon it in more recent times.

---

[1] It has been mentioned before that Agrippina had borne five sons and four daughters to Germanicus.   The deaths of Nero and Drusus have been recorded in their place : two other sons seem to have died in infancy.   Caius, the youngest of the five, was now the sole survivor.

[2] This Tiberius had also the name of Gemellus, which seems to show that he was one of the male twins whom Livilla bore to Drusus in the year 772. Tac. *Ann.* ii. 84.; see above, chap. xliii.   The other child, as has been said, probably died in infancy.

[3] Tac. *Ann.* vi. 15. Vinicius, the patron of Velleius Paterculus, was probably an adherent of Sejanus, and owed his alliance with the Cæsarean family to the favour of so powerful a friend.

A third daughter, who bore her mother's name, Agrippina, was affianced to a man of higher rank than either of these, a Cnæus Domitius Ahenobarbus, descended lineally from the three Domitii whose names have been successively signalized in these pages. A fourth, whose name has not been recorded, was united to the son of Quintilius Varus. Again, after the death of her husband Nero Germanicus, the younger Julia, daughter of Drusus and Livilla, had been espoused to Rubellius Blandus, a second connexion which might properly be regarded as an unworthy descent from the first, inasmuch as his nobility dated only from the last generation.[1] But in casting his eyes on these and perhaps other scions of the old aristocracy, Tiberius could discover none whose eminence entitled him to be exalted above all the rest of his order ; the levelling effects of his tyranny were already manifest in the general mediocrity of talent in the senate, and the public mind was not unprepared to admit the rule of hereditary succession as a state necessity.

The bitterest of Tiberius's enemies admits, not as it would seem without some inconsistency,

Tiberius appoints Caius and Tiberius Gemellus heirs of his private fortune.
A. D. 35.
A. U. 788.

that he was anxious at heart to settle the succession on a secure footing, and would have disregarded, in making his choice, the opinion of his contemporaries, could he have felt assured of the approbation of a grateful posterity. Nevertheless, after much restless

---

[1] Tac. *Ann.* vi. 27.: "Cujus avum Tiburtem equitem Romanum plerique meminerant." Juvenal (viii. 39.) employs the name of Rubellius to represent the pride of those who have greatness thrust upon them:

> " Tecum est mihi sermo, Rubelli
> Blande: tumes alto Drusorum stemmate tanquam
> Feceris ipse aliquid propter quod nobilis esses.
> Ut te conciperet quæ sanguine fulget Iuli ;
> Non quæ ventoso conducta sub aggere texit."

Domitius, Vinicius, Cassius, and Rubellius are mentioned together in *Ann.* vi. 45. as the four progeneri, grandsons-in-law, of Tiberius.

deliberation, the failing old man was constrained to leave it in all the uncertainty above described : he *abandoned to fate,* says Tacitus, *the decision to which he was himself unequal.*[1] But already in the year 788 he had made a testament, appointing Caius and Tiberius co-partners in his private heritage, with whatever advantage might thence accrue to them in regard to their public pretensions; and in the event of the death of either, the survivor was destined to inherit from the deceased.[2] The elder of the two princes at least was not unmoved by the prospect of the fortunes which seemed so likely to befall him. Caius was not insensible to the advantage he enjoyed in popular favour, and especially among the soldiers, as the son of Germanicus. Though actually born in the peaceful retirement of Antium, he had been carried in infancy to the stations of the Rhenish legions, and bred up in the midst of the soldiery, and he gladly countenanced, we may suppose, the common belief that he had first seen the light in the camp.[3] As a child, he had been accoutred in the military garb, and it was from the boots, or caligæ, which he was made to wear, that the soldiers gave him his familiar nickname of Caligula.[4] The mutiny on the Rhine was actually

(marginal note: Caius Germanicus Cæsar, nicknamed Caligula.)

---

[1] Tac. *Ann.* vi. 45.: " Quippe illi non perinde curæ gratia præsentium quam in posteros ambitio: mox incertus animi, fesso corpore consilium, cui impar erat, fato permisit."

[2] Suet. *Tib.* 76.

[3] Suet. *Calig.* 8.: " Ubi natus sit incertum diversitas tradentium facit. Cn. Lentulus Gætulicus Tiburi genitum scribit ; Plinius Secundus in Treveris, vico Ambiatino, supra confluentes . . . . Versiculi, imperante mox eo divulgati, apud hibernas legiones procreatum indicant:

In castris natus, patriis nutritus in armis,
Jam designati Principis omen erat.

Ego in actis Antii editum invenio."

[4] Tac. *Ann.* i. 41.; Dion. lvii. 5 ; Suet. *Calig.* 9.: " Caligulæ cognomen castrensi joco traxit, quia manipulario habitu inter milites

quelled, it was said, by showing to the troops their
young pet and playfellow. But these rude caresses
were not, as he early learnt, to be accepted without
danger, and he was careful to disguise the pleasure
he took in the favour in which the citizens held him.
Nor less anxiously did he conceal any emotions of an
opposite character, which the sufferings of his mother
or brothers may have awakened in his breast. A
practised dissembler from his early years, for from the
first dawn of consciousness he found himself the in-
habitant of a palace, and closely attached to the person
of the all-dreaded imperator, he studied to clothe his
countenance day by day with the expression assumed
by Tiberius himself, to penetrate his sentiments and
echo, as it were, his very words. He was ever on the
watch to anticipate the wishes of the tyrant, and at
a later time, the remark of the orator Passienus
obtained a great success, that no man was ever a better
servant, or a worse master.[1]

Caius Cæsar, by the direction of his grandsire, had
married in 786 Claudia, or Claudilla, the
daughter of M. Junius Silanus; but this
consort he had lost in the third year of
their union.[2] At this latter period the
end of Tiberius was visibly approaching. While
his bodily strength was failing his mind continued
unimpaired, and the power as well as the habit of dissimulation retained its full vigour to the last. No
consciousness of his own decay could extort from him

Macro obtains
ascendancy
over him.
A. D. 36.
A. U. 789.

educabatur . . . . post excessum Augusti tumultuantes . . . . solus
haud dubie conspectu suo flexit."

[1] Tac. *Ann.* vi. 20. : " Immanem animum subdola modestia tegens
. . . qualem diem Tiberius induisset, pari habitu, non multum dis-
tantibus verbis. Unde mox scitum Passieni oratoris dictum percre-
buit ; neque meliorem unquam servum, neque deteriorem dominum
fuisse."

[2] Tac. *Ann.* vi. 20. Suetonius (*Calig.* 12.) gives her name more
correctly, Junia Claudilla. Dion is inaccurate in placing the marriage in 788.: lviii. 25.

any disclosures of his actual views regarding the
imperial inheritance.   The ambitious and intriguing
spirits at Rome trembled in uncertainty as to the
future, and Tiberius kept his courtiers still attached
to his side by refusing to indicate by word or gesture
in what quarter they should look for his successor.
He even let it be supposed, it would seem, that,
dissatisfied with the prospect opened to him within
the limits of the Cæsarean family, he meditated removing both the grandson and the grand-nephew
by death.[1]   Nevertheless the arts of the veteran
dissembler could not blind the wariest of his observers.   Since the overthrow of Sejanus, the bold
and crafty Macro had wielded no small share of
that minister's power, but he had never succeeded
in gaining the personal favour and confidence of his
master.   Though at the head of the prætorians and
of the police of the city, he had not been advanced
to the more brilliant honours of the state.   For these
he must be content to look to the exigencies of a
new reign, in which his talents and position might
command still higher promotion; and it was now
his object to divine the future emperor, and bind
him to himself by some signal service.   As shrewd
in observation as he had proved himself bold in
action, he fixed without hesitation upon Caius as the
destined chief of the state.   To secure an ascendancy over him he employed the artifices of his wife
Ennia, who insinuated herself into the affections of
the young and idle voluptuary at a moment when
his fancy was unoccupied, and soon acquired for
her husband all the influence he desired.   *You
leave the setting sun to court the rising*, muttered
Tiberius, whom nothing could escape: but he gave
no further token of displeasure, and the people accepted the words, which were speedily noised abroad,

---

[1] Suet. *Tib.* 62.

as an intimation that already in his own mind he
had determined to transmit the empire to his grand-
nephew.   Another sentence, which was ascribed to
him, seemed not less significant of this intention.
Observing one day a cloud pass over the countenance
of Caius, on his making a gesture of kindness towards
the young Tiberius, for whom he seems to have felt
some yearning of natural affection, he was reported
to have said to him, *you will kill him, and another
will kill you.*[1]   The young dissembler had never been
able to impose on his uncle's practised sagacity.   Tiberius had observed, not, it is said, without a malignant satisfaction, the gross sensuality and cruel or
degrading sports in which he delighted, hoping, as
was commonly surmised, that they would divert him
from the aspirations of a premature ambition, expect-
ing, as some ventured to ·suggest, that the crimes of
the ensuing reign would extinguish the recollection
of his own.[2]

Tacitus, as we have seen, assures us that Tiberius
abandoned the imperial succession to fate ;
by which he evidently means that the emperor addressed no direct injunction or
recommendation to the senate upon a subject on which, as he well knew, he could exercise no
real authority.   In the phrase itself, the current language of the philosophy of the time, there is nothing
remarkable ; nor do I imagine that there is any allusion in it to the story upon this subject narrated by
Josephus, which deserves, however, to be recorded in
illustration of the character of the age.   Tiberius,
says the Jewish historian, on his return to
Capreæ from his last visit to the continent,
was seized with a consumptive attack, which at first

*Ideas regard-
ing the disposal
of the succes-
sion : expres-
sion of
Tacitus.*

*Anecdote told
by Josephus.*

---

[1] Tac. *Ann.* vi. 45.: "Occides tu hunc, et te alius." Dion, lviii. 23.
Comp. Philo, *l. c.*

[2] Suet. *Calig.* 11.; Dion, lviii. 23.

did not threaten danger : but as the disorder gained
ground he began to feel that his end was actually
approaching; whereupon he commanded Euodus, the
most confidential of his freedmen, to send his two
grandchildren to him betimes the next morning, that
he might address them before he died.   After giving
this direction, he prayed the gods to make known to
him by some token which of the two they destined
to succeed him : for although his wish was to leave
the empire to the young Tiberius, he felt that his
own inclination ought to yield to the manifestations
of the divine will.   Accordingly he proposed to himself a sign by which that will might be discovered;
and this was, that whichever of the princes should
first come into his presence, him he would regard as
called to the empire.   Having thus piously placed
himself in the hands of the gods, he proceeded, with
a natural inconsistency, to control, if possible, their
decrees, by desiring the tutor of Tiberius to make
sure and bring his charge at the earliest hour possible.   But this prince, spending some time over
his morning meal, was actually forestalled by Caius,
much to the emperor's regret, who was moved to
tears at the unhappy fortune of his own offspring,
not only excluded by providence from the sovereign
power, but exposed, as he well knew, to the direct
risk of destruction.   Commanding himself, however,
with a great effort, he said to Caius, *My son, although
Tiberius is nearer to myself than you are, yet both
of my own choice, and in obedience to the gods,
into your hands I commit the empire of Rome.*   To
these solemn words he added, according to the same
authority, an earnest entreaty that he would continue to love his unprotected kinsman, enforced by a
warning of the perils of his own position, and of the
pains which wait on human ingratitude.[1]

[1] Joseph. *Antiq. Jud.* xviii. 6. 9.

Of all our principal authorities for the history of
Last days of Tiberius. this period Josephus undoubtedly stands
the nearest in point of time ; nevertheless,
bred as he was in the ideas of a foreigner or a
provincial, his information on matters of constitutional principle is often at fault ; and the anecdote
just related is of little historical value, except as
showing the more indulgent way in which the character of Tiberius might be regarded beyond the
precincts of Rome or Italy. This writer is not indeed correct in the place he assigns for the death of
the emperor, a point on which a Roman historian
could hardly have made a mistake. It was early in
the year 790 that Tiberius, now in his seventy-eighth
year, quitted for the last time his retreat in Capreæ,
and moving slowly from villa to villa, arrived within
seven miles of the city on the Appian Way. Again,
having taken one more view of its distant buildings,
he turned his back finally upon them, terrified, so it
was reported, by an evil omen, and retraced his languid steps along the coast of Campania.[1] At Astura
he fell sick ; but having a little recovered he proceeded onwards to Circeii. Here, anxious to avert
suspicion of his illness, he not only presided at the
exercises of the camp, but even cast javelins with
his own hand at the beasts which were driven before
his seat in the amphitheatre. By this exertion the
old man both strained and overheated himself ; yet,
though his symptoms grew worse, he insisted on
continuing his progress as far as Misenum, where
he possessed the voluptuous villa of Lucullus ; nor
would he allow any change to be made in his sensual and perhaps intemperate habits at table.[2] His

---

[1] Suet. *Tib.* 72.: " Ostento territus."

[2] Suet. *l. c.*: " Nihil ex ordine quotidiano prætermitteret, se con-
vivia quidem ac cæteras voluptates, partim intemperantia, partim
dissimulatione." But Pliny, in the passage before cited (*Hist. Nat.*
xiv. 28), while he allows the intemperance of Tiberius in his youth,

courtiers and attendants looked on with awe and trepidation. Every one felt assured that the days of the tyrant were numbered; yet every one feared to pay his court too soon by a day or an hour to the expected heir of his fortunes. All eyes were turned on Charicles, the emperor's confidential physician; and Caius himself, perhaps, was the first to urge him to contrive to feel the dying man's pulse, for Tiberius persisted to the last in disguising his actual condition, and thus ascertain how much life was yet left in him. Charicles, it seems, was about to quit the court for a few days: possibly his master had dismissed him on purpose to blind the eyes of the watchful observers around him. Rising from the table, and taking the emperor's hand to kiss it, he managed to touch the wrist. Tiberius noticed the touch and immediately guessed its motive. He called for fresh dishes and more wine, nor would he consent to break up the festivities till a later hour than ordinary.[1] On rising he even received one by one the salutations of all his guests, according to his wont, keeping all the while an erect posture, and addressing to each a word in reply. But Charicles had attained his object, and his science was not to be deceived. He assured Macro that the patient could not survive beyond two days. Tiberius was the more anxious, it was said, to regain Capreæ, because he was offended at the neglect of the senate to expedite the condemnation of some criminals he had required it to sentence, and could not venture on a stroke of authority except from his inaccessible citadel. But whether or not this were so, his hopes and fears were all about

expressly declares that his abstemiousness was strict if not austere ("severus atque etiam sævus:" the words are perhaps corrupt) in this respect in his later years. Tac. *Ann.* vi. 50.: "Jam Tiberium corpus, jam vires, nondum dissimulatio deserebat: idem animi rigor; sermone ac vultu intentus, quæsita interdum comitate quamvis manifestam defectionem tegebat."

[1] Tac. *l. c.*: "Instaurari epulas jubet, discumbitque ultra solitum."

to close, and Capreæ he was destined never again to
visit. Unfavourable weather combined with the advance of his malady to retain him at Misenum; and
whether his dissolution was altogether natural, or
hastened by foul means, as commonly suspected, it
was not perhaps delayed beyond the term assigned
to it by the physician. The actual circumstances of
the tyrant's end were variously reported. On the
17th of the calends of April, or the 16th of
March, says Tacitus, he had fainted away,
and it was imagined he had ceased to breathe. The
courtiers trooped without delay to congratulate Caius,
who quitted the chamber to surround himself, as was
supposed, with the ensigns of power, when suddenly
it was reported that the sick man's voice and vision
had returned, and he had called to his attendants for
nourishment. The consternation was universal; the
crowd hastily dispersed, and every man framed his
countenance to a look of ignorance or anxiety. Caius
himself was struck speechless in expectation of immediate punishment. But Macro was at his side,
and Macro was resolute and prompt as ever. *Heap
more bedclothes upon him*, he whispered, *and leave
him.*[1] Tacitus insinuates without hesitation that he
was stifled, and his account has been most commonly
followed; he refers, however, to no authority.[2] On
the other hand, a contemporary of the events seems
to describe the old man's death as simply natural.
Feeling himself sinking, said Seneca, Tiberius took
off his ring, and held it for a little while, as if about
to present it to some one as an instrument of authority; but soon replaced it on his finger, and lay for

His death.

---

[1] Tac. *l. c.*: " Cæsar in silentium fixus a summa spe novissima ex-
spectabat: Macro intrepidus, opprimi senem injectu multæ vestis
jubet, discedique a limine."

[2] Thus Dion, lviii. 28.: δείσας οὖν ἐκεῖνος μὴ καὶ ἀληθῶς ἀνασω ῇ,
οὔτε ἐμφαγεῖν τι αἰτήσαντι αὐτῷ, ὡς καὶ βλαβησομένῳ, ἔδωκε, καὶ ἱμάτια
πολλὰ καὶ παχέα, ὡς καὶ θερμασίας τινὸς δεομένῳ, προσέβαλε· καὶ οὕτως
ἀπέπνιξεν αὐτὸν, συναραμένου ποι αὐτῷ καὶ τοῦ Μάκρωνος.

a time motionless: then suddenly he called for his attendants, and when no one answered, raised himself from his bed with failing strength, and immediately fell lifeless beside it.[1]   This account was distorted by others into the denial of necessary sustenance, and actual death by exhaustion, while some did not scruple to affirm that Caius had caused him to be poisoned.[2]

Cæsar, the high-handed usurper, met an usurper's death, by open violence in the light of day.   Augustus, after fifty years of the mildest and most equitable rule the times admitted, sank at last by a slow and painless decay into the arms of those dearest to him, amidst the respectful sympathies of an admiring people.   The end of Tiberius, whether consummated by treachery or not, was shrouded in gloom and obscurity; the chamber of mortality was agitated to the last by the intrigues and fears of the dying man and his survivors.   The fellow countrymen of the detested tyrant seem to have deemed it fitting that one whose life was to them a riddle should perish by a mysterious death.   For my own part, I would rather represent him as a man whose character was sufficiently transparent, whose apparent inconsistencies, often exaggerated and misrepresented, may generally be explained by the nature of his position, and the political illusions with which he was required to

The character of Tiberius not mysterious.

---

[1] Suet. *Tib.* 73.: "Seneca cum scribit, intellecta defectione," &c. The elder Seneca, who is known to have written a history of his own times, died towards the end of Tiberius, at an advanced age.   This must be the account of his son the philosopher ; but there is no such passage in his existing works.   Suetonius in another place (*Calig.* 12.) gives another account: "Caius veneno Tiberium aggressus est," &c.

[2] Tacitus gives March 16, for the date of this event, Dion, March 26.   Tiberius, born November, 712, was in the middle of his seventy-eighth year.   Dion, *l. c.*: ἐβίω δὲ ἑπτὰ καὶ ἐβδομήκοντα ἔτη, καὶ μῆνας τέσσαρας, καὶ ἡμέρας ἐννέα.

encircle himself. It is the character of the age in which he was placed, an age of rapid though silent transition, rather than of the man himself, which invests him with an historical interest. This is the point to which it will be well to direct our attention, before letting the curtain drop on the personage with whom the forms of the republic perished, and the despotism of the Cæsars finally dropped its mask.[1]

Judgment of the Romans on the character of Tiberius. The practice of delation, so rapidly developed under the rule of Tiberius, introduced a new principle into the government of his day, and marked it with features of its own.

It is hardly possible to overrate the effects of this practice on the general complexion of the Roman polity, nor is it easy to exaggerate the horror with which it came to be regarded. It was an attempt to reconcile the despotism of the monarch with the forms of a republic; to strengthen the sovereign power by weakening its subjects; to govern the people by dividing them, by destroying their means of combination among themselves, by generating among them habits of mutual distrust and fear, and finally plunging them into a state of politica imbecility. We have already seen how this system was in fact the product of peculiar circumstances rather than the creation of a deliberate will; nevertheless the chief of the state was made, not unnaturally, to bear the whole responsibility of

---

[1] Thus Ferguson concludes his history of the Roman republic with the death of Tiberius. Tacitus describes, according to his view, the different epochs in the character of Tiberius. *Ann.* vi. 51.: "Morum quoque tempora illi diversa: egregium vita famaque, quoad privatus, vel in imperiis sub Augusto fuit: occultum ac subdolum fingendis virtutibus, donec Germanicus ac Drusus superfuere: idem inter bona malaque mixtus, incolumi matre: intestabilis sævitia, sed obtectis libidinibus, dum Sejanum dilexit timuitve: postremo in scelera simul ac dedecora prorupit, postquam, remoto pudore et metu, suo tantum ingenio utebatur."

it, and the disgust of the nobler spirits of Rome at
the tyranny of spies and informers was turned against
the prince himself, in whose interest at least, if not
at whose instigation, their enormities were for the
most part perpetrated.   If we examine the authorities for the history of the reign we have been re-
viewing, we shall find that those who were nearest to
the times themselves have generally treated Tiberius
with the greatest indulgence.   Velleius Paterculus
indeed, and Valerius Maximus, his contemporaries
and subjects, must be regarded as mere courtly
panegyrists : but the adulation of the one, though it
jars on ears accustomed to the dignified self-respect
of the earlier Romans, is not more high-flown in
language and sentiment than what our own writers have addressed to the Georges, and even the
Charleses and Jameses, of the English monarchy;
while that of the other is chiefly offensive from the
connexion in which it stands with the lessons of
virtue and patriotism which his book was specially
designed to illustrate.   The elder Seneca, the master
of a school of rhetoric, to which science his writings
are devoted, makes no mention of the emperor
under whom he wrote ; but his son, better known
as the statesman and philosopher, though he was
under the temptation of contrasting the austere and
aged tyrant with the gay young prince to whom he
was himself attached, speaks of him with considerable moderation, and ascribes the worst of his deeds
to Sejanus and the delators rather than to his own
evil disposition.[1]   In the pages of Philo and Josephus, the government of Tiberius is represented as
mild and equitable : it is not till we come to Suetonius and Tacitus, in the third generation, that his
enormities are blazoned in the colours so painfully

[1] Seneca, *Ep.* 21.; *de Benef.* iii. 26.; *Consol. ad Marc.* 15.

familiar to us. It will suffice here to remark that
both these later writers belong to a period of strong
reaction against the Cæsarean despotism, when the
senate was permitted to raise its venerable head and
resume a show at least of imperial prerogatives;
when the secret police of Rome was abolished, delation firmly repressed, freedom of speech proclaimed
by the voice of the emperor himself, and the birthright of the citizen respectfully restored to him.
There ensued a strong revulsion of feeling, not
against monarchy, which had then become an accepted institution, but against the corruptions which
had turned it into tyranny; and Tiberius, as the
reputed founder of the system of delation, bore the
odium of all the crimes of all the tyrants who had
succeeded him. Tacitus admits that the *affairs of
Tiberius* were misrepresented during his power by
fear, and after his death by spite: yet we cannot
doubt that Tacitus himself often yields to the bias of
his detractors, while Suetonius is at best indifferent
to the truth.[1] After all, a sober discretion must
suspend its belief regarding many of the circumstances above recorded, and acknowledge that it is
only through a treacherous and distorting haze that
we have scanned the features of this ill-omened
principate.

Nevertheless, the terror which prevailed in the
last years of Tiberius, to whomsoever it is
chiefly to be ascribed, exercised a baleful
influence over society at Rome, and shows
by effects which are still discoverable that it has been
but little exaggerated. It has left permanent traces
of itself in the manifest decline and almost total

The reign of
terror at
Rome.

---

[1] Tac. *Ann.* i. 1.: "Tiberii Caiique, et Claudii, ac Neronis res,
florentibus ipsis ob metum falsæ, postquam occiderant *recentibus odiis*
compositæ sunt." There seems reason to believe that the hostility
to Tiberius's memory increased rather than diminished in the course
of the succeeding century.

extinction of literature under its pressure. The Roman writers addressed only a small class in the capital; to be popularly known in the provinces, to be read generally throughout the Roman world, was a privilege reserved for few, and anticipated perhaps rarely by any. Even in the capital the poet and historian composed their works for a circle of a few thousand knights and senators, for the friends and families of their own few hundreds of acquaintances, whom they invited to encourage their efforts by attending their recitations. The paralysis which benumbed the energies of the Roman nobility at this crisis of terror and despair, extended naturally to the organs of their sentiments and opinions. *Its effect upon literature.* Not history only and philosophy suffered an eclipse, but poetry also, which under Augustus had been the true expression of the national feelings, became mute when the feelings themselves could no longer be trusted with utterance. We have seen how Cremutius was subjected to persecution for pronouncing that Brutus and Cassius were the last of the Romans. A tragedian was accused, and if accused we may presume perhaps that he was condemned, for speaking evil of the king of men, Agamemnon; and various authors were assailed, and their writings sentenced to proscription, to whose recitations the last princeps had himself listened with indulgence.[1] The poems which were tolerated were generally the most trifling and perhaps licentious in character.[2] The sly irony of the fable, a style of composition adopted by slaves, and imitated from the servile Orientals, seems not unsuitable to these

---

[1] Suet. *Tib.* 61. It will be remembered by scholars that Atrides is the invidious nickname often applied by the poets to the Roman tyrants. Comp. Juvenal, iv. 65.: "Itur ad Atridem."

[2] Such seems to have been the character of the verses of Lentulus Gætulicus. Martial, *praf.* i.; Plin. *Ep.* v. 3.

perilous times.[1]   The name of Phædrus belongs in
all probability to the Tiberian period, but it is curious
that no later writer for four centuries should have
cared to notice him.[2]   Similar or worse has been the
fate of a more serious writer, Manilius, the author of
an elaborate poem on Astronomy and its spurious
sister Astrology, a theme of some danger under the
circumstances of the times, but which he has treated
with irreproachable discretion; it is owing perhaps
to the disgrace under which the forbidden science
fell that this innocent work lapsed into entire oblivion, and has escaped the mention of any writer of
antiquity.[3]

The deep gloom which settled on the face of higher
society at Rome was heightened by its contrast with the frivolous dissipation of the
populace, who though deprived of the glitter
of a brilliant court, and surrounded by signs of mourning and humiliation among their natural leaders, not
the less abandoned themselves to the sensual enjoyments which alone they relished, and rejoiced in their
utter indifference to political principles, to parties
and to men.   They clamoured with exultation over
the body of the traitor; nevertheless, *had the goddess
Nursia*, says the moralist, *but favoured her Etruscan
votary, had but the false intriguer circumvented the*

No traces of it among the populace.

---

[1] Phædrus says of his own style of composition (*Prol. ad.* iii. 33.):
   " Nunc fabularum cur sit inventum genus
      Brevi docebo.   Servitus obnoxia,
      Quia quæ volebat non audebat dicere,
      Affectus proprios in fabellas transtulit."

[2] Phædrus is supposed to have been a freedman of Tiberius.
Seneca exhorts Polybius, a freedman of Claudius, to divert his mind
by writing fables a few years later ; but even then he calls this kind
of composition, " Intentatum Romanis ingeniis opus." Senec. *Consol.
ad Polyb.* 27.   Martial (iii. 20.) alludes to a Phædrus, but not apparently as a fabulist.   " An æmulatur improbi jocos Phædri?"

[3] In this total absence of the " testimonia veterum," the date of
Manilius is ascertained from his allusions to the death of Varus
(i. 897.), to Augustus as still living (i. 922.), and again to the island
of Rhodes as the "hospitium recturi Principis orbem." iv. 764.

guileless old man, on the instant they would have been heard proclaiming Sejanus a Cæsar and an Augustus.[1] In the one class was abandonment of public life, shame, despair and suicide;—the intolerable evils of the time drove men not to religious consolations, but to a restless inquiry into the future, or a vain attempt to lull the sense of the present in philosophic apathy:—the other rushed headlong, hour by hour, to the baths, shows, and largesses, or shouted at the heels of the idol of the moment, or sighed and perhaps murmured at his loss, and speedily resigned itself to oblivion of the fitful emotion of the day.

We must be careful notwithstanding to observe that both the shame and the degradation were for the most part confined to the city and its vicinity, which lay in the very shadow of the despot. Tiberius was content to sacrifice Rome to the exigencies of his position; but he ruled the provinces on the whole in a Roman spirit, and maintained the dignity of the empire for the most part intact from the centre to the frontiers. The stability of the system, if decaying at the heart, might still be measured by the strength and solidity of its members. At no period did the bulwarks of the Roman power appear more secure and unassailable. The efforts of Drusus and his son to overpower the Germans on their own soil had been stupendous; they had wielded forces equal at least to those with which Cæsar had added Gaul to the empire, and yet had not permanently advanced the eagles in any direction. But, on the other hand, it was soon found that the Germans were only formidable under the pressure of an attack. When the assault relaxed, the power they had concentrated in resistance crumbled

General state of peace and security in the provinces.

---

[1] Juvenal, x. 74.: "Idem populus, si Nursia Tusco
  Favisset, si oppressa foret secura senectus
  Principis, hac ipsa Sejanum diceret hora
  Augustum."

readily away.   With the death of Arminius, all combined hostility to Rome ceased among them.   They
never dared to retort in concert the invasions under
which they had suffered.   Meanwhile the arts and
manners of the South advanced incessantly among
them; their political dissensions were fostered by
the enemy, and in the weakness caused by mutual
jealousy they turned with awe and wonder to the
image of the immense and undivided empire, the
skirt of whose robe trailed majestically on their
borders.   At the same time the long respite from
military exactions allowed the pursuits of ease and
luxury to fructify within the limits of the provinces.
Gaul was no longer drained from year to year by the
forced requisitions of men and horses, of arms and
stores, which had fed the exhausting campaigns of
Germanicus.   Her ancient cities decked themselves
with splendid edifices, with schools and theatres,
aqueducts and temples.   The camps on the Rhine
and Danube were gradually transformed into commercial stations, and became emporiums of traffic
with the north of Europe, where the fur and amber
of the Hercynian forests and the Baltic coast were
exchanged for wine and oil, or gold and silver, those
instruments of luxury which nature was supposed,
in mercy or in anger, to have denied to the German
barbarians.[1]   Such a state of affairs allowed the emperor to persist in his favourite plan of leaving the
provincial governors for years unchanged at their
posts.   Each succeeding proconsul was no longer in
a fever of haste to aggrandise himself by the plunder
or renown of a foray beyond the frontiers.   The ad-

---

[1] Tac. *Germ.* 5.: " Argentum et aurum propitii an irati Dî nega-
verint dubito." This well-known assertion, so remarkably inaccurate, as it has proved, in fact, was provoked perhaps by the failure of
the first speculation in Nassau mines. See Tac. *Ann.* xi. 20.: " Cur-
tius Rufus . . . in agro Mattiaco recluserat specus quærendis venis
argenti ; unde tenuis fructus, nec in longum fuit."

ministration of the provinces became a matter of ordinary routine; it lost its principal charms in the eyes of the senators, who could at last with difficulty be induced to exchange the brilliant pleasures of the capital, with all its mortifications and perils, for the dull honours of a distant prefecture. Nothing is more significant of the actual improvement in the condition of the subject than this fact, which is advanced by Tacitus as a proof of the decay of public spirit and the degeneracy of the age.[1]

Nor can I discover in general the justice of accusing Tiberius of neglecting the safety of his remote possessions, which seem, on the contrary, to have flourished securely in the armed peace of his august empire.[2]   In Gaul the revolt of Sacrovir and his Belgian confederates was effectually suppressed: the outbreak of the Frisians seems, though at some cost of blood, to have been speedily quelled.[3]   Nor have we any distinct confirmation of the assertion of Suetonius, that Tiberius suffered the province to be ravaged with impunity by the Germans, which, if true, can apply only to some transient violation of the frontiers.   That disgrace indeed to this extent actually attended the Roman government seems not improbable, from circumstances which have transpired regarding the conduct of the commander in those parts.   For many years the legions of the Upper Rhine were confided to a senator of high consideration; but he was said to have gained the devotion of both his own soldiers and those of the lower

Vigilance of Tiberius in guarding the frontiers.

Gaul and Germany.

---

[1] Tac. *Ann.* vi. 27.: "Egregium quemque et regendis exercitibus idoneum, abnuere id munus." The distrust, however, or indifference of Tiberius was more distinctly shown in his keeping some of his governors at home for years after nominally appointing them. Such were the cases of Ælius Lamia and Arruntius. Tac. *l. c.*

[2] Suet. *Tib.* 41.: "Armeniam a Parthis occupari, Mœsium a Dacis Sarmati-que, Gallias a Germanis vastari neglexit."

[3] Tac. *Ann.* iv. 72.

province, by the popularity of his manners and the
laxity of his discipline.[1]　Such conduct proceeded,
we may confidently affirm, either from culpable neg-
ligence or from criminal aspirations.　Tiberius was
doubtless alarmed.　Lentulus Gætulicus, such was
the officer's name, was denounced by a delator; but
his marriage with the daughter of Sejanus seemed a
surer ground of attack than a charge of incapacity or
treason.　Tiberius pretended to listen to an accusation thus artfully framed, the senators were blinded,
and Gætulicus was threatened with removal and disgrace.　Undismayed, he addressed from his camp a
letter to the emperor, urging that he had not sought
connexion with the minister of any motion of his own,
but at the suggestion of Tiberius himself; that if he
had been deceived by the arts of the traitor, his fault
was only the same as his master's: it was unjust that
he should suffer for an error which had been in fact
common to both.　His loyalty, he protested, was un-
shaken, and so it would remain as long as he was
himself trusted; but the arrival of a successor to
his command he should regard as no other than a
sentence of death, and to such he would refuse to
bow.　The emperor, he boldly added, might continue
to rule the state, but he would retain the government
of his own province.　The rumour of so proud a
defiance struck the citizens with astonishment; but
Gætulicus kept his place, and the impunity which
was thus accorded to a son-in-law of Sejanus engaged
them to believe it.　Tiberius, they whispered, knew
well how deep was the general dissatisfaction with
his rule; he was conscious also of the infirmities of
age, and aware that his authority rested after all on
opinion rather than on its own intrinsic force.　He
refrained from risking a collision.[2]

---

[1] Tac. *Ann.* vi. 30.: "Effusæ clementiæ, modicus severitate."

[2] Tac. *l. c.*: "Reputante Tiberio publicum sibi odium, extremam
ætatem, magisque fama quam vi stare res suas." We shall see reason

Nor does the assertion of Tiberius's indifference
seem to be better founded with regard to
Mœsia. Tacitus steps frequently aside from
Mœsia.
his domestic narrative to record the affairs of this
region and the exploits of the emperor's lieutenants;
while Appian makes special mention of the conquest
of Mœsia under Tiberius, and of the establishment of
provincial government in this quarter by his hand.[1]
Sabinus, Pandus, and Labeo seem to have held the
command there successively during the first half of
this principate, and these men at least were not allowed to indulge in indolence, for their exertions and
victories are a theme to which the historian repeatedly
refers.   At a later period, indeed, we shall read of
an incursion of the Roxolani, a people of Sarmatia,
during a season of commotion at Rome, and this is
not improbably the occurrence which Suetonius had
actually in view.[2]   Mœsia, in the reign of the second
princeps, was one of the best appointed of the imperial provinces.   Two legions were quartered in it,
and a military road from the borders of Pannonia
led along the bank of the Danube to the Euxine
at Tomi, thus securing the communications of the
presidiary cohorts through the whole length of the
only exposed frontier.   The north-eastern corner of
the province, for the Romans did not care to occupy
the pestilential marshes of the Dobrudscha, was also
connected by a coast-road with Byzantium on the
Thracian Bosphorus.[3]

But the emptiness of these charges can be more
clearly shown in the case of the dependent
kingdom of Armenia, which, according to
Armenia.
the same authority, Tiberius suffered to be seized by

---

at a later period to believe that the command of Gætulicus was really
fraught with danger to the imperial interests.

[1] Tac. *Ann.* ii. 66., iv. 5.; Appian, *Illyrica*, 30.

[2] Tac. *Hist.* i. 76.—A.U. 823, A.D. 70.   Comp. Suet. *l. c.*

[3] Bergier, *Grands Chemins*, p. 509.

the Parthians, and wrested from the patronage of the
empire.　It appears, on the contrary, from the particular recital of Tacitus, that the bold occupation
of this kingdom by Artabanus was immediately resented by the emperor with the energy of a youngei
man.　Not only were the wild mountaineers of the
Caucasus, the Iberians and Albanians, invited to descend upon the intruders; not only were the sons
of Phraates released from their long detention at
Rome, and directed to present themselves on their
native soil, and claim-the allegiance of their father's
subjects; but a Roman general, L. Vitellius, a man
of distinguished valour and experience, was deputed
to lead the forces of Asia and Syria against the
enemy; and while it was hoped that a vigorous demonstration would suffice to hurl him back from the
territory in dispute, instructions were not withheld,
it would appear, to push on if necessary, and smite
the Parthians with the strong hand of the empire.
But these combinations proved speedily successful.
Artabanus, already detested by many of his most
powerful subjects, was compelled to descend from his
throne, and take refuge in the far wilds of Hyrcania;
while Tiridates, the son of Phraates, was accepted in
his room.　The army, which had crossed the Euphrates, returned victorious without striking a blow,
though, by a subsequent revolution, Artabanus was
not long afterwards restored, and admitted, upon
giving the required hostages, to the friendship of his
lordly rivals.[1]

　　If Tiberius refrained from enlarging his empire
by fresh conquests, he was not the less in-
Thrace,
Cappadocia,
and Syria.
tent on consolidating the unwieldy mass
by the gradual incorporation of the dependent kingdoms enclosed within its limits.　The contests between two rival brothers, Cotys and Rhascu-

---

[1] Tac. *Ann.* vi. 31—37.; Joseph. *Antiq.* xviii. 5.

poris, in Thrace, gave him a pretext for placing the fairest part of that country under the control of a Roman officer, thus preparing the way for its ultimate annexation.[1] On the death of Archelaus, king of Cappadocia in 770, his country was declared a Roman province, and subjected to the rule of an imperial procurator.[2] At the same period the frontier kingdom of Commagene was placed under the government of a propraetor.[3] Syria, the great stronghold of the Roman power in the East, was still skirted by several tributary kingdoms or ethnarchies, such as Chalcis, Emesa, Damascus, and Abilene; but the dependency of Judea, the wealthiest and proudest of all these vassal states, had been wrested under Augustus from the dynasty to which it had been entrusted, and was still subjected by his successor to the control of the proconsul at Antioch.

Herod the Great, on his death-bed, had sent his seal, together with an ample present, to Augustus, in token of the entire dependence upon Rome in which he held his dominions. This act of vassalage procured him, perhaps, the ratification of the disposition he had made of his territories between Archelaus, Herod Antipas, and Philippus. To the first was allotted the kingdom of Judea, including Samaria and Idumea, but with the loss of the cities of Gaza, Gadara, and Hippo, which were now annexed to the government of Syria. To the second fell the districts of Galilæa to the west, and Peræa to the east of the Jordan; while the Trachonitis, Auranitis, and Gaulonitis formed with Ituræa the tetrarchy of Philip, extending northward to the borders of Damascus.[4] But the rival kinsmen were not satisfied with this

[margin note: Division of Palestine between the sons of Herod the Great.]

---

[1] Tac. *Ann.* ii. 67.

[2] Tac. *Ann.* ii. 42.; Dion, lvii. 17.; Suet. *Tib.* 28.; Strabo, xii. p. 534.

[3] Tac. *Ann.* ii. 56.   [4] Joseph. *Antiq.* xvii. 11. 4.

division.   Archelaus and Antipas repaired to Rome
to plead against one another; but while they were
urging their suits before the tribunal of the senate,
the provisional government which the Romans had
established in Judea was suddenly attacked on all
sides by bodies of armed insurgents.   Their leaders,
however, were not men of rank or commanding influence, and the revolt was in no sense a national
movement.   It was speedily crushed by Varus, then
proconsul of Syria, the same who ten years afterwards perished so miserably in Germany, and punished with the atrocious severity too commonly employed in such cases.[1]   Archelaus, confirmed in his
sovereignty, continued to reign under these lamentable auspices in Judea.   His subjects, still mindful
of the sons of their beloved Mariamne, never regarded him with favour; and it has been
mentioned how they complained to Augustus
of his tyranny, and obtained his removal
from the throne.   He was finally sent into exile at
Vienna in Gaul.

Disgrace and banishment of Archelaus.

The fall of Archelaus left the throne of Judea and
Samaria without a direct claimant, and the
emperor took the opportunity of attaching
them to the Roman dominions.[2]   This acquisition was placed under the general administration
of the proconsul of Syria, but governed more directly
by an imperial procurator, who took up his abode
at Cæsarea Philippi.   Of the character of the new
government we find no complaints even in the Jewish writers whose accounts of this period have been
preserved to us.   Both Augustus and his successor
appear to have instructed their officers to continue
to respect the peculiar habits and prejudices of the

*Judea an-
nexed to the
Roman
empire.*

[1] Joseph. *Bell. Jud.* ii. 5.; *Antiq.* xvii. 10.
[2] Fischer (*Ræm. Zeit.* a. 759.) fixes the annexation of the province
to the last half of this year.   Comp. Dion, lv. 27.; Joseph. *Antiq.*
xviii. 2. 1.

Jews[1] : whatever may have been the ordinary severities of Roman domination, it was not till the arrival of Pontius Pilatus, about the middle of the reign of Tiberius, that any special grievance was inflicted upon them.　　They complained that the new procurator commenced his career with a grave and wanton insult.　　He entered Jerusalem with standards flying, upon which, according to the usage of the time, the image of the emperor was displayed.　　The old religious feeling of the Jews against the representation of the human figure was roused to indignation : they remonstrated with the procurator, nor would they listen to his excuse that the Romans had their customs as well as the Jews, and that the removal of the emperor's portrait from his ensigns by an officer of his own might be regarded as a crime against his majesty.　　But if Tiberius was merely the creature of the delators in his own capital, in the provinces he retained his good sense and independence.　　Perhaps it was by a special authorization from him that Pilate consented to withdraw the obnoxious images.[2]　Nevertheless, the Jews, under the guidance of their priests, continued to watch every act of his administration with inveterate jealousy, and when he ventured to apply a portion of the temple revenues to the construction of an aqueduct for the supply of their city, broke out into violence which provoked him to severe measures of repression.　　Mutual exasperation led probably to further riots, followed by sanguinary punishments : the government of Pilate was charged with cruelty and exaction, and at last the provincials addressed themselves to Vitellius, the governor of Syria.[3]　　Nor were

Government of Pontius Pilate.

---

[1] Philo, *legat. ad Cai*, 37.

[2] Joseph. *Antiq. Jud.* xviii 4.1.; *Bell Jud.* ii. 9. 3.

[3] Joseph. *Antiq Jud.* xviii. 5. 2.: καὶ Πιλάτος, δέκα ἔτεσιν διατρίψας ἐπὶ 'Ιουδαίους, εἰς 'Ρώμην ἠπείγετο, ταῖς 'Ουϊτελλίου ἐντολαῖς οὐκ ὃν ἀντειπεῖν.

their expectations disappointed. The proconsul required his procurator to quit the province,
and submit himself to the pleasure of the
offended emperor. Tiberius, indeed, was
already dead before his arrival, but the new ruler attended without delay to his lieutenant's representations, and Pilate was dismissed with ignominy to
Vienna.[1] From the confidence with which Tiberius
was appealed to on a matter of such remote concern,
it would seem that the vigilance of his control was not
generally relaxed even in the last moments of his life.

Recall and banishment of Pilate.

While Judea and Samaria were thus annexed to
the Roman province, Galilee and the out-
lying regions of Peræa and Ituræa were
still suffered to remain under their native
rulers; and the dominions of the great Herod became,
as we shall see, once more united transiently under
a single sceptre at no distant period. If, however,
we consider the condition of the Jewish provincials
under the Roman fasces, we shall find reason to believe that it was far from intolerable, and presented
probably a change for the better from the tyranny of
their own regal dynasties. Doubtless the national feeling, as far as it extended, was outraged in its cherished
prepossessions by the substitution of a foreign for a
native domination. The nobles and the priests, who
preserved and reflected this sentiment, and who suffered in consideration under foreign sway, fostered
the prejudices of the people to the utmost, excited
their discontent, fanned the flame of sedition, and
then betrayed their clients to the sword of relentless
executioners. It may be admitted that the fiscal exactions of the procurator were more uniformly rigid
than those of Herod, whose remission of a large portion of his people's taxes had gained him favour in
the midst of his atrocities. Yet the amount of free-

Condition of Judea under the Roman government.

---

[1] Joseph. *l. c.*; Euseb. *Hist. Eccl.* ii. 7

dom and security enjoyed by the Jews under a Quirinius and a Pilate shows the general leniency of the
Roman government at this period. The warm descriptions of provincial felicity by the Jewish authority
Philo, which will be cited hereafter, may be coloured
to suit a purpose, and it may be impossible to produce
any distinct facts to support this general conjecture.
Yet indications are not wanting in the writings of the
Evangelists, which contain, abstracted from their religious significance, the most interesting record in
existence of the social condition of antiquity,—for
they alone of all our ancient documents are the pro-
ductions of men of the people,—to show that the mass
of the population of Judea was contented and comparatively happy under the rule of the Roman procurator.[1] Such is the impression I receive from the
representations of common life in the Scriptures of
the New Testament. The instances they allege of
cruelty and injustice are drawn from the conduct of
the Jews towards one another, rather than of the
foreigner towards the native. The Scribe and the
Pharisee are held up to odium or contempt, not the
minister of police or the instrument of government.
The Romans are regarded in them as the protectors
of the people against their domestic tyrants. The
duty of paying them tribute is urged as the proper
price of the tranquillity they maintain ; their fiscal
officers are spoken of with forbearance ; their soldiers
are cited as examples of thoughtful toleration ; the
vice of the provincial ruler is indifference and unbelief rather than wanton violence ; and the tribunal
of the emperor himself is appealed to as the last
resort of injured innocence. The freedom of movement enjoyed by the subjects of Rome, the permis-

---

[1] These writings refer in point of time to the middle of the reign
of Tiberius. The dates variously assigned for the Crucifixion range
from A. D. 27 to A. D. 33. Clinton fixes it at A. D. 29, A. U. 782, the
sixteenth year of Tiberius.

sion so fully allowed them of passing from town to town, from frontier to frontier, of assembling together for social and religious objects, of flocking in crowds into the city or the wilderness, at the call of popular leaders or preachers, all indicate a state of personal liberty which might be envied throughout the continent of Europe at the present day.[1]

[1] It may be said perhaps that this indulgence was owing to the want of means of repression rather than of the desire to repress. The imperfections of the police of the empire, from the slenderness of its military force, were compensated by the severity of its punishments.

END OF THE FIFTH VOLUME.

www.ingramcontent.com/pod-product-compliance
Lightning Source LLC
Chambersburg PA
CBHW021326110726
47900CB00005B/1375